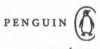

PENGUIN

JOSÉ M.
SELECTED WRITINGS

Born in 1853 to a humble family, JOSÉ MARTÍ embarked early on
a life of political struggle and literary achievement. At fifteen,
he wrote an epic poem in praise of Cuba's war of independence
against Spain, and at seventeen he was imprisoned and sentenced
to hard labor for his political activities. At eighteen, while in exile
in Spain, he published a thundering, implacable denunciation of
the Spanish treatment of Cuban political prisoners, which made
him an important voice in the Cuban nationalist movement and
had considerable impact on the thinking of Spanish liberals. For
the rest of his life, he wrote and worked unstoppably for the freedom of Cuba. He founded the Cuban Revolutionary Party and was
until his death the central architect of the Cuban independence
movement. His political involvement was accompanied and com-
plemented by a constant and relentless outpouring of poetry, literary prose, journalism, and political writing. In 1895 he returned to
Cuba with a military force to embark upon another revolution and
soon thereafter met a suicidally heroic death in battle.

ESTHER ALLEN has translated numerous works from Spanish and
French, including *The Book of Lamentations*, by Rosario Castellanos; portions of *Selected Non-Fictions*, by Jorge Luis Borges;
and, most recently, *Dark Back of Time*, by Javier Marías.

ROBERTO GONZÁLEZ ECHEVARRÍA is Sterling Professor of Hispanic
and Comparative Literatures at Yale and the author of many books
of criticism. He co-edited the monumental *Cambridge History of
Latin American Literature*.

JOSÉ MARTÍ
SELECTED WRITINGS

EDITED AND TRANSLATED BY
ESTHER ALLEN

with an introduction by
Roberto González Echevarría

PENGUIN BOOKS

PENGUIN BOOKS

Published by the Penguin Group

Penguin Group (USA) Inc., 375 Hudson Street, New York, New York 10014, U.S.A.
Penguin Group (Canada), 90 Eglinton Avenue East, Suite 700, Toronto,
Ontario, Canada M4P 2Y3 (a division of Pearson Penguin Canada Inc.)
Penguin Books Ltd, 80 Strand, London WC2R 0RL, England
Penguin Ireland, 25 St Stephen's Green, Dublin 2, Ireland
(a division of Penguin Books Ltd)
Penguin Group (Australia), 250 Camberwell Road, Camberwell, Victoria 3124, Australia
(a division of Pearson Australia Group Pty Ltd)
Penguin Books India Pvt Ltd, 11 Community Centre, Panchsheel Park,
New Delhi – 110 017, India
Penguin Group (NZ), 67 Apollo Drive, Rosedale, North Shore 0632, New Zealand
(a division of Pearson New Zealand Ltd)
Penguin Books (South Africa) (Pty) Ltd, 24 Sturdee Avenue,
Rosebank, Johannesburg 2196, South Africa

Penguin Books Ltd, Registered Offices: 80 Strand, London WC2R 0RL, England

First published in Penguin Books 2002

13 15 17 19 20 18 16 14

Translation and selection copyright © Esther Allen, 2002
Introduction copyright © Roberto González Echevarría, 2002
All rights reserved

LIBRARY OF CONGRESS CATALOGING-IN-PUBLICATION DATA
Martí, José, 1853–1895.
[Selections. English. 2002]
José Martí : selected writings / edited and translated by Esther Allen;
with an introduction by Roberto González Echevarría.
p.   cm.—(Penguin classics)
Includes bibliographical references.
ISBN 978-0-14-243704-9 (pbk.)
I. Title : Selected writings.   II. Allen, Esther, 1962–   III. Title.   IV. Series.
PQ7389.M2 A6   2002
861'.5—dc21   2001054865

Printed in the United States of America
Set in Stempel Garamond

CONTENTS

JOSÉ MARTÍ: AN INTRODUCTION

AGAINST THE ADVICE of General Máximo Gómez, military leader of the Cuban insurgent army, José Martí mounted his horse and rushed in to do battle with the Spanish troops. It was May 19, 1895, and the men had been in the Cuban countryside for a little more than a month. They had landed at La Playita, on Cuba's easternmost southern coast, having sailed there from nearby Haiti, where they had gathered after crossing over from the Dominican Republic. The war against Spanish rule had been launched on February 24 with an uprising that had not been as successful as expected. At Fernandina Beach, on Florida's east coast, the American authorities had confiscated three small steamships loaded with weapons and supplies that Martí, through his tireless fund-raising efforts, had managed to purchase. Undaunted, Martí had forged ahead with plans for what he had hoped would be Cuba's definitive war of independence. The skirmish into which Martí rode had flared up near the confluence of two rivers, the Contramaestre and the Cauto, the island's largest fluvial system. The area is known, laconically, as Dos Ríos ("Two Rivers"). Martí was felled by bullets to the head, chest, and thigh, which killed him instantly. His body was seized by the enemy and hastily buried in a common grave. But when the Spanish authorities realized who the dead man was, the corpse was disinterred, embalmed, and sent to Santiago de Cuba for proper entombment. Almost four months earlier, on January 28, Martí had turned forty-two.

Martí's death sealed his fate as a political and literary figure in Cuba and Latin America. His was the martyrdom of which religious creeds are made and the culminating event of a life that was Martí's greatest poetic creation. Martí's life and death are so intertwined with his literary pursuits that it is impossible to separate the political man from the poet—one does not make sense without the other. In the poetic realm, this radical symbiosis of life and work is his greatest claim to originality. Other nineteenth-century poets had found in early death an often desired and meaningful end to their lives. John Keats died of tuberculosis at twenty-six; Percy Bysshe Shelley drowned in an apparent accident at thirty; Gérard de Nerval hanged himself at forty-seven; Aleksandr Pushkin died in a duel at thirty-eight; Mariano José de Larra shot himself at twenty-eight; and Martí's fellow Cuban poets José María de Heredia and Julián del Casal died at thirty-six and thirty respectively. Some poets had even met their demise while engaged in political struggles. Lord Byron died of a fever at thirty-six, shortly after joining Greek insurgents. Yet Martí's immolation was in the name not just of freedom but of his country's independence and birth as a nation in a war that he had himself feverishly planned. He set an unsurpassable standard for future poets, who would work rebelliousness into their verse but were not quite ready to make the ultimate sacrifice. In Latin America, Martí represents an idealized fusion of politics and poetry.

Because of this, and because Martí's premature death did not allow him to test his political programs in practice, he became the object of a cult, and his writings a gospel with multiple interpreters claiming to know what he would have wanted Cuba and Latin America to become. Martí's martyrdom also put him beyond the reach of rigorous literary criticism; work on him by Cubans and Latin Americans verges on hagiography. The task seems to be not who can best interpret and evaluate Martí's work, but who is capable of praising him most extravagantly. Scholars and other writers, ashamed by their sedentary militancy, find comfort in exalting Martí, while those working under the aegis or sway of the current Cuban regime distort facts and texts to turn him into the unlikely herald of their doctrines. In Cuba, Havana's airport is named after Martí, as are the national library and countless other buildings and institutions, and his face appears on bills and on coins. Some of this is slowly beginning to give way, and a more sober reappraisal of Martí as poet and thinker has started in some quarters, particularly among young Cuban intellectuals and writers.

Simón Bolívar, José de San Martín, Miguel Hidalgo, and more-recent Latin American revolutionaries have all been writers of one sort or another, but Martí is the only bona fide poet among them. He figures securely in the canon of Latin American literature on his own merits as poet, orator, essayist, and chronicler. Martí was one of the greatest journalists ever, and he had no peer as an orator in an age when oratory was a highly respected literary genre. As a political organizer, Martí had no equal, either. His political and philosophic thought, though responding to the specific needs of his revolutionary plans, was charged with idealism, sympathy for the downtrodden, and a pan-Americanism that has found many followers. Martí's thought was not systematic enough to be a philosophy, and his political program was more hortative than practical—fit to encourage Cubans to battle yet not detailed enough to run a country in peacetime. Still, one must remember Martí's interest in education and his production of children's literature with a view to the development of better citizens for his imagined Cuban republic. A heady mixture of spiritualism, mystical nationalism, and compassion for the poor and abused, Martí's credo envisioned a free Cuba ruled by love and justice, free of prejudice and oppression, exempt from arbitrary rule by military leaders, in harmonious commerce with the rest of the world, and enjoying absolute self-determination. It is a poetic ideal whose reality he struggled to bring about through selfless work. But Martí was a man of the nineteenth century; he did not live to see the twentieth, which did not really "begin" until the First World War. A projection of his social and political programs beyond his time can be based only on the blind faith in his qualities as a seer, which he may have been, but only as a poet.

Martí's death brought unity and closure to all of his endeavors by eliminating the frail physical vessel that contained them and by giving them transcendental meaning on an ideal literary plane. In one of his more memorable poems, he says that he has two motherlands—Cuba and the night—and he wonders if they are not really the same. When he fell at Dos Ríos he did make them one. Love of country and love of death drove him inexorably to that place and moment where all would acquire a meaning too transcendental to express with mere words. Death sealed life and poetry as a unit. Martí's moving *War Diaries* *(Diarios de campaña)* is, of course, unfinished, as if to dramatize this point. Its end is death itself.

Cuba is a very large island. At the latitude of New York, if its eastern tip were placed on Sandy Hook, its western end would reach the environs of Chicago. It is half the size of the British Isles and larger than Ireland. Cuba's advantageous geographical location has given it a political and cultural relevance that larger Latin American countries have not had. From the beginning of Spanish settlement in the sixteenth century, the island played a critical role in the organization of the Spanish Empire in America. Havana was the port where the two annual fleets connecting the metropolis to its overseas possessions met. Products, peoples, and ideas from the Philippines, Mexico, and

Peru reached Havana, as did Spanish immigrants, government officials, troops, officers, and priests. This gave Cubans a sense of centeredness and worldwide significance that they have not lost. Cuba's wars of independence and Martí's role in them reflect this feature of early Cuban life. The Spanish-American War, with which these processes culminated, was a war of world historical importance in a way that the more massive and protracted wars of Latin American independence fought in the first half of the nineteenth century were not.

But it is the modern Cuba that is relevant to Martí. Its history begins in the early nineteenth century and is closely related to the development of the United States as a world power. The transformation of Cuba into a modern country resulted from an event beyond its shores: the Haitian Revolution in the waning years of the eighteenth century. Haiti had been the principal provider of sugar in the world, but this ended with the revolution. Cuba, led by native intellectuals like Francisco de Arango y Parreño, entered the "sugar race" to fill the void. The cultivation of sugar brought about drastic and lasting changes in the island's ecology, demography, and politics. The sugar barons began to import modern machinery from England and the United States, and thousands of slaves from Africa. By the 1830s, there were more blacks than whites in Cuba, and a class of powerful, forward-looking sugar barons was doing business principally with the United States and Europe instead of with Spain. Explosive ethical, social, and political contradictions were contained in this situation. The broadest had to do with the clash between modern industrial practices—represented by the machines and ideas imported from the United States and England— and the most archaic form of exploitation, slavery. Moreover, the new class of "sacharocrats," as Manuel Moreno Fraginals called them in his classic work *The Sugarmill*, had little access to political power. Spain still clung to its policy of forbidding Cubans to hold high political office—only the Spanish-born had access to government positions. The rich were disenfranchised, a situation that sooner or later leads to strife.

On October 10, 1868, after careful preparations, Carlos Manuel de Céspedes, the owner of a sugar plantation and mill at La Demajagua, in the easternmost province of Oriente, proclaimed Cuba's independence, freed his slaves, and took to arms. He was followed by other leaders of his class, like Ignacio Agramonte, from the neighboring province of Camagüey, and by many who would rise through the ranks, like Calixto García, the mulatto Antonio Maceo, and the Dominican-born Máximo Gómez. The war was fought mainly on the eastern part of the island, far from Havana, the seat of political and military power (this trend would continue through Cuban history). It was a bitter struggle, to which Spain committed thousands of troops, added to the many it had already deployed before the outbreak of war to suppress the ominous unrest. One of the men sent to Cuba, a first sergeant in the Royal Artillery Corps from Valencia, was Mariano Martí y Navarro, who would become Martí's father in 1853. In October 1869, a year after Céspedes's proclamation, the sixteen-year-old Martí was arrested and accused of activities disloyal to Spain. The war lasted a full ten years and in fact came to be known as the Ten Years War (also *la Guerra Grande,* or "the Big War"). It brought great devastation to Cuba, for the revolutionaries tried to inflict economic damage on Spain by destroying the sugar industry, whose revenues were crucial to the metropolis. Persecution, imprisonment, and deportation of those suspected of collaborating with the rebels increased as the movement gained momentum in the cities. Martí was sentenced to forced labor in 1870 and, granted clemency, deported to Spain the next year. He was lucky. On November 27, 1871, after a hasty trial, the Spanish sent eight medical students to the firing squad in Havana. They were accused of desecrating the tomb of a loyal Spanish journalist. Many Cubans left for the United States, where they settled in Key West, Tampa, Jacksonville, and New York; others sent their children to American academies and universities to protect them from the fate suffered by the medical students. From the United States, those Cubans contributed money, supplies, and men to the war.

But the Ten Years War ended in 1878 with the Cubans' capitulation at El Zanjón. To lay down arms was a painful decision on the part of the Cuban leaders. It exacerbated dissensions among them that had contributed in no small measure to their defeat in the first place. Antonio Maceo, for instance, refused to surrender and left Cuba only when there was no other recourse. The divisions in the Cuban camp were deep and older than the war itself. In a broad sense, there were three groups among those dissatisfied with Spanish rule: The *autonomistas* favored making Cuba an autonomous region of Spain. This movement echoed the yearnings and struggles of various regions in the Iberian Peninsula that have often wanted to be freed from the central government (some still do). The *anexionistas* wished to have Cuba annexed to the United States in some way, seeing that the country already had significant commercial and cultural ties with the Union. One could argue that by the second half of the nineteenth century,

Cuba was an economic colony of the United States while still a political one of Spain, an issue that was settled with the Spanish-American War. The third group, the *independentistas*, wanted Cuba to become a sovereign nation. The arguments of the first two groups were persuasive on pragmatic grounds, and the *anexionistas* had found attentive listeners among American politicians, in an age when the United States was flexing its muscles and in the process grabbed a large chunk of Mexico's territory.

But those favoring independence, whose undisputed leader Martí would become after 1878, wielded the force of nationalist emotion, long-term resentment, and ideals of freedom to which they clung with religious fervor. Founding a nation was the romantic ideal of nineteenth-century intellectuals, poets, and politicians, and many territories struggled to nationhood both in Europe and in the Americas. Germany, Italy, and even the United States in the wake of the Civil War were new nations, as were the Latin American republics that emerged after the Spanish Empire was dismantled in the first half of the nineteenth century. White Cubans felt alienated from Spain, which they saw as backward and crassly exploitative. For Cuba's black population, who had no mother country in which to find refuge (or be deported to), and many of whom knew of the dismal conditions under which their brethren lived in the United States, there was no option but total independence. Poor whites faced a similar predicament, and whether peasants in the countryside or workers in the tobacco industry in Cuba, Key West, or Tampa, they actively supported the war against Spain. But the Big War had been lost, some leaders like Céspedes and Agramonte were dead, and others, like Maceo and Gómez, were in exile and unhappy with one another. This is where Martí came in.

Martí's greatest political achievement was to bring together the disillusioned and fractious veterans of the Ten Years War by convincing them of his own and the new revolutionaries' commitment. The men who had fought the Big War were battle-hardened and suspicious of upstarts like Martí, who lacked combat experience. (Many suspect that it was to prove himself to them that he rode rashly into the skirmish at Dos Ríos.) But Martí had managed to persuade the veterans to join in a new venture and launch another war. In his fifteen years in New York, during which he traveled tirelessly up and down the east coast of the United States all the way to Key West, Martí accomplished this goal by the sheer force of his charisma, clarity of purpose, mesmerizing oratory, and unflagging spirit of sacrifice. He wrote voluminously for Latin American newspapers, such as *La Nación* in faraway Buenos Aires, for Spanish-language publications in the United States, and even in English for the *New York Sun* and others. He was founder, editor, and chief contributor of *Patria*, his main organ of propaganda among Cubans in the United States. Martí's crowning effort was the foundation in 1892 of the Partido Revolucionario Cubano (Cuban Revolutionary Party), the civil organization that would lead the revolutionaries to war.

Martí spoke to all sorts of groups but most memorably to Cuban cigar workers in Tampa and Key West, cities where he was idolized. In these speeches, Martí outlined his vision of a free Cuba, "with all and for the good of all," democratic, pluralistic, and capable of learning from the mistakes made by the recently established Latin American nations. The worst of these errors was militarism, or *caudillismo,* which had already created rifts among the Cuban leaders of the Ten Years War like Céspedes and Agramonte and would continue to haunt the Cuban independence movement. Martí had to rein in military-minded leaders like Gómez and Maceo, potential caudillos, and insist, without alienating them, on the civilian cast of the movement. It was not easy to hail civilian virtues during all-out war. Of Martí's fears about the future of Cuba, militarism was the most justified and the one that unfortunately became a nightmarish reality in postindependence Cuba. There was no place in the Cuba Martí envisioned for arbitrary rule in the hands of soldiers. His disagreement with the military leaders Maceo and Gómez continued until the very last days before that fateful May 19 at Dos Ríos. A page torn from Martí's *Diaries* by an unknown hand is purported to have contained the record of a violent confrontation with Gómez and Maceo.

After Martí's fall, the rest of the war was fought ferociously, with Maceo achieving the difficult task of spreading the fighting west to Havana's environs and beyond to Pinar del Río. He and other leaders followed a scorched-earth policy, leaving behind a trail of devastation. This time the Spanish seemed on the verge of losing and sent to the island thousands of ill-prepared soldiers, many mere boys in their teens, and engaged in brutal policies like relocating all the peasants to cities to keep them from aiding the rebels. This *reconcentración,* ordered by cruel Spanish governor Valeriano Weyler, caused widespread famine and disease, and people died by the thousands. Spanish atrocities were lavishly depicted in the American press, which urged the government to intervene on the side of the rebels. Eventually, another of Martí's fears was realized when the Americans intervened in the war after the battleship *Maine* was blown up in Havana harbor on February 15, 1898. Spain's defeat by the United States in 1898 deprived the Cuban insurgents of a hard-fought victory that was within their grasp, and installed yet a new colonial power in Havana. The condescending way that the American authorities dealt with the Cuban troops, and the Platt Amendment, which was attached to the Cuban constitution when the country was declared free in 1902, fueled anti-American feelings in Cuba. The amendment gave the United States the "right" to intervene in case of political unrest. These developments left open the question of how Martí would have conducted the war had he lived and, more urgently, how he would have led the new nation that emerged from it. We will never know, but there is no shortage of opinions and politically inspired would-be programs presumably derived from Martí's ideas.

In organizing the war and as a result of his numerous writings for Latin American newspapers and literary magazines, Martí became one of the leading prose writers of the Spanish language and a recognized poet in a new literary movement called *Modernismo*. The first literary trend to originate in Latin America, *Modernismo* was led by the Nicaraguan Rubén Darío, who in 1888 published *Azul,* a slim volume of poetic prose and poems that revolutionized literature written in Spanish. In 1896 his *Prosas profanas,* a book of poems, set the standard for the new poetry. Darío was a poet with continent-wide fame whose influence on Latin American and Spanish literatures can hardly be exaggerated. (Other important poets of the movement were the Colombian José Asunción Silva and the Cuban Julián del Casal.) *Modernismo* was a break from the Spanish tradition, seen as too local and wallowing in maudlin local color, and a reaction to Latin America's entrance into the world economy. As Cathy L. Jrade has proposed, *Modernismo* was made up of contradictory impulses. Modernity was the product of the rationalist forces that, through their effect in science and industry, made social life materialistic and crass, particularly in the growing cities of Europe, the United States, and increasingly Latin America. *Modernismo* countered these trends with refinement, spiritual and artistic elitism, and a rejection of the bourgeois life that the world economy engendered. Jrade writes in her authoritative *Modernism, Modernity, and the Development of Spanish American Literature:* "The *modernistas,* like the romantics before them, favored an alternative that was primarily 'spiritualist,' predicated on changes in consciousness and values. They proposed a worldview that imagined the universe as a system of correspondences, in which language is the universe's double capable of revealing profound truths regarding the order of the cosmos." Their critique of bourgeois values was grounded, she says, in the *modernistas'* belief "in the transformative capacity of art" (p. 4). This gave *Modernismo* a political edge, particularly in Martí's works.

Martí's verse and prose, particularly the prose, matched Darío's and the others' in their cosmopolitanism, decadent spirit, and uncompromising cultivation of beauty for its own sake. Beauty, the result of highly formal techniques, was contemplated in a slightly detached, unsentimental way, which is what separated *modernista* poets from their romantic predecessors. No gushing of emotions in *modernista* writing: the principal emotion sought was the sublime contemplation of the beautiful, of the "shape" that Darío famously stated he pursued. Not since the Baroque had Spanish been subjected to such craft, to such unnatural, untraditional artifice. Literary discourse had no pretense of reflecting common speech; it reveled in its literariness. The new models were French and American poets like Paul Verlaine and Charles Baudelaire, Walt Whitman and Edgar Allan Poe, all of whom, particularly the Americans, Martí read and admired in the original. Conservative Spanish writer and critic Juan Valera complained of Darío's "mental Gallicism." To the *modernistas* this was praise. They did not want Spanish works to be limited by regionalism but to enter the world literary economy as well and to reflect the Spanish-speaking world, not just Spain or any one Latin American country. Like Darío, Martí was a traveler, whose continent-wide conception of Latin American literature he expressed in his publications throughout the New World, from the United States and Mexico to Argentina. In one of his essays he referred memorably to Latin America as "Our America." Unlike Darío and the other *modernistas*, Martí imbued his poetry with an assertive ethical, sometimes (but not often) overtly political message and occasionally with a sentimental charge that still hearkened back to romanticism.

Martí did not have the time, because of his early death and his frenzied political activities, to publish a vast and influential corpus of poetry. Only two slim volumes of poems were printed in his life—*Ismaelillo* (1882) and *Versos sencillos* (1891)—but he did attain renown as a poet because his works appeared in periodicals in New York and throughout Latin America and were read and admired by the likes of Darió. *Ismaelillo,* a tender book about the son Martí's estranged wife had taken with her to Cuba, contains some striking poems revealing the poet's turbulent feelings and longings. *Versos sencillos,* made up of quatrains of deceptive simplicity and sounding very much like popular poetry, became Martí's most acclaimed book. Martí was known to all as a poet, in the broadest sense of the term. Not only Darío but other *modernista* poets recognized him as one of their own, and older writers like the Argentine Domingo Faustino Sarmiento admired him, though sometimes grudgingly because of his threatening originality. Martí's posthumous *Versos libres* is the most daring of his collections and the one that contains his best mature poetry. Some poems in this book, like *"Amor de ciudad grande"* ("Love in the City"), uncannily announce the work of avant-garde poets like Pablo Neruda. Martí was exposed in New York to a modern metropolis, hence to the atmosphere to which the poets of the 1920s were going to react. *Versos libres,* however, was not published until 1913, in a Cuban edition that included *Ismaelillo* and *Versos sencillos,* which probably had a limited circulation.

Martí's chronicles were his greatest literary success. These texts, as Susana Rotker has carefully shown, are a combination of the French sketches of life and manners and the Spanish and Latin American *costumbrista* tradition. They are a blend of reportage, tableau, and essay that Martí took to its highest form through his powerful imagination. He often wrote them not as an eye-witness report, but from a collection of press releases that he took from the wire or from American newspapers. The chronicles found an eager audience because they dealt with—indeed were written from within—the United States, a country whose rapid transformation into a major power inspired awe, admiration, fear, and in some cases resentment among many Latin Americans. The United States was becoming more powerful and important than the European nations from which the American republics had devolved and on which they had been modeled. The Venezuelan Andrés Bello had been to England in the late eighteenth century, and Simón Bolívar had been an officer in the Spanish army. France and Germany, like Great Britain, had far-flung, modern empires, and Paris was deemed the intellectual capital of the nineteenth century. Latin American poets, politicians, and intellectuals had been meeting in the French capital since the 1830s and forging a continental solidarity; indeed, they were founding Latin American literature. But

Martí was now writing from a country that dwarfed Europe in everything, particularly material progress and sheer physical size. It was the quintessentially modern nation, in which the gadgets and advances of industry were being produced in great volume, something that captivated not just Latin America but the rest of the world. The United States also possessed a compelling culture, with writers as original as Whitman, Poe, and Ralph Waldo Emerson, whom Martí introduced to Latin American audiences. It was a country that had just emerged from a bloody civil war and in which the Enlightenment ideas of democracy were being dramatically tested. Moreover, it was a country where thousands of immigrants from Europe struggled to adapt themselves and to become part of a nation in which the old class divisions of their mother countries could be abolished. Everyone could begin anew in America, a yearning Latin Americans also felt. All of this social, industrial, and political effervescence Martí was able to capture in his chronicles from the perspective of a Latin American that was both admiring and critical—detached from the events themselves, but not totally, for Martí was living in the United States and profiting from the opportunities and freedoms that the country offered to launch the liberation of his own. The mix, together with Martí's captivating style, was irresistible to his public, and the volume of Martí's publication attests to the recognition he enjoyed among newspaper editors in Latin America.

The literary value of those chronicles lies not just in Martí's journalistic eye for the unusual and for significant details, but in his uncanny ability to seize the collective dynamics of a situation and the drama of the individuals caught in it. Scenes of this kind evoke the likes of Charles Dickens and Victor Hugo. For instance, here is his description of the tumult surrounding the execution of four anarchists in Chicago and the scene of their death:

Spies's face is a prayer; Fischer's is steadfastness itself; Parsons's radiant pride; Engel ducks his head and makes his deputy laugh with a joke. Each one in turn has his legs bound with a strap. Then hoods are flung over the four heads like candlesnuffers putting out four flames: first Spies, then Fischer, then Engel, then Parsons. And while his companions' heads are being covered, Spies's voice rings out in a tone that strikes deep into the flesh of all who hear it: "The time will come when our silence will be more powerful than the voices you are throttling today." "This is the happiest moment of my life," Fischer says,

while the deputy is attending to Engel. "Hurray for anarchy!" says
Engel, who, beneath the grave-clothes, was moving his bound hands
toward the sheriff. "Will I be allowed to speak, O men of America . . ." Parsons begins. A signal, a sound, the trapdoor gives way, the
four bodies drop simultaneously, circling and knocking against each
other. Parsons has died in the fall; one quick turn, and he stops. Fischer swings, shuddering, tries to work his neck free of the knot, extends his legs, draws them in, and dies. Engel rocks in his floating
hangman's robes, his chest rising and falling like the swell of the sea,
and strangles. Spies dangles, twisting in a horrible dance like a sackful
of grimaces, doubles up and heaves himself to one side, banging his
knees against his forehead, lifts one leg, kicks out with both, shakes
his arms, beating against the air, and finally expires, his broken neck
bent forward, his head saluting the spectators.

In this unsurpassable page, Martí conveys the drama of the situation
by depicting not just the reaction of the men as they face death, but
also the response of their bodies as they die—in some meaningless
twists and jerks yet, in the case of Spies, in a salute to the audience as
his head bobs.

As Aníbal González has demonstrated, Martí's prose also gained by
contamination with his oratory, a mixture that one would expect to
lead to bombast and excessive rhetoric. But in his prose the oratorical
creates a sense of immediacy and urgency, and the customary repeti-
tions of speeches gives his prose a very compelling cadence and
rhythm. González writes:

It is important to remember that Martí was one of the most charis-
matic and powerful orators of his time and that part of the effective-
ness of his chronicles resides in their evocation of the spoken word.
The rhetorical tricks of oratory gave Martí's chronicles an air of immediacy and coherence, with the disparate events narrated being
"centered" and organized by the author's disembodied voice. As the
title *Escenas norteamericanas* suggests, events in Martí's chronicles
are usually described as a sequence of tableaux or scenes, not unlike
the dioramas that were so popular in the Parisian arcades of the mid-
nineteenth century—in which each immobile scene was brought to
life by the voice and presence of an orator—or like a museum, in
which disparate exhibits are linked together by the organizing discourse of the guide. [p. 92]

But above all, oratory gives Martí's prose, as González also points out, its aphoristic quality. Aphorisms, like maxims, are statements that express an idea concisely and with a rhetorical and even poetic flair that lifts them from ordinary prose to become independent of the texts in which they appear. They are like maxims and proverbs. Aphorisms are used in speeches to wind up a thought in a way that makes the idea memorable—that is to say, literally easy to remember. They are like slogans. For instance, *"La patria es ara, no pedestal"* ("The motherland is an altar, not a platform") means, of course, that one should sacrifice for one's country, not use it to elevate oneself. Such was Martí's aphoristic proficiency that volumes of his *pensamientos,* his thoughts, have been collected and made standard fare in schools, particularly in Cuba, where they are memorized by children. The relative independence of these utterances exempts them from having to cohere as a philosophical system, which is why a philosopher like Friedrich Nietzsche, wary of systems and a contemporary of Martí, also cultivated this subgenre. These aphorisms are the bridge between Martí's prose and his poetry.

The most compelling Martí as poet emerges sporadically in images of astounding freshness and daring, generally overlooked by readers and admirers distracted by the ethical imperatives of his verse. For instance, there is the arresting quatrain in *Versos sencillos* that begins *"Si ves un monte de espumas"* ("If you see a mountain of foam") and winds up with an agile enjambement punctuated by two lines stressed in the last syllable, unusual in Spanish:

> Si ves un monte de espumas,
> es mi verso lo que ves,
> mi verso es un monte, y es
> un abanico de plumas.

> If you see a mountain of foam,
> it is my verse you see,
> my verse is a mountain, and
> is a fan of feathers.

"Ves," "ves," and *"es,"* plus the reiteration of *"verso,"* make up a staccato rhythm softened by the last sentence, wrapped around the end of the third line to wind up in the last. This final line is accentuated in the next to the last syllable, the most common pattern in Spanish,

and hence sounds normal—a downbeat that inspires reflection. The suppleness of the line reflects its meaning, *"un abanico de plumas."* To call one's poetry a feather fan is a beautiful metaphor to evoke lightness, luxuriance, color, and an explosion of meanings emerging from a center and spreading in various directions. But what is a "mountain of foam," and who has ever seen one? "Mountain of foam" also conjures feelings of lightness, a lightness that contrasts with the volume of the mountain, a lurking oxymoron linking the opposing bulk and levity of the mountain. There is also a feeling of fleetingness; foam does not last, it melts, again in opposition to the mountain's solidity. *"Monte de espumas,"* "mountain of foam," is a nearly surreal image that one is at a loss to equate to any reality.

Did Martí ever see a mountain of foam, or is it a figment of his imagination? Such images are among the most modern, forward-looking elements of his verse and show his kinship with contemporary decadent poets like Baudelaire and Arthur Rimbaud who, as did Martí on occasion, indulged in mild hallucinogenic substances. It was a practice that he shared with *modernista* poets in Spain and Latin America, such as Rubén Darío, his compatriot Julián del Casal, and Ramón del Valle Inclán. Martí's dreams were not only those of living in a just and greatly run community of humans, joined by spiritual values. He shared with other late-nineteenth-century poets a more daring and dark visionary quality. To wit, his *"Copa con alas"* ("Winged Cup") in *Versos libres,* another image that seems to emerge from a nightmare and brings to mind Salvador Dalí.

The foregoing about the quatrain in *Versos sencillos* is striking without noting the elegant self-deprecation implicit in Martí describing his poetry as "foam" or "feathers," both of which usually signify something trifling. In other quatrains in *Versos sencillos,* Martí's characterization of his poetry is more dramatic, as in the color coding (reminiscent of Rimbaud's *"Voyelles"*) of *"Mi verso es de un verde claro / y de un carmín encendido"* ("My verse is light green / and burning crimson") another contrasting pair, which leads to the biblical-sounding *"Mi verso es un ciervo herido / que busca en el monte amparo"* ("My verse is a wounded fawn / seeking shelter in the mountain"). The mountain, the *"monte,"* is now the refuge for the wounded fawn. Why is Martí's poetry "hurt"? The fawn evokes innocence, guiltlessness, purity, and being wounded suggests that the animal has been shot by a hunter or attacked by a predator. There is a prophetic quality to these simple lines if one recalls Martí's death, of course. His verse is wounded, one assumes, by the violence and corruption of the world outside the poetic realm, which is why the fawn seeks shelter in a mountain that now stands for Martí's poetry. Wounded by the world, the poem seeks protection by running back into poetry itself. "*Monte,*" in fact, can also be Martí's own self, as he proclaims in another quatrain with pantheistic as well as, again, biblical resonances:

> Yo vengo de todas partes,
> y hacia todas partes voy,
> arte soy entre las artes,
> y en los montes, monte soy.

> I come from all places,
> and to all places go,
> I am art among the arts,
> and mountain among mountains.

"*Monte*" has a more solid connotation here than "mountain of foam," but the remarkable thing is Martí's conception of the poetic self as a spirit with no place or time, yet of all places and times. He is part of the real, not about it, but is free from the normal constraints of the material. This penchant for the mysterious is very much a part of *Versos sencillos,* the best part, not present consistently throughout the book. Some of the better-known verses, like the one popularized by the awfully monotonous song "Guántanamera," which begins "*Yo soy un hombre sincero*" ("I am an honest man"), lack originality, and the rhythm is dull. The only good line is the circumlocution that refers to Cuba as "*de donde crece la palma,*" flattened in the common English translation "from the land of the palm tree" (improved here by Esther Allen as "from where the palm tree grows"). In the better verses, the mysterious quality gives the quatrain a haiku-like conciseness and a compelling vagueness:

> Yo pienso, cuando me alegro,
> como un escolar sencillo,
> en el canario amarillo,
> que tiene el ojo tan negro.

> When I am happy, I wonder,
> like a simple schoolboy,
> about the yellow canary
> whose eye is so black.

Here the contrast between the presumably studious "schoolboy" and his mirthful musing on the canary's black eye in the midst of all that yellow lends the poem a delicious yet profound irony that is missing in the more declarative quatrains. There is more pleasure in the detached meditation on the unfathomable than in the contemplation of the obvious.

An often overlooked feature of Martí's poetry is the near absence of two of the most powerful drives in his life: politics and love. He wrote little openly political poetry. Even a poem about a Spanish dancer in New York, in which he refuses to enter the theater because the Spanish flag hangs there, is measured and even reticent in its critique of his father's motherland, the one whose citizenship he carried. There is nothing like Darío's *"Oda a Roosevelt,"* which pits Latin America, Catholic and Spanish-speaking, against the impetuous Protestant nation led by an impudent leader. Martí saved his political writing for his prose and his oratory. Nor is there any significant love poetry in his corpus, though Martí was a notorious lover, apparently irresistible to women and equally unable to resist them. The smallest evidence of this was his illegitimate daughter, María, with Carmen Miyares de Mantilla, his New York landlady, who had a crippled husband. (That daughter went on to become the mother of American actor César Romero.) Testimony from not an insignificant number of women attests to Martí's powers of seduction and to the ease with which he fell in love. There are few traces of this in his poetry. The exception is the well-known *"La niña de Guatemala,"* a tender yet boastful poem about a young woman who dies of lovesickness when Martí returns married to another woman. But there is no memorable love poem to a specific or idealized woman—a curious absence.

Much of Martí's poetry is elevated by his death, which gives a prophetic quality even to lines that are not, in themselves, great poetry, like the quatrain that winds up with *"moriré de cara al sol"* ("I will die with my face to the sun"). But he earned that at Dos Ríos by fulfilling poetic and political prophecies. Martí must have sensed that he had a historic date with death. Self-immolation for the cause of freedom was in the air in the Cuban camp. A minor exiled poet, Miguel Teurbe Tolón, had written a sonnet, popular among revolutionaries, that finishes: *"primero mi verdugo sea mi mano / —que merecer de un déspota insolente— / el perdón de ser libre y ser cubano"* ("I would rather die by my own hand / than to be granted by an insolent tyrant / the reprieve of being free and a Cuban). Earlier in the century, the major

Cuban poet José María Heredia, a rebel and an exile himself, had written:

> Al poder el aliento se oponga,
> y la muerte contraste la muerte:
> la constancia encadena la suerte;
> siempre vence el que sabe morir.

> Fervor should oppose dominance,
> and death countered with death:
> perseverance heralds good fortune;
> he who triumphs is prepared to die.

These feelings were encapsulated in a line of Perucho Figueredo's "*Himno de Bayamo,*" which became Cuba's national anthem, in the line: "*Que morir por la patria es vivir*" ("To die for the motherland is to live"). The heroes of the Ten Years War took this feeling to heart and lived up to it by dying or attempting to. On March 11, 1873, as Agramonte was inspecting battle lines in the Jimaguayú prairie, he was felled by an enemy bullet. And on February 27, 1874, Céspedes, who had already been deposed, was discovered by Spanish troops on a farm. They killed him as he bravely fought back with a mere revolver. In that same year, Calixto García miraculously survived his attempt at suicide when surrounded by the enemy. The bullet he shot into his mouth perforated the palate and came out through the middle of his forehead, where it left a starlike scar for the rest of his life. It was that star, perhaps, that Martí followed to Dos Ríos.

—Roberto González Echevarría

CHRONOLOGY

1853 January 28: José Julián Martí y Pérez is born in Havana to Mariano Martí y Navarro, a Spaniard from Valencia who is a first sergeant in the Royal Artillery Corps of the Spanish army, and Leonor Pérez Cabrera, originally from Tenerife in the Canary Islands. José, known to his family and friends throughout his life as "Pepe," is the couple's first child; they will eventually have seven more children, all daughters. The two youngest die in childhood.

1855 Renewing an offer previously extended in 1848, the U.S. government proposes to purchase Cuba from Spain for $100 million. Spain ignores the proposal.

1857 May: The Martí y Pérez family moves back to Spain.

1859 June: The family returns to Havana where they live under financial duress for the rest of Martí's childhood.

1862–63 Martí spends several months with his father in the rural town of Jaguey Grande, in the province of Matanzas, and develops a passion for the Cuban countryside.

1868 October 10: Carlos Manuel de Céspedes initiates an armed revolt against Spain with the *Grito de Yara* (Cry of Yara). This war, confined almost wholly to Cuba's eastern provinces, rages for a decade and becomes known as the Ten Years War.

1869 January: Martí publishes his earliest political texts in *El Diablo Cojuelo* (The Lame Devil), the newspaper of his close friend Fermín Valdés Domínguez, and in *La Patria Libre* (The Free Patria), his own paper, of which only one issue appears.

April 10: The Cuban rebels, gathered in the town of Guáimaro, declare all Cuban slaves free without payment or reparation.

October: Martí is arrested on charges of disloyalty to Spain.

1870 April: Sent to do hard labor in a stone quarry. Suffers for the rest of his life from a lesion to his groin incurred during this imprisonment.

October: Granted clemency and deported to Spain.

1871 February: Arrives in Spain and almost immediately publishes the tract "Political Prison in Cuba." Enrolls in the Universidad Central of Madrid.

Midyear: Undergoes two operations on a tumor resulting from his prison injury and decides to move to the provincial city of Zaragoza.

November 27: Eight Cuban medical students are executed by a firing squad in Havana for having profaned the tomb of a Spanish journalist. Thirty-five other medical students are sent to prison. Martí writes articles, appeals to the Spanish government, and mobilizes the Cuban community in Madrid. Finally, in May of the next year, the imprisoned students are pardoned.

1873 February: Spain proclaims itself a republic. Martí publishes "The Spanish Republic and the Cuban Revolution," arguing that Cubans should be given the same rights Spaniards are now claiming for themselves.

May: Enrolls in the University of Zaragoza.

1874 Graduates from the University of Zaragoza with degrees in Civil Law, Canonical Law, Philosophy, and Letters. At year's end, visits several European cities, including Paris, then embarks from Le Havre, via Southampton and New York City, for Mexico, where his family now lives.

1875 February: Arrives in Mexico City, where he rejoins his family shortly after the death of his beloved sister Ana.

For the next two years, works as a high school teacher and journalist, begins making a name for himself as a playwright and orator, and becomes engaged to Carmen Zayas-Bazán, a Cuban woman living in Mexico.

1877 January: Returns to Cuba under the name "Julián Pérez" but departs within less than two months for Guatemala.

May: Named Professor of French, English, Italian, and German

Literature and of the History of Philosophy at the Escuela Normal Central of Guatemala.

December: Marries Carmen Zayas-Bazán in Mexico.

1878 January: Returns to Guatemala with his bride.

April: Resigns his position at the Escuela Normal Central out of loyalty to its director, unjustly fired by the Guatemalan president.

September: Arrives in Havana with his pregnant wife and begins working in a law office there.

November 22: His only son, José Francisco Martí y Zayas-Bazán, is born in Havana.

1879 September: Martí is arrested for conspiring against Spain and deported, without his family, back to Spain.

December: Leaves Spain to pass through France on his way to the United States.

1880 January: Arrives in New York, where he lodges in a boarding house run by Carmen Miyares de Mantilla, a Cuban-born Venezuelan, the mother of three children, with an invalid husband.

Spring: Carmen Zayas-Bazán and José Francisco come from Cuba to join him in New York.

May: As interim president of the Comité Revolucionario Cubano of New York, Martí leads the exiled Cuban community through the rapidly checked uprising led by General Calixto García Iñiguez, later known as the *Guerra Chiquita*, or "Little War."

October: Carmen Zayas-Bazán returns to Cuba, taking José Francisco with her.

November 28: Carmen Miyares de Mantilla gives birth to María Mantilla, who is widely believed to have been Martí's daughter (and who later went on to become the mother of Hollywood actor César Romero).

1881 January: Martí arrives in Venezuela, where he teaches, gives lectures, writes articles, and founds a magazine, the *Revista Venezolana* (Venezuelan Review), of which only two issues appear.

July: Leaves Venezuela for New York, after an article in the second issue of his magazine upsets Venezuela's president Antonio Guzmán Blanco.

1882 Settles in New York and publishes his first volume of poems, *Ismaelillo*, about his absent son. Writes but does not publish most of the poems that comprise *Versos libres* (Free Verses).

In this and subsequent years, he writes for newspapers in Venezuela, Argentina, Uruguay, Honduras, and Mexico, as well as for both English- and Spanish-language publications in New York. He also writes for and becomes editor-in-chief of the magazine *La América*, published in New York; serves intermittently as Uruguay's consul in New York; consolidates his reputation as an orator and political organizer among Cubans in the United States; and translates several books into Spanish for D. Appleton and Company publishers.

December: Carmen Zayas-Bazán returns to New York with young José Francisco to live with her husband for the next two years.

1884 Martí breaks with Generals Máximo Gómez and Antonio Maceo over their vision of an independent Cuba with a military government.

1885 March: Carmen Zayas-Bazán returns to Cuba with José Francisco.

Amistad Funesta (Fatal Friendship) or *Lucía Jerez*, Martí's only novel, is published in installments in the New York magazine *El Latino-Americano*.

1886 The Spanish government abolishes slavery in Cuba.

1889 July: The first issue of *La Edad de Oro* (The Golden Age) appears, a magazine for "the children of America" of which Martí is editor, publisher, and sole author. Four issues appear in all.

September: The Pan-American Conference, in which Martí will play an active role, opens. Delegates from across Latin America converge on Washington, D.C., where the conference continues through May of the following year.

1890 January: Martí assists in founding La Liga ("The League"), a school for black Cubans and Puerto Ricans in New York, at which he teaches as well.

In the course of the year, he is named consul of Argentina and Paraguay, and begins teaching night courses in Spanish at the Central Evening High School, 63 East 74th Street, New York City.

1891 March: As the delegate of Uruguay, Martí attends sessions of the American International Monetary Commission in Washington, and delivers a speech opposing bimetallism, in Spanish and in English.

June: *Versos sencillos* (Simple Verses), the second and last volume of his poetry to be published during his lifetime, appears in New York.

Reunited in midyear with his wife and son, who, at his urging, return to New York to live with him. The reconciliation is unsuccessful; his wife soon returns to Cuba, taking the boy with her.

Begins resigning from his various posts as foreign correspondent and consul in order to devote himself entirely to the cause of Cuban independence.

November: Travels to Florida and delivers two famous speeches that instill revolutionary fervor in the Cuban communities of Tampa and Cayo Hueso (Key West). Founds a branch of La Liga in Florida.

1892 January: Participates in a meeting of the leaders of various exile groups in Cayo Hueso at which the Partido Revolucionario Cubano (Cuban Revolutionary Party) is formed, and its bases and secret statutes are drawn up and ratified.

March: The first issue of *Patria*, the last and most successful newspaper to be founded by Martí, appears in New York.

April 8: Martí is elected leader, or *Delegado*, of the Cuban Revolutionary Party. He will be re-elected in each of the remaining three years of his life.

Makes another trip to Florida in July, then, in September, leaves New York for Haiti, the Dominican Republic, and Jamaica, returning to New York in October and traveling back to Florida in early November.

1893-94 Travels continually up and down the east coast of the United States and throughout the Caribbean, twice going as far as Costa Rica to meet with General Antonio Maceo, who is living there.

1895 January 10: Catastrophe. A carefully planned armed expedition that was about to strike out for Cuba from Fernandina Beach, Florida, is stopped by the U.S. authorities, who seize the expedition's three ships along with all the supplies and weapons onboard.

February 7: Martí arrives in Montecristi, Dominican Republic, where he joins General Máximo Gómez.

February 24: Cuba's third war of independence begins with the *Grito de Baire* (Cry of Baire).

March 25: With Máximo Gómez, Martí draws up and signs the Montecristi Manifesto.

April 11: Martí disembarks clandestinely in Cuba, at La Playita, near the eastern tip of the island, with Gómez and four other men.

May 19: Though under orders from Gómez to stay back, Martí charges headlong into a skirmish with Spanish troops and is killed.

1896–97 In order to separate the Cuban rebels from their supporters in the countryside, Valeriano Weyler, the newly appointed Spanish governor of Cuba, institutes the policy of *reconcentración*. More than 300,000 people are forced off their land into centrally located towns where they are confined under appalling conditions. At least 100,000 of them die as a result. The atrocities receive extensive coverage in the U.S. press.

1898 January 1: The Spanish government grants limited autonomy to Cuba.

February 15: The U.S. battleship *Maine* blows up in the bay of Havana, killing 266 of the men onboard. Though the cause of the explosion is uncertain, the incident further inflames the U.S. public.

April: War between the United States and Spain is officially declared by both sides.

July: With the Spanish fleet largely sunk, the Spanish forces surrender the city of Santiago de Cuba to the United States, effectively ending the war.

August 12: An armistice between the United States and Spain is signed.

December 10: The Treaty of Paris, officially ending the war, is signed. Spain cedes control of Cuba, Guam, and Puerto Rico to the United States, and surrenders the Philippines for a payment of $25 million.

1902 The U.S. occupation of Cuba ends. Tomás Estrada Palma, Cuba's first democratically elected president, is inaugurated under a constitution that contains the U.S.-imposed Platt Amendment, which severely limits Cuba's sovereignty, granting the United States the right to intervene in Cuban affairs under a number of circumstances, as well as the right to lease a naval base on Cuba at Guantánamo Bay.

SUGGESTIONS FOR FURTHER READING

Abel, Christopher, and Nissa Torrents, eds. *José Martí: Revolutionary Democrat*. Athlone Press, 1986.

Arenas, Reinaldo. *The Doorman*. Translated by Dolores M. Koch. Grove Atlantic, 1994.

Benitez Rojo, Antonio. *The Repeating Island: The Caribbean and the Postmodern Perspective* (1989). Duke University Press, 1992.

Domínguez, Jorge I. *Cuba: Order and Revolution*. Harvard University Press, 1978.

Gónzalez, Manuel Pedro. *José Martí: Epic Chronicler of the United States in the Eighties*. University of North Carolina Press, 1953.

González, Aníbal. *Journalism and the Development of the Spanish American Narrative*. Cambridge University Press, 1993.

González Echevarría, Roberto, and Enrique Pupo-Walker, eds. *The Cambridge History of Latin American Literature*. Cambridge University Press, 1996.

Gray, Richard Butler. *José Martí, Cuban Patriot*. University of Florida Press, 1962.

Guerra Sánchez, Ramiro. *Sugar and Society in the Caribbean* (1927). Yale University Press, 1964.

Jrade, Cathy L. *Modernismo, Modernity, and the Development of Spanish American Literature*. University of Texas Press, 1998.

Kirk, John M. *José Martí: Mentor of the Cuban Nation*. University of South Florida Press, 1983.

Kutzinski, Vera M. *Sugar's Secrets: Race and the Erotics of Cuban Nationalism*. University Press of Virginia, 1993.

Lizaso, Felix. *Martí, Martyr of Cuban Independence*. Translated by Esther Elise Shuler. University of New Mexico Press, 1953.

Luis, William. *Literary Bondage: Slavery in Cuban Narrative*. University of Texas Press, 1990.

Mañach, Jorge. *Martí: Apostle of Freedom*. Translated by Coley Taylor, with a preface by Gabriela Mistral. Devin-Adair, 1950.

Martí. José. *The America of José Martí* (anthology). Translated by Juan de Onis, with a preface by Federico de Onis. The Noonday Press, 1953.

Moreno Fraginals, Manuel. *The Sugarmill: The Socioeconomic Complex of Sugar in Cuba.* New York: Monthly Review Press, 1976.

Opatrny, Josef. *U.S. Expansionism and Cuban Annexationism in the 1850s.* Translated by Dagmar Steinová. Charles University, 1990.

Ortiz, Fernando. *Cuban Counterpoint: Tobacco and Sugar.* Translated by Harriet de Onís, with an introduction by Bronislaw Malinowski (1970). New edition with an introduction by Fernando Coronil. Duke University Press, 1995.

Perez, Louis J., ed. *José Martí in the United States: The Florida Experience.* Arizona State University Center for Latin American Studies, 1995.

Pérez Firmat, Gustavo. *The Cuban Condition: Translation and Identity in Modern Cuban Literature.* Cambridge University Press, 1989.

Ripoll, Carlos. *The Falsification of José Martí in Cuba.* Translated by Manuel Tellechea, edited by Enrico Mario Santí. Center for Latin American Studies, 1994.

Ripoll, Carlos. *José Martí, the United States, and the Marxist Interpretation of Cuban History.* Transaction Books, 1984.

Ripoll, Carlos. Web site at www.eddosrios.org.

Rodríguez-Luis, Julio, ed. *Re-Reading José Martí (1853–1895) One Hundred Years Later.* State University of New York Press, 1999.

Rotker, Susana. *The American Chronicles of José Martí: Journalism and Modernity in Spanish America.* University Press of New England, 2000.

Santovenia, Emeterio S. *Lincoln in Martí: A Cuban View of Abraham Lincoln.* Translated by Donald F. Fogelquist. University of North Carolina Press, 1953.

Schulman, Ivan. "José Martí" in *Latin American Writers,* vol. I, ed. Carlos A. Solé and María Isabel Abreu. Charles Scribner's Sons, 1989, pp. 311–19.

Thomas, Hugh. *Cuba, or, Pursuit of Freedom.* Eyre & Spottiswoode, 1971.

Turton, Peter. *José Martí: Architect of Cuba's Freedom.* Zed Books, 1986.

JOSÉ MARTÍ
Selected Writings

EARLIEST WRITINGS

By the age of eighteen, Martí had published many poems and articles, had founded a newspaper that promoted the Cuban revolution, and had been tried, imprisoned, subjected to forced labor, and deported from Cuba for his views. Yet nothing in his background foretold that he would be a writer or a fervent advocate of Cuban independence. On the contrary, he was born to impecunious Spanish parents of minimal education, his father was a soldier in the Spanish army, and Martí even spent part of his childhood in Spain. Those of his contemporaries whose antecedents were similar generally gave their allegiance to Spain and became soldiers or functionaries in the colonial administration.

Against his father's objections, Martí's mother had struggled to ensure that her extraordinarily gifted son received the education he deserved. That education led him to Cuban nationalism. Under the guiding hand of Cuban poet Rafael María de Mendive, who was the director of the Havana Municipal School for Boys, Martí came to think of himself as a Cuban, and to do so in a very particular way. Cuban opinion at the time was divided among the autonomistas, *who wanted Cuba to remain a Spanish possession, but with greater autonomy, the* anexionistas, *who wanted to see Cuba become part of the United States, and the* independentistas, *like Mendive, who wanted independence. Martí was always, unwaveringly, in the latter camp. In 1868, when the Ten Years War—Cuba's unsuccessful first war of independence—broke out and put his convictions to the test, he was only fifteen, but he rose to the challenge.*

ABDALA

Published in La Patria Libre, *the only issue of the first newspaper to be founded by Martí, which appeared in the early months of the Ten Years War—on January 23, 1869, when its author had just turned sixteen—*Abdala *is a dramatic poem in eight scenes, whose plot is as follows: A senator begs the young warrior Abdala to save Nubia from the invaders closing in on it. Abdala gladly agrees and inflames a group of warriors with his patriotic ideals. His mother, Espirta, enters and begs him not to go. He sends the warriors away, argues with her, and leaves. Finally, Abdala is carried back from battle in the arms of his warriors.*

An 1867 census determined that Cuba had a total population of 1,370,211, of whom 764,750 were white, and 605,461 were black or "colored." Cuba's independence movement was strongest in the impoverished and predominantly black eastern provinces. As a result, the movement was often depicted by its enemies as a slave uprising, a race war bent on making Cuba into another Haiti. Martí's decision to use the ancient African kingdom of Nubia as the setting for his allegory of Cuban independence was therefore highly provocative.

Written expressly for *La Patria*

Characters

Abdala
Espirta, Abdala's mother
Elmira, Abdala's sister
Warriors

The action takes place in Nubia.

Scene II

ABDALA

Abdala: At last my strong, sinewy arm
        can brandish the hard scimitar,
        and my noble steed can fly
        fleet amid the din of battle!
        At last my head shall be garlanded with glory;
        I shall be the one to free my anguished patria,
        and wrest my people from the oppressor
        whose talons rip them apart!
        And the vile tyrant who threatens Nubia
        will weep for forgiveness and life at my feet!
        And those cowards who help him
        will groan, appalled by our strength!
        And into the quagmire that haughty forehead will sink,
        and in the vile quagmire his soul will wallow,
        and the plain where his camp sprawls
        will bear mute witness to his infamy,
        and the oppressor will bow before the free man,
        and the oppressed will avenge his stigma!

                                         . . .

        And so the raging enemies
        will hurl themselves, barbaric, at our ranks.
        And fight—run—retreat—fly—
        fall inert—rise up moaning—
        prepare for another encounter—and die!
        Now their cowardly and routed hosts
        flee across the plain: Oh! how joy
        gives strength and steadiness and life to my soul!
        How my valor grows! How the blood
        blazes in my veins! How this invincible
        fervor carries me away! How I long
        to go forth into battle!

                                         . . .

Scene V

ESPIRTA AND ABDALA

Abdala: Forgive me, oh Mother! for leaving you
and going to the battlefield. Oh! These tears are
witness to my terrible yearning,
and the hurricane that rages deep within me.
(ESPIRTA *weeps.*)
Do not weep, oh Mother! my own burning tears
are sufficient to my pain.
It is not the groans of the dying or the clash
and hard smiting of mighty weapons
that bring tears to my sad eyes
and fear to my brave heart!
Perhaps I shall return lifeless,
or shall, hidden amid the clamor of battle,
fall victim to blood and furor.
It matters not to me. If Abdala knew
that by his blood Nubia would be saved
from the terrible foreign claws,
I would stain those robes you wear,
my mother, with drops of my own blood.
I tremble for you alone, and though I do not show
my tears to the warriors of my patria,
see how they run down my face, oh Mother!
See how they spill across my cheeks!

Espirta: And so much love for this patch of earth?
Did it protect you in your childhood?
Did it bear you lovingly in its bosom?
Was it the land that gave birth to your daring,
your strength? Answer me! Was it your mother?
Or was it Nubia?

Abdala: Love, Mother, for the patria
is not a foolish love for the dirt
and grass where our feet walk;
it is an invincible hatred of those who oppress her,
an eternal hostility toward those who attack her—

and such a love awakens in our breast
a world of memories that call us back
to life once more when the blood
wells in anguish from the wounded soul—
the image of love that consoles us
and the placid memories it preserves!

Espirta: And this love is greater than that stirred
in your breast by your mother?

Abdala: Can it be that you believe
there exists a thing more sublime than the patria?

. . .

Scene VIII
(Enter warriors carrying a wounded ABDALA in their arms.)

Elmira and Espirta *(horrified):* Abdala!

(The warriors bear ABDALA to center stage.)

Abdala: Yes, Abdala, who returns a dying man
to throw himself in surrender at your feet,
then go where he cannot
brandish any blade or seize any spear.
I come to exhale in your arms, Mother,
my last sighs, and my soul!
To die! To die when Nubia is fighting;
when the noble blood of my brothers
is being spilled, Mother, when the patria
expects her freedom from our strength!
Oh, Mother, do not weep! Fly as
noble matrons fly on wings of valor
to cry to the warriors on the field:
"Fight! Fight, oh Nubians! Take heart!"

Espirta: Not to cry, you tell me? And will the patria
ever repay me for your life?

Abdala: The life of a noble man, my mother,
is to fight and die in obedience to the patria,

and, if need be, to rend
his entrails with his own steel, to save her!
But . . . I feel myself dying, in my final agony.
(To all.) Do not come near to disturb my sad calm.
Silence! . . . I want to hear . . . Oh! It seems
that the enemy host, in defeat,
is fleeing across the plain. . . . Listen! . . . Silence!
I see them running now. . . . Upon the cowards
the valiant warriors hurl themselves. . . .
Nubia has triumphed! I die happy; death
matters little to me, for I have saved her. . . .
Oh, how sweet it is to die, when I die
fighting boldly to defend my patria!
                    (He falls into the warriors' arms.)

LETTER TO HIS MOTHER FROM PRISON

*On October 21, 1869, Martí and his lifelong friend Fermín Valdés
Domínguez were arrested and imprisoned by the Spanish authorities after an unsent letter was found in Domínguez's room addressed to a schoolmate who had enlisted in a Spanish regiment.
The letter, signed by both boys, read: "Compañero: Have you ever
dreamed of the glory of the apostates? Do you know how apostasy
was punished in Antiquity? We hope that a disciple of Señor Rafael
María de Mendive[1] cannot allow this letter to go unanswered."[2]*

November 10

Madre mía:
Two days ago I sent you a letter with a Frenchman who comes to see
the Domínguezes—not the one who was there—and he told me he
wasn't able to take the letter. He promised me he would take it. Tell
me if he does.

The day before yesterday I wrote you as well, but I had no one to
send the letters with and I don't want to slip them under the door of
the prison canteen. Since I'm writing you today, I'll tear up the letter
from the day before yesterday.

Yesterday, the Fiscal was here and questioned me with considerable interest about my case and my condition. I told him what I knew, but it's very strange that the person who is to pass judgment on me must ask me why I am in prison. It appeared from what he told me that someone has talked to him about me. The Domínguezes and Sellén will go free in the end, and I will stay in jail. The results of imprisonment frighten me very little, but I haven't endured life as a prisoner for very long. And that is all I ask: that things move quickly; that to one who has done nothing, nothing be done. At least they cannot accuse me of anything I cannot undo.

I am sorry to be behind bars, but my imprisonment is very useful to me. It has given me plenty of lessons for my life, which I foresee will be short, and I will not fail to make use of them. I am sixteen years old, and many old men have told me I am like an old man. And they are right in a way: because while I have in full measure the recklessness and effervescence of my young age, I also have a heart as small as it is wounded. It is true that you are suffering greatly—but it is also true that I am suffering more. God willing, someday in happier times I will be able to tell you about the vicissitudes of my life!

I am a prisoner, and that is an undeniable truth, but I lack for nothing except two or three reales from time to time to have some coffee—but today is the first time that has happened. Still, when one is living without seeing one's family or any of those one loves, one can spend a day without coffee. Papá gave me five or six reales on Monday. I gave two or three away as alms and loaned two.

On Sunday, bring one of the little girls to see me.

This is an ugly school, for although decent women come here, there is no lack of others who are not.

So little lack is there that the visit occurs every day at four. Thank God that the women's bodies became like stone to me. Their soul is the immensely great thing, and if that is ugly they can proffer their beauties somewhere else. Nothing prison can do will be able to make me change my mind on this point.

In prison I've written not a line of poetry. In part, I'm glad, because you know what the poems I write are like, and will be like.

Here everyone talks to me about Señor Mendive, and that makes me happy. Send me books of poems, and a large one called *The Universal Museum*. Give your blessing to your son.

Pepe

POLITICAL PRISON IN CUBA

*After six months of forced labor in the San Lázaro stone quarries of
Havana (April 14–October 13, 1870), Martí was granted clemency
and placed under house arrest on the Isle of Pines to await deportation to Spain. On January 15, 1871, he left for Spain. One of his first
acts upon arriving was to publish this tract, addressed to the people
of Spain, which had considerable impact in Spanish liberal circles
and among Cuban exiles in Madrid.*

Madrid, 1871

I

Infinite pain should have been the only title of these pages.

Infinite pain: for the pain of imprisonment is the harshest, most
devastating pain, murdering the mind, searing the soul, leaving marks
that will never be erased.

It is born from a lump of iron, and quickly sweeps away this mysterious world that agitates every heart; it grows, feeding on every
shadowy sorrow, and finally it overflows, swollen by scalding tears.

Dante was never in prison.

If Dante had felt the dark vaults of that life of torment plummeting
down onto his mind, he would have ceased to paint his Inferno.
Merely by copying them, he would have painted a better one.

If a providential God existed and had seen this, he would have covered his face with one hand and flung this negation of himself into the
abyss with the other.

Yet God does exist in the idea of the good, which is present at the
birth of every being and leaves one pure tear in the soul thus incar-
nated. Goodness is God. That tear is the source of eternal feeling.

God does exist, and I come in his name to shatter the cold glass that
encloses that tear in the souls of Spaniards.

God does exist, and if you send me from this place before I have
torn away your cowardly and calamitous indifference, then give me

leave to despise you since I can hate no one; give me leave to pity you in the name of my God.

I will not hate you or curse you.

If I were to hate anyone, I would hate myself for having hated.

If my God were to curse, I would deny my God for having cursed. . . .

III

Men wrapped in black cloaks came by night and met together on an enormous emerald floating in the sea.

"*Gold! Gold! Gold!*" they chanted in unison, then threw off their cloaks and recognized one another, gripping each other's bony hands and moving their cadaverous heads in greeting.

"Listen," said one. "Despair is setting in below the haciendas' sugarcane; so many bones cover the earth that the grass cannot sprout; the battles are suns, shining so brightly that black skin is indistinguishable from white. I have seen from afar the ruin that advances, terrible, upon us; the demons of wrath have seized our cashbox, and I struggle, and all of you struggle, and the cashbox moves, and our arms grow tired and our strength is drained, and the cashbox will be gone. But far away, very far, there are new arms, new forces; there, the chord of honor often resounds and the name of the dismembered patria often exalts. If we go there and the chord resounds and the name exalts, then the cashbox stays; we will make servants of the despairing whites; their dead bodies will fertilize the earth while their living bodies dig and plow it, and Africa will give us wealth: gold will fill our coffers. New arms are there, new forces are there; let us go, let us go there."

"Let us go, let us go," said the men in cavernous voices, and then the first one sang, and the others sang with him.

> The country is ignorant, and sleeps.
> The first to reach its door sings beauteous verses and inflames it.
> And, inflamed, the country clamors.
> Let us sing, then.
> Our arms are tired, our strength is drained.
> New arms are there, new forces are there.
> Let us go, let us go there.

And the men mingled their bodies together and transformed into a vapor of blood; they crossed through space, robed themselves in honor, reached the ear of the country that was sleeping, and sang.

And the noble fiber that lies in the souls of countries contracted vigorously, and the country clamored to the chords of the lyre that swayed within the red cloud, and in the intoxication of its clamor raised the cry of anathema.

The country clamored unthinkingly. Even men who dream of a universal federation, of the free atom within the free molecule and of respect for the independence of others as the basis for one's own strength and independence,[1] denounced the petition of rights that was tendered, approved the persecution of the independence that was championed, and sanctified the heartless war of extermination as representative of peace and morality.

They forgot themselves and forgot this truth: since remorse is inexorable, countries, too, must expiate their sins.

They begged yesterday and are still begging today for greater freedom for themselves, and on the very same day they applaud an unconditional war to crush another's petition for freedom.

They did wrong.

Spain cannot be free while it is stained with blood. . . .

A lusty, sonorous name echoed in your ears and engraved itself upon your minds: *National Integrity!* And the vaulted roof of the national assembly hall echoed with the unanimous cry: *Integrity! Integrity!*

Oh! It is not really so beautiful or so heroic, this dream of yours, for there can be no doubt that you were dreaming. Look, look at the image I shall paint for you, and if you do not shudder with fear at the wrong you have done, if, aghast, you do not curse the face of national integrity that I present you with, then I will turn my eyes in shame from this Spain that has no heart. . . .

IV

You, who had not a thought of justice in your minds or a word of truth in your mouths for the most painfully sacrificed, most cruelly trampled race on earth; you, who immolated some on the altar of seductive words even as you were listening with pleasure to others who spoke of the simplest principles of right, the most common notions of sentiment: moan for your honor, weep at the sacrifice, cover your foreheads with dust and go on bare knees to collect the broken shards of your reputation that lie scattered across the earth.

What have you been doing for so many years?

What have you done?

There was a time when the sun never set on your territories. And today hardly a ray of sunlight illuminates those that lie far from here, as if the sun itself were ashamed to cast its light on possessions of yours.

Mexico, Peru, Chile, Venezuela, Bolivia, New Granada, the Antilles—all of them came in festive garments to kiss your feet, paving with gold the wide furrow that your ships made across the Atlantic. You put an end to each one's freedom; all were joined together to place one more sphere, one more world on your monarch's crown.

Spain reminded the earth of Rome.

Caesar had returned and had spread himself across your many shoulders, with his thirst for glory and his delirious ambitions.

The centuries passed. . . .

And the storm broke out at last; and it was as furious and inexorable in its unleashing upon you as it had been slow in the making.

Venezuela, Bolivia, New Granada, Mexico, Peru, Chile—all bit your hand, which clutched the reins of their freedom, and opened deep wounds in it, and when your spirits were flagging, weak and battered, an *Ay!* escaped from your lips; one doleful blow after another was struck into the gash, and the head of Spanish dominion rolled across the American continent and traveled over its plains and marked its trackless mountains and forded its rivers to fall at last into an abyss, never to rise there again.

The Antilles, the Antilles alone, Cuba above all, still dragged themselves to your feet and put their lips to your wounds and licked your hands, and tenderly, solicitously, fashioned a new head for your mutilated shoulders.

And as Cuba was benevolently restoring your strength, you put your arm under hers and reached for her heart, and ripped it out and tore open the arteries of morality and science.

And when she begged some miserable alms from you as a reward for her hardships, you stretched out your hand and showed her the shapeless mass of her trampled heart and laughed and threw it in her face. . . .

And she felt the blood rise to her throat, and it choked her and rose to her brain and needed to burst forth, and concentrated in the strength it found in her breast, and made her whole body boil with the heat provoked by mockery and outrage. And it burst forth in the end. It burst forth because you yourselves caused it to, because your cruelty made the opening of her veins necessary, because you had crushed her heart many times and she did not want you to crush it again.

And if this was what you wanted, then why do you find it strange?

And if it is a matter of honor for you to continue writing your colonial history on pages such as these, why do you not temper—with justice, even—your supreme effort to affix the tattered remains of your conquistador's cloak to Cuba forever? . . .

VII

"Martí! Martí!" a poor friend of mine said to me one morning, a friend from back there, a political prisoner and a good man who, like me, was that day, under unusual circumstances, ordered to stay in the cigar factory and not go outside to work. "Look; there's a little boy going by over there."

I looked. Sad eyes are mine to have seen such sadness!

It was true. He was a little boy. His full height barely reached a normal man's elbow. His eyes stared with a mixture of curiosity and fear at the coarse garments in which he had been clad, the strange chains that encircled his feet.

My soul flew toward his soul. My eyes gazed into his eyes. I would have given my life for him. And my arm was tied to the factory table, while his arm was moving, terrorized by the club and the pumping of the tanks.

Until then I had understood everything—I had been able to explain it all to myself, even my own absurd case—but in the presence of that innocent face, that delicate form, and those serene, pure eyes, my mind went astray; I had lost my reason, for it had left me in horror to go and weep at the feet of God. My poor mind! And how many times has it been made to weep thus for others!

The hours passed; exhaustion was etched on that face; the little arms moved heavily; the soft pink of the cheeks disappeared; the life was going out of the eyes; the strength of those fragile limbs was draining away. And my poor heart wept.

The hour finally came when the day's work was over. The child climbed the stairs, gasping for breath. He reached his ward. He threw himself to the floor, for the floor was the only seat we were given, the only rest for our weariness; the floor was our chair, our table, our bed, the handkerchief drenched with our tears, the bandage soaked with our blood, the longed-for refuge, the only asylum for our battered, lacerated flesh, our swollen, throbbing limbs.

Quickly I was at his side. If I were capable of cursing and hating, I would have cursed and hated at that moment. I, too, sat on the floor, I lay his head down on his wretched little jacket and waited for my agitation to permit me to speak.

"How old are you?" I asked him.

"Twelve, señor."

"Twelve, and they brought you here? And what is your name?"

"Lino Figueredo."

"And what did you do?"

"I don't know, señor. I was with Taitica and Mamita,[2] and the soldiers came and took Taitica away and then came back and took me away."

"And your mother?"

"They took her away."

"And what happened to your father?"

"They took him and I know nothing about him now, señor. What could I have done to make them bring me here and not let me stay with Taitica and Mamita?"

If indignation, sorrow, and anguished pain could speak, I would have spoken to that unfortunate boy. But something strange—and every man of honor knows what it was—inspired me with resignation and sadness and cooled the flames of vengeance and wrath; something strange put its iron hand upon my heart and wiped the tears from my eyelids and made the words freeze on my lips.

Twelve years old. Twelve years old: the words buzzed ceaselessly in my ears, and his mother and my mother, and his weakness and my powerlessness all merged into one in my breast, and roared, and overwhelmed my head and drowned my heart.

Twelve years old was Lino Figueredo, and the Spanish government sentenced him to ten years of imprisonment.

Twelve years old was Lino Figueredo, and the Spanish government put him in chains and threw him among criminals and perhaps displayed him as a trophy in the streets.

Oh! Twelve years old!

There is no moderate way to express it: What shame! There is no possible rationalization: What a vile blot! The government forgot its honor when it sentenced a twelve-year-old boy to imprisonment; forgot it even more when it was cruel, inexorable, and wicked to him. And that government must turn back, and quickly, to reclaim that honor, which in this case once again, as in so many others, was soiled and disgraced.

And it must turn back soon, horrified by its own handiwork, when it hears the whole series of events I do not name because the misery of others fills me with shame.

Lino Figueredo had been sentenced to imprisonment. That was not enough.

Lino Figueredo was already a prisoner; he was moaning, his feet bound by chains; he wore the black hat and the horrid uniform. But that was not enough.

This twelve-year-old boy had to be cast into the stone quarries, to be whipped there, to be beaten. And he was. Stones tore at his hands, clubs beat his back raw, quicklime scraped and opened sores on his feet.

And that was the first day. And they pummeled him.

And then another day. And they pummeled him again.

And many more days.

And a club ripped open the flesh of a twelve-year-old boy in the prison of Havana, while here in Spain the words *national integrity* strike a magical chord that never fails to resound, vibrant and powerful.

There, national integrity dishonors, whips, murders.

Here, it moves and enthuses and exults.

It moves and enthuses and exults: the same national integrity that whips, that dishonors, that murders!

The representatives of this country did not know the story of . . . Lino Figueredo when they gave their approval to their government's actions, intoxicated by the heady aroma of an opportunistic patriotism. They did not know the story, for in it their country speaks, and if this country knew the story and deliberately spoke thus, then this country has neither dignity nor heart. . . .

And there is that, and much more.

The stone quarries are the least of Lino Figueredo's martyrdom. There is more.

One morning, Lino's neck could not hold his head up; his knees tottered; his arms fell limply from his shoulders; a strange malady was vanquishing the unknown spirit within him that had kept him . . . and so many others like him, and me, from dying. A greenish black shadow surrounded his eyes; red spots dotted his body; his voice emerged in a moan; his eyes gazed out in lamentation. And in that agony, in the struggle of sickness in prison, which is the most terrible of all struggles, the boy approached the officer in charge of his crew and said to him, "Señor, I am sick; I cannot go on; my body is covered with spots."

"Go on, go on!" the officer said harshly. "Go on!" And he answered Lino's plaint with a blow from his club. "Go on!"

And Lino, leaning imperceptibly—for had it been noticed, his story would have had one bloody page more—on the shoulder of someone who was not as weak as he was that day, went on. Many things go on. Everything goes on. Eternal justice, as unfathomable as it is eternal, goes on as well, and one day it will stop!

Lino went on. Lino worked. But in the end the spots covered his body, the shadow blinded his eyes, his knees buckled. Lino fell, and smallpox appeared at his feet and stretched its claws over him and wrapped him up, quick and greedy, in its awful cloak. Poor Lino!

Only then, only because of the egotistical fear of contagion, did Lino go to the hospital. Prison is a real hell, a living hell. The prison hospital is another and even more real hell, on the threshold of unknown worlds. And to move us from one hell to the other, the political prison in Cuba requires that the shadow of death be upon us.

I remember it with horror. When cholera was gathering up its sheaf of victims, the body of a Chinaman was not sent to the hospital until one of his countrymen cut into the ill-fated man's vein and a drop welled up, a drop of black, coagulated blood. Then, only then, was it established that the sufferer was sick. Only then. And minutes later that sufferer died.

My hands have rubbed their rigid limbs; with my breath I have tried to resuscitate them; from my arms they have been taken, the poor cholera victims, unconscious, sightless, voiceless, who only then were acknowledged as such.

Beautiful, beautiful is the dream of National Integrity. Is it not truly beautiful, O you representatives of the nation? . . .

. . . When I left that graveyard of living ghosts, Lino was still there. When I was shipped off to this land, Lino was still there. Since then, a tombstone has closed that immense corpse off from me. But Lino lives on in my memory, and clings to my hand, and embraces me tenderly, and hovers about me, and his image is never absent from my memory.

When countries go astray and from cowardice or indifference commit or excuse grave errors, when the last vestige of energy disappears, when the last—or perhaps the first—expression of political will remains awkwardly silent, then countries weep long, pay for their crimes, and perish, mocked, humiliated, and torn to shreds, as they themselves once mocked and humiliated and tore to shreds.

No idea can ever justify an orgy of blood.

No idea can ever excuse crime, and barbaric refinement in crime. Spain speaks of its honor.

Lino Figueredo is there. There. And in my imagination's dreams I see the nation's representatives dancing, drunk with enthusiasm, eyes blindfolded, their movements dizzying, their momentum inexhaustible, illumined like Nero by human bodies tied to pillars and blazing like torches. Amid this sinister splendor, a red spectre lets out a strident cackle. They dance. . . .

Dance now, dance.

VIII

. . . Poor black Juan de Dios! He laughed when they put him in chains. He laughed when they put him to work at the pump. He laughed as he walked to the stone quarries. Only when the club was lacerating his shoulders, on which the sun's light had shone for more than a hundred years, did he stop laughing. Idiocy had replaced reason within him; his intelligence had changed to instinct; only his emotions lived on intact. His eyes preserved a faithful image of lands and things, but his memory randomly joined the latest with the earliest years of his life. In the long and strange tales he told me, which I greatly enjoyed hearing, what always stood out was his unlimited respect for gentlemen, and the trust and gratitude with which his masters rewarded his affection and loyalty. In one square yard his finger could mark out the exact contours of the greatest haciendas in Port-au-Prince, but in ten words he confused the great-grandson with the great-grandfather, and the fathers with the sons, and families of the most remote and separate origins.

The only response he gave to that which most wounded him was the goodhearted, frank, full laugh that is particular to the Negro nation. Only blows awoke his former life in him. When the club smashed against his flesh, the eternal smile disappeared from his lips, the lightning of African wrath shone fleeting and fierce in his dimmed eyes, and his broad, wiry hand squeezed the tool of his labor with feverish agitation.

The Spanish government has condemned a simpleton in Cuba.

The Spanish government has condemned a black man more than a hundred years old in Cuba. It has condemned him to prison. It has whipped him in prison. It looks on coldly as he labors in prison. . . .

XII

. . .

Look, look.

Here comes the stone, an enormous mass. Many arms with military stripes on their sleeves are pushing it. And it rolls and rolls, and at each turn the desperate eyes of a mother shine out from its black roundness and disappear. And the men go on laughing and pushing, and the mass goes on rolling, and at each turn a body is crushed, and a shackle clanks, and a tear jumps from the stone and lands on the necks of the men who laugh and push. And eyes glisten, and bones are broken, and the tears weigh heavy on the necks, and the mass rolls. Ay! When the mass has had done with its rolling, a body will be weighing on your heads, a body so cumbersome that you will never be able to lift it off. Never!

In the name of compassion, in the name of honor, in the name of God, stop the mass, stop it or it will turn on you and drag you beneath its horrible weight. Stop it, for it is sowing many tears upon the earth, and the tears of martyrs rise in a vapor to the sky and condense, and if you do not stop it the sky will plummet down upon you.

The terrible cholera, the snowy head, the appalling smallpox, the wide black mouth, the mass of stone. And as the corpse stands out in the coffin, as white flesh stands out against a black tunic, all of it moved against a wide, dense, suffocating, reddish background. Blood, always blood!

Oh! Look, look.

Spain cannot be free.

Spain's head is still covered in blood.

Now approve of the conduct of the Spanish government in Cuba.

Now, fathers of the patria, say in the patria's name that you endorse the wickedest violation of morality and the most complete abandonment of all sense of justice.

Say it, support it, approve it, if you can.

The breakneck pace of Martí's life continued unabated in the decade that followed his deportation to Spain. During his three years there, he became known throughout the Cuban exile community for his impassioned oratory, fiery political tracts, and unceasing efforts in defense of Cuba. He also found the time to take degrees in several subjects from the University of Zaragoza. Then he moved on, visiting Paris and New York for the first time before settling for a few years in Mexico, where he acquired a love for that country, a Mexican friend, Manuel Mercado, whom he would keep until his death, and a Cuban wife. After spending a year teaching in Guatemala, he returned to Cuba, where his only son was born. But the decade's end found him exiled for his political activities once more, this time in New York City, where he thought his stay would be brief.

NOTEBOOKS 1–3

*** SELECTIONS ***

Throughout his adult life, Martí kept notebooks, sometimes no more than assorted scraps of paper stitched together by hand. (The pages of Notebook 14 were cut from old U.S. War Department weather maps.) He jotted down everything: snatches of poetry, citations from books he was reading, random thoughts, aphorisms (his own and other people's), the addresses of friends and contacts, arguments with himself or with a book, incidents from his day, jokes, and various other literary and philosophical musings in Spanish, French, English, Greek, Latin, and German. Twenty of these notebooks remain, and though it is sometimes difficult to date them precisely, they have been arranged in more or less chronological order; the first of them were clearly written during his student days in Madrid and Zaragoza, and the last during his final years in New York.

from NOTEBOOK 1 (1871)

Thought acts independently of the will to think. Sometimes I want to think but do not, and sometimes I think without wanting to, and then nothing is left of things but their images.

North Americans put utility before sentiment. We put sentiment before utility.

And when there is such difference in organization, life, being; when they were selling while we were weeping; when we exchange their cold and calculating head for our imaginative head, and their hearts made of cotton and ships with a heart so special, so sensitive, so new that it can only be called the Cuban heart, then how can you ask us to govern ourselves by the same laws with which they govern themselves?

We imitate. No! We copy. No! It is good, they tell us. It is American, we say. We believe because we need to believe. Our life does not resemble theirs, and on many points it must not become like theirs.

Among us, sensibilities are extremely vehement. Our intelligence is less positive, our customs are purer: how can two different peoples be ruled by the same laws?

The American laws have given the North a high degree of prosperity and have also raised it to the highest degree of corruption. It has been metallized to make it prosper. Accursed be prosperity at such a cost![1]

And if the general state of enlightenment in the United States seduces you, despite the corruption and the glacial metallization, can't we aspire to enlighten without corrupting? This is happening. . . .

I want to educate a country that will save a drowning man and never go to Mass.

There is a soul in animals.

The Catholic priesthood is necessarily immoral.

There is no Providence.

Providence is nothing but the logical and precise result of our actions, facilitated or blocked by the actions of others.

If we accept the Catholic Providence then God would be an extremely overworked bookkeeper.

To prevent the abolishment of the death penalty, to seek to demonstrate its goodness, is to defend it. And, in truth, it takes a certain degree of courage to stand up for it—the same courage it takes to oppose the abolition of slavery.

From the moment I could feel, I have been horrified by this penalty. From the moment I could judge, I judged it to be completely immoral. I will never be known for my utilitarian solutions, but if there is one thing I know about utility, it is the complete uselessness of capital punishment.

And it seems to me that if I had had the misfortune to think and feel otherwise, I would never have dared say so.

Therefore I feel anguish when someone does say so. I feel pain because Karr's[2] original talent has come to champion a thing so bloody.

It may be an illusion of my overheated mind, but anything that advocates the death penalty seems to me to be stained with blood.

It is an illusion, those who advocate the death penalty would say with a laugh; but it now strikes me that it is not, and I firmly believe it is true.

Karr's *esprit* wounds me, and frankly I regret not having more of it than he does in order to crush and do away with his.

Even as they preach progress, many progressives prostitute themselves, in the moral sense of that word.

If he were a Jesuit, he would have added immense numbers of men to the Company of Jesus.

Let us look calmly, with all the calm of pain, upon these inconveniences of talent. Without them, the law of harmony, the immutable principle of equilibrium, would not be present in all things.

November 1871

from NOTEBOOK 2 (circa 1872–73)

Life is undoubtedly a contradiction. We desire what we cannot obtain; we want what we shall not have; and no contradiction could exist without the existence of two distinct and opposing forces.

For a book: ME.

My ideas about my own feelings are a little confused. Sometimes I acknowledge that I am good. Sometimes I berate myself angrily and exasperate myself because I think that wicked or egotistical thoughts are arising within me.

I must go inside myself and see myself for myself. I must be the one to analyze who I am; I must know myself; with my own will and my brave or weak nature, convinced of my absolute independence; I must found my own knowledge of myself, and overthrow all other ideas stemming from vanity or egotism.

I believe in the divinity of my essence; I feel and watch and believe in the wretchedness of my existence. And yet I seem, involuntarily, to acquiesce in my own wretchedness. What am I?

An absolute conviction. What I am I do not owe to myself. I was not born from my own will. Whatever in me is of worth I did not give to myself. What there is in me is mine only insofar as it temporarily exists within me. I am what I am, but I am not responsible for a spirit I could not choose; I cannot pride myself on a soul I did not create. Now I write. . . .

From NOTEBOOK 3 (1874–78)

Bakunin,[3] the Russian revolutionary.

Disciple of Panlof, who introduced Russia to the philosophy of Schelling.[4]

Stanekevith, youthful and eloquent, brought Hegel.

Belinsky,[5] the steely critic, was the Russian Voltaire.

He conspires:—reviled—spat: assembled.

Bakunin's collectivism: communism.

The communist municipal government: politically, subjected to an irresponsible ruler; administratively, to a standard functionary, implacable and impassible. Bakunin spoke in Berne: in Basel, he expanded his system.

Social Liquidation.

Collective ownership of the soil.

Common ownership of all instruments of labor.

Replacement of all political states with workers' associations.

To restore Slavicism: Is that, in private, the whole Russian idea? To extend the domination of the Slavs: Is that what the internal decompositions of the empire will give rise to? The right thing to fear is something else: the nature of the vengeful democracy that advances in darkness. That which Bakunin brought to the dreamers of the West—for would he not take the wrathful form of the nascent Russian freedom to the discontented workers of the West? But will it not assuage this fear, truly assuage it, to think that while the powerful Russian aristocracy exhausts all its weapons against the heroic breast of the nihilists—freedom, with the French example and its majestic development in enlightened peace, will have solidly and irrevocably affirmed its conquests, infecting the attentive bordering countries with astonishment and hope?

The Slavophiles have not been at rest. How much money they gave to Taz! 1840. They had a great enemy in Chaadayev,[6] the energetic and gloomy Hussar officer whom the czar declared mad.

The Slavophiles were divided: into Orthodox authoritarians and socialist republicans.

In Kornekoff, the former group had their rational constructor. The human will being powerless to rule mankind, all men must submit to the Greek church, vessel of the divine will. In Kireyevski,[7] they had their mystic, kneeling on the ground with his arms outspread before the altar, as if awaiting, like the Brahmans, the hour of the eternal mingling, the eternal sinking of man, steeped in his Maker: *Aham Brahma!* Aksakov[8] was the man of the sword and the spear.

Velocipedes:—bicycles. There is a factory that makes them now in Japan.

"But we cannot be lawyers if the law is taught in the schools"—a Guatemalan magistrate, on the promulgation of the Civil Code and my desire that it be taught in abridged form in the high schools.

   Me—"Then let us be something else, my friend. The economic principle must be to the benefit of the many."

EARLY JOURNALISM

During the two years Martí spent in Mexico City (1875–77), he consolidated his reputation as a writer and orator, contributing numerous articles to Mexican newspapers, especially El Universal, delivering the fiery speeches for which he was already renowned, and enjoying some success as a playwright. In this article he evinces the outspoken critical spirit that would eventually make Mexican dictator Porfirio Díaz (and, in succeeding years, the dictators of both Guatemala and Venezuela) pressure him to leave.

THE POOR NEIGHBORHOODS OF MEXICO CITY

We are obliged to turn our eyes from the beauties on offer in the books of poets, and must put off, as well, whatever we might have said about some recently published scientific works, in order to direct not our enthusiasm but our dismay toward the terribly sad state of the unhealthy and neglected City of Mexico.

Strange it seems that there should be poets at all in our imperturbable municipality. A poet is something like a clean, white soul, and one might imagine that such a soul by its very nature rejects whatever is tainted, unclean, or repugnant in its surroundings. Agapito Silva publishes his "Poetical Thoughts" in *El Porvenir*,[1] but how can he think poetically in this foul and contaminated atmosphere? And how can Eduardo Zárate fail to be appalled that the pure wings of his muse, elegantly outspread in the book of American poets that José Domingo Cortés[2] has just published in Paris, are being dragged and defiled across the muddy and wretched streets of Mexico? Clean thoughts have need of clean surroundings: the delicate spirit is upset by any grossness of form or concept. And to turn from individual entities to the impassive city itself, we would have good reason to resort to the crude and demanding language of the law. The councilmen do not go to City Hall simply in order to grace the city with the calm of their magnificent persons. City Hall is a test of public men; those who handle public funds have a duty to make useful, visible, and fully transparent employment of them, for doltishness is no longer the right of anyone who has had a sufficient concept of himself to aspire to public office. Since City Hall has been entrusted with the means to make the dense and pernicious atmosphere of Mexico City breathable, the municipal corporation is very much obliged to attend to the primary interests that it has taken in charge—all the more so given the special care it must take to avoid being perceived as having neglected to carry out its mission because that mission was unpaid and therefore fruitless.

A city demands something more of its citizens than the hollow vainglory of calling themselves councilmen. It asks, imperiously, for neatness and cleanliness; it asks that its parks be elegant, that its places of transit be easily accessible, and that its impoverished back streets be subject not to a neglect that exacerbates the misfortune of all the needy children, but to tenacious and persistent effort, even though the good thus done will yield no financial profit. It is wrong for a person who values his good name to accept a post whose high mission he does not fulfill and whose significance he does not understand or live up to.

The outcry being raised by the press is not vain and futile, nor is it right that City Hall should gainsay those who remind it of its duty. In the poor neighborhoods, death, garbed in misery and ever seated at the thresholds of the houses, is now taking on a new form; deadly miasmas are exuded by the layer of greenish scum that blankets swampy pools of water. One breathes as if the air were heavy with humidity, or as if there were a scarcity of air, and this poor population of ours, so weakened already by their hunger, their laziness, and their vices, suffers even more from the scourge of this vagabond death that lives, errant and threatening, in every dense undulation of the atmosphere.

The press does not complain out of habit or fixation but because more of the poor are dying as a result of City Hall's incomprehensible laxness. This is no simple matter that the municipality can afford to ignore: it is a matter of life or death, grave, immediate, and urgent. The accusation is all the more necessary the more it appears to go unheard, for the municipality has paid no heed to it at all. Why do the councilmen take so long to do what is right when it is their duty to do it and when the means to carry out most of it are certainly not lacking, though neither is there any surplus or abundance of them. If the wagons that transport objects to or from Mexico City must travel on the calzada de Buenavista, then why is the calzada an unusable road on which crowds of men are endlessly working to get stalled or toppled wagons under way again? It is the only road; how can City Hall neglect the only road? Why, in the center of the city, where limpid breezes cannot easily blow, are the eyes repelled and the lungs obstructed and harmful elements breathed in from the miasmas given off by puddles of stagnant water blanketed by a greenish layer of rot? It is distressing to have to occupy oneself with this, and it is injurious to City Hall's reputation not to have addressed the problem already. The city council does not do the city some gratuitous favor by repairing the streets, taking care of the parks, and energetically promoting more hygienic conditions; rather, that was the purpose for which the members of the council were raised to the office they occupy. They do us a double harm: by not carrying out their duty, and by preventing, through their presence in City Hall, that duty from being carried out by others more intelligent or conscientious than they.

Precisely because their office is unpaid, they should be all the more careful to carry out its duties in full.

Since the populace entrusts them with funds whose employment cannot easily be scrutinized, the members of the city council, arbiters and handlers of these public funds, should be at pains to display to everyone that they have responded with interest and zeal to the public confidence of which, on election day, they claimed to be worthy. For how could anyone who, out of laziness or doltishness, did not strive for or understand all the good he could achieve, ever aspire to public office again?

Do the city councilmen fail to understand that precisely because their services are unpaid, they must take care to show that the lack of remuneration does not make them slow, neglectful, and wayward in their work?

For did they not seek the office to which the public vote has elevated them?

How can they make a show of not being concerned by the public's reproaches? It may be that the white souls of the councilmen have not consulted their intelligence; certainly they would not deliberately seek to be unworthy of the honorable office they continue to hold.

—*Revista Universal* (Mexico City), September 4, 1875

SARAH BERNHARDT

It is not known whether or where this article was published, though it may have been written for the New York Sun *in 1880. The ver-*

sion of it found among Martí's papers is written in French, like the
art reviews written for The Hour *during the same period.*

During a brief stay in Paris on his way to New York from
Madrid in December 1879, Martí met Sarah Bernhardt at the
Parisian benefit for flood victims in Murcia that he mentions. On
his previous visit in 1875, he had seen her in the role of Racine's
Phaedre at the Comédie-Française.

The name is celebrated and already greatly beloved in New York. Great ladies are known to be in thrall to her. She is the symbol of energy triumphant. A poor woman who has made so much space for herself in the world must be a great woman.

Each century has its stars: the land of Rachel, Mademoiselle Mars, and Sophie Arnould has now been further enriched by Sarah Bernhardt, who is unquestionably a tragedian, but is also something even more valuable: a character. We are not going to say what has already been said: we have our own impressions to convey.

Sarah is supple, slim, svelte. When she is not shaken by the demon of tragedy, her body is full of grace and abandon; when the demon takes hold of her, she is full of strength and nobility. Her face, though feminine, exudes a lovely hauteur: it is not beauty that is imprinted there—though she is a fine-looking woman—but resolve. She will do what she wants. She has something of the first Bonaparte about her: her soul is full of friendship and frankness but she feigns disdain because she believes she must in order to make others respect her. Where does she come from? From poverty! Where is she going? To glory! She is feared, but loved, which is unusual: it is because she is hard, but good-natured, a haughty woman, but at the same time *"un bon garçon."* Mention a woman in distress to her: she will open her purse. Tell her there is a little painting of real genius chez Goupil—or that very close to the Passage Jouffroy there is a beautiful Chinese carpet. Sarah, member of the Théâtre Français, will not balk at the price. If the carpet is old, if the painting was made by a strong hand, she will buy it; sometimes she does not know how she will pay, but she will earn the money herself, honestly; she will paint another painting of her own, a seascape, a watercolor, or she will make a statue of love, since she lacks the power to make it a reality.

Alexandre Dumas has piled his house high with objets d'art, from little Japanese monsters to a pre-Adamite Christ, an overly realistic Christ; but Sarah Bernhardt arranges her things better than anyone else can, and everything she owns is first-rate. She is majestic even in her caprices; her fantasies are royal. There is no particular merit in being born a queen and knowing how to be one, but there is great proof of majesty in being born into a poor family and knowing how to make a land as artistic and intelligent as France into your own kingdom.

There she was at the great Paris-Murcia gala, given to benefit the flood victims of Murcia, that Spanish city beloved by the sun. *La Vie Moderne,* an illustrated magazine, had built a magnificent red velvet throne for Sarah, with thickly embroidered Spanish cushions. Sarah, dressed as Doña Sol, the heroine of Victor Hugo's *Hernani,* sat beneath the rich hangings, attended by a very beautiful lady in waiting, Mlle. Croizette. She is proud, Mlle. Croizette, but what a good woman next to the superbly arrogant Sarah!

When Sarah stretches out her arm, she commands. When she raises her rather Asiatic head, with its slanting eyes, delicate nose, haughty forehead, and fragile lips, she must be obeyed, she must be admired.

It is not beauty that dazzles us: she is not beautiful. It is not a voluptuous charm that intoxicates us; she knows how to love, no doubt, but does not trouble herself with such unduly feminine matters. It is her lofty soul, dreaming of every height, an eagle's soul—the soul of a lioness or of tempered steel. It is her gaze, penetrating as a Toledo blade; it is her irresistible superiority that makes us lower our heads.

That night she was selling *panderetas,* Spanish tambourines: great painters had employed all their talents upon them, in the service of the poor. The shoddy leather was exalted by the hand that was to sell it— and by Meissonier, Worms, Detaille, Neuville, Raimundo Madrazo, Dubufe, etc. The auction was dull at first, but by the third *pandereta,* what a crowd was gathered around Sarah! As far as the eye could see were women with their hair done *à la Capoul,* Russian princes, great writers, wealthy Englishmen, youthful dandies.

They barred the way, and others were forced to look upon her from afar. She seemed quite proud of her triumph; at that moment she felt a little like the queen of Spain.

The whole world knows what she does: her great roles, her delightful writings, lovely paintings, bold little statues.

As a painter, she draws well, colors flawlessly, lights up the canvas as if by a stroke of genius: a clarity, an effect of moonlight, a fallen tree.

But that is not enough. As a writer, she has sounded a piercing and magnificent cry in her Paris-Murcia journal: her whole soul is there! Her work as a sculptor reminds us of Gustave Doré; she does not have his flair for composition, she will never sculpt groups like his, but she is as elegant, original, and brave. As for her work as a tragedian, let us hear the words of M. Emile Girardin, the Gordon Bennett of the French press: "Rachel had more genius; Sarah possesses more talent. Rachel is well aware of everything she does; Sarah draws from her nature without much awareness. Sarah is worth more." Truly: one must be great in order to become great. Clearly: she has known how to triumph.

In his home, Girardin has two beautiful portraits: one of Rachel, the other of Sarah Bernhardt. He sees her as a father would: he is passionate in his praise of her. How well this admirable old man of seventy speaks! His brain is as strong today as it was when, with dire hand, he killed the gallant Armand Carrel.

Sarah wears her hair very simply. She likes long-waisted dresses that sweep the floor. Her eyes are fevered. At the sight of certain creatures, one says: Muscle! At the sight of Sarah, one says: Nerve! The llama is a poor, delightful sort of Peruvian goat; Sarah raises her head like an irritated llama, but not like the llama that dies of sorrow, its melancholy eyes turned toward the sky, when its Indian master scolds or punishes it. Sarah would kill the Indian.

Sarah receives guests on Wednesdays. A woman writer, Julie Lambert, also has a beautiful salon in Paris, where one converses well and sees the best of the Parisian writers, but chez Sarah one feels from afar the spirit of Victor Hugo, who loves her. In the actress's salon, one notices a power of thought, a virility of purpose, an anxious mobility that well reflect the tempestuous spirit of the mistress of the oceans—and of her century. One does not sense the presence of Moses, as in Victor Hugo's house,[1] but at times one believes that one senses Judith.

Last year in London she appeared with the actor Coquelin in one of her most important roles; the British could not find crowns enough for her: everything was taken in advance. Extraordinary prices were paid for her paintings: her precious little sculptures met with great success. When she was seen surrounded by all the world at the Murcia gala, everyone said; "Sarah is an immense success!"

Ah yes, that is true today, but how much strength, weeping, sorrow, and indomitable energy did she have to exert and endure to attain it! She deserves to be studied as a lesson in the force of the human will.

Young people who do not triumph fast enough put a bullet through their heads. Sarah may have wept the kind of hot tears that go unseen and do not flow from the eyes, but she worked. Fifteen years ago—alone, so young, and all in tears—she must have said to herself, "What is to become of me?" Today she must have asked herself more than once, "How can it be that I am not a queen?"

IMPRESSIONS OF AMERICA
(BY A VERY FRESH SPANIARD)[1]

During Martí's first extended stay in the United States, in 1880, he was invited by influential journalist and publisher Charles Anderson Dana[2] to contribute to a New York weekly literary magazine called The Hour. *All told, Martí published twenty-nine short essays in the magazine that year, most of them originally written in French, on diverse topics such as* "Raimundo Madrazo" *(February 21),* "Fortuny" *(March 20), and* "The Metropolitan Museum" *(April 3). Among them was the following series of articles on his initial impressions of the United States. These he wrote in English, with what seems to have been rather minimal intervention from his editors, and they appear here exactly as they did in* The Hour.

I

I am, at last, in a country where every one looks like his own master. One can breathe freely, freedom being here the foundation, the shield, the essence of life. One can be proud of his species here. Every one works; every one reads. Only does every one feel in the same degree that they read and work? Man, as a strong creature—made to support on his shoulders the burden of misfortune, never bent, never tired, never dismaying,—is unrivalled here. Are women, those beings that we, the Southern people, like,—feeble and souple, tender and voluptuous,—as perfect, in their way, as men are to theirs? Activity, devoted to trade, is truly immense. I was never surprised in any country of the world I have visited. Here, I was surprised. As I arrived, in one of this summer-days, when the face of hasty business men are at the same moment fountains and volcanoes; when, bag in hand, the vest open, the neck-tye detached, I saw the diligent New Yorkers running up and down, buying here, selling there, transpiring, working, going ahead; when I remarked that no one stood quietly in the corners, no door was shut an instant, no man was quiet, I stoped myself, I looked respectfully on this people, and I said good-bye for ever to that lazy life and poetical inutility of our European countries. I remembered a sentence of an old Spaniard, a healthy countryman, father of thirty-six sons: "Only those who dig their bread, have a right to eat it: and, as if they dig most deeply, they will eat it whiter." But is this activity devoted in the same extent to the development of these high and noble anxieties of soul, that cannot be forgotten by a people who want to escape from unavoidable ruin, and strepitous definitive crumbling? When the days of poverty may arrive—what richness, if not that of spiritual strength and intellectual comfort, will help this people in its colossal misfortune? Material power, as that of Carthage, if it rapidly increases, rapidly falls down. If this love of richness is not tempered and dignified by the ardent love of intellectual pleasures,—if kindness toward men, passion for all what is great, devotion to all what means sacrifice and glory, are not as developed as fervorous and absorbent passion for money, where shall they go? where shall they find sufficient cause to excuse this hard burden of life and feel relief to their sorrow? Life wants permanent roots; life is unpleasant without the comforts of intelligence, the pleasures of art and the internal gratification that the goodness of the soul and the exquisiteness of taste produce to us.

I am deeply obliged to this country, where the friendless find always a friend and a kind hand is always found by those who look honestly for work. A good idea finds always here a suitable, soft, grateful ground. You must be intelligent; that is all. Give something useful. You will have all what you want. Doors are shut for those who are dull and lazy; life is sure to those who are faithful to the law of work. When I was a child, I read with admiration,—born as I am in a country where there is no field for individual activity, a series of biographies as those who are called here with a magnificent simplicity—*self-made men.* My childhood was not entirely gone out when I admired again, in British Honduras,[3] a wealthy Southern family brought by misfortune to painful scantiness,—and raising by their hands, in the thick bossom of forest, a clean, elegant, prosperous sugar plantation. The father, an ancient governor of a powerful State, was the engineer; the charming mother, very simply dressed, with a perpetual smile on her lips,—the

smile of those who are courageous enough to support human sufferings,—was the most skillful housekeeper I have ever seen. Hot cakes,
fine pastry, fresh milk, sweet jelly—were always on hand. When she
came to me, the noble face illuminated by the most pure look, the
curled silver hair carefully dressed, a waiter with exquisite dishes in
her wrinkled hands—the sweetest feelings filled my heart, and tears of
pleasure came to my eyes. The sons helped the father in all kinds of
labors; they ploughed the field,—saw the sugar-cane, burn the woods,
build a new "sweet home,"—and as slightly dressed as miserable countrymen in those far forests do,—very early in the morning, merrily
singing, they drove the oxen to the hardest work of the plantation.
And they were elegant, gentle, learned young men. I will study a most
original country at its birth—in the school; at its development—in the
family; at its pleasures—in the theatre, in the clubs, in Fourteenth
Street, in large and small family party. I will go, in a brilliant Sunday,
walking down the fashionable Fifth Avenue, to the crowded church to
hear a preacher—the word of peace—speaking about politics or the
field of war. I will see many nonsenses, many high deeds; the politicians, who save the country, when they could—without any effort go
back to the days of arrogant militarism, violation of the public will,
corruption of the political morality; I will see benevolent faces of men,
defiant faces of women, the most capricious and uncommendable fancies, all the greatness of freedom and all the miseries of prejudices;
here, a powerful originality, there a vulgar imitation of transatlantic
extravagances. Liberty in politics, in customs, in enterprises; humble
slavery in taste. Frenchmen give the sacred word; great names, and not
great works are looked for. As there is not a fixed mind on art, the
most striking is the most loved. There is no taste for the sweet beauty
of Hélène or Galæthea—the taste being all devoted to old imperfect
works of China and Japan. If a scientific object would have been intended by the owners of these *bibelots*, it would be a matter of praise.
But it is only for the censurable pleasure of indiscreetly holding foreign goods bought at a high price.

At a first glance what else can I tell? I have all my impressions
vividly awaken. The crowds of Broadway; the quietness of the
evenings; the character of men; the most curious and noteworthy
character of women; the life in the hotel, that will never be understood
for us; that young lady, physically and mentally stronger than the
young man who courts her; that old gentleman, full of wisdom and capacity who writes in a sobrious language for a hundred newspapers;

this feverish life; this astonishing movement; this splendid sick people, in one side wonderfully extended, in other side—that of intellectual pleasures—childish and poor; this colossal giant, candorous and credulous; these women, too richly dressed to be happy; these men, too devoted to business of pocket, with remarkable neglectness of the spiritual business—all is, at the same time, coming to my lips, and begging to be prepared in this brief account of my impressions.

Size and number: these are here the elements of greatness. Nothing is absolutely neglected, however. If the common people, increased every day by a thirsty foreign population, that must not be confounded with the true American people, shows that anxious desire for money, and fights frightfully in this way,—the true Americans preserve national greatness, constitutional rights, old and honorable names, from the vulgar storm of immigration, that brings in strength and possibilities of wealth, what they lack of intellectual height, and moral deepness. In the columns of a newspaper, in the page of a magazine, in the familiar chit-chat, the most pure feelings, noble aspirations, and generous ideas bravely fight for the rapid improvement of the country, in the sense of moral development.

It will be reached. It has not yet been reached, because many strangers bring here their odiums, their wounds, their moral ulcers. What a terrible enemy the desperate want of money is for the achievement of virtues! How great a nation must be, to conduct in a quiet way, these bands of wolves, hungry and thirsty, these excrescences of old poor countries, ferocious or unuseful there,—and here, under the influence of work, good, kind and tame!

And, for the *mot de la fin*, let me tell you what it happened to me, as I came, a week ago, from Cape May, a charming watering-place, to Philadelphia. The train near to the station jumped off the tracks; the car where I was, fell side-way. The accident was without consequences; but, as everybody was compelled by the shaking and pulling of the car to abandon violently their seats, the moment was a solemn one. Women became deadly pales. Men forgot women, looking for their own salvation. I thought, first, what must occur to a man under such a case, and, in the same instant, I saw rolling a poor eighty years' woman on the floor. I ran to her, offering her my hands. The old lady, very elegant indeed, notwithstanding her large amount of years, looked at me gratefully, tended her hands toward me;—but, as she touched the extreme of my fingers with their own, she told me, with expressive frightened grimaces:

"By the hands, no! Go away! Go away!"
Was she an old Puritan?

—*The Hour* (New York), July 10, 1880

II

Let us begin this time by a curious confession. This is the only country, of all those I have visited, where I have remained a week without becoming particularly devoted and deeply attached to some woman. Even in Southampton, where in a brilliant half an hour, I saw a sweet girl, we loved ourselves, and we bid good-bye for ever; even while crossing a magnificent country, the Atlantic coast of Guatemala, where—like a Crown Venus, emerging from the spring of a clear river—a supple, slender but voluptuous Indian woman, showed herself to the thirsty traveler with all the majestic power of a new kind of impressive and suggestive beauty, I loved and was beloved. Everywhere, a woman's soul has come to bless and sweeten my exhausted life.

But I have not found in New York my two lovely eyes! That is a curious case, because I feel rapidly beauty of the body or the soul, and I pay both sudden and fervently vehement admiration. I attach myself most vigorously to a clear mind, a generous heart, a deep and tender eye. I have spent many a sunny afternoon between Fourteenth and 23d Street; I have visited, I have talked, I have dined with American women. I have been acquainted with serious ladies, with most gay young ladies; they have translated my verses; they have decorated the button-hole of my evening dress; they even have, in a noisy cordial party, crowned me with a bonbonnière, representing a chicken's head. But I am still as an inconsolable widow, awaiting the first powerful emotion. Education and politeness, although not of kind we like in Europe, is quite common here; beauty is the general endowment; culture is spreading, but French tastes invade and penetrate the elegant world. But where are the chaste abandon, the savory languor, the Haydée-like looks, the tender sweetness and gentle grace of our Southern women?

Man here is both strong-minded and strong-bodied; if he usually drowns in the stormy business tide, the intellectual and refined pleasures which charm us and occupy us in old romantic Europe,—he remains kind, because he is prosperous; he has the strength of gladness; he gains it by his vigorous efforts; he has an athletic development secured by his continual work in the red-hot forge of life. But why should women look so manly? Their fast going up and down stairs, up and down the streets, the resolute, well-defined object of all their actions, their too virile existence, deprive them of the calm beauty, the antique grace, the exquisite sensitiveness which make of women those superior beings—of whom Calderon said that they were "a brief world."

A friend of mine told me once, while we were paying a visit to an always-smiling, always-talking, never-resting Andalouse lady, "If your tired veins need a new, powerful blood, and you want to see a land less obstructed by the ruins of feudal castles, old heavy churches, go to that marvelous land, America. But if you want, as I want, a woman's smile to live upon, take with you this gentlewoman—there women never smile!"

The great heart of America cannot be judged by the distorted, morbid passion, ardent desires and anguishes of New York life. In this turbulent stream, natural currents of life cannot appear. All is darkened, unhinged, dusty; virtues and vices cannot be at first glance properly analyzed. They run away tumultuously mingled. Prejudice, vanity, ambition, every poison of the soul, effaces or stains the American nature. It is necessary to look for it—not in the crowded street, but in the sweet home quietness; not in the convulsive life of the city, but in the open-hearted existence of the country.

Young women in America are remarkable by their excessive gaiety or excessive seriousness. Their control over themselves, their surety of being respected, their calculated coldness, their contempt of passions, their dry, practical notions of life, give them a singular boldness and a very peculiar frankness in their relations with men. What I have seen and heard is, indeed, painfully suggestive. The love of riches moves and generally guides feminine actions in this country. American women seem to have only one necessary thought when they see a new man: "How much is that man worth?" Such thoughts deform and harden the most handsome faces, made by the Almighty to be the consolation of misfortune, the home of grace, tenderness, nobleness.

A conversation I have heard, sharp and cold as the end of a weapon, deserves to be remembered. God has never intended the young woman to speak in such a way. It was in a literary party. Arrogant New York ladies cruelly sneered at a Western wealthy family, whose recent prosperity and humble beginnings were denounced by the heavy luxury of the dresses, the striking colors of the silks and a certain provincial candor which inexpert parvenus bring always to their first excursions into society. But mockery of this kind is especially unreasonable in this country, where nobody has a right to disdain the modest cradle of others, all being born in a similar poor cradle. The New Yorkers who now mock at the showy, vulgar, amusing Western family, must not forget that the same natural pride and social inexperience marked undoubtedly the first business triumphs and prosperous years of their equally modest ancestors.

A plough or an engine are, gloriously indeed, the only blazons of American families. No gold fields, no plumed helmet, no fierce dragon in their coat-of-arms. Hard work and self-made prosperity are their only armorial ensigns. Sons of toil, they ought to be all brothers. An old rich man must not sneer at a new rich man, for they came, in one or two degress, from the same mother—poverty; from the same father—work. An old plough has no reason for disdaining a new one; the time that distances the one from the other is not a reason for mockery. For my own part, I like better the man who has just used the plough than another who has forgotten the manner of using it.

The Hour (New York), August 21, 1880

III

We read in Europe many wonderful statements about this country. The splendor of life, the abundance of money, the violent struggles for its possession, the golden currents, that dazzle and blind the vulgar people, the excellencies of instruction, the habit of working, the vision of that new country arising above the ruins of old nations, excite the attention of thoughtful men, who are anxiously looking for the definitive settlement of all the destructive forces that began during the last century to lay the foundations of a new era of mankind. This could be, and ought to be, the transcendental significance of the United States. But have the States the elements they are supposed to have? Can they do what they are expected to do? Do they impose their own character, or do they suffer the imposition of the character of others? Is America going to Europe or Europe coming to America? Error, both in politics and religion has been worshipped in the Old World. Truth, liberty and dignity are supposed to have reached, at last, a sure heart in the New World. We must ask for a response to these secrets of the home life from the benches of the schoolrooms, the daily newspaper and conversation in society. Eloquent answers to all mystifications strike the observer as he goes through the streets. We must ask women for the natural end of their unextinguishable thirst for pleasure and amusement. We must ask them if a being so exclusively devoted to the possession of silk dresses, dazzling diamonds and all kinds of costly fancies could afterwards carry into their homes those solid virtues, those sweet feelings, that kind resignation, that evangelic power of consolation which can only keep up a hearth shaken by misfortune and inspire children with contempt for regular pleasures and the love of internal satisfactions that make men happy and strong, as they did Ismael, against the days of poverty. We must ask a boy of fourteen what he knows and what he is taught. We must observe in the newspapers what they place before the public—news or ideas. We must look at what people read, what they applaud, and what they love. And, as these problems cannot be answered in a page, or understood and remembered by a new-comer, I have taken here and there some memoranda. Here, from my note-book, are some:

"What do I see? A girl seven years old goes to school. She talks with unusual ease to other girls; this miniature of a woman has all the self-control of a married woman; she looks and smiles at me as if she could know all the mysteries of mankind. Her ears are adorned with heavy earrings; her little fingers with rings. Where can this wonderful volubility come from? What will this little girl, so fond of jewelry at seven years, do for it at sixteen? Slavery would be better than this kind of liberty; ignorance would be better than this dangerous science."

"I went down town by the elevated railroad. As I travelled by this perilous but seductive way, I lost all hope of understanding Americans when I heard the name of a street, 'Chamber Street!' always pronounced in an indistinct way by the conductors. Is it Cham, Chem, Chamber or Chember? Is it Houston, House or Hous? Is it Franklin, Frank or Frenk? It is curious to observe that I can always understand an Englishman when he speaks to me; but among the Americans a word is a whisper; a sentence is an electric commotion. And if somebody asks me how can I know if a language that I so badly write, is badly spoken, I will tell frankly that it is very frequent that critics speak about what they absolutely ignore. There is, among the Americans, an excellent writer, the humorist Mark Twain[4]—and has he not presented the gifted king of Bavaria, a poet, an enthusiast, a knight of old times, as a savage who oblige the singers of his theatre to play the same opera twice in a night, under the most terrible rain that could fall over the poor Bavarians? He astonishes himself with the mastodontic composition of German words. All conversation is here in a single word: no breathe, no pause; not a distinct sound. We see that we are in the land of railroads. 'That's all'—'did'nt'—'won't'—'ain't'—'indeed'—'Nice weather'—'Very pleasant'—'Coney Island'—'Excursion.' That is all that I can seize, when I listen with anxious attention to the average American. When I listened to men and women of culture I have been able to appreciate how the correctness of Addison can be mingled wit the acuteness of Swift, and the strength of Carlyle with the charming melody of Longfellow.

"Among women, as their usual kindness inclines them to soften the asperity of their language, in order to be easily understood by the foreigner, the English tongue appears exceptionally harmonious. Everything could be pardoned to these indefatigable talkers, if they would speak in such a way, in order to employ the time that seems to be always short for them; but if—by a marvel—you can fathom the sense of those whirling words, you will remark that a vulgar subject is, commonly, too extensively developed."

"I love silence and quietness. Poor Chatterton[5] was right when he desperately longed for the delights of solitude. The pleasures of cities begin for me when the motives which make pleasure for others are fading away. The true day for my soul dawns in the midst of the night. As I took yesterday evening my usual nocturne walk, many pitiful sights made a painful impression upon me. One old man, dressed in that style which reveals at the same time that good fortune we have had and the bad times that begin for us, steps silently under a streetlamp. His eyes, fixed upon the passers by, were full of tears; his hand held a poor handkerchief. He could not articulate a single word. His sighs, not his words, begged for assistance. A little farther on, in Fourteenth Street, a periodic sound, as a distant lamentation, sprang from the shadow. A poor woman knelt on the sidewalk, as if looking for her grave, or for strength to lift on her shoulders the hoarse organ whose crank her dying hand was turning. I passed through Madison Square, and I saw a hundred robust men, evidently suffering from the pangs of misery. They moved painfully, as if they wished to blot out of their minds their sorrowful thoughts—and were all lying down on the grass or seated on the benches, shoeless, foodless, concealing their anguish under their dilapidated hats."

1882–1890

After a stay of several months in Venezuela that came to an end when his insistence on speaking his mind got him ejected from yet another country, Martí returned to New York, which would become his home base for the rest of his life. There he published his first volume of poetry and embarked upon a career as U.S. correspondent for a number of Latin American newspapers. The resulting cumulation of articles, with their detailed description, analysis, and critique of virtually every aspect of the young nation, would become one of the major facets of his lifework and one of the nineteenth century's most telling commentaries on democracy in the United States.

By consistently viewing the United States from the pan–Latin American perspective that was required for articles that were often reprinted in newspapers across the hemisphere, Martí used his "Letters from New York" not only to give Latin Americans a more complex and realistic view of the United States, but also to promote his ideal of Latin American unity. At the same time, he remained a leading figure in the Cuban exile community and—except for a period in the mid-1880s—continued to be very actively involved as a leader in the ongoing efforts to gain Cuban independence.

POETRY

PROLOGUE TO JUAN ANTONIO PÉREZ BONALDE'S *POEM OF NIAGARA*

*** SELECTIONS ***

In 1824 José María de Heredia (1803–39), a Cuban poet exiled for his political activities and living in the United States, wrote a famous ode titled "Niagara." A half century later, when Juan Antonio Pérez Bonalde[1] asked Martí to write a prologue to his poem about Niagara, an homage to Heredia was implicit. Over that period, Niagara Falls had become something of a literary topos for Latin American writers. Colombian poet and novelist Rafael Pombo (1833–1912) had written another well-known poem called "El Niagara" during his years as a diplomat in the United States in the late 1850s, and other Latin American travelers to the United States such as the Argentine Domingo Faustino Sarmiento had eloquently evoked the Falls in books about their journeys. Martí himself, however, was more interested in the man-made features of the U.S. landscape; aside from this prologue, his work makes scant mention of Niagara Falls or any other North American natural landmark.

. . . Contemptible times, these: when the only art that prevails is that of piling one's own granaries high, sitting on a seat of gold and living all in gold, without perceiving that human nature will never vary and the only result of digging up external gold is to live without gold inside! Contemptible times: when the love and exercise of greatness is a rare and outmoded quality. Men today are like certain young ladies who are much taken with virtue when they see it extolled by others or exalted in sounding prose or winged verse, but who, after embracing virtue, which has the shape of a cross, throw it off in horror as if it were a corroding shroud that would eat away the roses from their cheeks and the delight from their kisses and the necklace of vivid butterflies that women like to clasp around their throats. Contemptible times: when the priests no longer deserve the praise or reverence of the poets, but the poets have not yet begun to be priests! . . .

Females, weak females men would seem now if, crowned with garlands of roses, in the arms of Alexander and Cebetes, they were to drain the sweet Falernian wine that gave its bouquet to Horace's banquets. Sensuality has made the pagan lyric obsolete, and the Christian lyric, which once was beautiful, is obsolete as well because humanity has changed its idea of Christ, who yesterday was seen as the smallest of the gods and today is loved as perhaps the greatest of men. To the poets of today neither the lyric nor the epic mode comes naturally and calmly, nor is any lyric acceptable but that which each person draws from within, as if his own being were the only matter of whose existence he had no doubt, or as if the problem of human life had been addressed with such courage and explored with such eagerness that there could be no theme better, more stimulating, or more conducive to depth and grandeur than the study of oneself. No one nowadays is certain of his faith, and those who believe they are deceive themselves. Those who write the word *faith* gnaw at the fist they write with, tormented by gorgeous, savage inner beasts. There is no painter who succeeds in coloring the luminous aureoles of virgins with the novelty and transparency of other times, no religious cantor or preacher who puts unction and a tone of certainty into his stanzas and anathemas. All are soldiers in an army on the march. All have been kissed by the same sorceress. In everyone the new blood boils. Men can tear their innermost selves to shreds, but intranquillity, insecurity, vague hopes, and secret visions remain, famished and wrathful, in the most secret recesses of their beings. An immense, pale man, dressed in black, with gaunt face, weeping eyes, and dry lips, is walking gravely across the earth without rest or sleep—and he has taken a seat in every home and has put his trembling hand on every bedstead. Such a pounding in the brain! Such fear in the breast! Such demanding of things that do not come! Such unawareness of what one wants! And in the spirit, such a sense of mingled nausea and delight: nausea for the day that is dying, delight for the dawn!

There are no permanent works, because works produced during times of realignment and restructuring are shifting and unsettled in their very essence: there are no established paths. The new altars, vast and open as forests, have only just been glimpsed. The mind solicits diverse ideas from everywhere, and those ideas are like coral and like starlight and like the waves of the sea. There is a constant yearning for some knowledge that will confirm current beliefs and a fear of learning something that will alter them. The formation of new social conditions makes the struggle to earn a living uncertain and hampers the fulfilment of daily duties that, not finding broad roads, change form and direction at every instant, spurred on by the fear that arises from the probability or proximity of poverty. With the spirit thus divided among contradictory and intranquil loves, and the concept of literature shaken at every moment by some new gospel, with all the images that were once revered now naked and discredited while the future's images are as yet unknown, in this bewilderment of the mind, this restless life without fixed course, definite character or certain conclusion, in the biting fear of our own impoverishment and the varied and apprehensive labors we undertake to escape it, it is no longer possible to produce those long and patient works, those expansive tales in verse, those zealous imitations of Latin men that were written with great deliberation, year by year, in the repose of the monk's cell or amid the pleasant leisures of the ambitious courtier, seated in his ample chair of richly worked cordovan with studs of fine gold, in the beatific spiritual calm produced by the certainty that the good Indian was kneading the bread, the good king decreeing the laws, and the Mother Church giving shelter and sepulcher. Only in an era of stable elements, a general and established literary type, and well-known and established channels, when individual tranquillity is possible, is it easy to produce those massive works of ingenuity that, without exception, require such a conjunction of favorable conditions. Hatred, which hoards and concentrates, may still be able to produce this kind of work, but love brims over and flows out all around, and these are times of love, even for those who hate. Love intones fleeting songs, but because it is a vehement and climactic emotion whose tension is wearying and overwhelming, it does not produce works of unhurried inspiration and painstaking labor.

Today, there is a kind of dismantling of the human mind. Gone are the days of high fences; now is the time of broken fences. Now men are beginning to walk across the whole of the earth without stumbling; before now, they had hardly begun to move when they ran into the wall of a gentleman's estate or the ramparts of a convent. Now we love a God who penetrates and prevails over everything; it seems a profanation to give the Creator of all beings and of all that is to be the form of a single one of those beings. Since all human progress may consist in returning to the point of departure, we are returning to Christ, to the crucified Christ, the forgiving, captivating Christ of bare feet and open arms, and not to a heinous, Satanic, malevolent, hateful, bitter, lashing, impious, crucifying Christ. . . .

Cities have more tongues now than there are leaves on the trees of the forest; ideas mature in the public square where they are taught and passed from hand to hand. Speech is not a sin but a gala occasion; listening is not heresy, but a pleasure, a habit, and a style. The ears are ready for anything; thoughts have hardly sprung up when they are already laden with flowers and fruit and leaping off the page and penetrating every mind like a fine, rarefied dust. Trains vanquish the wilderness; newspapers, the human wilderness. Sunlight penetrates the fissures in old tree trunks. All is expansion, communication, florescence, contagion, diffusion. The newspapers deflower grandiose ideas. Ideas do not form families in the mind, as before, or build homes, or live long lives. They go at a gallop, mounted on lightning, winged. They do not grow within a solitary mind but emerge through commerce among all ideas. They do not laboriously come forth to benefit a handful of readers, but benefit all from the moment they are born. They are wrung out, placed on a pedestal, worn as a crown, stuck on a spike, worshiped as idols, overturned, raised up, and torn down. Even when their glitter seems genuine, spurious ideas cannot withstand rough handling, heavy weather, much trafficking and thrashing. Genuine ideas emerge in the end, bruised but whole and compact, with the power of spontaneous healing. We arise in the morning with one problem, and by the time we go to bed at night we have exchanged it for another. Images devour each other in the mind. There is not enough time to give form to thought. Ideas are lost in each other in the sea of our minds, as when a stone strikes blue water and the circles in the water lose themselves in each other. Before, ideas stood silently in the mind like fortified towers, and when they arose they were seen from afar. Today they emerge in clusters from the lips, like golden seeds that fall on seething ground; they break open, radiate, evaporate, come to nothing—oh beautiful sacrifice!—for the one who creates them; they dissolve into glowing sparks; they crumble. And hence the small, shimmering works of our time, and the absence of those great, culminating works that are intense, sustained, and majestic.

It happens, as well, that in the great common labor of humanity— the commendable habit of examining ourselves and asking one another to account for our lives, and the glorious need for each man to store up by his own efforts the bread served at his table—our era does not esteem or perhaps even permit the isolated appearance of super-human entities immured in a single labor that is taken to be marvelous and supreme. A high mountain looks lower when it is surrounded by hills. And ours is an era when hills are rising higher than mountains, when peaks are subsiding into plains. Already the new era approaches when all plains will be peaks. As the lofty heights descend, the flat-lands rise, and this will make the earth more easily transitable. Indi-vidual geniuses are less distinguishable, for they are beginning to lack the surrounding lowliness that once heightened their stature. And since all are learning to harvest the fruits of nature and esteem its flow-ers, fewer flowers and fruits are awarded to the old masters and more to the new generations who were once a mere host of venerators of the good harvesters. We are witnessing something like a decentralization of intelligence. Beauty has become the dominion of all. The number of good secondary poets is startling, as is the scarcity of lone, eminent poets. Genius is moving from the individual to the collectivity. Man is losing out to men. The traits of the privileged are being diluted and ex-panded to the masses, which will not please those among the privi-leged with ignoble souls, but will gladden those of generous and gallant heart who know that however grand a creature you may be on the earth, you are no more than a reflection of the Creator's gaze and a golden sand that will return to the beautiful source of gold.

And as the man of Auvergne dies in glad Paris more of homesick-ness than of bedazzlement, and every man who pauses to look at himself languishes with a sweet nostalgia for heaven, the poets of today—simple men of Auvergne in a sumptuous, turbulent Lutèce—are nostalgic for great deeds. War, once a source of glory, is becoming obsolete, and what once seemed greatness is now beginning to be crime. The princely court, once the haven of bards for hire, looks with frightened eyes at the modern bards, who though they sometimes rent out their lyres no longer rent them out permanently, and usually do not rent them out at all. God moves about in confusion, women as if unmoored and bewildered, but nature still sets the solemn sun ablaze in the middle of space; the woodland gods still speak the tongue no longer spoken by the divinities of the altars. Man casts his talking-headed serpents across the seas, from the wild crags of England to the merry American coast, and captures the light of the stars in a crystal bauble, and hurls his black and smoking tritons over the waters and the mountain ranges—and within the human soul, even as the suns that gave light to the earth for dozens of centuries are going out, the sun itself has not gone out. There is no West for the human spirit; there is nothing but the North, with its corona of light. The mountain ends in a peak, the rearing wave churned up and hurled to the sky by the tempest ends in a crest, the tree ends in a crown, and human life must end upon a summit. In the structural change we are witnessing—this remaking of the world by men along which the new life gallops like a fiery steed pursued by barking dogs—in this walling off of sources and clouding over of the gods, nature, human labor, and the spirit of man open like pure and inexhaustible springs to the thirsty lips of the poets who empty out the bitter old wine from their goblets carved of precious stones, and set them down where they will be filled with the sun's rays, the echoes of toil, and good, simple pearls drawn up from the depths of the soul—and then, before mankind's astonished eyes, their fevered hands lift high the sonorous cup!

Thus, his feet and eyes aching from seeing and walking across these smoking ruins, the lyric poet, who was always more or less a personal poet, re-enters himself, while he who, in epochs of courts, convents, and bloodshed, would have been an epic poet, fixes his eye instead on the battles and solemnities of nature. The battlefield is in the factories; glory, in peace; the temple, throughout the earth; the poem, in nature. When life has settled down, the Dante to come will arise, not because he has greater power than today's aspiring Dantes, but because of the greater power of the times. What is arrogant man but the spokesman of the unknown, an echo of the supernatural, a mirror of eternal lights, a more or less finished copy of the world in which he lives? Today Dante lives within himself, and by his own labors. Ugolino[2] gnawed his son, but today's poet gnaws himself; no beggar's hard crust is more pocked with toothmarks than a poet's soul; the eyes of the soul can see the blood that drips from the poet's lacerated fists and from the hollows where his wings were ripped out.

Historic life, then, is suddenly suspended; the nascent institutions are as yet too new and too confused to have yielded up the elements of poetry—for countries acquire their bouquet as wine does, with the years. The roots of the old poetry are in decay, shaken by the wind and the critical spirit; personal life is full of doubt, unsettled, questioning, restless, Luciferian; and feverish inner life, dynamic, clamorous, not fully anchored, has become the principal and, with nature itself, only legitimate subject of modern poetry.

But what hard work it is to find oneself! Man hardly enjoys the use of his own reason, for it is obscured when he is still in his cradle; before he can truly enter into himself he must dissolve himself. His is a Herculean struggle against the obstacles placed in his path by his own nature and by the conventional ideas on which, in waning hour, and by unholy council and culpable arrogance, he is nourished. There is no more difficult task than that of distinguishing the life that is parasitic and acquired from the life that is spontaneous and innate, that which arrives with man from that which is added to him by the lessons, legacies, and orders of those who came before him. Pretending to complete the human being, they interrupt him. He is hardly born when the philosophers—or the religions, the parents' passions, the political systems—are already standing over his cradle with thick, durable blindfolds in their hands. And they swaddle and they bind, and then, for the whole of his life on the earth, man is a blinkered horse. Thus is the earth now a vast abode of masqueraders. We come into life like wax, and chance pours us into prefabricated molds. Established conventions deform true existence, and true life comes to be like a silent current that slips invisible beneath the life that is apparent, sometimes not sensed even by the very one in which it does its stealthy work, like the mysterious Guadiana that runs silently for long stretches beneath Andalusian soil. To safeguard human free will and leave human spirits in their own seductive form, to refrain from marring virgin natures by imposing the prejudices of others upon them, to make them capable of taking for themselves what is useful without warping them or compelling them to follow a well-marked route—this is the only way to populate the earth with the vigorous and creative generation it needs. Redemptions are becoming theoretical and formal, when they must be effective and essential. If spiritual freedom is not safeguarded, then literary originality has no place and political freedom does not long endure. Man's first task is to reconquer himself. It is urgent that men be returned to themselves and extricated from the bad government of convention that suffocates or poisons their sentiments, accelerates the awakening of their senses, and overtaxes their intelligence with a pernicious, alien, cold, and false abundance. Only what is genuine is fruitful. Only what is direct is powerful. What another bequeaths on us is like a warmed-over meal. It is up to each man to reconstruct life, and no sooner does he look inside himself than he reconstructs it. He who, claiming to guide the new generations, teaches them a circumscribed and absolute set of doctrines and fills their ears with the barbarous gospel of hatred instead of the sweet speech of love commits premeditated murder; he is ungrateful to God and the enemy of man. He who obstructs, in any way, the free, direct, and spontaneous employment of the magnificent faculties of man is guilty of betraying nature. Now enters the good and valiant lancer, the robust jouster, the knight of human freedom—a high order of knighthood—he who comes, free of violent desires derived from Valbuena or leavings from Ojeda,[3] straight from epic poetry to our own time; he who raised his generous hands to the sky in supplication, and withdrew them from his prayer transformed into a sonorous vessel, overflowing with vibrant, opulent verses, caressed by reflections of Olympus! The poem lies within mankind, intent on tasting every apple, extracting all the sap from the tree of Paradise, and transforming into a comfortable hearth the fire in which God long ago forged the exterminating sword. The poem lies in nature, a mother with bounteous breasts, a wife who never ceases to love, an oracle that always responds, a poet with a thousand tongues, a sorceress who makes us hear what she does not say, a giver of solace who fortifies and anoints! Enter now the good bard of Niagara, who has written an extraordinary and resplendent song of the endless poem of nature! . . .

The poem of Niagara! The halo of spirit that hovers about the halo of multicolored water; the battle in its bosom, less thunderous than the human battle; the simultaneous surge of all that lives which, bounding, churning, and pushed by forces unseen, will end in the unknown down below; the law of existence, an inexorable, incomprehensible logic that senselessly annihilates martyrs and villains and downs a clutch of evangelists at one gulp like a famished ogre while leaving squads of criminals alive on the earth, as if gory-mouthed predators amused it; the ready channel along which men and thundering waterfalls explode, crash, rebel, leap to the sky, and plunge to the depths; the outcry and angelic resistance of a man borne off by the onrush of the law, who even as he yields and dies, blasphemes, struggles like an earth-shaking Titan and roars; the booming voice of the cascade that is pushed along by an equal law and foams and groans whether it falls to the sea or into a dank cave; and beyond all that, the tears that now veil all of it, and the heartrending wail of the solitary soul: such is the monumental poem that this man of his time saw in Niagara. . . .

You have done well, sincere and honorable poet, to feed on yourself! . . . You have done well, Poet of the Torrent, to dare to be free in a time of pretentious slaves, for so accustomed are men to servitude that now that they have ceased to be the slaves of kings, they are beginning, with even more shameless degradation, to be the slaves of Liberty! You have done well, illustrious cantor—and note that I know the worth of this word I speak to you! You have done well, lord of the flaming sword, rider of a winged horse, rhapsodist with an oaken lyre, man who opens your breast to nature! Cultivate what is great, since such cultivation is what brought you to the earth. Leave all other pettinesses to the petty. May these solemn winds always move you. Put aside the hollow rhymes of common usage, strung with pearls and mantled with artificial flowers, which are more often the diversion and legerdemain of idle spirits than a blast from the soul and a deed worthy of the mind's magnates. Gather all contracted sorrows, Latin tepidness, reflexive rhymes, doubts acquired from others, woes learned from books and preordained faith into a heap and throw them on the fire, and warm yourself at the wholesome flame from the chill of these painful times when, the sleeping embryo already awake within the mind, all men stand upon the earth, their lips clamped shut, their brave chests bare, and their fists raised to the sky, demanding that life reveal its secret.

ISMAELILLO

Among the many photographs of Martí, only one shows him with a
smile on his face: a picture in which he holds his toddler son in his
arms. Separated from the boy after his wife took him back to Cuba
with her toward the end of 1881, Martí shaped his loss into his first
published book of poems, Ismaelillo, *or "Little Ishmael." In a note*
accompanying the copy of it that he sent to Charles Anderson
Dana, Martí wrote: "This is a novel about my love affair with my
son: one grows weary of reading so many novels about love affairs
with women."

New York, 1882

Son:

Appalled by everything I take refuge in you.

I have faith in the betterment of humanity, in a future life, in the
usefulness of virtue, and in you.

If anyone tells you that these pages are like other pages, say to them
that I love you too much to profane you like that. As I paint you here,
so my eyes have seen you. In this festive garb you have appeared to
me. When I have ceased to see you in a certain way, I have ceased to
paint you. These streams have passed through my heart.

May they reach yours!

SUEÑO DESPIERTO

Yo sueño con los ojos
Abiertos, y de día
Y noche siempre sueño.
Y sobre las espumas
Del ancho mar revuelto,
Y por entre las crespas
Arenas del desierto,
Y del león pujante,
Monarca de mi pecho,
Montada alegremente
Sobre el sumiso cuello,
Un niño que me llama
Flotando siempre veo!

WAKING DREAM

I dream with my eyes
open and always, by day
and night, I dream.
And over the foam
of the wide and restless sea,
and through the spiraling
sands of the desert,
upon a mighty lion,
monarch of my breast,
blithely astride
its docile neck,
always I see, floating,
a boy, who calls to me!

BRAZOS FRAGANTES

Sé de brazos robustos,
Blandos, fragantes;
Y sé que cuando envuelven
El cuello frágil,
Mi cuerpo, como rosa
Besada, se abre.
Y en su propio pérfume
Lánguido exhálase.
Ricas en sangre nueva
Las sienes laten;
Mueven las rojas plumas
Internas aves;
Sobre la piel, curtida
De humanos aires,
Mariposas inquietas
Sus alas baten;
Savia de rosa enciende
Las muertas carnes!—
¡Y yo doy los redondos
Brazos fragantes,
Por dos brazos menudos
Que halarme saben,
Y a mi pálido cuello
Recios colgarse,
Y de místicos lirios
Collar labrarme!
¡Lejos de mí por siempre,
Brazos fragantes!

MI REYECILLO

Los persas tienen
Un rey sombrío;
Los hunos foscos
Un rey altivo;
Un rey ameno
Tienen los íberos;
Rey tiene el hombre,

FRAGRANT ARMS

I know arms that are strong,
soft and fragrant;
I know when they encircle
my fragile neck,
my body, like a kissed
rose, opens,
and breathes in its own
languid perfume.
Rich in new blood
the temples throb;
and the red plumage of
internal birds begins to stir;
across skin weathered
by human winds
restless butterflies
beat their wings;
elixir of rose ignites
dead flesh!—
And I give up those rounded
fragrant arms,
for two small arms
that know how to tug at me,
and cling tightly
to my pale neck
and of mystic lilies
weave me a chain!
Away from me forever,
fragrant arms!

MY KINGLET

The Persians have
a gloomy king;
the sullen Huns
an arrogant king;
the Iberians have
a congenial king;
and men have a king,

Rey amarillo:
¡Mal van los hombres
Con su dominio!
Mas yo vasallo
De otro rey vivo,—
Un rey desnudo,
Blanco y rollizo:
Su cetro—un beso!
Mi premio—un mimo!
Oh! cual los áureos
Reyes divinos
De tierras muertas,
De pueblos idos
—¡Cuando te vayas,
Llévame, hijo!—
Toca en mi frente
Tu cetro omnímodo;
Úngeme siervo,
Siervo sumiso:
¡No he de cansarme
De verme ungido!
¡Lealtad te juro,
Mi reyecillo!
Sea mi espalda
Pavés de mi hijo:
Pasa en mis hombros
El mar sombrío:
Muera al ponerte
En tierra vivo:—
Mas si amar piensas
El amarillo
Rey de los hombres,
¡Muere conmigo!
¿Vivir impuro?
¡No vivas, hijo!

a yellow king,
and fare badly
beneath his dominion!
But as vassal
to another king I live,
a naked king,
plump and white.
His scepter—a kiss!
My reward—a caress!
Oh! Like the golden
god-kings
of dead lands
and departed peoples
—take me with you, son
when you go!—
Touch my forehead
with your almighty scepter;
anoint me your vassal,
your meek vassal;
Never shall I tire
of being so anointed!
My fealty I swear to you,
my kinglet!
Let my back be
a pavais to my son:
cross, on my shoulders,
the gloomy sea:
and let me die when I set you,
alive, on the earth:—
but if you think of loving
the yellow god
of men,
die with me!
Live impure?
Son, do not live!

HIJO DEL ALMA

Tú flotas sobre todo!
Hijo del alma!

SON OF MY SOUL

You float over everything!
Son of my soul!

De la revuelta noche
Las oleadas,
En mi seno desnudo
Déjante al alba;
Y del día la espuma
Turbia y amarga,
De la noche revueltas
Te echan las aguas.
Guardiancillo magnánimo,
La no cerrada
Puerta de mi hondo espíritu
Amante guardas;
Y si en la sombra ocultas
Búscanme avaras,
De mi calma celosas,
Mis penas varias,—
En el umbral oscuro
Fiero te alzas
Y les cierran el paso
Tus alas blancas!
Ondas de luz y flores
Trae la mañana,
Y tú en las luminosas
Ondas cabalgas.
No es, no, la luz del día
La que me llama,
Sino tus manecitas
En mi almohada.
Me hablan de que estás lejos:
¡Locuras me hablan!
Ellos tienen tu sombra;
¡Yo tengo tu alma!
Esas son cosas nuevas,
Mías y extrañas.
Yo sé que tus dos ojos
Allá en lejanas
Tierras relampaguean,—
Y en las doradas
Olas de aire que baten
Mi frente pálida,

The crashing waves
of restless night
in my naked breast
set you down at dawn:
and from the bitter, tainted
seafoam of the day,
the night's restless waters
hurl you.
Small, magnanimous sentry,
you guard the unclosed
door of my deep spirit
with love:
and if, hidden in shadow,
and jealous of my calm,
my many griefs
seek me, ravenous—
on the dark threshold
you stand, fierce,
and your white wings
bar their way!
Morning brings
waves of light and flowers,
and you upon those
luminous waves are riding.
No, it is not the day's light
that calls me,
but your little hands
on my pillow.
They tell me you are far:
What madness!
They have your shadow;
I have your soul!
These are new things,
mine and strange.
I know that your two eyes,
flash there
in far-off lands
and in the golden
waves of air that beat against
my pale forehead

Pudiera con mi mano,	I could, with my hand,
Cual si haz segara	as if reaping a sheaf
De estrellas, segar haces	of stars, reap sheaves
De tus miradas!	of your gazes!
¡Tu flotas sobre todo,	You float over everything,
Hijo del alma!	son of my soul!

FREE VERSES / *VERSOS LIBRES*

Written around the same time as Ismaelillo, *the* Versos libres *(Free Verses), like most of Martí's poetry, were not published until 1913, long after his death. He mentions them—"those bristling hendeca-syllables born of great fear and great hope"—in the preface to his* Versos sencillos *(Simple Verses), but only to ask, rhetorically, why he has not published them. He also mentioned them to his friend Gonzalo de Quesada in a letter known as his literary testament, written near the end of his life. A rough table of contents for the volume was found among his papers, along with a rough draft of a preface.*

*Though his published poetic output during his lifetime was mea-ger, consisting only of two slim volumes—*Ismaelillo *and* Versos sencillos*—Martí's poetry had a tremendous impact on the Latin American literature of his time, for he was one of the leading pre-cursors of the far-reaching Latin American literary movement of Modernismo, whose central figure, the Nicaraguan poet Rubén Darío (1867–1916), revered Martí and wrote of him in 1888, "This man . . . writes more brilliantly than any other in Spain or America today." Martí's work would also have a profound influence on the Nobel Prize–winning Chilean poet Gabriela Mistral (1889–1957), who wrote, "All gratitude is in my love for Martí, gratitude for the writer who is the American Master most ostensible in my work, and gratitude, as well, for the terribly pure guide of men that America produced in him as an enormous compensation for the sordid guides we have endured, are enduring and will yet endure."*

MY VERSES

These are my verses. They are as they are. I borrowed them from no one. As long as I was unable to enclose my visions whole within a form that befitted them, I let them fly away: oh friends so golden who have yet to return! But poetry has its honor, and I have always sought to be honorable. I, too, know how to pare down a poem, but I do not want to. Just as each man wears his own physiognomy, each inspiration wears its own language. I like difficult sonorities, a sculptural line, vibrant as porcelain, airborne as a bird, fiery and devastating as a tongue of lava. The poem must be like a glittering sword, leaving onlookers with the memory of a warrior whose path leads to the heavens and who sprouts wings as he sheathes his sword in the sun.

These—my warriors—are gashes in my own entrails. None of them has emerged from my mind, warmed over, artful and beautified; they have come like tears springing from the eyes or blood spurting out from a wound.

I did not stitch together bits of this and that, but cut deep into myself. These poems emerged written not in academic ink but in my own blood. Whatever I place on view here I once have seen (*I* have seen it: me), and I have seen much more, which fled before I could copy its features. From strangeness, singularity, haste, and hoarding, I wrest my visions, and any fault was my own, for I have made them rise up before me as I copy them. I am responsible for the copy. I found some garments that were torn and others that were whole, and I wore these colors. I know they are not worn out. I love difficult sonorities and sincerity, even when it may seem brutal.

All that they have to say I know and have confirmed for myself. I have sought to be loyal, and if I sinned I feel no shame at having sinned.

EL PADRE SUIZO

LITTLE ROCK, ARKANSAS, SETIEMBRE 1.—"El Miércoles por
la noche, cerca de París, condado de Logan, un suizo, llamado Edward
Schwerzmann, llevó a sus tres hijos, de 18 meses el uno y 4 y 5 años los
otros, al borde de un pozo, y los echó en el pozo, y él se echó tras ellos.
Dicen que Schwerzmann obró en un momento de locura." Telegrama
publicado en N. York.

Dicen que un suizo, de cabello rubio
Y ojos secos y cóncavos, mirando
Con desolado amor a sus tres hijos,
Besó sus pies, sus manos, sus delgadas,
Secas, enfermas, amarillas manos:—
Y súbito, tremendo, cual airado
Tigre que al cazador sus hijos roba,
Dio con los tres, y con sí mismo luego,
En hondo pozo,—y los robó a la vida!
Dicen que el bosque iluminó radiante
Una rojiza luz, y que a la boca
Del pozo oscuro—sueltos los cabellos,
Cual corona de llamas que al monarca
Doloroso, al humano, sólo al borde
Del antro funeral la sien desciñe,—
La mano ruda a un tronco seco asida,—
Contra el pecho huesoso, que sus uñas
Mismas sajaron, los hijuelos mudos
Por su brazo sujetos, como en noche
De tempestad las aves en su nido,—
El alma a Dios, los ojos a la selva,
Retaba el suizo al cielo, y en su torno
Pareció que la tierra iluminaba
Luz de héroe, y que el reino de la sombra
La muerte de un gigante estremecía!

¡Padre sublime, espíritu supremo
Que por salvar los delicados hombros
De sus hijuelos, de la carga dura
De la vida sin fe, sin patria, torva
Vida sin fin seguro y cauce abierto,

THE SWISS FATHER

LITTLE ROCK, ARKANSAS, SEPTEMBER 1.—"On Wednesday
night, near Paris, in Logan County, a Swiss named Edward Schwerzmann took his three children, one 18 months, the others 4 and 5 years
old, to the edge of a well and threw them in, and threw himself in after
them. Schwerzmann is said to have acted in a moment of madness."—
News cable published in New York

> A Swiss, they say, hair blond,
> eyes dry and hollow, gazing
> with heartsick love at his three children,
> kissed their feet, their hands,
> their thin, dry, sickly, yellow hands:
> and suddenly, tremendous as the enraged
> tiger who robs the hunter of his offspring,
> he sent all three, and then himself,
> down a deep well—and robbed life of them!
> They say the forest glowed with reddish
> light; and at the dark well's mouth
> —his hair flying like the crown of flames
> that only at the funeral cavern's edge
> does the doleful human monarch's brow divest—
> his rough hand tightly clutched to a dead tree—
> the silent little ones held fast
> by his arm, their nails digging
> into his bony chest, like fledglings
> in their nest on a raging night—
> his soul fixed on God, his eyes upon the wilderness,
> the Swiss defied the heavens, and all around
> a heroic light shone down
> upon the earth, and the kingdom of shadow
> was shaken by the death of a giant!

> Sublime father, supreme spirit
> who to save the fragile shoulders
> of his little ones from the hard burden
> of a life without faith or patria, grim
> life with no certain end or open channel,

Sobre sus hombros colosales puso
De su crimen feroz la carga horrenda!
Los árboles temblaban, y en su pecho
Huesoso, los seis ojos espantados
De los pálidos niños, seis estrellas
Para guiar al padre iluminadas,
Por el reino del crimen, parecían!
¡Ve, bravo! ve, gigante! ve, amoroso
Loco! y las venenosas zarzas pisa
Que roen como tósigos las plantas
del criminal, en el dominio lóbrego
Donde andan sin cesar los asesinos!

    ¡Ve!—que las seis estrellas luminosas
Te seguirán, y te guiarán, y ayuda
A tus hombros darán cuantos hubieran
Bebido el vino amargo de la vida!

ISLA FAMOSA

    Aquí estoy, solo estoy, despedazado.
Ruge el cielo: las nubes se aglomeran,
Y aprietan, y ennegrecen, y desgajan:
Los vapores del mar la roca ciñen.
Sacra angustia y horror mis ojos comen:
A qué, Naturaleza embravecida,
A qué la estéril soledad en torno
De quien de ansia de amor rebosa y muere?
Dónde, Cristo sin cruz, los ojos pones?
Dónde, oh sombra enemiga, dónde el ara
Digna por fin de recibir mi frente?
En pro de quién derramaré mi vida?

    —Rasgóse el velo: por un tajo ameno
De claro azul, como en sus lienzos abre
Entre mazos de sombra Díaz famoso,
El hombre triste de la roca mira
En lindo campo tropical, galanes
Blancos, y Venus negras, de unas flores

upon his colossal shoulders took
the horrendous burden of his ghastly crime!
The trees quaked; against his bony
chest, the six terrified eyes
of the ashen children seemed six stars
shining to guide their father
through the realms of crime!
Go, brave man! Go, giant! Go, loving
madman! And tread the venomous brambles
that like poison gnaw the soles
of the criminal in that grim domain
where murderers must walk forever!

Go!—and those six luminous stars
shall follow and guide you, and your
shoulders will be helped to bear their burden
by all who've ever drunk the bitter wine of life!

FAMOUS ISLAND

Here I am, alone, and torn asunder.
The heavens roar: clouds gather
and press down, and darken, and break away:
sea vapors encircle the rock:
sacred anguish, horror, that my eyes devour:
why, oh furious nature, why
this sterile solitude that surrounds
one who brims with thirst for love, and dies?
Where, oh Christ without a cross, do you turn your gaze?
Where, oh enemy darkness, where is the altar
that will at last prove worthy of my head?
For whom shall I spill out my life?

—The veil is rent: through a fair slash
of clear blue, like those famed Díaz[1] cuts
across the shadowy reaches of his scenes,
the sad man on the rock sees,
in lovely tropic landscape,
white gallants and black Venuses,

Fétidas y fangosas coronados:
Danzando van: a cada giro nuevo
Bajo los muelles pies la tierra cede!
Y cuando en ancho beso los gastados
Labios sin lustre, ya, trémulos juntan,
Sáltanles de los labios agoreras
Aves tintas en hiel, aves de muerte.

AMOR DE CIUDAD GRANDE

De gorja son y rapidez los tiempos.
Corre cual luz la voz; en alta aguja,
Cual nave despeñada en sirte horrenda,
Húndese el rayo, y en ligera barca
El hombre, como alado, el aire hiende.
¡Así el amor, sin pompa ni misterio
Muere, apenas nacido, de saciado!
Jaula es la villa de palomas muertas
Y ávidos cazadores! Si los pechos
Se rompen de los hombres, y las carnes
Rotas por tierra ruedan, no han de verse
Dentro más que frutillas estrujadas!

Se ama de pie, en las calles, entre el polvo
De los salones y las plazas; muere
La flor que nace. Aquella virgen
Trémula que antes a la muerte daba
La mano pura que a ignorado mozo;
El goce de temer; aquel salirse
Del pecho el corazón; el inefable
Placer de merecer; el grato susto
De caminar de prisa en derechura
Del hogar de la amada, y a sus puertas
Como un niño feliz romper en llanto;—
Y aquel mirar, de nuestro amor al fuego,
Irse tiñendo de color las rosas,—
Ea, que son patrañas! Pues ¿quién tiene
tiempo de ser hidalgo? Bien que sienta
Cual áureo vaso o lienzo suntuoso,
Dama gentil en casa de magnate!

crowned with foul and filthy flowers,
and dancing as they go: with each new spin
the earth yields beneath their lewd feet!
And when the spent lips, their luster lost,
join, tremulous, in long kiss,
from those dire lips there spring
birds inked in bile, birds of death.

LOVE IN THE CITY

Times of gorge and rush are these:
Voices fly like light: lightning,
like a ship hurled upon dread quicksand,
plunges down the high rod, and in delicate craft
man, as if winged, cleaves the air.
And love, without splendor or mystery,
dies when newly born, of glut.
The city is a cage of dead doves
and avid hunters! If men's bosoms
were to open and their torn flesh
fall to the earth, inside would be
nothing but a scatter of small, crushed fruit!

Love happens in the street, standing in the dust
of saloons and public squares: the flower
dies the day it's born. The trembling
virgin who would rather death
have her than some unknown youth;
the joy of trepidation; that feeling of heart
set free from chest; the ineffable
pleasure of deserving; the sweet alarm
of walking quick and straight
from your love's home and breaking
into tears like a happy child;—
and that gazing of our love at the fire,
as roses slowly blush a deeper color,—
Bah, it's all a sham! Who has the time
to be noble? Though like a golden
bowl or sumptuous painting
a genteel lady sits in the magnate's home!

O si se tiene sed, se alarga el brazo
Y a la copa que pasa se la apura!
Luego, la copa turbia al polvo rueda,
Y el hábil catador,—manchado el pecho
De una sangre invisible,—sigue alegre,
Coronado de mirtos, su camino!
No son los cuerpos ya sino desechos,
Y fosas, y jirones! Y las almas
No son como en el árbol fruta rica
En cuya blanda piel la almíbar dulce
En su sazón de madurez rebosa,—
Sino fruta de plaza que a brutales
Golpes el rudo labrador madura!

¡La edad es ésta de los labios secos!
De las noches sin sueño! De la vida
Estrujada en agraz! Qué es lo que falta
Que la ventura falta? Como liebre
Azorada, el espíritu se esconde,
Trémulo huyendo al cazador que ríe,
cual en soto selvoso, en nuestro pecho;
Y el deseo, de brazo de la fiebre,
Cual rico cazador recorre el soto.

¡Me espanta la ciudad! ¡Toda está llena
De copas por vaciar, o huecas copas!
!Tengo miedo !ay de mi! de que este vino
Tósigo sea, y en mis venas luego
Cual duende vengador los dientes clave!
¡Tengo sed,—mas de un vino que en la tierra
No se sabe beber! ¡No he padecido
Bastante aún, para romper el muro
Que me aparta ¡oh dolor! de mi viñedo!
¡Tomad vosotros, catadores ruines
De vinillos humanos, esos vasos
Donde el jugo de lirio a grandes sorbos
Sin compasión y sin temor se bebe!
Tomad! You soy honrado, y tengo miedo!

New York, abril—1882

But if you're thirsty, reach out your arm,
and drain some passing cup!
The dirtied cup rolls to the dust, then,
and the expert taster—breast blotted
with invisible blood—goes happily,
crowned with myrtle, on his way!
Bodies are nothing now but trash,
pits, and tatters! And souls
are not the tree's lush fruit
down whose tender skin runs
sweet juice in time of ripeness,—
but fruit of the marketplace, ripened
by the hardened laborer's brutal blows!

It is an age of dry lips!
Of undreaming nights! Of life
crushed unripe! What is it that we lack,
without which there is no gladness? Like a startled
hare in the wild thicket of our breast,
fleeing, tremulous, from a gleeful hunter,
the spirit takes cover;
and Desire, on Fever's arm,
beats the thicket, like the rich hunter.

The city appals me! Full
of cups to be emptied, and empty cups!
I fear—ah me!—that this wine
may be poison, and sink its teeth,
vengeful imp, in my veins!
I thirst—but for a wine that none on earth
knows how to drink! I have not yet
endured enough to break through the wall
that keeps me, ah grief!, from my vineyard!
Take, oh squalid tasters
of humble human wines, these cups
from which, with no fear or pity,
you swill the lily's juice!
Take them! I am honorable, and I am afraid!

—New York, April 1882

ODIO EL MAR

Odio el mar, sólo hermoso cuando gime
Del barco domador bajo la hendente
Quilla, y como fantástico demonio,
De un manto negro colosal tapado,
Encórvase a los vientos de la noche
Ante el sublime vencedor que pasa:—
Y a la luz de los astros, encerrada
En globos de cristales, sobre el puente
Vuelve un hombre impasible la hoja a un libro.—

Odio el mar: vasto y llano, igual y frío
No cual la selva hojosa echa sus ramas
Como sus brazos, a apretar al triste
Que herido viene de los hombres duros
Y del bien de la vida desconfía,
No cual honrado luchador, en suelo
Firme y seguro pecho, al hombre aguarda
Sino en traidora arena y movediza,
Cual serpiente letal.—También los mares,
El sol también, también Naturaleza
Para mover el hombre a las virtudes,
Franca ha de ser, y ha de vivir honrada.
Sin palmeras, sin flores, me parece
Siempre una tenebrosa alma desierta.

Que yo voy muerto, es claro: a nadie importa
Y ni siquiera a mí: pero por bella
Ígnea, varia, inmortal amo la vida.

Lo que me duele no es vivir: me duele
Vivir sin hacer bien. Mis penas amo,
Mis penas, mis escudos de nobleza.
No a la próvida vida haré culpable
De mi propio infortunio, ni el ajeno
Goce envenenaré con mis dolores.
Buena es la tierra, la existencia es santa.
Y en el mismo dolor, razones nuevas
Se hallan para vivir, y goce sumo,

I HATE THE SEA

I hate the sea, beautiful only when it howls
beneath the cleaving keel of a conquering
ship and like some fantastic demon
cloaked in colossal black
bends in the winds of night
before the sublime victor who passes:—
and by the light of stars enclosed
in crystal globes, upon the bridge,
a man, impassive, turns the page of a book.—

I hate the sea: huge and flat, cold and level,
not as the leafy jungle, stretching branches
like arms to clasp the sad soul
that comes wounded by men's hardness
and doubts the good of life,
nor as an honorable fighter, firm
on the ground, solid-chested, does it await us,
but on perfidious shifting sands
like the deadly snake.—The sea, too,
and the sun, and Nature
must be frank to move man
to virtue, must live in honor.
No palm trees, no flowers: to me
it is ever a dark and abandoned soul.

That I am a dead man, still walking, is clear and matters not,
even to me; but for its beauty, fire,
variety and deathlessness, I love life.

It isn't living that pains me: it hurts
to live and not do good. I love my pain,
the pain that is my noble coat of arms.
I will not blame provident life
for my own misfortune, or poison
others' joy with my sorrows.
The earth is good, existence is holy.
And in sorrow itself new reasons
to live are discovered, and highest joy,

Claro como una aurora y penetrante.
Mueran de un tiempo y de una vez los necios
Que porque el llanto de sus ojos surge
Lo imaginan más grande y más hermoso
Que el cielo azul y los repletos mares!—

Odio el mar, muerto enorme, triste muerto
De torpes y glotonas criaturas
Odiosas habitado: se parecen
A los ojos del pez que de harto expira
Los del gañán de amor que en brazos tiembla
De la horrible mujer libidinosa:—
Vilo, y lo dije:—algunos son cobardes,
Y lo que ven y lo que sienten callan:
Yo no: si hallo un infame al paso mío,
Dígole en lengua clara: ahí va un infame,
Y no, como hace el mar, escondo el pecho
Ni mi sagrado verso nimio guardo
Para tejer rosarios a las damas
Y mascaras de honor a los ladrones:

Odio el mar, que sin cólera soporta
Sobre su lomo complaciente, el buque
Que entre música y flor trae a un tirano.

COPA CON ALAS

Una copa con alas: quién la ha visto
Antes que yo? Yo ayer la ví. Subía
Con lenta majestad, como quien vierte
Óleo sagrado: y a sus bordes dulces
Mis regalados labios apretaba:—
Ni una gota siquiera, ni una gota
Del bálsamo perdí que hubo en tu beso!

Tu cabeza de negra cabellera
—Te acuerdas?—con mi mano requería,
Porque de mí tus labios generosos
No se apartaran.—Blanda como el beso
Que a ti me transfundía, era la suave

clear as a dawn and penetrating.
May they die once and for all, those fools
who think the tears that spill from their eyes
a greater and more beautiful thing
than the blue sky and thronging sea!—

    I hate the sea, enormous corpse, sad corpse
where hateful creatures dwell,
torpid and gluttonous: like the eyes
of a fish dying of its own excesses
are those of love's hired hand who trembles
in the arms of some horrid, rutting woman:—
I saw it and I said it:—some men are cowards,
and silence what they see and feel.
Not I: if I find a wicked man before me,
I say so in clear speech: there walks a wicked man.
Unlike the sea I do not hide my breast
or clutter my sacred verse with trifles,
weaving rosaries for the ladies
and masks of honor for thieves:

    I hate the sea, which unraging bears
on its complacent back the ship
that 'mid flowers and music brings a tyrant.

WINGED CUP

    A winged cup: who before me has
seen one? I saw it yesterday. It rose
with slow majesty, as though pouring out
sacred oil: and against the sweetness of its rim
I pressed my feasting lips:—
not a single drop, not one, did I lose
of the balm of your kiss!

    Your mane of black hair
—remember?—I wooed with my hand
so your indulgent lips would not
move from me—soft as the kiss
that transfused me into you was the gentle

Atmósfera en redor: la vida entera
Sentí que a mí abrazándote, abrazaba!
Perdí el mundo de vista, y sus ruidos
Y su envidiosa y bárbara batalla!
Una copa en los aires ascendía
Y yo, en brazos no vistos reclinado
Tras ella, asido de sus dulces bordes:
Por el espacio azul me remontaba!

　　Oh amor, oh inmenso, oh acabado artista:
En rueda o riel funde el herrero el hierro:
Una flor o mujer o águila o ángel
En oro o plata el joyador cincela:
Tú sólo, sólo tú, sabes el modo
De reducir el Universo a un beso!

air around us: all of life I felt,
as I embraced you, embracing me!
I lost sight of the world and its noises,
its envious, barbaric battle!
A cup soared in the air
and I, in your unseen arms, lay
behind it, clutching its sweet rim:
through the blue of space I rose!

Oh love, oh immense and consummate artist:
Into the form of wheel or rail the blacksmith casts his iron:
flower or woman, eagle or angel,
on gold or silver the jeweler engraves:
but you alone, only you, know how
to reduce the Universe to a kiss!

NOTEBOOKS 4–15

*** SELECTIONS ***

from NOTEBOOK 4

Sorrows—like benevolent angels—lift the veils from my life.

"Why," Todboys asked me, "can't we do anything like this here?"—and he showed me a Meissonier[1] cartoon in three colors published by *Vanity Fair*.

"Because," I told him, "art isn't the isolated product of an active mind, but the result of a common artistic aptitude that is continually exercised. It isn't an exclusive manifestation, but an essential condition. To be in anything, it must be in everything. Artistic impressions pass through the eyes to the mind, which then guides the hand, which gives back what was sent to it. The hand produces in analogy with what the eyes see. A country of painters will always be a country of elegant women, beautiful buildings, well-printed books, well-decorated houses."

"But these craftsmen whose work isn't right are the same as those elsewhere whose work is right."

"Some of them, yes, but not all; only a very small minority. And even if they were, they would still be damaged by the enslaving influence that the consumer's taste exerts on the producer's faculties. The industries are the same, the craftsmen are not. The means, but not the agents. Beauty is something more intimate and sublime than the mere work of the hand. Only from its cultivation is the best means of cultivating it born. This is the sickly side of this great, hemiplegic country—candid and elemental in one sense, consummate and penetrating in another: gigantic and puerile, astute and simpleminded. It has no faculties of creation."

"Power confers elegance."—Thiers[2]
On one who is elegant.

For as long as man lasts, the representation of the human personality will be what moves and interests him most.

There is only one way of living on after death: to have been a man for all times—or a man for one's own time.

Love: renews. I feel, when loving, a generous oblivion, an invigorating hope. A woman told me, "This is my second youth." Another told me, "This is another wedding day for me." Poor rejuvenator that as it gives us life makes us old! Fortunate indeed are the vile—egotists!

I am not—and God save me from being—an inveterate revolutionary. I do not bind my life to tumults. But it doesn't matter to me whether the fulfilment of a duty is unpopular: I fulfil it, even if it is unpopular.

What do you want, my wife? For me to do the work that will be applauded on earth—or for me to live, gnawed by rancor, without the sound of applause, without the profits of one who bows low—serene and doing the work whose applause we will not live to hear?

from NOTEBOOK 5

1881

Movement is contagious.

Before assembling a collection of my poems I would like to assemble a collection of my actions.

The action of morphine.
What does it put to sleep?
What does it consist of?
To deduce, in this way, what *the soul* might be?

A great confederation of the countries of Latin America—not in Cuba—in Colombia (thus avoiding the danger of a forcible annexation of the Island).
Tribunal of all for each one's disputes.
Monetary aid for the States at war with foreign nations.
Full freedom of each of the republics to join with every country at war.
Prior visit to the States of South America.

Work gives me wings.
Others are intoxicated by wine; myself by overwork.
From wine—foam; from overwork, poems.

And so many noble things that could be done in life! But we have stomachs. And that other stomach that hangs down below: which is subject to terrible hungers.

In Cuba, the idea of annexation, which was born to accelerate the enjoyment of liberty, has changed in intention and motive, and today is no more than the desire to avoid a Revolution. Why do they want to be annexed? Because of the greatness of this land. And why is this land great, if not for its Revolution? But in these times, and with the relations that exist between the two parties, we will be able to enjoy the benefits of a Revolution without exposing ourselves to its dangers. But that is not rational: what you buy, you own. No one buys anything for another's benefit. If they give it, it will be because they stand to profit by it.

To live in exile—to sculpt clouds.

from NOTEBOOK 6

Oh! what a lesson! The Dutch, who had withstood all the cruelties of the Duke of Alba and the Inquisition, could not withstand an increase in their taxes. With taxes, everyone feels wounded! With the Inquisition, each one could still hope that the executioner would knock at the neighbor's door, not at his own.

I will die without pain: it will be an inner breakage, a gentle fall, and a smile.

And he makes the defect of some into the defect of all—which is why the book seems false to those who are not defective. We must always keep in mind that we will not be read in the same exaltation with which we write.

—

When I need to wrap up the little straw hat and boots that my son wore a year ago, I check to see if the newspaper I'm wrapping them in is written by the passions of men, or if it defends what is just, and only if it defends what is just do I wrap them in it. I believe in these contagions.

Women poets! Sorrow must be manly.

from NOTEBOOK 7

"Because it is necessary that this son of mine, beyond all other things on earth, and equally with those of heaven—beyond those of heaven!—beloved; this son of mine whom we must not name José but Ismael—not suffer what I have suffered." (For *Ismaelillo*)

The "Ruba-iyat" of Omar Khaiyam of Indostan. Oh secondhand erudition!—*Of Persia.*
   Fauch—translator of Valnuk.
   Ollantai—drama in Quechua verses of the era of the Incas.—by G. Zegarra—Paris, 1878.

from NOTEBOOK 8

They are unacquainted here with the fevered, melancholy youth of our Latin lands—the pale poets, the premature despair. Neither Shelley nor Leopardi could have been American. Longfellow, who is American, is truly great, because he feels things very deeply and is a daring reformer—though in new nations everything can be dared with less risk and greater probability of good fortune than in old ones—and yet he retains the spirit of his people. He has not written his verses running through forests, clambering up to some wretched garret, warming himself by the light of old books. His verses are tranquil, soft, perfumed, as if written in an elegant dining room or a richly furnished study: something of Tennyson. There is *comfort* and wealth in them. It is the literature of a prosperous country. This country does not live from internal passions—but from the clash and progress of external elements. It moves, grows, laughs, fattens, roars, steams! This country is a magnificent landscape—at noon.

A life of Abraham Lincoln was published in 1866—Appleton—by D. F. Sarmiento.[3] There is a singular mixture of classic sobriety, Castilian decorum, and Gallic impurity in the style. The man evinces a habit of elevated reading and a capacity for honorable thoughts.

There is something of the ship in every house in a foreign land. A certain sensation of indefinable unease persists. We feel the earth oscillating, and our feet are unsteady upon it. At times, we clutch the walls—and where others find solid footing, we lurch. The spirit is off balance.

In Eten, in the new province of Otuzco, a language is spoken that no one in the rest of Peru understands. The inhabitants shun any intermixture. They say that in Lima a man from Eten had no trouble speaking with a Chinaman. Lovely hats, towels, and cigarette cases are woven by the people of Eten. Eten: place from where the Sun is born.

Paz Soldán[4] believes that coca is only a vice—like tobacco.

Back there, in other worlds, in previous lands, in which I firmly believe—because we have the astonishing intuition of them, a prior knowledge of life that reveals a prior life—just as I believe in the lands to come to which we must take the excess of ardor, unused force, unfulfilled yearnings, and wrenching energies with which we emerge from this life; back there, in previous lands, I must have committed toward what was then my patria some grave offense, given how great my punishment has been for as long as I have lived, to live perpetually in exile from my natural country, not knowing where it is—from the very beautiful country where I was born, where all the flowers are poisonous, yours and his. Human life, because of the moral straits to which it condemns us, loses grandeur and significance in my eyes each day. What kind of existence is this, in which a singular ability and a decided will to do good are not sufficient to do it? in which accidental conditions of coloration and atmosphere determine the transcendence and usefulness of the most noble human forces? in which the absence of all vice, and the fervent love and austere practice of all virtue, is insufficient to achieve the soul's peace or to leave behind—for the immense pleasure of doing good and not the puerile vanity of achieving fame—a visible and lasting trace?

from NOTEBOOK 9

Nothing so terrifies a great soul as the little things.

For me, the word *universe* explains the Universe: *Versus uni:* the many in the one.

Language must be mathematical, geometric, sculptural. The idea must fit precisely into the sentence, so precisely that nothing can be eliminated from the sentence without eliminating that same thing from the idea.

The jug of milk. The sea inside the jug.
    Every mother should be named Wonder.

I am not understood: what joy!—and what sorrow, if I am understood!

Nothing seems more right to me, or more proven, or more revealing of the deep-delving mind than Tacitus's method of explaining great events by trivial causes. For so it is in actuality, and so goes the world. A rivalry between two leaders creates two different political systems. And how the reasons for supporting these newly created systems pour forth! Zeal and the fear of seeing the rival get ahead, how eloquent they are!

from NOTEBOOK 12

Mr. Rumbold, minister of Great Britain in Chile, attributes, in a report to his government, Chile's orderly condition (in addition to attributing it to the traditions of the founders of the republic, the leadership of the country by the educated and wealthy class, and "the cultivation of the innate conservative instincts in the country") to the "happy extinction of militarism, the almost complete absence of accidental sources of wealth—the need to resort to extensive labor—and beyond all that, perhaps, to the negligence of her former masters, which forced her to create everything for herself."

from NOTEBOOK 15

Didn't men look at the wondrous Mont Blanc for thousands of years without ever alluding to it? There was a map, published in 1570, on which the mountain does not appear.

TWO MYTHOLOGIES

Eve	Pandora
Picks the apple.	Opens the box.
The labor of the whole	At the bottom, hope:
race for the mistake	how beautiful.
of one frivolous young woman;	
how barbaric!	

"Having no inward resources, they hunger for tumultuous externals."

Charm lies more in the will to be charmed than in the charmer.

The entrails of suffrage are ugly, like all entrails.

Victory awakens an instinct for aristocracy and a love of conservation.

UNDATED FRAGMENT

To write: *The Supreme Moments:*
(of my life, of The Life of a Man: the little that is remembered, like the peaks of a mountain: the hours that count).

The afternoon of Emerson.
Ingratitude. (In jail, on learning of the departure of M.'s family.)
María's bee.

The mountaintop in Guatemala.

Papa's kiss, on leaving for Guatemala in the ship—and on coming back to Mexico, in Borell's house.

The afternoon in the amphitheater: (hands on the club's balcony:) in Catskill.

Sybilla.

When they showed me Pepe, just born.

The letter from Adriano Páez.

A PASSION

(Undated fragment of an unfinished novel)

The novel was not a literary form for which Martí felt much affinity. He did write one, titled Amistad Funesta *(Fatal Friendship) or* Lucía Jerez; *it was published serially in 1885 in a bimonthly New York magazine called* El Latino-Americano, *under the pseudonym Adelaida Ral. He did it as a favor to a friend, and it took him all of a week. "The genre does not please [me]," he wrote in a draft preface, "because there is much feigning in it and the joys of artistic creation do not make up for the pain of moving through a prolonged fiction, amid dialogues that have never been heard between persons who have never lived."*

A few fragments of incomplete fictions were found among Martí's papers, including this one, in which he speaks in the voice of a woman who has fallen under the spell of a man much like Martí himself.

June 14—He is the only man who has ever spoken to me without looking at my body. I have learned—in my need to captivate men in order to gain, through their flattered vanity or false confidence, the means of freeing myself from them—the power of a shift in perspective, a fleeting and only apparent abandonment of form, which is immediately recovered. I know—oh unhappy me!—what the tip of a prettily shod foot can do when it brushes for an instant, as if by accident, against the toe of a sturdy boot. I, who love my virtue, let its dust fall to the ground, certain that it will shine forth all the more. Men are brutal, but they are even more vain. They all have their vanities—this one about his intelligence, another about his wealth, another about his good looks, another about his goodness—but their greatest vanity, the one that most gratifies them, is that of believing that a woman has developed a weakness for them.

By their vanity are men led. They decide to be good only in order to appear good. They would not be good if it were not for their desire to appear good. They do it not for the inner delight of goodness but because of the stigma of revealing that they are not good. I know men as well as I know the keyboard of my piano.

I know which man responds to the black key, which one has to be spoken to "in sad." I have yet to meet one who responds to the white key. In all of them, in their eyes, lips, nostrils, in the quick gestures of their hands and the restlessness of their bodies, I read their appetite. I read it in him, too, but it is a strange appetite, both gentle and impassioned, which does not repel me; it disturbs me a little but does not offend me. It would be futile for me to feel for him what I feel for others. I almost think he would be grateful if I felt for him in a different way. He knows all there is to know about the world, that much is clear from his wisdom, so strange in a man his age, and the solid judgments he makes, like one who sees the root of everything, and the forking prongs of every root, and the tree trunk and the branches. At times, listening to him speak, I think he is dissecting the world. But without cruelty, without bitterness, as if to let me see where a danger might lie in wait for me, without ever giving me to understand that he thinks I might actually be threatened by it. There are moments when the desire to throw myself into his arms is irresistible, though I don't know whether it would be to love him or to console him. To console him, though he never complains. It must not be love, or it must be something more than love, or something different from what the world thinks of as love, because I see the same desires in my poor aunt, who is no longer of an age for passions. This man is good; he is undoubtedly good. But it is certain that he is not as good as he wants to appear. And of course he must be vain—vain about his goodness. One must make him believe one has recognized his goodness, one must rejoice in it and tell as many people as one can about it, one must make him believe, as one makes them all believe, that for him I have a special greeting, a more intense gaze, a slight but exclusive preference. And what if this new tactic were to make him believe he was entering my heart—he, a stranger? But no. He has never sought me out. He has always eluded me. He could have cultivated the friendship he inspired in me.

In three years, he could have seen me a hundred times instead of five. No. This man does not defile me, as the others do, with his desire. This is another desire, deep, almost impalpable, that seems to protect rather than threaten. If I believed in angels, I would think that there was something of the angel in his way of gazing. The very clarity of it is unsettling. He never lowers his eyes, or makes others lower theirs. There is something in his gaze that comes from far away. It is energetic, like the gaze of a military man. It is gentle, like the gaze of a dog. If he could kiss me, where would this man give me his first kiss? When we see each other again, I will give him my hand with aversion, because yesterday he held it a moment too long. It was imperceptible, but I perceived it. He did not grip my hand, no: he kept it and no more. It was as though he were giving me the kiss he could not give me. But what's strangest to me is this. He is the only man who has ever spoken to me without looking at my body.

June 14—For what, for what, wretched soul? You don't know that the world is closed off to you now, that a mistaken love closed it off to you forever, that your honor prevents you from returning to life, accepting tenderness or awakening it, that your goodness seems false precisely because it is so true: that you must hide your great goodness so that all that is most delectable and beautiful in life does not seem like self-interest, the passion of

—*Daughter, not son.*—

FROM *THE GOLDEN AGE*

In 1889 Martí embarked on a new career in children's publishing, founding, editing, and writing his own magazine for "the children of America" called La Edad de Oro (The Golden Age). The venture was very much in character: Martí had long had a passionate interest in education and had taken a very active role in educating the younger children of his companion Carmen Miyares.

La Edad de Oro *contained, among other things, original stories and poems; adaptations of fairy tales by Laboulaye; an article on Homer's* Iliad; *a "History of the Knife and Fork"; a "History of Man as Told by His Houses"; pieces on Bartolomé de Las Casas and Bolívar, San Martín, and Hidalgo (three heroes of Latin American independence); a description of the Paris Exposition; an account of a journey through "the Land of the Annamites" in central Vietnam; and the following digressive disquisition on the latest craze in the United States: pin the tail on the donkey. Four issues appeared in all before the magazine shut down because its financial backer, a wealthy Brazilian named A. d'Acosta Gómez, withdrew his funding in anger at its absolute lack of religious content.*

PIN THE TAIL ON THE DONKEY:
A NEW GAME AND SOME OLD ONES

Today in the United States there is a very curious game that they call "Donkey." In summertime, when you hear gales of laughter coming from a house, it's because they're playing "Donkey." It isn't only children who play it but grown-ups as well. And it's the easiest thing to do. On a large sheet of paper or a piece of white fabric you draw a donkey, about the size of a dog. You can use charcoal to do it, because coal doesn't leave a mark, only charcoal does, the kind made by burning wood beneath a mound of dirt. You could also draw the donkey with a brush dipped in ink, because you don't need to paint the whole figure black, only the outline, the shape. You draw the whole donkey, except the tail. The tail you draw somewhere else, on another bit of paper or fabric, and then you cut it out so that it looks like a real tail. And that's the game: putting the tail where it should be on the donkey. Which isn't as easy as it seems, because the player is blindfolded and given three spins before he's allowed to walk. And he walks and walks, and people stifle their laughter. And some players pin the tail on the donkey's muzzle or its rib cage or its forehead, while others pin it to the back of the door, thinking it's the donkey.

In the United States they say that this is a new game that has never existed before, but it isn't really very new; it's just another way of playing "the blind hen." It's very curious; children today play in the same way as children did long ago. The peoples of distant lands, who

Los niños griegos y la diosa Diana

have never seen each other, play in the same ways. We often speak of
the Greeks and the Romans, who lived two thousand years ago, but
Roman children played with balls the same way we do, and little
Greek girls had dolls with real hair, just as little girls have nowadays.
In the picture, some Greek girls are placing their dolls before the
statue of Diana, who was a kind of saint of that era, for the Greeks also
believed that there were saints in the heavens, and little girls prayed to
Diana to let them live and keep them pretty always. It wasn't only
dolls that the children brought her, for the small gentleman in the picture who is gazing at the goddess with the face of an emperor has
brought her his little wooden chariot so that Diana can ride in it when
she goes out hunting, as they say she did every morning. There never
was any Diana, of course, nor any of the other gods the Greeks prayed
to in their very beautiful poems and their processions and songs. The

Greeks were like all new peoples, who believe themselves to be the masters of the earth, just as children think they are. They see that sun and rain come from the sky, and that the earth yields wheat and corn and that there are birds and animals that are good to eat in the forests, and so they pray to the earth and the rain and the forest and the sun, and give them the names of men and women and depict them in human form, believing that they think and desire just as humans do and that they must have the same form. Diana was the goddess of the forest. In the Louvre Museum in Paris there is a very beautiful statue of Diana out hunting with her dog, so fine that she looks as if she were really walking. But her legs are like a man's, to show that she is a goddess who does a lot of walking. And the Greek girls loved their dolls so much that when they died they were buried with their dolls.

Not all games are as old as playing with balls or dolls, or cricket, or the ball game, or swinging, or jumping. "The blind hen" isn't that old, though it's been played for about a thousand years in France. And children don't know, when they are blindfolded, that this game is played to honor a very valiant knight who lived in France and who was blinded one day while fighting, but didn't drop his sword or ask to be attended to and went on fighting until he died. The knight was named Colin-Maillard. Then the king ordered that in all the mock fights, which were called tourneys, one knight would always fight with a blindfold over his eyes, so that the people of France would never forget that knight's great valor. And that is where the game comes from.

A pastime that seems unfit for men was that of the friends of Henry III, who was also king of France—not a brave and generous king like Henry IV of Navarre, who came later, but a ridiculous little man of the kind who thinks only of doing his hair and powdering himself like a woman and trimming his beard into a point. That king's friends spent their lives playing and jealously quarreling with the court jesters, who hated them for their slothfulness and told them so to their faces. Poor France was in misery; the working people paid a huge tax so that the king and his friends would have silken clothing and swords with golden hilts. Back then, there were no newspapers to tell people the truth. The jesters were something like the newspapers back then; the kings didn't keep them in their palaces just to make them laugh, but also so that the jesters could find out what was going on and tell the truth, which the jesters always spoke as if it were a joke, to the nobles and even to the kings themselves. The jesters were almost always very ugly men, either skinny or fat or hunchbacked. One of the saddest

La danza del palo en Nueva Zelandia

paintings in the world is a painting of jesters by the Spaniard Zamacois. All of those unhappy men are waiting for the king to call them so they can make him laugh, wearing costumes the color of an ape or a parrot, embellished with horns and little bells.

Naked as they are, the blacks who are dancing their pole dance in the other picture are happier than the jesters. Countries, like children, sometimes need to run a lot, laugh a lot, and shout and jump. That's because you can't do everything you want to do in life, and all the things you don't do come bursting out like that sometimes, like a craziness. The Moors have a festival of horses they call the "fantasy." Another Spanish painter—poor Fortuny[1]—has painted that festival very well. His painting shows the Moors galloping into their city at top speed on horses as crazed as they are, firing their long Moorish flintlocks into the air, stretched over the necks of their mounts, kissing them, biting them, throwing themselves to the ground, and remounting in the middle of their mad dash. They shout as if their chests were tearing open and the air is dark with the dust they raise. Men of all countries, white or black, Japanese or Indian, need to do something beautiful and daring, something dangerous and fast, like the pole dance of the New Zealand blacks. It's very hot in New Zealand, and the blacks there are men with arrogant bodies—the bodies of people who do a lot of walking—brave men, who fight for their land as well as they dance around the pole. They go up and down on cords, winding half the cord's length around the pole, then letting themselves drop. They send the cord flying like a swing, and they hang on by one hand, by their teeth, by a foot, or by a knee, bouncing off the pole like balls, shouting to each other and embracing.

When the Spaniards arrived, the Indians of Mexico had this same pole dance. The Mexican Indians had beautiful games. They were fine, hardworking men; they knew nothing about gunpowder and bullets as the soldiers of the Spaniard Cortés did, but their city seemed to be made of silver, and they knew how to work silver into something like lace, with all the delicacy of the very best jewelers. They were as light-hearted and original in play as at work. Among the Indians, the pole dance was a pastime that demanded great agility and daring, because they threw themselves from the top of the pole, which was about twenty yards high, and came hurtling down through the air, spinning and doing acrobatic tricks without hanging on to anything but the strong, slender cord that they made themselves, and called *mecate*. Their daring is said to have been staggering to behold; according to an old book, it was "horrible and appalling, and seeing it frightens and fills one with dismay."

The English believe that the pole game belongs to them and that they're the only ones who know how to display their skill at fairs: with the cudgel, which they grasp by one end and in the middle, or with sticks, which they handle very well. The Canary Islanders, who are people of great strength, believe that the pole was not invented by the English, but by the islanders, and it is something to see a Canary Islander playing with a pole and spinning it like a pinwheel—and fighting, too, which the children of the Canary Islands are taught to do in school. And there is a dance with a beribboned pole, a very difficult dance in which each man has a ribbon of one color, and they go braiding and unbraiding them around the pole, making loops and pretty designs with never a mistake. But the Indians of Mexico played the pole game as well as the blondest Englishman or the most muscular Canary Islander; and they didn't just defend themselves with it, but also knew how to balance on the pole as the Japanese and the Moorish Kabyles do now. And there we have five peoples who have done the same as the Indians: those of New Zealand, the English, the Canary Islanders, the Japanese, and the Moors. Without counting the ball game, which all peoples play, and which was a passion among the Indians, for they believed that a good player was a man come down from heaven, and that the Mexican gods, who were different from the Greek gods, descended to tell him how he should throw or catch the ball. The story of the ball game, which is very curious, will be for another day.

Right now we're talking about the pole, and the extremely difficult balancing tricks the Indians did on it. The Indians lay down on the ground, as the Japanese do when they're about to play with balls or barrels in circuses; they laid the pole across the soles of their feet and held up to four men on it, which is more than the Moors did, because the Moors were held up by the shoulders of their strongest man, not by the soles of his feet. *Tzaà* they called this game: first two Indians got up on each end of the pole, then two more climbed up onto those two, and the four of them did many tricks and turns, without falling. And the Indians had their chess, and their prestidigitators, who ate burning wool and then brought it back out through their noses, but that, like the ball game, will be for another day. Because when you're telling stories you have to do what Chichá, a pretty little Guatemalan girl, told me:

"Chichá, why do you eat that olive so slowly?"

"Because I like it a lot."

LETTERS FROM NEW YORK

The following essay is one of the earliest and most famous of what were to be more than a decade's worth of "North American Scenes," filling five thick volumes in Martí's Complete Works. *Virtually no aspect of life in the United States was left unexamined: news events were reported alongside the doings of high society, the struggles of the working classes, profiles of the leading men and women of the day, descriptions of elections, sporting events, famous trials, plays, buildings, education, family life, murders, and snatches of conversation overheard in the street. Taken together, the articles comprise one of the most sustained, detailed, and perceptive portrayals of life in the United States ever written by an outside observer.*

Though some of the articles, like the one that follows and the later description of the great blizzard of 1888 in New York, were clearly based on his personal experience, others derived largely from information gleaned in the New York newspapers, then shaped and stamped by Martí's unique perspective and unmistakable narrative style. In his articles about the United States, Martí developed a kaleidoscopic new form of journalism that juxtaposed a dizzying diversity of stories—sometimes within a single sentence—and mingled fact and poetry, the personal and the political, the heroic and the banal, the colossal and the petty, admiration and alarm.

CONEY ISLAND

Nothing in the annals of humanity can compare to the marvelous prosperity of the United States of the North. Does the country lack deep roots? Are ties of sacrifice and shared suffering more lasting within countries than those of common interest? Does this colossal nation contain ferocious and terrible elements? Does the absence of the feminine spirit, source of artistic sensibility and complement to national identity, harden and corrupt the heart of this astonishing people? Only time will tell.

For now it is certain that never has a happier, more joyous, better equipped, more densely packed, more jovial, or more frenetic multitude lived in such useful labor in any land on earth, or generated and enjoyed greater wealth, or covered rivers and seas with more gaily bedecked steamers, or spread out with more bustling order and naive merriment across gentle coastlines, gigantic piers, and fantastical, glittering promenades.

The North American newspapers are full of hyperbolic descriptions of the original beauties and unique attractions of one of those summer resorts, overflowing with people, dotted with sumptuous hotels, crosshatched by an aerial tramway, and colored in with gardens, kiosks, small theaters, saloons, circuses, tents, droves of carriages, picturesque assemblies, bathing machines, auctioneers, fountains.

Echoes of its fame have reached the French newspapers.

From the farthest reaches of the American Union, legions of intrepid ladies and gallant rustics arrive to admire the splendid landscapes, the unrivaled wealth, the bedazzling variety, the Herculean effort, the astonishing sight of the now world-famous Coney Island. Four years ago it was a barren heap of dirt, but today it is a spacious place of relaxation, shelter, and amusement for the hundred thousand or so New Yorkers who repair to its glad beaches each day.

There are four little towns, joined by carriage roads, tramways, and steam trains. One of them—which has a hotel with a dining room that can comfortably seat four thousand—is called Manhattan Beach. Another, which has sprung up like Minerva with her helmet and spear, armed with ferries, plazas, boardwalks, softly crooning orchestras, and hotels that are not like towns but like nations, is called Rockaway;[1] another, the smallest of them, which takes its name from a hotel of extraordinary capacity and ponderous construction, is called Brighton. But the main attraction of the island is not far-off Rockaway or monotonous Brighton or grave and aristocratic Manhattan Beach: it is Gable,[2] laughing Gable, with its elevator that goes higher than the spire of Trinity Church in New York—twice as high as the spire of our cathedral—and allows travelers to rise to the dizzying heights of its summit, suspended in a tiny, fragile cage. Gable, with its two iron piers that advance on elegant pillars for three blocks out over the sea, and its Sea Beach Palace, which is only a hotel now but was the famous Agricultural Building at the Philadelphia Centennial Exposition, transported to New York as if by magic and rebuilt in its original form down to the last shingle on the coast of Coney Island. Gable, with its fifty-cent museums exhibiting human freaks, preposterous fish, bearded ladies, melancholy dwarves, and stunted elephants grandiloquently advertised as the largest on earth; Gable, with its hundred orchestras, its mirthful dances, its battalions of baby carriages, its gigantic cow, perpetually milked and perpetually giving milk, its twenty-five-cent glasses of fresh cider, its innumerable pairs of amorous wanderers who bring the tender lines of García Gutiérrez[3] to the lips:

> Two by two they go
> over the hills
> the crested larks
> and the turtledoves.

Gable, where families gather to seek respite from the rank, unwholesome New York air in the healthy and invigorating seaside breeze; where impoverished mothers—as they empty the enormous box containing the family's lunch onto one of the tables provided without cost in vast pavilions—clasp to their hearts their unlucky little ones, who appear to have been gnawed, devoured, consumed by infantile cholera, the terrible summer disease that cuts children down as the scythe cuts wheat.

Ferries come and go; trains blow their whistles, belch smoke, depart, and arrive, their serpentine bosoms swollen with families they disgorge onto the beach. The women rent blue flannel bathing costumes and rough straw hats that they tie under their chins; the men, in less complicated garments, hold the women's hands and go into the sea, while barefoot children wait along the shore for the roaring wave to drench them, and flee as it reaches them, hiding their terror behind gales of laughter, then return in bands—the better to defy the enemy—to this game of which these innocents, prostrate an hour earlier from the terrible heat, never tire. Like marine butterflies, they flit in and out of the cool surf. Each one has his little pail and shovel, and they play at filling their pails with the beach's burning sand. Once they have had a swim they throw themselves down on the sand—in imitation of more serious persons of both sexes, who are indifferent to the reproachful astonishment of those who think as we do in our lands—and let themselves be covered, pounded, kneaded, and buried beneath the blazing hot sand, for this is considered a healthy exercise and provides, as well, an unparalleled occasion for that superficial, vulgar, and boisterous intimacy of which these prosperous folk seem so fond.

But the amazing thing here is not this manner of having a sea-bath, or the cadaverous faces of the little children, or the capricious headgear and incomprehensible garments of the demoiselles, who are notable for their prodigality, their outlandish behavior, and their exaggerated gaiety; nor is it the colloquies of lovers, or the bathhouses, or the operas sung over café tables by waiters dressed as Edgar and Romeo, Lucía and Juliet, or the grins and shrieks of the black minstrels who cannot, alas, much resemble the minstrels of Scotland, or the majestic beach, or the serene, gentle sunlight. The amazing thing here is the size, the quantity, this sudden result of human activity, this immense valve of pleasure opened to an immense people, these dining rooms that, seen from afar, look like the encampments of armies, these roads that from two miles away are not roads at all but long carpets of heads, the daily surge of a prodigious people onto a prodigious beach, this mobility, this faculty for progress, this enterprise, this altered form, this fevered rivalry in wealth, the monumentality of the whole, which makes this seaside resort comparable in majesty to the earth that bears it, the sea that caresses it, and the sky that crowns it, this rising tide, this overwhelming and invincible, constant and frenetic drive to expand, and the taking for granted of these very wonders—that is the amazing thing here.

Other peoples—ourselves among them—live in prey to a sublime inner demon that drives us to relentless pursuit of an ideal of love or glory. And when, with the joy of grasping an eagle, we seize the degree of ideal we were pursuing, a new zeal inflames us, a new ambition spurs us on, a new aspiration catapults us into a new and vehement longing, and from the captured eagle goes a free, rebellious butterfly, as if defying us to follow it and chaining us to its restless flight.

Not so these tranquil spirits, disturbed only by their eagerness to possess wealth. The eyes travel across these reverberating beaches; the traveler goes in and out of these dining rooms, vast as the pampas, and climbs to the tops of these colossal buildings, high as mountains; seated in a comfortable chair by the sea, the passerby fills his lungs with that powerful and salubrious air, and yet it is well known that a sad melancholy steals over the men of our Hispanoamerican peoples who live here. They seek each other in vain, and however much the first impressions may have gratified their senses, enamored their eyes, and dazzled and befuddled their minds, the anguish of solitude possesses them in the end. Nostalgia for a superior spiritual world invades and afflicts them; they feel like lambs with no mother or shepherd, lost from the flock, and though their eyes may be dry, the frightened spirit breaks into a torrent of the bitterest tears because this great land is devoid of spirit.

But what comings and goings! What spendings of money! What opportunities for every pleasure! What absolute absence of any visible sadness or poverty! Everything is out in the open: the noisy groups, the vast dining rooms, the peculiar courtship of the North Americans— almost wholly devoid of the elements that comprise the bashful, tender, and elevated courtship of our lands—the theater, the photographer, the bathhouse—all of it out in the open. Some weigh themselves, because for the North Americans it is a matter of positive joy or real grief to weigh a pound more or less; others, for fifty cents, receive from the hands of a robust German girl an envelope containing their fortune; others, with incomprehensible delight, drink unpalatable mineral waters from glasses as long and narrow as artillery shells.

Some ride in spacious carriages that take them at twilight's tender hour from Manhattan to Brighton; one man, who has been out rowing with a laughing lady friend, beaches his boat, and she, resting a determined hand on his shoulder, leaps, happy as a little girl, onto the lively beach. A group watches in open-mouthed admiration as an artist cuts from black paper, which he then pastes onto white cardboard, the silhouette of anyone who wants to have so singular a portrait of himself made; another group celebrates the skill of a lady who, in a little stall no more than three quarters of a yard wide, creates curious flowers out of fish skins. With great bursts of laughter others applaud the skill of someone who has succeeded in bouncing a ball off the nose of an unfortunate man of color, who, in exchange for a paltry day's wage, stands day and night with his head poking out through a piece of cloth, dodging the pitches with ridiculous movements and extravagant grimaces. Others, even some who are bearded and venerable, sit gravely atop a wooden tiger, a hippogriff, a boa constrictor, all ranged in a circle like horses, which revolve for a few minutes around a central mast while a handful of self-styled musicians play off-key sonatas. Those with less money eat crabs and oysters on the beach, or cakes and meats at the free tables some of the large hotels provide for such meals; those with money throw away enormous sums on the purplish infusions that pass for wine, and on strange, leaden dishes that our palates, preferring lighter and more artistic fare, would surely reject.

These people eat quantity; we, class.

And this squandering, this uproar, these crowds, this astonishing swarm of people, lasts from June to October, from morning until late night, without pause, without interruption, without any change whatsoever.

And by night, such beauty! It is true that a thinking man is startled to see so many married women without their husbands, so many mothers who stroll along the damp seashore, their little ones on their shoulders, concerned only with their own pleasure and never fearing that the biting air will harm the child's natural delicacy, so many ladies who abandon their babies in hotel rooms to the arms of some harsh Irishwoman and who, on returning from their long walks, do not take their children in their arms, or kiss their lips, or sate their hunger.

But no city in the world offers a more splendid panorama than that of the beach of Gable by night. Were there heads by day? Well, by night there are even more lights. Seen from the water, the four towns are radiant against the darkness; it looks as if the stars that populate the sky had gathered together in four colossal clusters and fallen suddenly to the sea.

With its magical, caressing clarity, electric light floods the hotels' little plazas, the English gardens, the bandstands, and even the beach itself, where in its bright glow every grain of sand can be counted. From afar, the electric lights look like blithely superior spirits, laughing and diabolical, cavorting among the sickly gaslights, and the rows of red streetlights, Chinese lanterns, and Venetian lamps. Everywhere, newspapers, programs, advertisements, and letters are being read as if it were broad daylight. It is a town of stars—and of orchestras, dances, chatter, surf sounds, human sounds, choruses of laughter and praise for the air, hawkers' loud cries, swift trains and speedy carriages, until it is time to go home. Then, like a monster emptying out its entrails into the ravenous jaws of another monster, this immense crush of humanity squeezes onto trains that seem to groan under its weight in their packed trajectory across the barren stretches to cede their turbulent cargo to gigantic ferries, enlivened by the sound of harps and violins, which carry the weary day-trippers back to the piers and pour them out into the thousand trams and thousand tracks that crisscross the slumbering city of New York like iron veins.

—*La Pluma* (Bogotá, Colombia), December 3, 1881

THE TRIAL OF GUITEAU

On July 2, 1881, Charles J. Guiteau shot James Abram Garfield, the twentieth president of the United States, who had been in office only four months. Garfield died two and a half months later and

*was succeeded in office by Chester Arthur. Guiteau was tried and
sentenced to death, and in July 1882, he was hanged.*

*Martí reported extensively on the shooting of Garfield, the slow
process of his death, and his funeral; the following is one of six long
articles he devoted to Guiteau's trial and execution. The case was of
particular interest to the readers of the Caracas newspaper where
the articles were originally published because the Venezuelan ambassador, Simon Camacho, had been standing at Garfield's side
when he was shot, and took the witness stand during the trial.*

Interest in the trial of Garfield's killer has not waned or tapered off. It's
as if a wild beast were on exhibit and the entire nation were gathering
to have a look at it. Guiteau is a cold, demonic, livid figure. He resembles nothing so much as a wild pig: he has the gleaming eyes, full of hatred, the thick, bristling hair, the same way of charging to the attack,
taking fright, running away. It would be impossible to imagine him
any uglier than he is—he is a fantastical creature out of the tales of
Hoffmann. The moral gamut that runs from the wild beast to man has
its degrees, like the zoological gamut. Victory consists in subduing the
wild beast. In this criminal—for the court of human opinion holds
him to be a criminal—the wild beast has gnawed away the man and
seated itself in the hollow space that was left in his spirit. And little by
little, shining in his eyes, speaking through his lips, working through
his hands, it gave the external creature its own appearance. He does
not arouse pity; he does not arouse forgiveness; he arouses no desire to
excuse him. There is no place for him in men's hearts, only in their hatred. Reason demands that his life be spared, because of the futility of
his horrendous act and because killing the monster is an inadequate
way of ending nature's power to grow monsters—for, in the end,
moved by prolonged solitude and fear and watered by tears, the
gnawed-away man may revive deep within his body, and in these days
of wrath justice might appear to be vengeance. One should not kill a
wild beast at a time when one feels oneself to be a wild beast: that is to
be the same as he is, and not his judge. Man must always keep a tight
hold on his own reins and not release them or let the tempest carry
them away. Tremendous winds can blow from within, as from a deep
cavern. One must be very sure of one's own path before accusing others of having gone astray. For what greater punishment could be dealt

this man than that of seeing all his calculations go up in smoke, and his misery revealed, and his desires unfulfillable, and his final effort frustrated, and his decaying mind revealed to itself, and all the advantages that he hoped to gain by his act irrevocably gone? In truth, there was never a greater villain! The indictment shows it, the trial reveals it. The man does not even have the dignity of his crime. He toys with it, makes it a matter for laughter and sophistries. Neither the image of the death he caused nor the image of himself as a skeleton that now taps him on the shoulder and threatens him has settled in beside him or is reflected in any sadness in his eyes. He seems already a creature of the netherworlds where the judges of his crime may hurl him. He loves life with abominable adhesion. He remains a source of confusion to the mind, but he will always be a source of displeasure to the eyes. He is like a sea of ice floes that drift apart at the slightest push from the wind.

Good Scoville [Guiteau's brother-in-law and defense lawyer] has called on a retinue of favorable witnesses: the sister of the accused has on his behalf told the story of his downfalls, extravagances, and miseries; his brother, who once believed he was guilty, has come to prove, in his honorable and forthright testimony, that he no longer believes him to be master of himself, but mentally deranged. The defense has turned up a host of experts who proclaim him to be demented. But he himself, though he took a seat in the witness box with jocose tone and friendly smile to testify on his own behalf, arose from it haggard and rattled, as if he could still feel his able prosecutor's iron hand on his skull.

And the prosecution has brought on its witnesses, who contradict and combat the defense's affirmations; it has lined up its experts and readied them for the fight.

Guiteau's very brother—infuriated because in the quest to excuse the killer, a good, kind sister of theirs, just starting out in life, was made out to be mad—has come to vigorously stamp out the belief in some permanent family madness on which good Scoville is basing his defense of the killer, and on which the experts based their declarations.

What a singular spectacle this courtroom presents! To one side, where they have been from the beginning, are the jurors who are forbidden to have any contact with anything unrelated to the trial: they are mute as oracles, and later they will break into oracular speech. There is the judge who is enhancing his own and his nation's reputation with his exceptionally benevolent treatment of the prisoner, which the courtroom and the whole world beholds so that it cannot later be said that he was put to death without a defense, or was deprived of any chance of saving himself, or was unjustly condemned. There is the defense counsel, with his weary, benevolent face and anxious eyes. There is the accused's sister, sad and shaken. The prosecutors are in their place. Protecting the prisoner's back is a wall of policemen. And the public section is full of magnificent ladies and suffocating old men who call for help as they struggle out of the throng—the public: curious, laughing, profane, which, as if watching the convulsions of a drunken animal, rejoices in the spasms, outbursts, jeers, cynical jokes, and brutal gestures of the accused. The onlookers rock with gales of laughter; the prisoner shares in the laughter he provokes; the ushers call for silence; and the judge scolds in vain. The mournful ghost of the venerated victim does not come to trouble the merriment of the room.

One of the prosecutors, the grave and solemn Judge Porter, placed his implacable hand on the prisoner's entrails and felt him convulse, and wrested from him his only honorable cry, his only moan of remorse, his only sign of deference to human nature. Another of them—Davidge, who cross-examined the experts—makes a show of his refined language and dexterity, his ability to arouse fear and his mischievousness: and he squeezes the witnesses, exasperates, shakes and wounds them, provoking taunts from Guiteau and shooting back his own witticisms, squabbling with the defense, and bragging that his jokes are always met with choruses of laughter. His services are high-priced and valuable; his laugh is chilling, his perspicacity great, and his conduct in the courtroom puerile and reprehensible. The widow of a cousin of Guiteau who died in an insane asylum states that Guiteau took a fancy to her daughter and wanted to bring her up himself so as later to make her his wife.

"Oh!" Davidge exclaims. "That's a very common form of madness!"

He then repeats the words of another witness, saying of the prisoner, "A blabbermouth and swaggerer who's a little shaky in the upper storey? Well, there are a lot of madmen like that walking around!"

One of the experts estimates that among every five men who appear to be sane, one is actually mad, and Davidge says, "That means there are two and a half madmen on the jury!"

"Careful, Judge, that's close to home," says Guiteau.

"Perhaps certain of the lawyers could stand in for the jurors," Scoville snorts angrily.

Scenes like this one send the public into raptures, and they happen every day. Now Guiteau, like a wilful child, turns his back on the prosecutor who is questioning him and silently starts reading a newspaper; now he hurls insults at him in a frenzy of rage, pounding the table in front of him, threatening the prosecutors with a fulminating gaze, his arm held high, pushing away the guards who try to calm him with his elbows and his irreverent words; now, like a schoolboy, he recites part of a speech in a dramatic tone, announcing it and commenting on it afterward in a vulgar tone; now he reads a newspaper extracted from the bundle of newspapers he carries to the courtroom each morning in his shackled hands, and hands a page from it to the guards who form a wall behind him; now, affecting gentility, he speaks with senatorial tongue and manner to his highly cultured prosecutor, and all is honeyed words, delight, and dandified charm; now, as if he knows he is clutching at the last plank of his life, pale, threatening, wrathful, anguished, terrible, both hands gripping the table, he disputes, shouts, pushes at the table as if he were seeking to escape from himself and from his prison, and snarlingly defends the fragile fabric that his defense has woven: he acted on God's orders, not out of rage at seeing himself passed over or in the hope of gaining something by his crime; the division within the Republican party was not a pretext, concealing the real reason for his act, it was the real reason for it; from his mother's breast and his father's thoughts of love he came away a madman, and men must deem insanity that which for him was a spontaneous and irresponsible fulfillment of a divine command.

Meanwhile, the prosecution maintains that he acted out of a despicable hope of extracting some advantage from his act; that he planned to commit for his own benefit the act by which, at the same time, he gratified his vengeful instincts; that he prepared the crime carefully so that it would appear to be the work of a political hothead to whom those borne to triumph by his act would then be indebted, and not the work of a religious fanatic, because if that were what he was, he would not have thought, as he did, that those men should repay him; that in the Republican dissensions he saw, with his fatal perspicacity, a pretext to excuse him and a thing to be taken advantage of, but that those dissensions were not the cause of his crime, which he began to conceive of as soon as he began to see that his ambition was being rebuffed.

Listen to his sister, who tells the prisoner's strange story very quickly, as if she wanted to have done with it, and in a very low voice that seems to emerge from an exhausted soul. The prisoner contradicts, interrupts, insults her. What a strange case! The lawyer questioning her is her husband; the man on whose behalf she is testifying is her brother. She is at once the person on trial and the witness. In a more energetic tone she checks the prosecutor who is trying to fluster her. Her voice is supplicating; her unhappiness makes the room fall silent; her narration is clear.

"My poor mother was always ill; she was dying when he was born, and died not long after. He was a strange boy; he still wasn't talking at the age of six; but later he was very loving. When he was sixteen I visited him at his school and found him already possessed by his strange mania for redemption and reformation; he was full of extravagant lectures and wanted to go off with the Christian Socialists of Oneida,[1] and did. When I went to see him in the Oneida community, I thought they had destroyed him, given him a hard blow to the head, or jarred his mind. Then came all the misfortunes: his mad ambitions, his marriage, his impoverishment, his absurd, audacious enterprises, and his constant mishaps. He came back to my house, where he had lived as a child. His every action was that of a madman: he wouldn't obey any direct order; he looked askance at my children; the Bible was always in his hands and he did not conceal his loathing or his wrath. Finally one day he raised the ax he was using to chop wood against me: I held my daughter close: 'Get him away from here! Get him away from here!' and what terrified me most was not the ax but his eyes. I've never been able to forget those eyes! He disappeared and then came back to the house. He learned that we believed he was insane and that if we could have persuaded his father and brothers to agree to it we would have put him in an asylum, and then he ran away. Who doesn't know the rest of his sad story?"

Now listen to his brother. His brother is an unusual, fierce, exalted, truthful man. He tells how, after a bitter quarrel with the prisoner, he went to see him in his cell, afraid of him. At first, he spoke to him from a distance, like one fearing an assault. Then he approached him, reassured. "I want to honor our name!" the prisoner was saying loudly. "I want to be called 'Guiteau the patriot'; I want it understood that no one must say 'Guiteau the assassin.'"

His brother went closer to him and told him in a low voice, "I believe you are honorable in what you say."

"I acted on God's orders; it doesn't matter to me if I die or suffer for it."

"But you are honorable?"

"I am honorable."

"And you wish to die for this principle, as Christ died?"

"Yes, I do."

"But you know that the jury that is to pass judgment on you will not accept your concept of divine inspiration."

"I know."

"And you will suffer the penalty that the jury gives you if it does not accept it?"

"Yes, I will suffer it."

"They say you're afraid of dying."

"I'm not afraid; my life doesn't matter to me in the least."

And all of that in the dank air of the dark cell, in rapid voices.

"And would you rather be hung by the law or killed by a lynch mob?"

"'Aaagh!' shouted the prisoner, running to a corner of the cell and hiding behind a table, 'neither lynched nor hung!'"

"And immediately he burst out laughing at his own cowardly behavior, and we all laughed. Since then I believe he is telling the truth: I believe he is insane. Before then, I had thought him responsible for his actions, for I judged that in his prior life he had always voluntarily chosen the path of evil over the path of good. In Boston, he came to pick a quarrel with me because he'd been told I was spreading information that was prejudicial to him and accusing him of not paying his debts, and in Boston I told him what I've just said. And when we were talking about how he did not pay his rent on time, he answered that he wanted to live like Christ. Christ went to a house and if people took him in he blessed them. He was working for God, and it was up to God to pay his landlords. I spoke approvingly of the Oneida community, and he, who hated them by then, flew into a rage. In his rage he wanted me to leave my own office. As I was pushing him toward the door, he called me a thief and a scoundrel: I hit him on the nape of the neck with the back of my hand, and he hit me back in the face, so hard it gave me new respect for him. And I thought he was demon-possessed. Religious theory holds that there are two forces in the Universe: one led by Satan, or the devil, the other by God or Jesus Christ: my father maintained that some people were possessed by the devil or Satan and others by Christ or God: he believed that the two powers were at war with each other and that after the fall of man Satan came to captivate as many men as he could, those who were not good believers in the Savior and had not saved themselves from the power of sin by a complete union with Jesus. He believed that all evil, all sickness, all deformity, was a defect caused by sin or by the power of the devil who is the spirit of evil, the wicked side of nature. And my brother and I held the same beliefs as my father. And I believe that my brother, out of wickedness, willfulness, and pride, allowed Satan to dominate him to such a degree that he was left in Satan's power. And therefore I believed that my brother was responsible before God for having chosen Satan as his master, but not responsible before the law for the deeds that Satan had inspired him to commit, given that he was already in one sense deprived of his reason. But that must not be said of my father, who followed God and was not mad. That was why I said, when I took out a life insurance policy, that there had been no cases of dementia in my family."

"No one would have had the slightest doubt that he was deranged," said the widow of the cousin of Guiteau who died insane, in an asylum, "if they had seen him constantly watching, pursuing, courting, importuning my daughter, who was still just a child then and became terrified of him."

But it was the prisoner himself who really had to be heard.

"Listen to him," Scoville had said, as if the prisoner's dementia were so clear that it was proven just by hearing him. He toys with his judges; he feigns resistance; he must not be forced to speak when he doesn't feel like it; he will acknowledge a few letters, but he will not speak.

Watch him as—fearful that if he turns to face the public some attempt on his life will be made—he looks to the right and the left with ceremonious and self-satisfied gestures, and a fleeting smile, like an orator certain of his own prowess who is about to address an enthusiastic public. But then fear overcomes him and he asks for a seat so as to make less of a target for murderous hands: it is good that God watches over his life but he does not think it improper for the wooden boxes of the courtroom to protect him as well. He pushes his stylish glasses up his straight nose, and with the air of a satisfied author reads some letters that he identifies one by one. He has many talents as a writer and as a penman. He seems to overflow with gloating enjoyment. "Oh, what script!" "Beautiful script!" "This one is even better." "And this letter looks as if it were a steel engraving." "Magnificent script." He looks like a boy warming to a new toy. Then the letters he identifies are read aloud, and he adds to them, refutes them, clarifies them, delights in them. In one he writes, "My eternal marriage to Jesus and his followers in this world takes precedence within me over all other attractions." And in another, "I have forgotten everything for Christ:

reputation, my manly honor, wealth, fame, and worldly renown. For me, the pursuit of the world's goods is over and may God grant that it be so forever. This community of Oneida is the seed of the kingdom of God, and we hope that through the calm and vigorous progress of the association the whole world will soon be his kingdom." But now he has begun to testify, and you have to see the way he starts out serenely but soon gives a shudder and then explodes, pounding the table, grasping the wooden bar that separates him from the jury box in sudden flashes of wrath, with grotesque words and a loud, violent tone, and you have to see the way that—as if unaware of it—he comes out with all the statements or versions of events that concur with the defense's theory, while staying away from anything that could strengthen the prosecution's case. And you have to hear his flowing, self-assured, vaulting, lashing words.

Like a fox, he sidesteps the dangers of his narration. And like a hungry dog he sinks his teeth into the episodes he can base his hopes on. As if he were fighting a rival dog for them, he shakes them, chews them, holds them high. He makes the public laugh; he is applauded. And after wounding the wooden railing with his closed fist and abandoning himself to scandalous transports, after disturbing the judge, who demands that he be silent, and his lawyer, who tries to soothe him, and the public, which is moved, and his guards, who try to restrain him, he stares at the public and at his judges, as if he were peering out from beneath his own gaze. And this was the story of his life that he told:

"I always felt motherless. I saw her when she was dying and then never again. Already at the age of twelve I was living in Scoville's house and going to school. My father then remarried without my consent, which was a very strange way of doing things. Oh, my father! I wanted to get an education and he wanted to save my soul. I wanted to study history, law, languages, and he wanted me, as the only way of preparing me for divine glory, to enter the Oneida community. He made me go to that stinking den of iniquity! And he told me that even were I the greatest man on earth it would be worth nothing if I did not save my soul! He sent me the *Bereano*, which is the Bible of the community, and their magazines. All of it poisoned me: as I read it I lost my eyes, my will, my zeal for science. At last I went to the community; there I beheld the theory of inspiration of which Noyes,[2] the Christ of that communion, said he was the repository. Noyes said that his community was the beginning of the kingdom of God on earth and that he was God's partner and that only through him would men be saved because he was greater and more divine than the Lord Jesus Christ. And I have to say that as a boy I once received a great blow to the head: I can still fit half an inch of my little finger into the wound. My father was fanatical about such things and believed that the devil entered human bodies, and therefore I myself, when my head was hurting in Oneida, didn't try any cure but said to the devil, 'Get out of me, old devil!' But my father was very sincere, very intense, very vehement, very impetuous in his beliefs! And I left Oneida and went to New York to found a newspaper—*The Theocrat*—which I wasn't able to found, but which was a royal idea. Then I studied law for three or four months in a lawyer's office and went to see the district attorney who asked me three or four questions, of which I answered one wrong, and he gave me a certificate that said: 'This certifies that Charles J. Guiteau has been examined by us and we consider him fit for the practice of law in the Supreme Court of the State of Illinois.' And that was how I became a lawyer. And because of my appearance I was given very good cases. I went to the wealthy businesses and asked for cases, and I didn't stop going until they gave them to me, and so I earned thousands of dollars in Chicago and New York. But the *Herald* called me a swindler, and ruined all of it for me. Then I went to hotels, and one day they threw me into a cell in the Tombs. Horrible cell! Scoville got me out of there and I rushed to soak my body in hot water. Oh, I would have made good money if it hadn't been for the *Herald*."

The accused went on to recount an extraordinary undertaking of his, a plan to buy the *Inter-Ocean*, a famous Chicago newspaper, for $75,000—for which purpose he asked one of the people he considered his friends for $200,000. And it was interesting to see how he didn't leave a thing undone that might have been advantageous to the deal. He didn't see underlings—he went right to the top. It was his plan to bring together upon the colossal page the ad-selling genius of the *Tribune* (a well-known Chicago paper), the enterprising spirit of the founder of the *Herald,* and the brilliant Republicanism of the greatly celebrated journalist Horace Greeley. He sought out the best editors. He agreed on a splendid building. He left nothing undone. He tried to establish an excellent wire service; he looked over and chose printing presses; and he wrote to the *Herald,* which of course did not reply, demanding the right to publish at the same time as the *Herald* all the highly detailed news cables which at great cost that New York newspaper receives from all parts of the earth. And what did he offer the famous paper in exchange for this tremendous benefit? Since the *Herald* had called him a swindler, he had filed suit against the *Herald* for $100,000 in damages—a dead lawsuit!—the quarrel of a desperate man. And he promised the *Herald*, in exchange for its wire service, that he would abandon his strange lawsuit! He had already grown scornful of his own lawsuit because he was of the opinion, and still is, that "though it no longer matters to me, and I would give up the position," he was destined to become president of the United States, and he doesn't believe a president should have the *Herald* against him!

At that juncture of his life there arrived in Chicago a pair of grotesque, frenzied preachers who attracted an enormous public to their revival meetings there, just as they are now doing in London where equally large crowds gather for their "Hosannah Testimonies" and their "Invitations to Paradise." Predictably enough, Guiteau became an usher for Moody and Shaddey.[3]

"And that was when, after a sermon I heard a pastor give, I began to study the second coming of Christ. Oh, great researches! I never left the Chicago Public Library. I wrote my lecture, the subject of which I had been pondering for years, and which did no less than prove that the second coming of Christ occurred at the time of the destruction of Jerusalem, up in the clouds, directly over the city, and that the destruction of Jerusalem was nothing less than the visible sign of the coming of Christ. Because that is the truth, and not, as they believe in the churches, that Christ will come in the future. And then I set off like Saint Peter, falling and getting back on my feet, thrown out of a house today and out of a train tomorrow, to publish my religious discovery and read my speech. For the same thing happened to Peter: neither he nor I had the money to pay for a room, and neither of us had any success because we had discovered new ideas in theology. And wasn't I working for the Lord? Well, the Lord would take care of me, as he has said he would do for whoever works for him. I went on my way, always thinking of Saint Peter and running from conductors. I still laugh and enjoy myself when I remember those good times. And the Lord always protected me. One day he did it so well that when I was forced to leave one car of a train, I changed seats and went on traveling to Washington and the Lord sat me next to a man who asked me if I wanted a good place to stay in the city. And that was precisely what I was praying to the Lord for—a good house I could stay in."

Good Scoville, eager to prove how the extravagant ideas of fanatics were embedded in the prisoner's fragile mind as if in wax, possessing

him utterly, stripping him of all self-control, and making him capable
of his future crime, then had him describe the belief of the Oneida
Community that any man who enters the community is a man of God,
and inspired by God; and that the Leader is in direct communication
with the heavens and a prophet of the Lord among men, whom the
members of the community obey and in whose hands they place their
goods, their thoughts, their wills, and every possession of their bodies
and souls.

"And I went on lecturing without any luck; in Boston that great
heretic Ingersoll[4] was going to give his speech denying the existence of
hell, and he had a full, overflowing house: and I, who wanted to prove
that there is a hell, had no more than a dozen people. They paid fifty
cents to hear that there was no infernal torment, but they didn't want
to pay a cent to hear that there was one. I set up a law practice and that
went badly. I went on another lecture tour and that went badly. I published my 'Truth, or the Bible Companion' and no one took any notice. And then came the presidential election and I decided to become
a politician. I fashioned my speech, the one titled 'Garfield against
Hancock,' which I had to rewrite so that it would support Garfield,
because I first wrote it in the belief that Grant would be the Republican candidate. That speech"—said Guiteau in a grave tone, the tone of
one telling the centuries to come about the work of a colossus—"was
written in the Boston State Library!"

In such insolent, naked, shameless, shifting, restless terms as these,
he recounted his futile visits to leading figures—"those friends," as he
calls them—such as Arthur, Logan,[5] who is an Olympian personage,
and others of no less stature. He told of his forays into the campaign
offices that sent his speech out in every direction, of how he delivered
part of it to a meeting of men of color and "those friends treated me
very well and were glad to see me and all of that." He said that as soon
as Garfield was elected he wrote to him demanding the ambassadorship to Austria, because there was a possibility that he was going to
marry a rich woman, and the ambassadorship would be most welcome; he said he saw Blaine[6] in Washington when he was seeking the
position of consul in Paris, and was finally rejected, and that he
watched his party boil over and break apart and read about the dispute
in the newspapers,[7] and wrote pacifying letters to Garfield—in which,
of course, his advice was followed by questions about the position of
consul he now desired—that went unanswered. He said that on the
night when the rift within the party came to a head with the resigna-

tion of the two senators who were offended by Garfield, he received from God the inspiration for his act.

He spoke in lugubrious, sad, or dramatic tones like one who hears and sees marvels and is the cause of them. "I went to sleep that night tormented by somber ideas about those dissensions, and like a bolt of lightning the thought came to my mind that if Garfield was no longer in the way all problems would be resolved. In the morning, the thought returned. And after that the idea of removing the president did not leave me; it worked on me, tortured me, oppressed me for two weeks. I was filled with horror and shook it, strangled it, cast it far from me, but it went on growing and growing until after two weeks my mind was certain of the necessity of removing the president. As for the divinity of the inspiration—I say to all of you that it was divine!" he exclaimed in a tremendous voice. "I then believed and I still believe now that it was divine. I prayed, prayed, prayed, because I wanted the Lord to reveal himself to me in some way and tell me if it was not his will that I remove the president. And the Lord did not reveal himself to me, because this act was inspired by him for the good of the great American people."

"How was it for the good of the American people?" asked Scoville, who was extracting these answers and clarifications from him.

"To unite the factions within the Republican party, which was then in bitter and deplorable schism, and to prevent war from breaking out anew in this nation because of the destruction of the Republican party. Yes, God inspired me when I entered Oneida; when I tried to found the *Theocrat,* when I went out to preach like Saint Peter, and when I had the idea of removing the president! God is taking care of me. See how he has kept me safe from murderers! God is protecting me, God and the government: these soldiers, these jurors, these experts, this court, all are here to serve God and to protect me!" Like fiery lava the words flow from his lips. "I wished no harm to the president. I was in great spiritual agitation, distraught and drowning: I had no relief until it was all done: then I felt happy, and gave thanks to God."

—M. de Z.[8]
—December 10, 1881;
published in *La Opinión Nacional* (Caracas), December 26, 1881

PRIZEFIGHT

*** SELECTIONS ***

Martí's "Letters from New York" often veer from one subject to another—from prizefighting, in the following case, to Valentines—and sometimes seem to correspond only to whatever topics of conversation were in the air at the moment of writing—or even to be wholly random. While the spontaneity of these writings is undeniable, their diversity of subject matter also embodies a consistent will to present the most complex picture possible, to round out one image with another that contradicts or serves as a counterpoint to it, rather than reaching for a simplistic conclusion. Here the subject is the United States at play: a masculine sport and a more feminine social custom. In the end, both reflect curiously similar traits of the national character, for both involve an element of entertainment, an element of cruelty, and a very large element of commerce.

The pen soars when it has great things to narrate but plods along heavily when it must, as now, give an account of brutal things that are devoid of beauty or nobility. The pen should be as immaculate as a virgin. It twists away like an enslaved woman, lifts from the paper as if trying to escape and droops in the hand that holds it, as if there were some iniquity in describing iniquitous things. Men charge at each other like bulls here. They gamble on the strength of their necks, bite and claw in the fight, and then go—covered in blood, their teeth knocked out, their foreheads bruised, their knuckles raw, weaving and falling, through the mob that shouts and flings its hats in the air and surges around them, cheering—to collect the bag of money they have just won in the fight. And the other contender lies unconscious in the arms of his trainers, his vertebrae shattered, while women's hands weave wreaths of flowers that will perfume the crowded dressing rooms of these sordid ruffians.

And this is a national holiday. It sets trains and telegraphs in motion and brings business to a halt for hours while workers and bankers throng the streets. Considerable sums are exchanged amid the clink of glasses, and the newspapers, which occasionally spend a few lines condemning what they describe elsewhere at copious length, narrate the comings and goings, utterances, leisure activities, training, disputes, fights, and falls of the rivals. The heartbeat of one of these scoundrels is invoked as if it were the heartbeat of a martyr. Their physiques and the whiteness and sheen of their skins are described in detail. The muscles they use for hitting are measured. Their habits, meals, weights, and witticisms are all reported. Their fighting insignia are depicted; the footgear they wear in the ring is sketched.

This is a prizefight of the kind that the Giant of Troy and the Boston Strong Boy just fought, at the end of which the Giant slumped to the ground, bloody and unconscious, in front of two thousand spectators. This is why there is merrymaking in New Orleans; this is what has kept every town in the Union on tenterhooks, and Boston, New York, and Philadelphia in a state of visible agitation. I can still see the street urchins, who are like green fruit that has rotted on the vine, hanging from the wheels and windows of the newspaper wagon, as if a beehive had been knocked over. A horde of buyers waits around the wagon, which the dray horse is already pulling away, while the children go scrabbling along the ground among heaps of newspapers: wretched little girls in rags, well-dressed lasses whose fine garments lay bare their souls, and rapacious Irish lads who curse as they retrieve their tattered hats, fallen off in the scuffle, from the mud. And new wagons pull in, and new scufflings ensue. Those vendors who manage to grab some newspapers can't sell them fast enough to the eager buyers who besiege them. Crowds stand shivering in the rain, waiting for news of the fight from the bulletins the famous newspapers post on their walls. Children can read, in the newspapers their parents bring home, which blow hit which eye, and that a good punch was delivered to a fallen adversary's nose, and that an enemy can be killed by a polite shove in the face with one hand while the other delivers a blow to the back of the neck, near the brain. The newspapers publish pictures of the fighters and the banners under which they fight and sketches of the blows. And over dinner the family talks of how this friend lost a hundred dollars while another won a thousand, and others thousands more, because many wagered on the Giant but in the end the Strong Boy won. This was New York, the evening after the fight.

And on the field of battle itself? It took place in the South, beside the sea, beneath oaks and cedars. These are not the quarrels of thugs, sparked by hot tempers, cooled by danger, and governed by caprice. These brutes have previously reached an agreement in which—as in the jousting tourneys of old—the field is divided into equal parts of sun and shade, and the weights of the participants and the tactics to be used are predetermined, as in a horse race. A detailed contract stipulates that the boxers will fight standing up, without rocks or brass knuckles in their hands or any more than three half-inch cleats with rounded tips in the soles of their shoes. To promote greater decorum, it is established that they will not bite or scratch this time, or throw any punches when the opponent has one hand and one knee on the ground or when he is caught in a chokehold against the ropes or poles of the ring, which must be on level ground and no larger than twenty-four feet square. In the sunlight, attached to the center poles of the ring, the fighting insignia of both ruffians must be displayed, in this case, for the Giant of Troy, a harp, a sun, a moon, a shield, and an eagle with outstretched wings atop a star-spangled globe, and for the Boston Strong Boy, an eagle, aloft among the clouds, holding an American shield and flanked by small North American and Irish flags. For this barbaric practice came here from Ireland, along with much of the population.

History is no more than this: the transition from the beast-man to the man-man. Are there not hours of beasthood in every human being, when the teeth need to bite, the throat feels a murderous thirst, the eyes flame, and the clenched fist seeks bodies to pound? To restrain that beast and seat an angel over it: that is the human victory. But while industrious Aztecs and cultured Peruvians built roads over mountain peaks, diverted rivers into cyclopean conduits, and fashioned delicate jewelry for their women's hands, the men of these Northern lands, like Cormon's Cain,[1] confronted the spears of Caesar's legions with their backs clothed in furs and their hairy chests exposed, pitched their nomadic tents in craggy lands, and ate the barely smoked flesh, cooked in the skin, of animals they had throttled between their iron hands. Their arms were like mountain slopes, their legs tree trunks, their hands drop hammers, their heads forests. In the beginning, life was no more than a struggle against wild beasts for control of the forests. But today life is not a mountain wilderness; it is a statue carved out of the mountainside.

The eyes take fright, as if they had suddenly caught sight of Cain walking through the streets of a modern city, when they see how the arts of printing and painting submissively lick the callused feet of these human beasts, and publish and celebrate the magnificent brute, and ogle him longingly when, his mountainous torso naked and his massive arm curled back, he pummels a leather bag, sending it swinging toward the ceiling from which it hangs by a leather cord, with the

same blows he will later deal, amid cheers and hurrahs, to the splinter-
ing skull, swollen lips, and reeling body of his shuddering adversary.
They train for the match, build up their strength, burn off the super-
fluous flesh that weighs them down and does not withstand assault.
They retreat to isolated spots in the countryside with their coaches
who teach them the best techniques for slugging, keep them from in-
dulging in any physical excess, and display them to professional gamblers who want to see their man before putting any money down on
him because "this is business," and they want to bet on "the best man."
And it is strictly business as well for the fighters, who sometimes see
each other for the first time in the ring. But a horse trader has put
down two thousand dollars on one man and a reporter has wagered
two thousand more on another, and so the fight is arranged, the
bloody fight, because it is a fine thing to win money and fame as
"Heavyweight Champion of America" by shattering bones and rat-
tling brains in their skulls. There are 130-pound runts who compete to
be known as the best-paid hitter among the lightweights, while 200-
pounders contend for the heavyweight championship.

And hardly is the news out that the fight is on than the coaches, who
call themselves his "seconds," take charge of the fighter and make sure
he doesn't jeopardize the earnings of those who have put money "on
his back" by drinking or womanizing. And the whole nation is a cock-
fighting pit. The two men go on tour, fighting with gloves, naked from
the waist up, in theaters, town squares, and barroom platforms; their
banners wave, their feats are recounted, their muscles are squeezed, and
their chances of winning or losing are calculated before a bet is exchanged with the next gambler. The towns are divided into opposing
factions that often end up leaping into the ring or onto the platform, revolvers in the air and knives drawn. Troy, which loves its giant, who is
the owner of a theater and a family man, and like all good ruffians
is famously generous, burns with jealousy of Boston, which is proud of
its brute because every man who has stood up to the Strong Boy has
fallen bleeding to the ground. Don't bother asking who is preventing
this, for it happens in town squares month after month and it is clear
that no one is preventing it. There are laws, but of the same type as in
Mexico, where bullfights—which serve only to reduce men to bulls—
are prohibited within the boundaries of Tenochtitlán and allowed in
the nearby town of Tlalnepantla. There the great Netzahualcóyotl[2]
once prayed in his high tower, but today dumb beasts are hamstrung by

men dressed up as matadors who, for the greatness of the land that bred them, were born for more glorious tasks.

As the day of the fight approaches the pugilists are constantly on the move, one jump ahead of jail, for each state has different statutes, and abominators of this sport abound among the nation's distinguished lawmakers. But the fighters always find a state that will take them in, and there the fight becomes a public holiday. The trains come from afar, loaded with gamblers who have shut down their businesses and left their families fatherless to arrive by the hundreds of thousands and wedge into the roaring crowd that, with red faces, hats pushed back and hands waving in the air, will surround the boxing ring on the long-awaited morning of the fight. These are not just horse traders and riffraff: there are bankers, judges, men of position, churchgoers, and young men from rich families who should exchange their money for some serious responsibilities. Every city has at least one club devoted to this diversion and some cities have many. Each of these groups sends its deputies; every gambler who put money down sends his man to watch the fight; every lover of the sport goes to enjoy the spectacle at first hand. The doors of the hotels and saloons are never closed. With their displays of wealth or strong muscles, respectively, the prodigal sons of Lady Luck and the professional fighters astonish the ladies of the city, old and young, who, instead of averting their eyes from the sight of these repellent creatures, gaze at them with curiosity and delectation as if upon great men and privileged beings.

In New Orleans, on whose outskirts the fight took place, old purses were opened—purses whose strings had been tightly knotted since the terrible war—so that their rusting contents could be staked on the ferocity of these bruisers. The streets were like the hallways of a house; it was a family affair. The whole city was nothing but clinking glasses, boisterous talk, heated debates in stores and on street corners over the merits of the fighters, and droves of people going to feast their greedy eyes on the athletes' powerful backs, bulging shoulders, and agile hips. And some came away fretting because their bruiser had too much flesh on his ribs, while others were all abuzz because their man was solid muscle and bone. Groups of doctors went to see these splendid specimens of the human brute. And ladies went to place their slender hands in the sinewy hands of the heroes.

The night before the massive decampment to the scene of the fight, the entire city seemed already on the move. Afraid that the train would leave without them, those who had paid ten dollars for the right to witness the much-anticipated match slept on armchairs and sofas, or with their elbows propped on balcony railings. To keep from being robbed along the way, they stood at hotel counters emptying their pockets of jewels, which reprobates are always fond of. Then at last the train departed, speeding across the Louisiana bayous with the fighters, their seconds, their sponges and curative concoctions, and the purse for the fight; the coaches were so jammed that passengers were sitting on the roof and spilling out of the cars. Then came the drinking, the vociferating, the laying of bets. The old saying that a good fighter's got to have guts, agility, and endurance makes the rounds. A general reminiscing ensues about how in the old days New Yorkers used to settle their electoral disputes with their fists; how McCoy killed Chris Lilly in the ring; how, when Hyer beat Sullivan in "a whirlwind fight," festive lights were set out along Park Row, the famous old street that now runs alongside the post office, where for a long time a huge, transparent sign hung that read "Tom Hyer, Champion of America." Next comes the recollection, between gulps of burning liquor, that Morrisey left Heenan for dead; that when Jones fought McCoole he got such a blow to the temple that it left him retching and addled his brain; and that Mace was a great hitter who threw punches like a wind-mill and broke Allen's neck with one good jab. And sunlight was streaming in through the windows of the coaches.

At the site of the match, in the city of Mississippi, people were crowding around the spot chosen for the ring, men were sitting in the trees, the balconies were full of the curious, and clumps of spectators formed crenellations along the rooftops. The train emptied out its cargo. The ring was put up, with another, larger ring around it so that privileged onlookers could stroll in the space between the two. Singing merrily, a cheerful battalion of journalists sat down on the sand. Then the air was filled with hurrahs and every hand was waving a hat as the standoffish Sullivan appeared in his short pants and green jersey, fol-lowed by the handsome Ryan, the Giant of Troy, clad in white. There were ladies in the inner circle. As the two bruisers exchanged a hand-shake and the blood that would soon be flowing copiously began to boil, the seconds, squatting on the ground, counted up the money that had been wagered. But why watch them? Soon enough they are sprawled on the ground. Each is carried back to his corner and their limbs are rubbed with ointments; they charge at each other once more, blows pound against their skulls with the sound of a hammer against a damaged anvil; Ryan's clothing is stained with blood and he falls to his knees while the Boston Strong Boy skips back to his corner, smiling. There is a thunderous roar as Ryan stands up, weaving; Sullivan runs at him with a laugh; they clutch each other's necks and squeeze each other's faces, then stumble back against the ropes. Nine times they go at each other; nine times they injure each other. Now the Giant is dragging, his spiked shoes can no longer hold him up; now he is knocked out by a punch in the neck and falls, and seeing him unconscious, his second throws the sponge in the air in token of defeat. Three hundred thousand dollars has changed hands, wagered in all the cities of the nation on this fight. Specially commissioned telegraph wires have delivered a blow-by-blow account to anxious crowds thronging in the streets of the great cities, who greet the news of the victory with clamorous applause or wrathful booing. The triumphant Bostonian is hailed with music and parties, and the two are exhibited once more in rings and saloons, honored and regaled, the Giant and the Strong Boy. The sand on the seashore in the city of Mississippi is still red and trampled by their feet! This country is like a great tree; perhaps it is a law of nature that in the roots of great trees live worms.[3]

. . .

What is this messenger boy who knocks at my door in his uniform and blue cloth cap bringing? Ah! This is the time of year when lovers and loyal friends, who suffer to see souls that are alone, send pretty cards with anonymous greetings. On this card, bordered with a blue fringe, someone has sent me a winged boy astride a camel, and on this one, which, like most of them, has two lovely verses at the bottom—though the verses are not always lovely—is an eagle perched on a rock, who gazes into the sky. . . . And this little boy who's arriving now, what is he bringing? Why, a comic Valentine that shows a sad man dressed for sailing who stands beside an ocean on which not a boat can be seen! For Valentines, which were the invention of an English lady, fill their manufacturers' bags, the shops' counters, and the mailmen's leather sacks right now. There isn't a house that doesn't send or receive them. The custom was once limited to lovers, and at that time, on Saint Valentine's Day—when, as everyone knows, the birds greet the dawn chirping and fluttering around the branch where the one they choose as the companion of their nest will alight—the maidens of England did not go to bed without having placed four leaves at the corners of their pillow and one in the center, because these leaves had the power to make a vision of the suitor they should choose to marry appear to them in their dreams, a power that was even more certain if the maiden had previously boiled an egg and extracted its yoke, then filled the empty space with salt and eaten the rest, without eating or drinking afterward or removing the egg from its shell, because that would rob it of its power. It was also customary for the one chosen as the Valentine to make a valuable gift to his lady, in the manner of the Duke of York—a most excellent duke, who gave Miss Stuart (later to become the famous Duchess of Richmond) a piece of jewelry that cost him no less than eight hundred pounds sterling. "On that day when the birds were bountiful," as the old line goes, the shepherdesses went out early in the morning to fetch the milk and took for their sweetheart the first shepherd their eyes fell on, which naturally made every shepherd a very early riser on Saint Valentine's Day.

On this side of the ocean, the practice was different; it consisted of sending allegorical sketches, accompanied by rhyming explanations of the defects or peculiarities of the person for whom the sketch was destined. The cards were always anonymous, and over time malice took root in what had at first been the practice only of lovers, and anyone with a crooked back or a crossed eye or a big nose, or who was a miser or a braggart or a degenerate, received from unknown hands a large, colorful card that in foolish rhymes mocked, sometimes vaguely and sometimes cruelly and pointedly, the defect of the Valentined individual. And even today, you need only enter a shop and request a Valentine for a tailor, and the shopkeeper will scan his counters for the tailors' packet and take from it a card featuring a half-dressed little old man who is mending and refurbishing an aged dinner jacket to make it look new in cut and fabric. Nowadays only the lower classes engage in this kind of malice, but it was once so widespread that there wasn't a human presumption or ridiculous habit in these territories for which the Valentines didn't have a stinging little poem. One Valentine, meant for a housewife who does her own housework and then steps forth bejeweled and swathed in silks to show off all her finery on her Thursday nights out, shows the lady with a gigantic bucket for a hat, a scullery maid's apron as the front of her dress, forks for earrings, a slotted spoon for a fan, and a teaspoon as a brooch, being greeted by a lean pair of tongs dressed as gallant gentlemen. The Valentines that remain in fashion are original sketches drawn by a friend's hand to arouse another friend's curiosity, or enchanting little figures, tender or comical, in so numerous and rich a variety that the sea's beaches have no more sand than the shops have Valentines. They are stiff cards, edged or encircled in lace or fringes, or little blue or pink pillows on which a sweet boy wearing a beret smiles; they are angels, lovers, bunches of wildflowers, lilies, daisies, or a little black boy who is floundering beneath a colossal cap that a little black girl is tying under his chin, or sunflowers, which are now in vogue among aesthetes, or tulips, which once fetched such high prices here that they were sold off by shares. And all of them are captioned with laughing rhymes, April Fool's Day rhymes, the kind of sky-blue rhymes that one writes before embarking on the rigors of life, and not the red or black ones that are written later, until the kind years cloak the hair and the soul in white, the color of light.

People bustle about contented, busy, active. After a brilliant debate, the Senate has passed a law depriving the Mormon polygamists of the right to vote or be elected. The Academy of Music resounds with the clamor of happy masqueraders: children escorting a regally garbed Esmeralda and Phoebus in a carriage pulled by goats, and actors who recreate onstage the cart of Thespis where comedy was born, and send Frou Frou and the Duke of Buckingham, Camille and Louis XI dancing in pairs across the room. New Orleans is celebrating its carnival with a sumptuous procession that brings the great wonders of the Hindustani poems to life.

Portland plucks the loveliest roses from its gardens to ornament the house where Longfellow's birthday will soon be celebrated. Already here at home, the flagstaffs for the festive banners are being polished in honor of George Washington, that serene, glorious man who was more fortunate than Bolívar because he was not as great. We will listen to these hymns and attach wings of gold to them, and they will cross the sea.

—New York, February 17, 1882;
published in *La Opinión Nacional* (Caracas), March 4, 1882

EMERSON

On an undated fragment found among his papers, Martí listed "The afternoon of Emerson" first among the supreme moments of his life (see page 78). Since he never met Emerson in person, he may have been referring to the afternoon on which he wrote this essay.

At times the pen trembles like a priest capable of sin who feels unworthy of his ministry. Agitated, the spirit takes flight and wants wings to lift it, not a pen to hone and sculpt it like a chisel. Writing is pain, abasement: it yokes a condor to a cart. For when a great man vanishes from the earth, he leaves behind him a pure clarity, a hunger for peace, a hatred of noise. The Universe seems a temple; the city's commerce, the tumult of life and the commotion of men, a profanation. There is a sprouting of wings, a vanishing of feet. Life goes on, but as if by the light of a star, as if seated in a meadow of white flowers. A soft, fresh luminescence fills the immense, silent atmosphere. All is summit, and we are atop it. The earth lies at our feet, wrapped in shadow like some distant world once long ago visited. And these wagons that go rumbling by, these hawkers with their loud cries, these tall chimneys blasting their powerful whistles into the air, all the to-and-fro, the strutting, arguing, and living of mankind, strikes us, in our pure and caressing retreat, as the sound of a barbarous army that invades our mountaintops, tramples our foothills, and in its rage rends asunder the great shadow behind which looms—like a colossal battlefield where warriors made of stone wear golden armor and bear red spears—the tumultuous and resplendent city. Emerson is dead and sweet tears fill the eyes. The news brings envy, not pain. The breast fills not with anguish but with tenderness. Death is a victory. When a person has lived well, the hearse is a triumphal chariot. Our tears are of pleasure, not mourning, for rose petals already cover the wounds that life made on the dead man's hands and feet. The death of a just man is a celebration; all the earth pauses to watch the parting of the heavens. And the faces of men are radiant with hope, and in their arms they carry bundles of palm fronds to carpet the ground, and with their swords they make a high arch beneath which the body of the victorious warrior passes, covered with boughs of oak and golden straw. The man who gave fully of himself and did good unto others goes to his rest, while the man who labored badly in this life goes to labor anew. And the young warriors, having watched with envious eyes the passage of the great victor, whose warm corpse glows with all the greatness of repose, turn back to the tasks of the living, to make themselves worthy of their own palm fronds and arches!

You ask who he was, this man who has died? The whole world knows who he was. He was a man who found himself alive, and shook from his shoulders and his eyes all the mantles and blindfolds that the past casts over men: a man who lived face to face with nature as if all the world were his home and the sun his own sun and he a patriarch. He was one of those to whom Nature reveals herself and opens and stretches out her many arms as if to envelop the whole body of her child in them. He was one of those to whom the utmost wisdom, the utmost serenity, and the utmost delight are given. All of nature thrilled before him like a bride, and he lived in happiness because he bestowed his loves beyond the earth. The whole of his life was an awakening from a wedding night. What raptures his soul knew! What visions his eyes saw! What tablets of laws his books are, what flights of angels his poems! He was a reserved, slender child, who reminded those who saw him of a young eagle, a young pine. Later, he was serene, kind, and radiant; adults and children would stop to watch him go by. His step was firm, the step of a man who knows where he must go; his body was tall and frail, like a tree whose crown sways in the pure breezes. His visage was lean, that of a man made for detachment and eager to venture beyond himself. His forehead was like the slope of a mountain, his nose like the beak of a bird that soars above mountain peaks. And his eyes were captivating, for they were brimming with love, and calm, the eyes of one who has seen the unseen. All who saw him felt a desire to kiss his forehead. For Carlyle, the great English philosopher who turned against the earth with the strength and brilliance of Satan, Emerson's visit was "a celestial vision." For Whitman, who has discovered a new poetry in nature, to see Emerson was "to spend a blessed hour." For Stedman,[1] a good critic, "there was a white light in the wise man's village." For Alcott,[2] a noble, youthful old man who thinks and sings, it seemed "a misfortune not to have known him." People left his side as if coming away from a living monument or a supreme being. Some men are like mountains; they leave the earth flat before and behind them. He was not familiar, but he was tender, for his was an imperial family whose members all had to be emperors. He loved his friends as if they were cherished women: for him friendship had something of the solemnity of twilight in a forest. Love is superior to friendship in that it creates children; friendship is superior to love in that it does not create desires, or the weariness of having satisfied them, or the sorrow of abandoning the temple of sated desires for that of new desires. Around him was enchantment. His voice was heard as if it were the voice of a messenger from the future speaking from amid incandescent clouds. An impalpable thread made of moonlight seemed to bind the men who gathered to listen to him together. The wise went to see him, and came away rejoicing and chastened. Young men walked many miles to see him, and he received those tremulous pilgrims with a smile and bade them sit around his sturdy mahogany table, piled with large books, and served them fine aged sherry, attending to them like a servant. And those who read him but do not understand him accuse him of a lack of tenderness because, accustomed to permanent commerce with grandeur, he saw his personal affairs as small, random, and inessential, undeserving of narration. These petty poets with their jeremiads are no more than the Phrynes[3] of their own pain! Men must be told of things that are worthy of men and capable of exalting them! To go about telling of one's own little pains in swooning rhymes is a task fit only for ants! Pain must be modest.

His mind was priestly, his tenderness angelic, his wrath sacred. When he saw or thought of men who were enslaved, he spoke—and it was as if the Tablets of the Law were once again being smashed at the foot of a new biblical mountain. His wrath was the wrath of Moses. He shook off the trivialities of vulgar minds as a lion shakes off flies. For him, argument was merely a distraction from the discovery of truth. Since he said what he saw, he was irritated when the things he said were questioned. His anger stemmed not from vanity but from sincerity. In what way was it his fault that the eyes of others were not equipped with the elucidating light of his own? Must the caterpillar deny that the eagle flies? He disdained sophistries. The extraordinary was commonplace for him, so he was surprised by the need to demonstrate the extraordinary to other men. If they didn't understand him, he shrugged: nature had spoken to him: he was a priest of nature. He did not feign revelations; he did not construct mental worlds; he put no will or effort of his mind into what he wrote in prose or in poetry. All of his prose was poetry, and his poetry and prose are like echoes. He perceived beyond himself the creating Spirit that spoke through him to nature. He saw himself as the eye's transparent pupil that sees everything, reflects everything, and is only a pupil. His writings are like shards of light that shone into him and bathed his soul and intoxicated him with the intoxication of light and emerged from him. What must the vain little minds who go about perched on conventions, as if on stilts, have seemed to him? Or the unworthy men who have eyes and do not wish to see? Or the shirkers, the men of the herd, who do not use their own eyes but see through the eyes of others? Or the clay creatures who go about the earth being fashioned by tailors and shoemakers and milliners and enameled by jewelers, and who are endowed with senses and the power of speech but nothing more? Or the pompous phrasemakers who do not know that every thought is the peak of a mountain and a pain shooting through the mind and a light that consumes the oil of the thinker's own life?

Never was a man freer of the pressures of mankind and of his time. The future did not make him tremble or blind him as it came to pass. The light he bore within protected him from this journey across ruins that is life. He knew no limitations, no shackles. He was not a man of his nation; he was a man of the human nation. He saw the earth, found it out of step with himself, felt the melancholy of answering questions that men do not ask, and withdrew into himself. He was tender with men, and faithful to himself. He was educated to teach a creed, and returned his ministerial coat to the believers because he felt the august cloak of nature upon his shoulders. He followed no system, for that struck him as the act of a blind man or a servant; he believed in no system, for that struck him as the act of a weak, low, and envious mind. He plunged into nature and emerged from her radiant. He felt himself to be a man, and, as such, God. He said what he saw; and where he could not see, he said nothing. He revealed what he perceived and venerated what he could not perceive. He gazed upon the Universe with his own eyes and spoke his own language. He was a creator because he did not want to be one. He experienced divine pleasures and lived amid delightful, even celestial, exchanges. He knew the ineffable sweetness of ecstasy. Neither his mind nor his tongue nor his conscience was for hire. From him, as from a star, came light. In him, mankind was entirely worthy.

Thus he lived: seeing the invisible and revealing it. He lived in a sacred city, for there, tired of enslavement, men decided to be free and knelt upon the earth of Concord, his town, to fire off the first bullet—from whose metal that nation was forged—against the redcoats. He lived in Concord, which is like Tusculum,[4] a place where thinkers, hermits, and poets live. His house, like him, was spacious and solemn,

surrounded by tall pines, as if to symbolize its owner, and shady chestnuts. In the wise man's rooms, the books did not seem like books, but
like guests: all of them wore workaday clothes, stained pages, worn
spines. He read them all, like a plunging eagle. The roof of the house
was raised high at the center, as befit the dwelling of one whose life
was an endless soaring through the heights. And from the steep roof
rose plumes of smoke, like the vapor of ideas that is sometimes seen
emanating from a great and thoughtful head. There he read Mon-
taigne, who saw for himself and said true things; Swedenborg the mystic, whose mind was oceanic; Plotinus, who searched for God and
came close to finding him; the Hindus, who observe the evaporation
of their own souls, tremulous and submissive; and Plato, who gazed
fearlessly and with unequaled fruition into the divine mind. Or he
would shut his books and his bodily eyes to give himself over to the
supreme indulgence of seeing with the soul. Or he paced, restless and
agitated, like one who is moved by a will other than his own, catching
fire when an idea that craved precise expression lashed at his lips like a
man caught in a thicket and battling to make his way out into the open
air. Or he would sit down, weary, with a sweet smile, like one who sees
a solemn thing and gratefully caresses his own spirit, which has discovered it. Oh, what satisfaction it is to think well! And what a delight
it is to understand the objects of life—a kingly delight! One smiles at
the appearance of a truth as if it were the loveliest of maidens. And one
trembles, as in a mysterious betrothal. Life, which is often terrible, is
often ineffable. The common pleasures are the birthright of scoundrels;
life has far more exquisite delights, which come from loving and
thinking. What clouds in the sky are lovelier than those that gather,
ripple, and ascend in the soul of a father who gazes upon his child?
Why must a man envy the sacred sufferings, the childbearings of a
woman? For a thought, in the agony of its birth and the joy that follows, is a child. The hour of the knowledge of truth is intoxicating and
august; the feeling is not of elevation but of repose, of filial tenderness
and paternal confusion. Joy makes the eyes very bright, brings calm to
the soul, and softly caresses the mind with its wings. It is as if the skull
were lit with stars—an inner vault, silent and vast, illuminating the
tranquil mind in solemn darkness! Magnificent world. He who returns from it gently pushes away all the works of mankind with one
hand, as if out of pity for what is small, as if to ask that his sacred self-
communion not be disturbed. The books that seemed mountains a
short while before now look like shriveled grapes. And men seem in-

valids about to receive a cure. And the trees and the mountains, the immense sky and the mighty sea, are like our brothers, our friends. Man feels himself to be in some way the creator of nature. Reading stimulates, arouses, inflames, and is like a gust of wind on a covered fire, which carries away the ashes and leaves the flames exposed to the air. We read what is great, and if we ourselves are capable of greatness we are left with a higher capacity for it. The noble lion awakens and shakes his mane and from it fall thoughts like flakes of gold.

He was a subtle seer, who saw how the delicate air becomes wise, melodious words in the throats of men, and who wrote as a seer, not as a ponderer. Every line he writes is an axiom. His pen is not a paintbrush that dilutes but a chisel that cuts and sculpts. He shapes a pure sentence just as a good sculptor shapes a pure line. A single unnecessary word is, to him, like a bump on a curving form. With one blow of his chisel, the bump flies off and the sentence is left sharp and clear. He abhorred the unnecessary. When he speaks, he says all he has to say. At times he seems to leap from one thing to another and at first the relationship between two adjacent ideas remains unclear. That is because what seems a leap to others is, to him, a natural step. He goes from summit to summit like a giant, rather than along the tracks and pathways of the ordinary, overburdened pedestrians, who see the tall giant as tiny because they look up at him from so far below. He writes in catalogs, not sentences. His books are compendiums, not demonstrations. His thoughts seem insular because he sees a great deal all at once, and wants to say everything once and for all, and he says them as he sees them, like words read by the light of a thunderbolt or a thing glimpsed in a light so beautiful that one knows it must disappear. He leaves further development to others: he has no time to lose; he announces. His style is limpid, not luxuriant. He purified, refined, and tested it, then boiled it down and took from it only the essence. His style is not a green hill covered with fragrant, blooming plants: it is a mountain of solid rock. He was not the servant of language; he made it serve him. Language is the creation of mankind; man must not be the slave of language. Some have difficulty understanding him, for a mountain cannot be measured in inches. He is accused of obscurity, but what great mind has not been? It would be less mortifying to reproach what we read with being incomprehensible—for thus we would tacitly acknowledge our own inability to understand it. Emerson does not argue; he establishes. He prefers the teachings of nature to the teachings of man. In his eyes, a tree knows more than a book, a star teaches more than a university, a farm is a gospel, and an un-schooled farmer's boy stands closer to universal truth than an anti-quary; no candle can rival the stars, no altar the mountains, no preacher the deep, throbbing nights. The sight of the glad, fair-haired morning stripping off its veils to reveal its nakedness fills him with an-gelic emotions. He feels more powerful than an Assyrian monarch or a Persian king when he watches a sunset or a laughing dawn. To be good, he needs only to see beauty. Those are the flames by whose light he writes. His ideas fall into the mind like small white pebbles on a lu-minous sea: what sparks! what flashes! what veins of fire! There is a sense of vertigo, as if we were riding on the back of a lion in flight. He himself felt it, and emerged from it strengthened. And we clasp the book to our bosom as if it were a good, generous friend; we stroke it tenderly as if it were the pure face of a faithful woman.

He thought of all that is profound. He wanted to penetrate the mystery of life, to discover the universal laws of existence. As a child he felt strong and set out in search of the Creator. And he came back from his journey contented, saying he had found him. He spent the rest of his life in the beatitude that follows such a meeting. He trem-bled like a leaf during those expansions of his spirit, those outpourings into the universal spirit; and he returned to himself fragrant and fresh, like a leaf. When he was born, all the trammels that centuries of pre-sumptuous men had accumulated to set before the cradle of the new generation were set before him: books full of subtle poisons that in-flame the imagination and corrupt the mind. He drained all of those cups and went his own way, scarcely affected by the venom. It is our human torment that in order to see clearly we must be wise and forget that we are wise. The possession of truth is merely a struggle between the various revelations imposed by others. Some give in, and are then no more than the voices of other spirits. Others triumph, and add a new voice to nature's. Emerson triumphed: that is his philosophy. His best book is called *Nature;* in it, he abandons himself to exquisite de-lights, narrates marvelous rambles, turns with magnificent brio against those who ask for eyes to see with and forget their own eyes; there he envisions man as lord, with the Universe meek and yielding, and all that lives emerging from his bosom and returning to his bosom, and beyond all that lives, the Spirit, which will endure, with man in its arms. He gives an account of himself and of what he has seen. Of what he has not experienced, he gives no account. He would rather be per-ceived as inconsistent than as fanciful. Where his eyes do not see, he announces that he does not see. He does not deny what others have seen, but defends what he has seen. If what he sees is contradictory in any way, it is left to others to comment and draw distinctions; he simply narrates. He sees nothing but analogies, for he finds no contradictions in nature; he sees that all within her is a symbol of man, and that all within man is in nature. He sees that nature influences man and that man, at his whim, makes nature glad or sad, eloquent or mute, absent or present. He sees human ideas as the masters of universal matter. He sees that physical beauty invigorates and predisposes man's spirit to moral beauty. He sees that the barren spirit deems the universe barren. He sees that the panorama of nature inspires faith, love, and respect. He senses that the Universe refuses to respond to man in formulas and responds instead by inspiring feelings that allay his anxieties and allow him to live strong, proud, and happy. And he holds that all things are alike; that everything has the same object; that everything leads to man, who embellishes everything with his mind; that all the currents of nature pass through every creature; that the Creator dwells within every man and every created thing has something of the Creator within it and all will ultimately flow into the bosom of the Creating Spirit. He sees that there is a central unity in events, thoughts, and actions; that the human soul, as it journeys across nature, finds itself everywhere; that the beauty of the Universe was created to inspire desire and assuage the pain of virtue, and stimulate man to seek and find himself; that "within man is the soul of the whole; the wise silence; the universal beauty, to which every part and particle is equally related; the Eternal ONE." Life does not dismay him. He is content, for he does what is right; the important thing is to be virtuous: "virtue is that Golden Key / That opes the Palace of Eternity." Life is not merely commerce or government but something more: a commerce with the forces of nature and the government of oneself. From these premises arises this conclusion: the order of the universe inspires individual order; happiness is certain and is the supreme sensation; therefore, whatever the truth about all mysteries may be, it is rational to conclude that we must act in keeping with that which produces real happiness, superior to all other classes of happiness, and that is virtue, for life is no more than "a season in nature." And thus do the reader's eyes flow over these serene and radiant pages that seem to have been written out of superhuman benevolence, on the crest of a mountain, by a light not human: thus do the eyes, burning with desire to see these seductive marvels, stare and wander through this palace of truths, this procession of glowing pages like steel mirrors that reflect glorious images to eyes burning from the excess of light. Ah, to read when you feel the buffeting of flames within your brain—it is like holding down a live eagle! If only our hands were bolts of lightning and could vaporize our skulls without committing murder!

And death? Death does not trouble Emerson. Death does not trouble or frighten the man who has lived nobly; it is feared only by the man who has reason to fear it. He who deserves to be immortal shall be: to die is to restore what is finite to the infinite. Emerson sees no good reason to rebel against this. Life is a fact; its existence is its justification. Only imbeciles see it as a plaything, for true men it is a temple. A life spent growing in the honest exercise of the thinking and feeling spirit is better than one of rebellion.

And the sciences? The sciences confirm what the spirit possesses: the analogy of all the forces of nature, the similarity of all living beings, the equal composition of all the elements of the Universe, and the sovereignty of man who knows of beings that are inferior to himself but of none that is superior. The spirit foresees; scientific conviction ratifies. The spirit, submerged in the abstract, sees the whole; science, crawling like an insect through matter, sees nothing but details. That the Universe was formed by slow, methodical, and analogous procedures neither announces the end of nature nor contradicts the existence of the spiritual realm. When the cycle of the sciences is complete and they know all there is to know, they will know no more than what the spirit knows now, and they will know what it knows. It is true that the hand of the dinosaur resembles the hand of man, but it is also true that the spirit of man arrives at the tomb still young, though the body may be old, and feels in its immersion in the universal spirit such acute and ravishing pleasures—and an energy so fresh and potent, a serenity so majestic, and a need so strong to love and forgive—that this law of life, which is true for those to whom it is true, and not true for those who do not attain it, is every bit as certain as the resemblance between the hand of the dinosaur and that of man.

And the object of life? The object of life is the satisfaction of the yearning toward perfect beauty, for just as virtue beautifies the places in which it acts, so do beautiful places act upon man's virtue. There is a moral character in all the elements of nature, for all of them stimulate man's moral character: all of them have it, all of them produce it. Therefore truth, which is the beauty of the mind, goodness, which is the beauty of the emotions, and mere beauty, which is the beauty of the arts, are one. Art is no more than nature created by man. From this intermingling we never emerge. Nature bows down before man and gives him her variety to perfect his judgment; her marvels to stimulate his will to imitate them; and her demands to educate his spirit through work, vicissitudes, and the virtue that overcomes them. Nature gives man her objects, which are reflected in his mind, which in its turn governs his speech, in which every object is transformed into a sound. The stars are messengers of beauty and of the eternal sublime. The forest restores man's faith and reason: it is eternal youth. The forest gladdens, like a good deed. Nature inspires, heals, consoles, and fortifies man, and prepares him for virtue. And man does not find himself fully, is not revealed to himself, does not see the invisible, except in his intimate relationship with nature. The Universe in all its multiple forms leads to man, as radii converge in the center of a circle, and men set out to act upon the Universe by the many deeds of their wills, like radii leaving the center. The Universe, though multiple, is one: music can imitate the colors and movement of a serpent. The locomotive is the elephant of man's creation—as potent and colossal as an elephant. Only a different degree of heat makes the water flowing across the riverbed different from the stones it washes over. And in all this multiple Universe, just as in man, everything occurs as a symbol of the human being. Smoke rises into the air as thought does into Infinity. The waters of the sea flow and grow tempestuous like the sentiments of the soul. The mimosa, or sensitive plant, is fragile like a sensitive woman. Every quality of man is represented in an animal. The trees speak to us in a language we understand. The night leaves something in our ears, for the heart that went into it tormented by doubts awakens full of peace. The appearance of truth suddenly illuminates the soul, as the sun illuminates nature. The morning makes birds trill and men speak. The evening twilight makes birds tuck in their wings and men their words. Virtue, toward which everything in nature conspires, leaves man in peace, as if he had completed his task, like a curve that rejoins itself and closes off the circle and need go no further. The Universe is the servant and the human being is king. The Universe has been created to teach, feed, gratify, and educate man. Man, confronting nature, which changes and passes by, feels something solid within himself. He feels at once eternally young and old beyond memory. He knows himself to be aware of things he is certain he did not learn here, and this reveals to him a former life during which he acquired that knowledge. He turns his eyes toward a Father he does not see, but of whose presence he is sure, and whose kiss, which fills all of space and comes to him on the perfumed night air, leaves on his forehead a light in whose soft pallor are confusedly revealed the interior universe where all of the exterior exists in miniature, and the exterior universe where the interior is magnified, and the fearful and beautiful universe of death. But is God outside the earth? Is God the earth itself? Is he above Nature? Is Nature able to create and does the immense spiritual being to whose bosom the human soul aspires therefore not exist? Was the world in which we live born of itself? And will it always move ahead as it moves today or will it evaporate, and will we, floating on its vapors, become one in august and delicious commingling with a being whose nature is mere appearance? And thus the powerful mind of this gigantic man turns and turns; eyes wide open, he seeks the divine mind in the darkness and finds it, diligent, invisible, uniform, and pulsating in the sun's light, on the earth, in the waters and in himself. He feels that he knows what he cannot say, and that man will eternally spend his life groping without ever managing to touch the wing of the golden eagle upon which, in the end, he will sit. This man has stood erect before the Universe, and has not succumbed. He has dared to analyze the synthesis, and he has made no mistake.

He has stretched out his arms and held the secret of life within them. From his body, the frail basket that holds his winged spirit, he ascended through painful effort and mortal forebodings to those pure peaks where the traveler's zeal is rewarded with a glimpse of the robes of infinite beings, interwoven with starlight. He has felt the mysterious overflowing of the soul within the body, a solemn joy that fills the lips with kisses, the hands with caresses, and the eyes with weeping, like the sudden swell and cascade of nature in the spring. And then he felt the calm that arises from conversation with the divine, and the magnificent, regal arrogance that a consciousness of his own power gives to man. For what man who is master of himself does not laugh at a king?

Sometimes, dazzled by the resplendent books of the Hindus who believe that the human creature, purified by virtue, will fly like a flaming butterfly out of its terrestrial carapace and into the bosom of Brahma, he sits down to do what he criticizes, to see nature through the eyes of another because he has found those eyes to be in agreement with his own, and at such times he sees darkly and tarnishes his own visions. For Indian philosophy intoxicates, like a grove of orange trees in flower or the sight of flying birds that inspires a longing to fly.

When he enters into this philosophy, a man feels gently annihilated, as if lapped by blue flames on his ascent to the heights. And he wonders then if nature is not a phantasmagoria and man a fantasizer and the whole Universe an idea and God the pure idea and man the aspiring idea which will in the end come to rest, like a pearl in its shell or an arrow in a tree trunk, in the bosom of God. And he begins erecting a scaffold and constructing the Universe. But immediately he tears down the scaffolding, ashamed of the meanness of his edifice and the poverty of the mind that, when it sets itself to building worlds, seems like an ant dragging a mountain range behind it.

Once more he feels vague and mystical essences coursing through his veins; once more he begins to see how the torments of his soul are soothed in the friendly silence, charged with promise, of the forest; to observe that when the mind falls silent, like a ship run aground on dry rock, intuition bursts forth like a caged bird certain of the sky, and makes its escape from the broken mind, to translate into a language as craggy, brutal, and recalcitrant as stone the lucid transports, chaste ecstasies, soothing delights, and intoxicating pleasures of the tremulous spirit that captive nature, surprised by this audacious lover, admits into her company. And he announces to every man that since the Universe reveals itself to him entirely and directly, he has the right to see it for himself and to quench with his own lips the ardent thirst that it inspires. And having learned in these colloquies that pure thought and pure feeling produce delights so strong that the soul feels a sweet death in them, followed by a radiant resurrection, he announces to mankind that only he who is pure can be happy.

Once he knew this, and was certain that the stars are man's crown and that even when his skull grows cold his serene spirit will cleave the air, cloaked in light, he placed his loving hand upon his tormented fellow men and turned his lively and penetrating eyes upon the rude combats of the earth. His gaze swept away all the rubble. He takes his seat at the table of heroes, fully at ease. He narrates the exploits of nations with Homeric tongue. He has the naïveté of a giant. He allows himself to be guided by his intuition, which opens the grave and the clouds to him. And just as he sat in the parliament of stars and came back strong, he now sits in the parliament of nations as if in his brother's house. He speaks of remote history and recent history. He analyzes nations as a geologist does fossils. And his sentences are like the vertebrae of mastodons, like golden statues, like Greek porticos. Of other men it may be said, "He is a brother"; of this one it must be said, "He is a father." He wrote a marvelous book, a summation of humanity, in which he enshrined and studied the various types of great men. He saw old England, which his Puritan forefathers left behind, and out of that visit he created another mighty book called *English Traits*. He divided the facts of life into groups, and studied them in magical essays, and gave them laws. And his laws of life all revolve on the axis of this one truth: All of nature trembles before the consciousness of a child. Religion, destiny, power, wealth, illusions, greatness are all, as if by a chemist's hand, broken down and analyzed. He leaves what is beautiful standing, and overthrows what is false. He is no respecter of practices. Vile things are vile, however widely they may be accepted. Man must begin to be angelic. Tenderness is law; resignation is law; prudence is law. These essays are legal codes. Their vitality is overwhelming. They have the grandiose monotony of a mountain range. And they are further enhanced by their tireless imagination and singular good sense. For Emerson, no contradiction exists between the great and the small or between the ideal and the practical, and the laws that will bring about the definitive triumph and give man the right to crown himself with stars also bring happiness on earth. There are no contradictions in nature, but only in the men who are unable to discern its analogies. He disparages science not as false but as slow. Open his books and scientific truths spill out of them. Tyndall[5] says he owes all his science to Emerson. The whole doctrine of evolution is contained in a handful of Emerson's sentences. But he does not believe that reason alone is capable of penetrating the mystery of life and bringing peace to man and putting him in possession of the means to grow. He believes that intuition completes what reason commences. He believes that the eternal spirit divines what human science only chases after. The scientist sniffs like a dog, but like a great condor the spirit crosses the abyss in which the engrossed naturalist wanders. Emerson constantly observed, noted down what he saw, grouped similar facts together in his notebooks, and spoke when he had something to reveal. There was in him something of Calderón,[6] of Plato and of Pindar,[7] and something of Franklin, too. He was not like the leafy bamboo, whose hollow stem cannot sustain its weighty foliage and bends to the ground; he was a baobab, a red cedar or a great *samán* whose flourishing crown rises upon a strong trunk. Idealism itself walked upon the earth, little loved by judgmental men and seemingly disdainful of being here. Emerson made idealism human. He does not wait for science, because the bird needs no stilts in order to rise to the heights, nor does the eagle need rails. He leaves science behind, as the impatient captain, riding at full gallop, leaves behind the plodding soldier, burdened with heavy armaments. In him, idealism is not a vague desire for death, but the conviction of another life that must be earned by the serene practice of virtue in this one. And life is as beautiful and ideal as death. Do you want to see how he conceives of things? Thus does he conceive of them: he wishes to say that man does not devote all his powers but only that of reason—which is not the richest of them—to the study of nature, and that is why he does not penetrate very far, and he says: "The axis of vision is not coincident with the axis of things." When he wishes to explain how all the moral and physical truths are contained in each other, and each one is in all the others, he says, "It is like a great circle on a sphere, comprising all possible circles; which, however, may be drawn and comprise it in like manner." Do you wish to hear him speak? This is how he speaks: "To a man laboring under calamity, the heat of his own fire hath sadness in it." "We are not built like a ship, to be tossed, but like a house to stand." "Cut these words, and they would bleed." "Leonidas and his three hundred martyrs consume one day in dying." "All the facts in natural history taken by themselves, have no value, but are barren, like a single sex." And he describes a man as wallowing in the mire of dialectics.

His poetry is made like a Florentine palace, of colossal and irregular blocks of stone. It pounds and surges like the waters of the seas. Or else it is a basket of flowers in the hand of a naked child. It is a poetry of patriarchs, of primitive men, of cyclops. Some of his poems are like a grove of oak trees in bloom. His are the only poetic lines that enshrine the greatest struggle on the earth. And other poems of his are like trickles of precious stones, or shreds of cloud, or shards of lightning. Do we know yet what his verses are? Sometimes they are like a wise old man with a serpentine beard, curly locks, and a burning gaze, who leans against an oaken staff at the mouth of a white stone cave and sings; at other times they are like a gigantic angel with golden wings who plummets down from a high green mountain into the abyss. Marvelous old man, I lay my sheaf of green palm fronds and my silver sword at your feet!

—*La Opinión Nacional* (Caracas), May 19, 1882

TRIBUTES TO KARL MARX, WHO HAS DIED[1]

*** SELECTIONS ***

In the twenty-seven volumes of Martí's Complete Works, *he mentions Karl Marx only twice outside of the following evocation of the famous memorial meeting in New York City: once in a citation from a French author that he copied into Notebook 8 and a second time in an article discussing the formation of trade unions in the United States, published in* La Nación *on February 20, 1890. There he wrote: "Each nation finds its own cure, in keeping with its nature, which either requires varying doses of the medicine, depending on whether this or that factor is present in the ailment—or requires a different medicine. Neither Saint-Simon, nor Karl Marx, nor Marlo, nor Bakunin. Instead, the reforms that are best suited to our own bodies."*

Through gloomy taverns, boxing clubs, and dark streets the youthful throng makes its way with broad shoulders and hands like clubs, which can drain the life from a man as if draining the beer from a glass. But cities are like bodies; they have some noble viscera and some that are foul. And the angry army of workingmen is full of other soldiers, as well. There are some with broad foreheads, long disheveled hair, skin the color of straw, flashing eyes, and an air of rebellion about them, like a blade of Toledo steel: they are the ones who lead, mobilize, anathematize, publish newspapers, organize meetings, and speak. There are others with narrow foreheads, shaggy heads, prominent cheekbones, high color, and eyes that are motionless, as if doubting, hearing distant winds and scrutinizing, or that swell and become bloodshot, like the eyes of one who charges to attack: they are the patient and suffering multitude, who listen and hope. Some of them have become fanatics out of love, others are fanatics out of hatred. All that can be seen of some is their teeth. Others—Justice's gentlemen—are handsome and well groomed and have unctuous voices. On these fields, the Frenchman does not hate the German nor the German the Russian, nor does the Italian abominate the Austrian, for all are united in a shared hatred. And this is the weakness of their institutions and the reason they inspire fear, for those who know that Justice herself bears no children—for love alone engenders them!—keep their distance from the battlefields of wrath. The future must be conquered with clean hands. The workmen of the United States would be more prudent if the most aggrieved and enraged workmen of Europe were not emptying the dregs of their hatred into their ears. Germans, Frenchmen, and Russians guide these discussions. The Americans tend to resolve the concrete matter at hand in their meetings, while those from abroad raise it to an abstract plane. Good sense and the fact of having been born into a free cradle make the men of this place slow to wrath. The rage of those from abroad is roiling and explosive because their prolonged enslavement has repressed and concentrated it. But the rotten apple must not be allowed to spoil the whole healthy barrel—though it could! The excrescences of monarchy, which rot and gnaw at Liberty's bosom like a poison, cannot match Liberty's power![2]

Look at this great hall. Karl Marx has died. He deserves to be honored, for he placed himself on the side of the weak. But it is not the man who points out the harm and burns with generous eagerness to remedy it who does well—it is the man who advocates a mild remedy. To set men against men is an appalling task. The forced bestialization of some men for the profit of others stirs our indignation. But that indignation must be vented in such a way that the beast ceases to be, without escaping its bonds and causing fear. Look at this hall. Presiding over it, wreathed in green leaves, is the portrait of that ardent reformer, uniter of men of different nations, tireless and forceful organizer. The International was his work, and men of all nations are come to pay tribute to him. The throng, made up of valiant laborers whose gazes are touching and comforting, displays more muscles than adornments, more honest faces than silken clothes. Work makes men beautiful. The sight of a field hand, an ironworker, or a sailor is rejuvenating. As they grapple with nature's forces, they come to be as fair as nature.

New York is becoming a kind of vortex: whatever boils over anywhere else in the world spills into New York. Elsewhere they make men flee, but here they welcome the fleeing man with a smile. From this goodness has arisen the strength of this nation. Karl Marx studied the means of establishing the world on new bases; he awoke the sleepers and showed them how to cast down the cracked pillars. But he went very fast and sometimes in darkness; he did not see that without a natural and laborious gestation, children are not born viable, from a nation in history or from a woman in the home. Here tonight are good friends of Karl Marx, who was not only a titanic instigator of the wrath of European workers but also a profound seer into the causes of human misery and the destinies of men, and a man consumed with the desire to do good. He saw in everything what he bore within: rebellion, the high road, combat.

Here is a Mr. Lecovitch,[3] a newspaperman: look how he speaks. At times he seems a reflection of the tender and radiant Bakunin. He begins speaking in English, then turns toward others in German. "*Da! Da!*" his compatriots answer enthusiastically when he speaks to them in Russian. The Russians are the whip of reform, but these impatient, generous men, defiled by wrath, will not be the ones to lay the foundations of the new world: they are the spur, and serve their purpose, like the voice of conscience that can fall asleep, but the long sharp steel of a horseman's goad is of little use as a founding hammer.

Here is Swinton,[4] an old man inflamed by injustice, who saw Karl Marx as a man with the stature of a mountain and the voice of Socrates. Here is the German, Johann Most,[5] a relentless and none-too-likable firebrand whose right hand carries no balm with which to heal the wounds inflicted by his left. So many people have come to hear them speak that the crowd is overflowing into the street. Choirs sing. Among the many men there are also many women. To applause, they repeat lines from Karl Marx in chorus, and hang posters bearing his words on the walls. Millot,[6] a Frenchman, says something very fine: "Freedom has fallen many times in France, but it has arisen more beautiful from each fall." Johann Most speaks these fanatical words: "After I read Marx's book in a Saxon prison, I took up the sword against human vampires." A certain Magure[7] says, "Rejoice to see united, without hatred, so many men of all countries. All the workers of the world belong to a single nation and do not quarrel among themselves but are united against those who oppress them. Rejoice to have seen six thousand French and English workers meeting together near what had been the ominous Paris Bastille." A Bohemian speaks. A letter is read from Henry George,[8] the famous new economist, friend to those who suffer, beloved by the people and famous here and in England. And amid bursts of thunderous applause and frenetic hurrahs, the impassioned assembly rises unanimously to its feet while on the platform two men with broad foreheads and knife-sharp gazes read aloud, in German and English, the resolutions with which the great meeting concludes, in which Karl Marx is called the most noble hero and the most powerful thinker of the working world. Music is heard and choirs ring out, but it is not the music of peace.

On another day, they return by the tens of thousands. They want to have their own newspaper, and are holding a series of dances in order to raise the money to found it.

Good women! They've brought along all their little ones; how happy their men are tonight, who are usually so sad! And the night and their little dancing clothes disguise the children's sickly pallor and sunken cheeks! Health-giving air is in short supply where the workers live. Morgan,[9] the former governor, has just left millions to theological societies and seminaries—but rather than working to force men to a faith in heaven, would it not be better to create that faith naturally by giving them faith in the earth? Morgan has also left considerable sums to homes where invalids, the elderly, children, and the poor are given assistance: couldn't he have left some money to help construct houses full of air and light? For those who dwell long in the darkness begin to feel it in their souls and to make it felt in the souls of others. These populous cities, which are human granaries rather than marble palaces, should joyfully build healthy, happy, elegant, and luminous neighborhoods for the poor, rather than amassing people who work with their hands in immense pigsties. Today, simple cleanliness and sunlight are an unaccustomed elegance for them, and without seeing beauty, who has ever felt goodness? Without experiencing kindness from others, who was ever kind? He who would clear his own head of torment must first clear it from the heads of others. If you could see them, now that the summer months are coming, groups of them, the mothers' arms full of pale, dying children, returning from the boating excursions on which some charitable society or benign person allows them to cross the river for free. You would bite your lips in anger and wish you could go across the earth tirelessly waving the standard of their redemption!

But the city does not speak much of those things. It looks on as Democrats and Republicans struggle to see who can reform the most and the fastest, so as not to be accused of lacking the spirit of reform. There is talk of Butler,[10] the brilliant governor of Massachusetts, who is said to be like a strong eagle who shakes the tree on which he perches: all the abuses of the state fall to the ground like overripe fruit at the eagle's blows. Governor Butler is ubiquitous, insomniac, omnipresent, and alarming: he sees the hidden folds of human consciences and all the arts of cunning in laws, contracts, and accounts. It was told of a certain Spanish nobleman that he took pleasure in releasing a young bull from his herds among his guests, and the employees of the State of Massachusetts are like that Spanish nobleman's guests. Butler says and does everything in a high-spirited, sudden, and novel way, and he is as secure in his acts as he is polished and careful in his speech. He is a governmental romantic: he shakes the dust from the state as the young France of 1830 shook it from the academies. The city is also talking about the substantial sum that the *Herald* has raised to benefit the unfortunates in Ohio,[11] and it is gladdening to see that by joining their humble mites, the workers of the state's factories have given so much, and more rapidly than the state's people of distinction and authority. There is much talk, as well, about a gentleman of the cloth who in his Easter sermons painted such a picture of the ladies of fashion and their life, and sought to confine female life within such narrow limits, that though where the lives of ladies of fashion were concerned he was justly applauded, when it came to confining women to their distaffs and convents once again, both the clergy and lay-people raised an outcry against him. A prayerful Sister of Mercy is what the reverend would have a woman be. "And life?" an eloquent woman answers him in tones of inspiration from a pulpit. "What of inevitable, implacable life which forces her to work or be impure? What of all the orphaned girls and widows, alone in the vast crowd of people that carries them along like the desert wind and drowns them?" "And what of my mind, which grasps all that yours grasps; and this heart of mine, which is tenderer than yours; and my disdain, which so often condemns the barbaric tastes and practices of your gender—must I repress them as criminal, when they are powers given to me by nature?" Thus does another angry lady reprove the reverend. "Why do you deprive us of any real part in your earnings, when we would not use them for anything worse than men do when they pay ten dollars to see how two professional boxers or gentlemen of the city or students at a top college make each other's faces swell up with blows, and knock each other down and struggle on the ground with all the force and rage of wild beasts?" That was said by another woman, and a clergyman said, "Saints! Sisters of Mercy! Women of prayer! The best saints of the nineteenth century were outside the convents. Mary Carpenter, who spent sixty years of her life educating the children of the streets of London, is a saint, and there is no prayerful lady among those who adorn the stained-glass windows of your church whose face gives off a more radiant light than Mary Carpenter's, which brims with love." An ardent female reformer recalls how Wosley, the rector of Yale University, recommended that a convention of women be held to study and decide upon a divorce law; and she maintains, her sharp satire seasoned with jokes about the mistakes of the men currently in the government, that the Board of Education, the police stations, and all the positions of state that are poorly managed by ambitious and unloving men would be better off in the hands of women, in whom the development of reason does not extinguish tenderness—which is indeed a great gift for a governor.

In the middle of all this clamor comes the decision of Columbia University in this very State of New York. It does not dare open its lecture halls to men and women alike, because though Cambridge University[12] is said to have so opened them in England, it is not true that the young female students there have taken advantage of the concession; rather, they study at the famous college of Girton, which trains them in all the arts and sciences, just as the male students are trained, and Cambridge gives them no more than examinations, grades, and degrees. And that is what Columbia University is now offering to do; it recommends the creation of a college similar to Girton.[13]

This may be a mistake, or perhaps, in these nations where the excess of population—or of self-interest in the male portion of it—entrains such problems, the only way to save women from the appetites engendered by their external beauty is to inspire men, by continual conversation and intellectual commerce, with love for other more noble and lasting conditions! We are still at the first letter of the alphabet of life. Until today, the law of all existence has been based on a caprice of the eyes, exalted to a necessity of the soul and obscurely mistaken for one by the generous and aggrandizing imagination. No one looks askance on the toughening of the feminine soul, for that is the outcome of the virile existence to which women are led by the need to take care of themselves and defend themselves from the men who are moved by appetite. Better that the soul be toughened than that it be debased. For there is so much goodness in the souls of women that even after having been deceived, plunged into despair, and toughened, they still exude a perfume. All of life is there: in finding a good flower. In this great city where women must look after themselves and save themselves from the wolf of poverty and the wolves of life that are at their doors, they must become thick-skinned to protect themselves, and must learn all the science and art that can fit into their minds—

where there is room for everything—in order to acquire an honest way of living. Impurity is so terrible that it can never be voluntary. An educated woman will be purer. Yet how painful it is to see how the habits of a virile life gradually change these beauteous flowers into flowers of stone! What will become of men on the day when they can no longer rest their heads on a warm, female bosom?

But this week began with an event that had been conversational fodder in the press, at home and in the clubs for a month already, as if it were a symbolic act involving some fundamental element of the nation's life. Rome prided itself on its generals: the United States prides itself on its rich men. It does not raise them high upon a shield, however, but mocks them even as it worships them. They are admired but are seen as usurpers and temporary holders of the public wealth, and this happens to an even greater degree when the wealth of a single man or family takes on the proportions of the wealth of a nation. The popular eye, which sees only broad generalities, turns in anger against those who, on the same night that two famished wretches are arrested in the corner of a church, whirl amid torrents of light and perfume, bedecked in roses made of gold and diamonds and bejeweled like the saddle of a Persian horse, making ostentatious display of the wealth that overflows from their coffers. Broad is Fifth Avenue, like an imperial highway. Along it are palaces that timidly imitate the sumptuous, gloomy portals of the ducal houses of Venice, the turrets of gothic abbeys, the balconies of the Louvre, the barbicans of feudal castles, the minarets of Arabia. This wealthy street is the place for late-afternoon strolling and the sought-out and costly abode of the opulent. Fifth Avenue is the New Yorker's patent of nobility. There the leisured dandies, wearing tight clothes that emphasize the strength of their limbs, parade their Celtic heads and the medal of some rich men's club that hangs round their necks—though there are not many such men, for here, work is the law, and even he who has no work pretends he does, out of shame at appearing not to. But the ladies fill the street, carrying in arms born for sweeter and more noble uses, the little dogs with long hair and horrid faces that are now in vogue. They are ladies of singular beauty but they do not enliven the solemn street. It is the vast space, the dark and imposing buildings, and the regal calm that move the soul to grandeur.

Near the ambitious cathedral which in vain copies that of proud Milan—man's felicitous challenge to his Creator—there rises, penned in by dark and gloomy houses, one glad, bright palace that seems built of delicate lace. Austere windows are set within solid walls, all of them bearing paintings and sculptures. Its stone is chiseled. Its roof, which draws back into a pyramid, is completed by a graceful, pointed tourelle. And from front door to rooftop, all of it is intricately carved, sculpted, worked in bas-relief, caressed, embroidered. Grace, which is the finest sort of beauty, predominates everywhere. There is not a more beautiful house on earth, and in it dwells a Vanderbilt.[14] The house is such that when the eye, in perusing the wonders of its interior, falls on a graceful portrait of a "Castilian Lady" by the hand of Madrazo,[15] it seems not a canvas brought from elsewhere but part of the house itself, slender and luminous. Madrazo swirls his brush in sunlight and makes it his paint. Into this palace, between walls of attendants, all of New York high society walked on Easter Monday, and no court ever awaited a monarch's ball more eagerly than the people of New York awaited Vanderbilt's. In a city where wealth is held in such high esteem, the ball at which the monarch of the wealthy inaugurates his palace is inevitably seen as a royal affair. In anticipation, what discussions there were of the house's luxuries, the price of jewels and dresses and of the wines that were to be drunk and the lesser accoutrements of that night of dancing! What whisperings of millions! What appraisals of diamonds! What publication of the price of the fabrics! The sumptuous night at last arrived. All was curiosity and movement in the wealthy neighborhoods. It seemed to be everyone's party, not just one man's. Wagonloads of flowers were emptied out through that lavish doorway. At times the kind of silence that monuments inspire could be felt around the house. Already, as twilight came on, swords with languets, necklaces of the highest order, and gleaming short cloaks could be glimpsed through the windows of the carriages arriving rapidly from all directions.

The clock struck ten, and all in that house of wonders was alight. A thousand carriages pulled up at its doorway. Monarchs, gentlemen, dukes, and colonists of former days stepped out. A bullfighter helped down a Scottish lady. Van Dyck princesses, duchesses out of Holbein, and ladies by Rubens seemed to have emerged from their frames to walk down the majestic hallway with its walls of richly wrought stone and skillfully coffered oak. The guests can barely conceal the astonishment the house inspires. All that they behold is sculpted, gilded, chiseled. All that they set foot upon is stone so fine it is worth more than gold. Ascending the broad staircase that still winds upward at the third floor, beneath a high arch that ennobles it and makes it seem even larger, one thinks of immensity, of stately temples. The "Gymnasium" is what they call the vast room where, at the center of the curious crowd, the quadrilles of honor that are to guide the procession and commence the dance gather. Oh! How curious: a quadrille of ladies and gentlemen mounted on horses that seem real, with long cloaks to conceal the dancers' feet, and covered in real skins and manes that were alive not long ago. This quadrille is being danced in memory of the court festivals! The horsemen are wearing red hunting coats, with vests and stockings of white satin, and yellow knee breeches, like gentlemen out hunting in the time of Louis XIV. And how richly embroidered the huntresses' white skirts are, and how well the short red jacket looks on them! And the next quadrille, in celebration of the Opera Buffa, how brilliant it is! That man is Scopolette, who gives his hand to M. le Diable, and over there are the Angel Pitou and La Perricholi, and Mme. Angot and the Petit Duc! And those others, who have dressed in dazzling white moiré, and suits of snow-white silk, with powdered wigs and a white narcissus in the buttonhole, like gentlemen of the old German court, so as to look like the Dresden porcelain figurines whose famous brand name is embroidered on their clothes! And now a quadrille of stars: how ingenious! They wear pale colors, white, blue, delicate mauve, and soft yellow! The procession moves on: now, behind the quadrilles, comes the opulent retinue. Hardly a word is spoken: the eyes do not look, but count. Everyone is a Duke of Buckingham, a trainload of rich jewelry. Is it the house or the wealth of the guests that inspires the greater wonder? . . .

When the morning post arrives, the costume ball is still the subject, but not its witticisms and repartee, or its comedies of love in the shade of palm trees and the perfume of climbing roses, or the lively retorts that copious Burgundy provokes and fine champagne further gilds, or the charming deliria that flutter around the forehead after an animated dance like prettily colored butterflies or fleeting kisses. The ball is spoken of as if it had been a gigantic parade or an exhibition of luxury goods, a jewelry competition, or a probe of the depth of certain money boxes. Indeed, it seems in retrospect to have been a mute procession of people who ate a heavy meal, moved ponderously, and went home grim. The peruser of the newspapers' accounts of the dance reads descriptions of its scenery but not of its soul. The party has been taken amiss, and it's beginning to be said that such displays of excessive luxury and gracefulness of garment are ill suited to these times of wrath, revolt, and ravenous, inflamed masses. The unfortunate do not understand them and the gravity of the times does not bear well with them; they are inappropriate to a republican country and are neither forgiven nor forgotten by the army that advances in darkness, those men with swollen hearts and narrow foreheads who are captained by others with broad foreheads and gazes of sharp Toledo steel. For the ball was given as a display of wealth and has been received like a slap in the face by the envious, discontented, and wretched masses. The French Revolution's Convention is still in session! But here, wisdom is seated at its side.

—New York, March 29, 1883;
published in *La Nación* (Buenos Aires), May 13 and 16, 1883

from LA AMÉRICA

La América, *headquartered at 756 Broadway, New York City, was a magazine of "Agriculture, Industry, and Commerce," aimed at better acquainting readers in Latin America with the United States. In June 1883, the month the article on the Brooklyn Bridge came out, Martí assumed a position as literary editor of the magazine; six months later, when the magazine changed hands, he became its editor-in-chief.*

In an article published at the time of that promotion, Martí listed as the goals of La América, *"to explain the mind of the United States of the North to the minds of those who are in spirit, and will someday be in form, the United States of South America"; "to serve, at a moment when both hemispheres are drawing together and asking questions of each other, as an introducer of the products that, with the sacred salt and seasoning of liberty, have accelerated to a marvelous degree the maturity of English America"; and "to define, advise, alert, and reveal the secrets of the seemingly—and only seemingly—marvelous success of this country; and to promote, with clear and timely explanations and studies of applicable advances, the achievement of an equal—or perhaps greater, yes, greater and more lasting—success in our own countries."*

THE BROOKLYN BRIDGE

∗∗∗ SELECTIONS *∗∗∗*

The blood throbs more generously in the veins of the joyfully astonished people of New York these days. A crown seems to have descended upon the city, and each of its inhabitants can feel it on his brow. A dense throng, moving at the pace of those who go to see wonders, flows down the avenues toward the banks of the East River, for there, in stone and steel, rises what was once no more than a fine line traced by the tip of a daring builder's pencil. After fifteen years of work, Brooklyn and New York are at last connected by a 3,455-foot suspension bridge.

On June 7, 1870, the work of clearing the space in Brooklyn where the great tower would rise to support the massive structure began. On May 24, 1883, the bridge was opened to the public, stretching solidly between its two towers, which are like elongated Egyptian pyramids, with its five broad lanes along which a hundred thousand men, packed together and panting, now rush from dawn to midnight. Watching this vast, well-scrubbed, teeming, and ever-growing multitude gather to swarm rapidly across this airborne tendril, you can imagine that you are seeing Liberty herself seated on high, her radiant head at the summit of the heavens and her white hands, large as eagles, spread open in a sign of peace on earth: Liberty, who has given birth to this daughter in this city. Liberty, who is the mother of the new world that is only now dawning. It is as if a sun were rising over these two towers.

We shall take the readers of *La América* by the hand and lead them in for a closer look at the bridge's exterior, standing out in clean lines against the sky, its foundation, which bites into the rock of the riverbed, and its entrails, protected and sheltered from the weather's erosion by immense bulwarks on both banks. Between the bridge's high walls of steel wire, suspended—as if from the tusk of a mammoth that could knock over a mountain with a single thrust—from four long, parallel, cyclopean cables, there now crowd together, as if into a row of gashes cut deep into the heart of a mountain, avid-eyed Hebrews with sharp profiles, jovial Irishmen, fleshy, robust Germans, ruddy, muscular Scotsmen, handsome Hungarians, resplendent Negroes, Russians with burning eyes, redheaded Norwegians, elegant Japanese, and lean and listless Chinamen. The Chinaman is the unfortunate son of the ancient world: thus does despotism wring men dry. Like worms in a trough its slaves writhe among vices. The sons of despotic societies are like statues carved out of mud. Their lives are not censers of incense, but are rank with the smoke of opium.

And the creators of this bridge, and those who maintain it, and those who cross it seem—but for the excessive love of wealth that gnaws at their intestines like a worm—men carved out of granite, like the bridge itself. And there the structure rises! It starts on the New York side from beneath a solemn mass of masonry that presses down upon its roots with a weight of 120 million pounds; it emerges from this tremendous anchorage into the open air, travels 930 feet, and then, suspended from the cables that hang from the top of the 276½-foot towers, it passes through the first of those Pelasgian towers at a point 118 feet above the waterline. Halfway through its journey it rises to a point 135 feet above the river to meet the cables that descend in a solemn and graceful curve from the top of the tower; then, as the cables rise once more to the top of the Brooklyn tower, the bridge descends to the foot of that tower's arches, again at a height of 118 feet above the river, and then all its tremendous lacework glides on through the air to re-enter the Brooklyn anchorage, which with the same mass as the one in New York, its bosom pierced by deep and noble arches, holds down the cables' other roots. And when on the four steel plates buried beneath each one of the anchorages, the four cables from which the bridge is suspended reach their end, they have crossed 3,578 feet, from one bank of the East River to the other. Oh clasp worthy of these two marvelous cities! Oh steel hyphen between these two words of the New Gospel!

We are pounding at the doors of the New York station. Our way is blocked by a crush of thousands of men at the main entrance. Rising above the crowd in their humble blue cloth caps are the eminent heads of the city policemen who are instilling order. To our right, along the carriage road, wagons holding pieces of wall and columns are going in, along with red mail wagons overflowing with letters, stunted little carts carrying bottles of milk, sumptuous coaches full of wealthy ladies, rough lads riding bareback on dray horses to rival that of Troy, and handsome youths who caper around the coaches on skittish steeds. Now the throng gives way and we leave a penny, the price of the crossing, on the counter at the entrance. The bridge's colossal towers can barely be glimpsed from the windows of the New York station. From over our heads comes the drumming of powerful hammers, pounding on the rails of the still incomplete train track that will cross the bridge. Pushed along by the crowd, we rapidly climb to the top of the anchorage. Before us open five lanes that begin on robust masonry: the two outer ones are for horses and carriages, the next two in—between which runs the pedestrian lane—are where the train, whose spacious cars sit idle at the entrance, will come and go. After about 700 feet the masonry ends and the hanging bridge begins, suspended from the four parallel cables, which are held down by iron chains. The cables cross through the masonry like an immense curving scimitar with its pointed tip above the earth, the top of its hilt at the river and the other end in the city, to take root deep in their anchorage. Now the roadway is no longer stone, but wood, and through the cracks between the boards trains can be seen going by like speedy messenger boys or minor monsters on the elevated railway that runs along this bank of the river to the right and left. Beneath our feet is a web, a network, a fine tissue of steel: steel bars, light and delicate as threads, gracefully intertwine in the pavement and in the walls that separate the five wide lanes; before us rise, like curtains of invisible fabric slashed with long white stripes, the four taut walls that hang down from the four curving cables like the doors of a grandiose world that fills the spirit with rejoicing. In the presence of this gigantic brace, we feel tidings of majesty and we yield to gratitude, as if mountain peaks were rising within our minds, which are moved by an almost religious fervor. The pedestrian walkway, now reaching the tower, opens at the foot of the wall that separates the two arches, and forms a square around it, whose two sides rejoin each other between the colossal skein of wires hanging from the four thick cables, which descend in long braids, tall as the spires of a Gothic cathedral near the tower, shorter as the curve descends toward the center of the bridge and, in the center, at the level of the bridge. And the bridge, which rises at its center to a height of 135 feet so that the tallest ship can pass beneath it without losing the tip of a mast or getting its pennants entangled, begins to descend at the same rate at which it first rose: the imposing wire rigging now rises to the summit of the second tower in a reverse curve; the walkway at its foot opens into a square again and then closes; beneath its steel plates steamboats whistle, chimneys smoke, the crowds that travel back and forth in now-antiquated steamers disembark; barges unload; boats weigh anchor. Finally, the crowded steel roadway changes into the stone road borne on the back of the Brooklyn anchorage that, over arcades like hollow mountains, extends, curves, serves as a roof for the great streets that tunnel under it, and at last ends in another iron station, to pour forth the throng that has been jostling us along all the way from New York amid cheering, astonishment, jokes, witticisms, and song, and that now flows impetuous and ebullient through the streets. Immensity brings joy.

But still there remain before the eyes, like sappers of the Universe to come opening the path for the progress of mankind, those four colossal boa constrictors, those four parallel cables, thick and white, which uncoil like ravening serpents, lifting their sibilant bodies from one side of the river, rising to heroic heights, stretching out over the water upon sovereign pillars, and falling back to earth on the opposite side. And our feet seem even now to be walking on that framework which from afar looks like a tenuous surface, a monstrous anthill; and at close range is a very tight weave that relies on the cables alone to support it, and on the iron cords that descend like a fan in four walls, intersecting with the walls of vertical braces on all sides of the towers. Like sated boas the four great cables sway upon concave plates in the holes at the top of the towers, where they rest on wheels—or like the strings of a powerful lyre now breaking into song. . . .[1]

There is no fear that the structure will collapse, because even if all 278 braided suspension cords that support it from each of the four cables were to break, the branching supplementary cords that, like a tremendous hand opening out from a slender wrist, extend almost halfway down each cable on both sides from the top of each tower would be sufficient to hold it up, with all its weight and the weight of the traffic upon it. There is no fear that the structure will shift or be shaken by the play of the wind or a storm's wrath, because at its base the towers bite into it with steel teeth, and to keep even the strongest wind from affecting it, the two outer cables curve inward as they reach the middle of the bridge, and the two inner ones bend toward the outer ones, to give the bridge greater resistance. No, the mischievous winds will not be able to tip carriages into the river, because the edges of the bridge are 8 feet high, and between the carriage and the railway lanes stretches a network of strong wires to contain the gusting winds. There is no risk that the cables will break, for no weight greater than 3,000 tons will ever be placed on any one of them, and they are made to hold, in their 294 arms, 12,000 tons. Nor will the bridge twist, splinter, or buckle when the summer heat swells it as the sun swells the spirit with love, or when the rigor of winter shortens it, for this quintuple roadway is divided into halves, to prevent swelling and shrinking by means of an extension plate midway between them. That plate is attached to the ends of both halves, and sits on moving joints. And when, at the foot of one of the towers, thousands of sobbing women, screaming children, and shouting policemen are piled into a blockade without exit and fighting to make their way across, the cables, in their grooved beds at the top of the towers, will move no more than a lordly inch, like giants giving a nod of greeting.

Thus they have built it and thus it stands, the monumental structure, less beautiful than grand, like a ponderous arm of the human mind. No longer are deep trenches dug around embattled fortresses; now cities embrace one another with arms of steel. No longer do sentry posts manned by soldiers guard populations; now there are booths with employees bearing neither spear nor rifle who collect the penny of peace from the laborers that go past. Bridges are the fortresses of the modern world. Better to bring cities together than to cleave human chests. Today, all men are called upon to be soldiers of the bridge.

—New York City, June 1883

THE GLOSSOGRAPH

It appears that the instrument long hungered after by volcanic-minded thinkers and true poets, whose ideas generally come in compact and ephemeral bundles like sheaves of lightning bolts, has now been invented. Such thinkers say that sometimes, after extended lulls, their ideas arrive like armies of butterflies beating at their temples with their wings and brushing against their lips as if summoning up the words that can depict them, words that never arrive quickly enough to color in those restless and assailing butterflies on the page.

A certain Gentilli—who is worthy of his name—has invented the glossograph and has exhibited it at the Vienna Exposition of Electricity.

The glossograph is a small, highly ingenious device that, when placed inside the mouth, to which it adjusts effortlessly, does not prevent speech and reproduces it on paper as perfectly as a fifteenth-century scribe. It requires only that you speak with the utmost clarity, and each syllable, as it is pronounced, is immediately set down on the expectant page, without any further effort by the speaker, and without confusion for the reader, either, once he has learned what the new signs correspond to. The *Pall Mall Gazette,* known to be a highly respected newspaper, says that the only difficulty the new mechanism presents is that of deciphering these new characters; if this is true, what joy! The characters must be clearer or at least no more difficult than musical notes, and musical notes can be read on sight. Never, never will the fastest hand be able to reproduce the prancings, dashes, sudden pauses, unexpected outbursts, wavelike swellings, and galloping revelations of ignited thought! Blessed be the inventor of the glossograph. And yet, any friction or obstacle is ill suited to thought, and inevitably, the knowledge that one is about to think, the placement of the apparatus in one's mouth, and one's inner preparation for the event, will make one think less. Inspiration is a perpetual maiden. Solitude is its friend. And the spouse who impregnates it is silence.

The device is built so that, once positioned in the mouth, it remains in contact with the upper palate, the lips, and the tongue. An electromagnetic recorder receives the sounds and transmits them to the paper.

"There is no need to raise your voice," says Gentilli. "With a softer tone, you achieve a more accurate reproduction. You do need to pronounce your words clearly."

"Put the man who claims to write faster with his pen on one side," says a commentator, "and the one who speaks into a glossograph on the other. There is no question that the man with the mechanism will write five times faster than even the speediest scrivener."

It may be that the glossograph is nothing more than an improvement on Edison's phonograph—they claim it is not—which is of much earlier date but which, since it is based on a different acoustic principle, does not reproduce sounds in microscopic form.

Oh, everything, everything can be invented—except wings!

—New York, November 1883

INDIGENOUS ART

None of our readers will be fatigued by a brief review of the objects made by Indians that are being exhibited as part of an arts festival to raise money for a pedestal for Bartholdi's statue.[1]

The Indian, who, in North America, is disappearing, crushed beneath the white man's tremendous pressure, or diluted within the invading race, is a constant factor in Central and South America, for whose benefit little is done, with whom no one has yet tried to reckon, and without whom, in certain countries at least, nothing can be done. Either the Indian is made to advance, or his weight will impede the march.

The Indian is discreet, imaginative, intelligent, and predisposed by nature toward elegance and culture. Among all primitive peoples, he is the most beautiful and the least repugnant. No savage people rushes so quickly to embellish itself, or does so with such grace, dignity, and profusion of color.

The modern art of the North American Indian tribes can be taken in at a glance. The robes are made of skins, covered with beads and fringes. The ornaments are made of feathers. No garment or weapon is not fully ornamented. Everything, everything, is covered with colored beads, in capricious and variable combinations, forming rhomboids, squares, triangles. The straight line, in artistic and geometrical proportions and elegant groupings, predominates in all the designs. When the line curves, which seems rarely to happen, it is imperfect. Beads cover the moccasins, the leggings, the belt, a kind of ridiculous long, narrow handbag, the sleeves and open skirts of the robes. Despite all their embellishments, the garments, which are long, still have the shape of the beast's skin. This can be seen in all early peoples: then, when they enter into their second period, their garments adopt the shape of a bird, with its wings extended. The Indians love white leather, and they are such skilled tanners that it looks like the softest lambskin. On the skirts of the dresses of their valiant women, their *squaws*, the Tuscaroras hang a great profusion of little clinking trimmings or tiny hollow tin pyramids that look like silver fringes and tinkle merrily.

Everywhere the Indian's vehement love of well-ordered color and ornament stands out. He covers his battle shield in leather adorned with feathers. From eagle feathers the warriors make the finery they wear into battle. They tie a band around their heads, and along it, opening out like the fronds of a young palm tree, stand stiff eagle feathers. From this helmet, a long, narrow strip of leather hangs down their backs, with a strip of red velvet in the middle, adorned with a crest of bristling feathers, that runs all the way to the ground. The *tomahawk* is like the Indian: slim, aquiline, terrible, deft. Men have always resembled the weapons they use. The rough-hewn man of Brittany wielded a brutal mace. The Indian, slender and swift, uses the quick, sharp arrow and the tomahawk with its slim, elegant handle and long, flat blade, its curved edge like an eagle's beak.

When we look at the ceramics, though there were few in this exhibit, the same spontaneous tendency toward formal beauty can be seen, the same dislike of wide, bare spaces, the same happy passion for adornment. There is no pot made by the Pueblo Indians, however primitive and elementary, that does not flaunt branching lines, strange caprices, claws, wings, clouds, and suns, outlined in black on its red or white clay.

In the crude displays of sculpture, including one piece in volcanic lava, another in granite, and the rest in fired clay, what stands out is the excessive fidelity of detail that distinguishes the art of primitive peoples and the first drawings of young children, as well as the singular power—which seems to belong only to aboriginal American art, among the arts of all rudimentary peoples—of giving perfect expression and spiritual meaning to a set of uneven features, and sometimes to an entire figure. The three most noteworthy of the sculptures were a seated woman, a figure in repose, reclining on its back, and a comical little god of pain made of clay that gleamed as if it contained golden sand.

In the figure of the woman, everything wept: the half-closed eyes, the furrowed cheeks, the braids that unravel against the brittle back, the burning breasts. The figure of the reclining man, which may have adorned a tomb, has the affable smile of a satisfied spirit that breathes its last, and the still warm repose of recent death was visible in it. The god of pain, made with extremely modern artistry, brought on involuntary laughter, not so much for the elementary quality of its design and execution, as for the sparkling and felicitous mockery of the white man it reveals. The little statue, unclothed, lifts its hands to its belly; its head, stuck atop a languid neck, makes a grimace that is reminiscent of Thackeray's naked Louis XIV—for when Thackeray[2] drew caricatures he did it as well as he wrote novels. And the Indian sculptor has adorned the face of this clay god with a mustache made of flax that adds its blond and hirsute comedy to the mischievous figure.

What little of the Indians' ancient art there was was made out of the objects that nature presents to primitive man at the very same hour when civilized art is contriving means and inventing adornments that are unlikely ever to be surpassed by human artifice. Within the same period, and at the same time, some men work to transform nature's most rebellious and recondite elements, and others use only the most superficial and rough of them. The Stone Age subsists in modern times. No law of life assigns separate eras to human history. Whenever a new nation is born, life—new, grandiose, and feral—is reborn with it. In another room the paintings of Passini, who paints light, were on view, and one by Fortuny, who paints air; in the exhibit of indigenous art there are hundreds of silex arrows, crafted almost before our eyes, some of them so diminutive and skillfully wrought that they seemed beautiful.

Above all, these objects appear to be the tools of a period of transition from wild beast to man, from the slender, high-strung wild beast of America to the restless, brilliant man of modern America. Above the display cases filled with moccasins, straps, shoulder belts, sheaths, and breechclouts completely covered with or made entirely out of colored beads, above the curious paraphernalia of the Sun dance made entirely of colorfully painted cardboard dolls with large and intricate branches arrayed like halos around the heads, there floated, like a symbol of the era from which they come and of the transition to the era with which they are now merging, the white flag, with its eight red stars and three red and blue dots, of the old and long-since conquered Tuscaroras, once the fear and scourge of the land, who now are prosperous inhabitants of New Carolina.

And in the middle of the flag's rectangular white canvas, above a row of animals—bear, horse, dog, duck, turtle, cut out of colored cloth and sewn on—an eagle, its wings outspread, rises into the sky, clutching in its claws a horrible serpent.

—New York, January 1884

MEXICO, THE UNITED STATES, AND PROTECTIONISM

More important than any words of my own which, coming from Latin lips, might seem a mere trotting-out of theories, are those we have translated below from the *Herald,* a newspaper that sees the facts with a clear, cold, and often brutal eye, and censures, in its own way, with a clarity to equal its crudeness, the protectionist system. For that system barely compensates the country with the benefit of acquiring a few imperfect industries for the harm done by the obstacles erected out of love for those industries, by the harsh dispute between the favored, stubborn industrialists and the overburdened and strangling nation, and by the danger to the country of amassing an industrial population that, because of costly and excessive production, too plentiful for the domestic market and too expensive for foreign ones, must ultimately find itself in a state of hunger and wrathful revolt. This is the worst of the protectionist system: the idea behind it is always that it will only be maintained as long as it promotes the creation of national industries, but those very industries then do not allow it to end when it should, but, spoiled by the easy profits they first earn in a country that is enthusiastic and in need of supplies, do not want to abandon their privileges even when the country for whose benefit those privileges were instituted suffers from them. The protectionist system, which is put in place so that the nation will become industrialized and hence rich and powerful, is then maintained only by a group of rich, powerful industrialists, at the price of the discomfort and increasing deprivation of the nation.

About seven years ago, when the *Herald* did not foresee with any certainty what it now laments, the same hand that is now writing these things about Mexico in *La América* wrote them in Mexico about that country of warm heart and rich soil, and about this other land whose current difficulties the clear-sighted could already grasp even then. We recall this here because it is an unshakable conviction among people of little sense, blindly given to factions and generalizations, that because I write this from the United States, all that I write, though it be dipped in my own blood and extracted from the purest metal the mines of my brain can yield, must be North American; the soldier in the ranks never sees the dreams of glory or the delight in sacrifice that softens or illuminates his captain's eyes at the hour of combat.

About seven years ago, we said, with our Latin foresight, what now, after their Saxon experience, those who have learned it at their own expense acknowledge.

The United States, a living example until now of the apparent advantages of the protectionist system, is turning against it, as Nessus turned against his tunic,[1] and through the mouthpiece of the *Herald*, which is echoed by all the country's newspapers on this point, points out, with regard to the current and perhaps future failure of its trade with Mexico to take root, the cause of its present economic position, which is a grave if not formidable consequence of the inattentive and unchecked use of protectionism.

Since the *Herald* typifies, in many cases guides, and in all ways mirrors its country, none of what it says on these matters should be overlooked. The *Herald* says:

> Even now the railroads which are being run into Mexico from this country are almost exclusively controlled by citizens of the United States, and American capital has been largely invested in Mexican ventures. Whatever our disadvantages were when the maritime commerce alone existed, we will possess [and the *Herald* expresses this future with an absolute *will*, not the *shall* that leaves room for probability or doubt, the polite *shall*] every advantage in the trade that ought to spring up with the completion of the railroads.
>
> Every advantage, however, only if we choose to avail ourselves of them. Naturally the market of Mexico belongs to this country, but unfortunately natural conditions were not allowed to remain, and a purely artificial, and therefore unnatural, set of circumstances were introduced, with the result of giving to other nations a trade which we might have, and which is capable of being almost indefinitely increased as more favorable conditions are created. In the years 1882 and 1883 the exports from Mexico to England increased nearly seven millions, while those to this country increased only three millions. And the showing is even worse when the exports of precious metals are not considered, for England took in 1883 nearly five hundred thousand dollars more than in 1882, and the United States more than six hundred thousand dollars less.

Again we ask, Shall the United States have Mexico for a market? Not unless a change is made in our commercial policy. Mexico has an abundance of the raw materials of manufacture, and the manufacturers of this United States stand in need of these very raw materials in order that they may so reduce the cost of production as to be able to export their commodities to Mexico and sell them in competition with European nations which are now securing these cheap materials. What possible conditions could be more favorable to an exchange in which each country would gain an advantage? And how shall we characterize the stupid and almost suicidal policy embodied in our tariff and navigation laws which prevents such an exchange? The selfishness of the protective policy is too well known to require an illustration, but if one was needed the rejection of the reciprocity treaty with Mexico would serve as an excellent example. Mexico has done much to invite trade with this country; the wares it displays are such as we wish, and the liberal aid granted to railroads shows its earnestness in seeking trade relations with us. We calmly reject the offers of intercourse and choose to maintain a policy of isolation which is ruining our industries and depressing all branches of trade and manufacture. We coolly invite other nations to reap the great advantages that a trade with Mexico offers, and we must pay dearly for this course if we persist in it.

That is what the *Herald* says.

As for the treaty, it is true that there should be a treaty between Mexico and the United States, and that those on the Latin side who, foreseeing dangers, did not want it, are unaware that by closing the door entirely they will have worse dangers in store for them than those they sought to avoid. However, so will those who, coming from another direction, but with the same destination, are hastily instigating and contriving treaties of so grave a nature. A treaty there must be, but not the one that was proposed, which now rightly rests in peace.

As for the effects of the protectionist system, and what has happened in the United States, might the protectionist system not be like those wooden stakes to which young saplings are bound in their earliest years, but which then, when the young tree grows strong and full of grace, must be removed so as not to oppress the trunk, which in any case will ultimately throw the stake to the ground?

—New York, February 1884

GRADUATION DAY

We are at a famous college in the United States on graduation day. There are thirty fortunate students whose diplomas, tied with green, blue, and scarlet ribbons, shine in their hands. They grasp them with pleasure, as if grasping the keys to life. From here, they will go forth to shine their light, to better the lot of the ignorant, to soothe, elevate, and lead. The French word *élever*, meaning "to educate," is a great one. Those who have lived already look sadly upon those who are just beginning to live; casting these college students out into life is, in their eyes, like cutting off the wings of birds. The ground is strewn with white wings. But life, which consumes human strength, demands that new forces periodically surge through its tired veins to replenish its store. The candor and drive of these college students reanimate hope, honor, and public faith, even for those who do not feel these emotions within themselves, just as the generous waters of new rains come down bearing flowers and fragrant herbs from the virgin mountains to enrich with their burden the impoverished currents of the rivers.

A Protestant pastor opens the proceedings: in the United States, all public or private ceremonies, joyous or mournful, a university festivity or the convention of a political party, begin with a prayer. The pastor, dressed all in black, raises his eyes to the sky and blasts forth his congratulations; his listeners, seated on their pews, cover their faces with their hands and lean forward against the back of the pew in front of them as the spontaneous prayer of free men resonates. In later days, after the churches have quarreled among themselves, the power of prayer diminishes. A church with no dogma but the great and solid creed inspired by the majesty of the Universe and the good, immortal soul—what a great church that would be! And how it would dignify discredited religion! How it would help keep the spirit alight in these anxious, money-grubbing times! How it would bring together all men who love wonders and need contact with them, but who cannot conceive that nature, which is all harmony, can have created inharmonious faculties in man, and who do not wish to pay with their reason and their liberty for their contact with wonder!

We are at a famous college. After the prayer is over, one of the graduating students goes to the podium. And then another, and then another. They speak of profound matters in solid language. They do not repeat from memory the proof that the earth is round, nor do they hold forth in paragraphs modeled after Balmes[1] on the nature and description of knowledge, nor do they chorus the ancient names of every inlet, pool, and bend in the road mentioned in Greek history, as they made us do in our times, to the great satisfaction of parents and teachers who in truth are satisfied with very little, for the plumage gains in color with all that highly useful knowledge, but the brain does not benefit, nor does the life of the student, who must flail about with no ability to steer through it and guard against its anguishes. The colleges barely open the book that should always be open: the book of life.

The students of the college where we are do not speak of such hollow matters; their speeches take up the most urgent questions of the time, and other matters of physics and psychology that are always of great moment. Their speeches do not flutter in the air as dry leaves and many speeches do, but instead have all the weight of a bough laden down with fruit. And these are not doctoral students, but mere bachelors of arts. One student reads aloud a study of imagination in mathematics, and says that imagination has as much part in mathematical constructs as it does in the painful and luminous conceptions of poetry, and that the same degree of imaginative power required to write *Paradise Lost* was needed to establish the fundamental principles of conical sections. Another student examines the reasons for the harmful influx of ignorant Irish immigrants into the cities, where their sheer numbers smother the voting process and take control of it, even though their habit of mingling only with others of their kind and the fact that idealism is not a distinctive element of their nature mean that their level of education does not rise along with their influence and authority as voters in the nation that receives them as if they were its own children. On the hills of the cities' outskirts, the Irish raise geese, ducks, goats, and barefoot children who can find no model for a better life in their beer-sodden fathers and bedraggled mothers and the squalid parish priest, but leave their shoddy wooden shacks impoverished in both body and spirit—and since immigrants come from Ireland to New York in such quantities, that great city is very seriously threatened with mental and moral misery. The Germans could alleviate this problem if they were not so given to their own enjoyment and so indifferent to the good of others. Brutishness and egotism are clearly poor building blocks for a mighty nation. Of course there are the schools; but whatever the school coaxes to grow in the Irish children is quickly gobbled up by the goat. The children of the Germans, whose parents generally get ahead in life and do not live in such ruinous communities, take advantage of their books, in addition to which the German is a family man and a hard worker, who gradually and effortlessly instills good habits in his children. The graduate's speech did not say that, but it did say other things that were excellent.

Another young recipient of a bachelor of arts degree takes the podium and reads ... but what is it that everyone is applauding so vigorously? Nothing less than a study in which the right and capacity of the Egyptian people to govern their own land is defended, and the unseemly pretext for denying that right is accused of being no more than a mask for English ambition that, like a boa squeezing a dove, has been tightening its grip on Egypt—the pretext, that is, that a few ambitious men who know Latin have a natural right to rob some Africans who speak Arabic of their land; the pretext that civilization, which is the vulgar name for the current state of man in Europe, has a natural right to take possession of other lands belonging to barbarity, which is the name that those who desire other lands give to the current condition of any man who is not from Europe or from European America: as if head for head and heart for heart, a batterer of Irishmen or a shooter of sepoys[2] were worth more than one of those prudent, loving, and selfless Arabs who, unchastened by defeat and undaunted by numbers, defend their patria with their faith in Allah, a spear in each hand, and a pistol between their teeth. However, since liberty lives from respect and the power of reason is nourished by controversy, the young people of this country are educated in the virile and redemptive practice of speaking their minds without fear, and of hearing what others think without wrath or suspicion, so that no sooner has the applause with which we all salute the defender of human decorum died down than another graduate is on the platform defending the perfect right of England to put its hand definitively upon the abandoned people of Egypt and hang on to them with all its might, just as the United States took over the territory of the Indians.

Another graduate pays tribute to the system of public education in North America and says that the homogeneity of the nation's newest citizens offers proof that this way of teaching is worthy of a strong nation; but the next graduate stands up to criticize the current system, and says that they are the greatest possible failure, for the schools teach children to be like the children of the rich who will live from their inheritance and not from their labor, and there is hardly another nation where the children must leave school at fifteen with a more deficient and rudimentary education: they can spell, write, and count, but their appetite for knowledge has not been awakened, nor have they been instilled with that human sympathy and intuition without which men become that empty, harmful, and horrendous creature: the egoist.

A very young graduate who attracts every eye is the one who next recounts, not without historical style and sound critical acumen, the life of the two Elizabeths: the hateful Elizabeth of England and the great Isabella of Spain. The following one seems a veritable science professor, denying with ingenious arguments and picturesque phrases that the vital forces and the physical forces are equivalent, and that the latter can ever achieve the original potency of creation that resides only in the unknown and colossal will: "Chemistry," says this young scholar, "has been able to fabricate eggs, but not to hatch them." And the graduate who closes these animated exercises perorates, with exquisite tenderness, dense words, and profound vision, upon the sad and healthy philosophy of George Eliot, the noble and unfortunate English novelist: a new stoic, for whom life prepared a bitter cup, as it always does for lofty souls, a cup she drained to the dregs so there would be nothing left for others to drink, but without allowing the vapors of her bitterness, which cloud the eyes of so many, to dim her sight, so that she could see the element of unwavering happiness in every well-educated consciousness and in nature. A definitive and universal justice arises from all that lives, assuring us of forthcoming compensation for the earth's inequalities and injustices. This brave mind, towering among men like an unconquered giant among Lilliputians, encourages and caresses us.

We have not yet said—we avoided saying it on purpose—that these gallant graduates, who stride with such mastery through the inner workings of character and depict past empires and raise the flag of free men and weigh nature's body and soul, were women. The graduates of Vassar College that day were girls of eighteen to twenty.

On the day when woman is no longer frivolous, how happy man will be! She will be transformed from a mere vessel of fragrant flesh into an urn of spirit against which men will always press their anxious lips! Oh! what a day it will be when the power of reason no longer need be divorced from the natural love of beauty! The day when the sorrow of discovering that the vase once believed to be full of spirit is empty no longer drives fevered and desperate men from one vase to another in search of a beauteous soul! Oh! what a day it will be when one is no longer forced to disdain what one loves! Women will not necessarily become dry bluestockings because of it; just as men of

knowledge are not inevitably dull pedants. May the education of
women become so common that she who possesses it is not marked
out, and she herself does not notice it, and then wearied love will stay
home.

Thus, when a man has need of one who understands his sorrow, admires his virtue, and stimulates his mind, he will not have to go searching outside of his home, as now. It will not be compassion, duty, and
habit that keep him united to his wife, but an ineffable intermingling of
the spirit that does not involve the servile yielding of one spouse to the
opinions of the other: the delicious embrace of souls whose opinions,
capabilities, and nourishment are similar, even though their outer appearance is different.

The husband expands with the excellences of his wife, and by them
she sinks roots into him. And that is good, for the only pleasure that
redeems this sorrowful life, and perfumes, uplifts, and fortifies it, is the
feeling of having sunk roots into a warm and loving soul, like a tree in
the earth.

Moreover, like water, nations seek a level surface. Every nation, if it
is to save itself, requires a certain component of feminine intellect and
qualities. Just as no child is born without father and mother, so there is
no nation without happy communion between the virile and feminine
elements of the spirit. Though unaware of their own excess, the nations are dying of a hypertrophied strength that bewilders and intoxicates them, makes them haughty and causes pain and upheaval, just as
a hypertrophying of feeling and art would weaken them and make
them effeminate. Spiritual conditions have their hygiene, just as physical conditions do, and one must rest from one condition in another,
which tempers and modifies it. One must repose from strength in tenderness. There exists, in nations given to fatigue, frenetic labor, and eagerness for wealth, an urgent need to balance out by the education of
women, which brings sensitivity and the seeds of intellect to the life of
the nation, the natural scarcity of those conditions arising from the almost exclusive dedication of the majority of the nation to the battles,
emotions, and delights of the possession of wealth. Like stars that shed
soft light and illuminate the darkness along their way, these graduates
with long hair and harmonious forms pour out each year across the
country. The wealthy yokels who court and desire them improve
themselves out of shame at not being like them; their contact, example,
and teaching sweeten and spiritualize the lives around them. And just
as good wine tastes better in a cup that is well wrought or made of fine,

clear crystal, so is spiritual influence received from a cultured and beautiful woman with all the more meekness, pleasure, and benefit.

—New York, June 1884

THE INDIANS IN THE UNITED STATES

The Mohonk Conferences began in 1883 and were one of the forces behind the passage of the Dawes General Allotment Act of 1887, a federal law that gave plots of reservation land to individual Indians provided they renounced their tribal allegiance and became U.S. citizens. At the 1885 Mohonk Conference, which Martí reports on here, Senator Henry Dawes of Massachusetts said, "They [the Indians] have got as far as they can go, because they hold their land in common. It is Henry George's[1] system, and under that there is no enterprise to make your home any better than that of your neighbors. There is no selfishness, which is at the bottom of civilization. Till these people will consent to give up their lands, and divide them among their citizens so that each can own the land he cultivates, they will not make much progress."

Though the reformers of the time saw it as a progressive measure, the Dawes Act is now widely regarded as having done the Indians far more harm than good. By 1932 whites had acquired two-thirds of the 138 million acres held by Indians in 1887.

Lake Mohonk is a lovely spot in New York State. The forests of the nearby Adirondacks are conducive to grandeur, though they are being unsystematically cut down by clumsy speculators; in forests, as in politics, it is wrong to demolish except in order to build on the ruins. The lake invokes serenity, and the river that flows nearby gives an example of noiseless fecundation and progress toward the sea. This fall, as the leaves turned yellow and red, the friends of the Indians availed themselves of this picturesque retreat for a calm discussion of how to attract them to a peaceful and intelligent life in which their rights will not be flouted, their trust will not be betrayed, their character will not be corrupted, and their rebellions will not be frequent and justified, as is presently the case. Particularly notable in that gathering of benevolent

men and women was the absence of the spirit of theory, which obstructs or renders ugly and sterile the well-meaning efforts of so many
reformers, and generally alienates—by the repulsion that disjuncture
and imbalance inspire in a healthy mind—the solicitous support of
moderate spirits who would otherwise be useful allies of reform. Genius, which is bedazzling and explosive, need not do away with the
common sense that makes its terrestrial existence productive. Senators, commissioners, and superintendents were there to share the generous task with enthusiastic journalists and Protestant ministers.

In the United States, it was a woman who opened many hearts to
pity for the Negroes, for no one helped to liberate them more than
Harriet Beecher Stowe, who, ever impassioned on behalf of justice,
had no fear of tarnishing with tremendous revelations about Lord Byron[2] the fruitful success of *Uncle Tom's Cabin*—a tear that spoke! And
it was also a woman who, with greater sensitivity and tenderness, has
worked year after year to alleviate the misfortunes of the Indians: Helen Hunt Jackson,[3] of strong mind and loving soul, who has just died
as she was writing a letter of thanks to President Cleveland for his determination to recognize the Indians' humanity and right to justice.
There were people of apostolic speech and a gift for statecraft at the
convention, but the incomprehensible statistics, the precise account-
ing, and the implacable numbers did not come from any superinten-
dent, commissioner, or senator, but from a woman, Alice Fletcher,[4] a
lively orator, sure in her reasonings and skilled in debate.

The Mohonk Convention was not a gathering of breathless philan-
thropists who see Indians as seraphic creatures just because they are
Indians, or of those butterfly-like politicians who only pause momen-
tarily on the surface of things, and judge by mere appearances and results, without seeing that there is no way to cure maladies except by
eliminating their causes.

It was a gathering of men and women of action. One of the more
ardent among them, "shivered upon recalling the sad scenes that occur
in the Indian reservations when rations, clothing, or the money for the
year is apportioned among them like meat to wild beasts." He has seen
these marks of degradation and, since he is a man, has felt ashamed and
wants to raise up the unhappy Indians, for one is responsible for any
malady one knows of and does not remedy; it is a criminal idleness, a
passive guilt that differs only in degree from the guilt of doing, for
apostleship is a daily and constant duty. Another of those in atten-
dance has seen the Indians squatting in circles to gamble away their

year's pay, wagering nine out of every ten pesos they were given, just as the Chinamen in the cigar factories of a Spanish prison do the moment they receive, on Saturday evening, the part of their daily wage that is left after their debt to the establishment is deducted. That the Indians on the reservations are lazy and given to drink and gambling was something everyone at the convention knew. Accustomed by a bad system of government to an ignoble idleness, they do not like to work now, and since they are used to receiving a yearly sum, and food and clothing, from the government, they will resist any reform that tends to elevate their character by compelling them to earn their sustenance by their own work. Lacking the civic pleasures and social aspirations of white people, they take no interest in the system of public schools that is being offered them and do not give up the savage existence of the tribes—nor does that strike them as necessary. The convention knew all of that, but it also knew that the Indian is not so by nature, but has been made so by the system of idleness and debasement in which he has been kept for a hundred years.

Wherever the Indian has most successfully defended himself and continued as he was, he can be seen as he is by race: strong of mind and will, courageous, hospitable, worthy. Wild still, like all men and all peoples that are close to nature, it is his own noble characteristics of personal pride and attachment to his land that make him whirl around like a wild beast when he is robbed of the fields he has sown for centuries, when his sacred trees are brought crashing to the earth, when the hot wind from his burning village singes the manes of his fleeing horses—and then he burns the one who burned his village, and hunts down the one who hunted him and steals from the one who stole from him, and exterminates the one who is exterminating him.

And then, reduced in numbers—a poor nation of 300,000 scattered savages that fights untiringly with a nation of 50 million men!—he does not enter the cities of his conquerors; he does not take a desk in the conquerors' school; he is not taught their industries; no human soul is recognized in him. He is forced by onerous treaties to give up his land; he is cut off from the place where he was born, which is like cutting the roots off a tree, and he thereby loses the greatest object of life; he is forced, under the pretext of making a farmer of him, to buy animals to work a patch of land that does not belong to him; he is compelled, under the pretext of schooling him, to study in a foreign language, the hated language of his masters, textbooks that give him some vague notion of literature and the sciences, whose usefulness is never

explained and whose application he never understands. He is imprisoned in a confined space, where he mills around among his corralled
companions, their only horizon the hucksters who sell shiny geegaws,
weapons, and alcohol for the money that, in accordance with the
treaties, the government distributes on the reservations each year. If a
wish to see the world and leave this human paddock comes to him, he
cannot; he has no land of his own that he can work and that will stimulate him to cultivate it with care so as to leave an honorable name to
his children; in many of the tribes he has nothing at all to do, because
the government, under a system of degrading tutelage that began a
century ago, gives him a plot of common land to live off of, and supplies him with clothing, food, medicine, schools, and all that is the natural object of man's effort, on top of which it gives him a yearly sum
of money that, without property to improve or journey to undertake
or any unsatisfied material need, he wastes on colorful baubles that
flatter his rudimentary artistic taste, or on liquor and gambling, which
excite him and heighten the brutal pleasures to which he is condemned. The Indian is dead under this ignoble system, which extin-
guishes his personality; man grows through the exercise of his own
faculties, just as a rolling wheel picks up speed, and when he does not
exercise them he rusts and rots away like the wheel. A sentiment of
downtrodden fierceness that is never entirely extinguished in enslaved
races—arising from the memory of their lost homes, the counsel of the
old men who saw freer days in the native forests, the presence of their
own men, jailed, reviled, and idle—explodes in intermittent bursts
each time the hardhearted and rapacious government agents skim
from or deny the benefits that are stipulated in the treaties; and since
by virtue of those treaties whatever is noble in man is barred to them
and only what is beastlike is permitted, it naturally happens that in
their revolts the beast that the system has developed emerges to distort
the sense of justice that caused them to rebel.

This is the case of all enslaved men, not just the Indian, and it is why
revolutions that follow prolonged tyrannies are so cruel. What white
man who has his brain in the right place does not understand that he
cannot throw in the Indian's face the fact that he is as the whites have
made him? "He is fine and brave," said the venerable Erastus Brooks,[5]
whose words are loving and carry weight; "we have dozens, hundreds
of examples from American history to demonstrate that the Indian,
under equal conditions, is mentally, morally, and physically capable of
all that a white man can do." But we have made a vagabond of him, a

haunter of taverns, a professional beggar. We do not give him work to do for himself, work that gladdens and elevates, but at most, and in violation of treaties, we force him to earn, by work from which he does not profit directly, the value of the rations and medicines that we promised him in exchange for his land; we instill in him the habit of dependence, we habituate him to a life of idleness, without other needs or pleasures than those of naked, primitive man; we deprive him of the means of procuring for himself what he needs, and force him to ask the government agent for everything, head lowered and hat in hand: bread, quinine, clothes for his wife and children. The only white man he knows is the saloonkeeper who corrupts him, the peddler who cheats him, the distributor of rations who finds a way to reduce his ration, the untrained schoolteacher who repeats meaningless, joyless words to him in a language he barely speaks, the agent who sends him away with a laugh or a harsh shout when he goes to demand justice. Without work, without property, without hope, without native land, with no family delights other than the merely physical ones, what else can the Indians on the reservations be but irritable, lazy, sensual men, born from fathers who saw their own fathers, pipe and soul extinguished, squatting on the ground and weeping for the lost nation and the shade of the great tree that century after century bore witness to their marriages, their judgments, their celebrations, and their councils? A slave is a very sad thing to see, but even sadder is the son of a slave: traces of mud can be seen even in his complexion! Great developers of men are these Indian reservations. Cutting the Indians down altogether would have been better than debasing them.

In 1783 the first treaty in which the government of the United States took upon itself the right to supervise the tribes and regulate their traffic was signed; and today the three hundred thousand Indians, subjugated after a war whose greatest cruelties were not theirs, are distributed among fifty reservations that have no other law than the will of the president, and another seventy-nine that are called treaty reservations, whose law is a pact established between the tribes and the government. Thirty-nine of those pacts permit the redistribution of reservation land into individual properties, an ennobling measure that has been attempted with only twelve of the tribes. "What Congress allocates for food," said Alice Fletcher, "is distributed among the Indians, and because of that it passes through many hands and some part of it remains in each pair; but the money for schools is not distributed because it can only be obtained by government employees who steer the scanty schoolteacher's salary to their wives or daughters to supplement their domestic finances, in such a way that of the $2 million that from '71 to '81 should have been spent, tallying up the obligations under all the treaties, only about $200,000 has been spent on schools." Many tribes have been offered even more than the private property that is not distributed to them and the school that is not established for them: they have been offered citizenship.

And all of this was heard without contradiction and was even approved and confirmed by the vice inspector of Indian schools, the authors of the draft legislation on reservation reform in the House and the Senate, and the members of the Indian delegation. The top government employees approved of and confirmed all of it, and applauded the inspired defense of the Indian's nature made by the good Erastus Brooks. "He has no vice for which we are not responsible! There is no bestiality in the Indian that is not our fault! The agents whose only concern is to keep him dull-witted and in their control are lying about the Indian!"

The government debases them with a system of treaties that condemn them to vice and inertia, and in their greed the government's agents give out a false notion of the Indians and hide the cause of the Indians' corruption and rebellions, so that they can go on skimming at their ease from the flow of wealth that Congress sends for the Indians' upkeep.

Let he who governs keep an eye on these rapacious employees!

All hail President Cleveland, who without fuss or fanatical display has ordered that the Indians be asked what they are enduring, and instead of blaming them for the ignominy in which they are kept, has decided to bear the guilt for it and uplift them through just government to the status of men. President Cleveland does not want drunken insects; he wants human beings. "They are drunkards and thieves because that is what we made them: so we must beg their pardon for having made them drunkards and thieves, and rather than exploiting them and breaking our promises to them, we must give them work on their lands, and stimuli that will incite them to live, for they are good, even though we have given them the right not to be."

In unison, therefore, the convention agreed, in the shadow of the Adirondack Mountains, which are conducive to grandeur, to recommend these practical reforms made out of mere justice, which can transform a costly multitude of weary and restless men into a picturesque and useful element of American civilization.

Now that the republic, for its own reasons, has taken their rights as free nations from them, the Indians must not be deprived as well of their rights as men. The theft of their lands, even if it was reasonable and necessary, was nevertheless a violent deed that any civilized nation would resist with hatred and centuries of warfare, which must not be aggravated by repression and inhuman traffickings. The goal must be to eliminate the corrupting and unjust system of the reservations, and to open the national land to them little by little, mingling them with the white population so that they may soon own land in this nation's states and enjoy the rights that other citizens have, and attend to their obligations. The annual payment must be abolished because it promotes mendacity and vagrancy and habituates the Indian to non-self-reliance. The Indian's education should conform to his needs and abilities, and he should be convinced or where necessary compelled to learn and work, which, debased by his current style of life as a slothful ward of the state, he may resist. The Indian must recover his soul's clarity and ascend to citizenship.

And so that they may thus become useful men, and their lands, today no more than very expensive prisons, may become peaceful and prosperous regions, let the whole current, unwieldy system of education be changed—said the convention—and let the working of lands held in common, which neither stimulates nor yields any visible reward, be replaced with a redistribution of the land as the property of each family, untransferable for twenty-five years, in accordance with the type of land and the size of each family; let the government buy the lands that are not redistributed for a good price—and since it must pay itself for them, for it is the tutor of the Indians who are selling, let the price for which these lands are sold be reserved for the industrial education and betterment of the Indians—and open up the purchased areas to colonization. Let the tribes agree to revoke the treaties that have brought them to their miserable state, and let citizenship be granted to all tribes who accept the individual redistribution of their lands, and to the Indians who abandon the tribes that do not accept it and adapt themselves to the customs of civilization. Let the nation cease to drag the Indians from the lands of their elders and gather them in populous centers beneath the self-interested vigil of offensive and greedy government employees. "Put schools everywhere," said the vice inspector of Indian schools, in conclusion, "useful schools, lively schools: all efforts to promote education are in vain when the education is out of step with the needs, nature, and future of the person who receives it. And no more secondhand schoolteachers who know nothing about what they teach and are chosen only in order to increase the family pittance of some employee, or to please political strongmen; good teachers will be hired, and the Indians will be compelled to send their children to school, even if we must resort, while the dire system of rationing lasts, to cutting off the family's rations. Not education out of books—a storing up of words that then weigh too heavily in the head to be a good guide to the hands. What the field that must be tilled consists of, and who he is, and the nature of the nation in which he lives: these are the things the Indian must be taught. He must understand and admire; he must learn something of practical politics so that he can attain the appropriate degree of mutual respect; he must know the lay of the land, and what rights men have to own and to think within it, and he must have the means of exercising them. The school must teach him to be sufficient to his life: country people must have a rustic school.

Neither verbiage nor fine points of grammar, but the best methods of raising animals and tilling the earth, along with all the trades that will make him the master of himself and a useful member of the community of laborers. Teachers of letters alone must not be sent to the Indians or to any rural people. The teacher is the living letter. Teachers of agriculture and useful skills must also be sent. It progressed well and finished well, that convention of the Friends of the Indians, in the serenity of Lake Mohonk, where the mountains draw near and beautiful squares of land, cultivated with elegant care, spread out before the eyes of men worthy to contemplate them, like colossal green flowers.

—New York, October 25, 1885;
published in *La Nación* (Buenos Aires), December 4, 1885

THE WORLD'S BIGGEST EXPLOSION

While the road to civilization was being opened to the Indians in a peaceful country town, the islet of Flood Rock flew through the air in tiny shards at the impact of 280,000 pounds of explosives, opening a clear route for ships through the mouth of the East River, until now obstructed by the sharp points of Hell Gate where for centuries the current had crashed into tempestuous rapids that were the fear of the river people.

In nine years of work, man has broken the high mound of mud that was forged in the heat of the earth and deposited there over centuries by the murky river that used to flow through the channel now filled by the solemn waters of the East River.

For nine years tenacious workers have labored within the bosom of Flood Rock, lowered into it down a wide shaft to tunnel perfect streets through its entrails, twenty-four of them running from north to south, through which the current flows, and forty-six from east to west, perpendicular to it; and those running north to south were 1,200 feet long, a distance of about four blocks. The mules and men down below carted the rubble from the excavations to the shaft, through which they rose to heap it up on the surface; for nine years mules and men glistened with the water that flowed from the broken rock.

Not in vain did the city gather, in awe and fear, on the riverbanks and in a floating encampment of little steamers and boats that populated the water, to watch a whole island rise a hundred feet into the air, dashed to bits when a little girl's finger touched the button that activated the electrical battery whose current ignited the platinum wires that set off the primary detonators and made 13,300 sticks of dynamite explode. And above the river, which was tinged with gray, then yellow, then green, there rose a colossal crest of water, compact, foaming, and swirling, and crowned with high peaks like the massive walls of polar crevasses.

Let us go down into the vault before the island explodes. Such a marvel must not be celebrated in convulsive phrases: simply to enumerate it is humbling. Let us go down to the charged tunnels: the entire ceiling is full of boreholes that open out like the points of a crown, and each one of them, three inches wide and nine feet deep, is full of sticks of *rackarock*, a new explosive composed of potassium chlorate and nitrobenzene. Through the mouth of each borehole about six inches of a stick of dynamite emerges, tipped with an explosive even more sensitive than the tremendous charge contained within the stick. The ceiling of the tunnels is coffered with these little prongs, and when it vanished into the four winds, it left behind the 486 pillars that now support the 25-foot layer of rock that flew into the air when the little girl touched the button. Oh, no! What if someone stumbles against the instrument that stands in a little wooden hut on the other side of the river, while we, wrapped in rubber capes, are seeing the tunnels! What if, over our heads, the workers, who have forgotten the meaning of fear, connect the electrical wires in the cable that runs to the hut on the other bank! Ay! What if the blast is detonated before the reckless boats and steamers that are crossing the river to gaze at the islet as if it were a man about to die are far enough away! We have just seen, before retreating up the shaft, how the explosion was prepared. The tunnels are from 6 to 8 feet wide, and wooden crossbars have been placed across all of them every 25 feet; two sticks of dynamite are tied to each crossbar and each of them has a mine detonator attached to it: a steel cylinder, 7½ inches long and 1½ inches in diameter, also filled with dynamite, plugged at one end with a copper tube containing 30 grains of mercury fulminate, and at the other with a smaller tube filled with sulfur, which stabilizes the two united strands carrying electrical current that enter the cartridge through the second tube. The two strands end in an arc of platinum wire, and that is how the mine will explode. Not every borehole is wired, for 13,286 wires would have been needed! Nothing connects the sticks of dynamite that are sticking out through the boreholes to each other, or joins them to the ones on the crossbars every 25 feet throughout the tunnels. The boreholes contain 240,000 pounds of *rackarock* and 40,000 pounds of dynamite. There are 300 crossbars, and hence 600 mine detonators.

From each of the detonators on the crossbars, a double electric wire emerges, 600 electric wires in all, which then run outside into a cable that crosses the river from the island to the neighboring bank. There, the eleven-year-old girl—the same girl who, at the age of three, blew up Hell Gate in the same way; the daughter of General Newton,[1] who directed this project—will push the button that activates the battery. The electricity, running at once to the tip of each wire, will heat up the platinum arc that unites them; the ignited arcs will set off the mine detonators in which the electrical wires end; each of those detonators will make the stick of dynamite it is attached to on the wooden crossbar explode, and as those 600 sticks of dynamite simultaneously explode, the 13,286 that are sticking out through the mouths of the boreholes will go off, along with all the sticks of *rackarock* that are in the vault behind them; at the impact the river will burst into flame, and over its broken back the uprooted rock will rise through the air. Up the shaft we rose: no one is left on the island now, and not a steamer or little boat remains on the river, only the river police, whose quick steam launches with their red flags warning of danger circle near the islet so that no imprudent small craft will venture too close. It is 1:15 in the afternoon; 100,000 curious onlookers crowd the riverbanks, the rooftops, and the towers. Like immense spiders perched atop their long tentacles, photographers line the river on the New York side, and the crowd makes room for them; some newspapers have as many as seven photographers here to shoot instantaneous views of the enormous explosion that they can show their readers tomorrow. Not a sound can be heard: you might say that the silence is audible.

The ground all around oscillated half an inch. The river water trembled. The river opened out into two colossal waves that subsided on its banks. Through the broken river came a black mass, as if the giant who stokes the fire in the earth's belly were pushing it up through the water with his back, hands braced against his thighs. Was it mud or rock? There was no time to find out; up rose the water, up, up, and like an ice floe composed of the purest crystals it stayed there for a few seconds, 150 feet high, its peaks crowned with a rainbow: a watery Andes.

Soon the mass collapsed into drops that rained across the riverbed, which rose and then rose again with less force, until, a few seconds later, only the thick yellow smoke of the *rackarock* drifted over the placid waters. From every nook and inlet of the riverbanks, like water ants, came little boats loaded with people who picked dead fish from the water's dark surface in memory of the big event.

New York, October 25, 1885;
published in *La Nación* (Buenos Aires), December 6, 1885

IMPRESSIONIST PAINTERS

When the workers themselves are demonstrating exemplary restraint, it is not for the powers that be in this republic to evince less of it than they do. The lesson of the strikes has not been in vain: both in New York and in the Southeast the initial mistakes are in the past and the reins now appear to be firmly in the hands of the executive committee of the Knights of Labor.[1]

The committee is present at the site of the strikes and will not allow any illegal act, just as, with the deftness of an expert fencer, it does not permit any attack from the companies to go without a response.

It gladdens the heart to see them settle their dispute by the arts of peace. The companies can withstand the strikes because they have accumulated capital; the workers have learned the lesson and have imagined ways of accumulating capital of their own.

There is no poverty among the ten thousand striking railroad workers: the committee receives a regular flow of thousands of dollars a day that comes in from everywhere and is distributed in an orderly fashion. The strike, which initially escaped from its directors' hands, is now back in their control; they do not hope to win by "killing" locomotives or derailing trains, burning up stocks of hay or riddling constables' chests with bullet holes: they hope to win in the court of public opinion, in the state legislatures, and in the courts of law.

The railway companies, with legislatures and venal judges as their accomplices, have falsified the public laws and have wrongfully gained and distributed their wealth. Wounding them in their ill-gotten wealth, forcing them to confess their inner organization, dismantling bit by bit the enormous fortune that they have amassed by illegally merging competing companies, and depriving them of new employees by the simple means of paying what the company would have paid out of the Order's own funds, thus leaving the company with no one to repair the locomotives or make new parts, or attend to the many tasks along the railway tracks and the daily care they require: these are the means that the Order of the Knights of Labor promotes and employs to compel the railway company to treat the united workers as a necessary and respectable guild.

In New York, the way these associations work is even more strikingly on view this very day.

Thirteen hundred employees of a tramway company are on strike. Altogether the united employees of the tramway companies of the three cities of New York, New Jersey, and Brooklyn number around 12,000. Each one of them agrees to give up a day's wages—$1.50—each week for the expenses of the strike.

The strike, then, can distribute $18,000 each week to its idled workers, to be shared among 1,300 workers. Their salary doesn't give them much more than that.

Meanwhile, the company is losing horses and credit, and spending great sums importing inept conductors from neighboring cities and attracting new customers with outmoded free gifts.

There you see the practical and fearsome way in which these battles are now undertaken, battles whose meaning comes from so deep and is so far-reaching that the grave excesses that have marked these workers' movements have not sufficed to extinguish the sympathy inspired by the general conviction of their justice.

During these Easter days, clusters of young girls in bloom, showing off their brand-new finery as if they were garbed in light, stroll through the street alongside clusters of blue-clad men who are the patrols maintained by the strike so that no disorderly conduct takes place in its name—and clusters of grand gentlemen with faces like Henry III, who, with sumptuous ladies on their arms, are going to have a look at the lilac-tinted mountains, vivid clothing, beautiful landscapes, and disorderly conduct in green and blue of the Impressionist painters. Durand-Ruel[2] is their apostle in Paris, and he has sent a lavish exhibit to New York.

We enter. The whole world enters. There is a great love in this country for all that is Japanese and extravagant, which has unhinged the minds of the good school of open-air painters.

Why do they disfigure their sacred love for what is true with a voluntary worship of what is violent and ugly?

Manet is splendid; Laurens[3] we admire; Roll,[4] Lenolle, and Huguet we love. The technique is crude but the idea is healthy, and the effect is strong and beautiful; but why strive, as the Neo-Impressionists do, for such a brutal treatment of nature? The planes are superimposed as on a Chinese panel, with no shading to connect and soften them; over scaly waters a green beach looms without grace or nobility, like a knifeblade.

But, why speak of what is bad? It falls away on its own. Saying nothing is reproach enough. Only in cases of repeated infraction does criticism cease to be mere pedantry. Admiration is healthy and beneficial.

What first carries off the eyes is Roll's *Study:* a naked, half-swooning woman amid the mysteries of the jungle, who embraces a robust calf. On closer scrutiny: patches, impastos, rivulets of color, and thickly caked edifices of paint.

From afar, the calf's muzzle seems to emerge from the illuminated canvas, the admirable, closed muzzle of a being who concentrates all that gives him pleasure within himself; the calf's eye is satisfied, half-closed, languid, mysterious, full, and tender. The woman, half-fallen, her face flushed, her mouth smiling, presses the thick muzzle against her inclining head with her left hand, and with the right hand grasps one flank: great swaths of light are cast across her naked body and bring out her human beauty, the ample waist, the concise ornaments of her bosom, the fulfilment of the thirty Latin graces. The background is thick and green, with a few jungle flowers in white: the earth beneath them is broken, grassy, trampled.

Who does not know Laurens's *Dead Marceau*?[5] The grief it contains is not varnished but alive: these are men who weep, and glory that departs—not rented garments on models from the Academy! The whole world knows the daring foreshortening of this *Marceau:* the adored face still bears the shadows of the soul's wings: a green uniform trimmed with white braid and a pink sash, boots, and the hand, clad in a yellow glove, which grasps in its rigid fingers the hilt of a curved sabre that is tipped with light.

There is no luxury in the camp bed: over the sheet, a bright red bedspread with white roses; over the spread, a red cloth; beneath the head, a white pillow; and behind, as background and headboard, a yellow screen.

And the old man who weeps, sitting on the white chair near the camp bed—what an old man he is! His face cannot be seen; but the hand that covers it and his rumpled garments speak all his sorrow.

And what a sad man, too, who weeps against the top of the camp bed. Blue jacket, white wig. The soldier in the gray cape, how incurable is his anguish! What terrible pain is felt by the women who are lowering the body to the ground, and the gentleman in the white jacket with gold stripes and a green sash! As one gazes at the painting, a cry springs from the lips: How great the dead man must have been!

Over here is a portrait of Jaure dressed as Hamlet. Manet painted it. He is the true Hamlet, not one of those caveman Hamlets who look like emanations from the lower depths, but a tender soul, who in the furor of his indignation conceives of acts of vengeance that the educated mind does not dare carry out; with one outstretched hand, which drags his cape, he expresses his doubt, while with the other he seizes his sword, almost on the attack; the blackness of his doublet is enlivened by a short ruff trimmed with blue; his eye is fixed, the eye of a man who wants to know immensity itself, and does not know it; the thigh is slender; the calf swells; there is no line to separate the ground from the surroundings; the figure stands out against a gray background.

Another Manet is titled *Horse Race;* this is Manet in all his power and all his blunders. Manet had two fathers: Velázquez and Goya. In his *Absinthe Drinker,* his *Beggar,* his *Philosopher,* he has not yet left Velázquez behind, but in his *Fifer,* a kiss planted on a soldier's uniform and a little fellow laboriously playing his fife are Manet's own doing; it is he who detaches the figure from its surroundings without any shadows and with masterful fidelity and daring color.

In *Horse Race,* as in other paintings, Manet is the Goya of the punishments and prophecies, the Goya of bishops and madmen who paints caves for eyes, and remorse for faces, and rags for limbs—all in blots and jabs.

But such excess is appropriate in fantasy, for there all is distorted and seen through a mist, and that orgy of forms adds to the mental effect of the canvases. In the human realm of this horse race, only one beauty suits the painting, a beauty it has to the utmost degree: in dots, specks, scumblings, and mounds of color, without a single line, we see carriages, horses, the occasional very friendly couple, the stands crowded with people, waves of hats, ribbons, and parasols: behind the hill are houses, little trees, gullies, and the sun, which washes over and inundates everything; near the viewer, along the edge of the painting, burnished like the figures of Alma-Tadema,[6] two magnificent horses go by, whose round, bulging eyes shoot out flames like the chimera's.

There is no time for anything more: not for the great painting of an organ by Lenolle, not for Marcet's Spanish ballerina, and not even for the Arab landscapes by Huguet, which are seawater, living horses, and the color of the sky, or for a most admirable creature by Renoir, which, like the eyes of Goya's maja, captures the soul.

The lesser Impressionists, with all the fury of adolescence, are a frenzy of blue, green, and violet.

—New York, May 2, 1886;
published in *La Nación* (Buenos Aires), June 19, 1886

A GREAT CONFEDERATE CELEBRATION

Tolerance in peacetime is as grand as heroism in war. The victors should not resent the tributes that are paid to the memory of the defeated side's virtues.

Any brave and brilliant act carried out by one of a nation's sons is the patrimony of the whole nation, there for it to treasure and glory in. A country must be a column of virtue, for if virtue is not the material from which it is formed or the main ingredient in its mortar, the country crumbles away like a man who loses his faith in life or a beam gnawed by insects.

The United States has just witnessed a magnificent thing in peacetime. The South, which rabidly waged a vast war to separate itself from the North, has just congregated beneath its own flag, the rebel flag, with its former leader at its head, to inaugurate monuments that commemorate the soldiers who died in battle against this nation's government and the patriarchs who led and advised those soldiers.

Never has there been a more beautiful thing. From this nation of the North there is much to fear, and much that appears to be virtue and is not, and many forms of greatness that are hollow, like statues made of sugar, but the way every man here has his own magnificent concept of freedom and manly decency, in which all stand firm and united, is very much to be admired and gives rise to spectacles of immense, virile indulgence and peaceful and radical transformation that are in all respects equal to the epic life force and marble splendor of the public grandeur of Greece.

Who does not remember the battles that held the world in suspense and were like a test of human sovereignty and of the capacity of government by the people to lead a nation and maintain its unity?

It wasn't that the South wanted to have slaves while the North was opposed to slavery; it wasn't that the patrician plantation owners of the warmer climes repudiated the laws drawn up for the whole nation by the industrial inhabitants of the Northern states; it wasn't that the South, having lost all hope of keeping the Northern Yankee, whom it despised, beneath its rule, determined, in its blind and lordly arrogance, to "subdue the beast by force" or terrify it with the threat of force—and the beast became Lincoln, and shone as if a canopy of justice were stretched across the sky from East to West; the beast became Grant, and fell upon the Confederate States like a hammer on a nail that bends and twists, or like a mountain.

No, it was that throughout the universe the half-dead caste of monarchists and adherents to tradition who do not enjoy seeing mankind evolve and assert itself, like a broad-shouldered divinity seated upon its natural throne, the earth, maintained that a country could not exist without a royal head and mysterious prestiges, nor could a nation govern itself freely without catastrophe.

And it governed itself. And it battled in a new, singular, and brutal way that corresponded to the diverse and enterprising elements of which this young country is formed. And, in victory, it forgave with a fullness and truth that no people on earth had ever before demonstrated.

Who does not remember those sanguinary battles, the chain of rivers within which the Confederacy enclosed itself, the bridges of corpses on which the victorious Union soldiers slowly crossed them, the heroic good cheer and patriarchal grandeur with which, in its unjust fight, the South defended the land and government it considered legitimately its own, and the soldiers who shone in their ragged uniforms like a banner in bright sunlight, to whom the town matrons gave, with their slender hands, the bread they had willingly kneaded in homes without fathers or sons, because the war had carried them all off.

It is the manner of dying; the proud attachment to one's native land; the mad insistence on upholding what one believes to be one's rights; the sublime simplicity in the abandonment of gifts and fortune, equaled only by the strength of the women in their misery and the bravery of the men in war; the terrible hecatomb that had to be displayed as a warning to the ages, as the sepulchre of the institution of slavery in whose defense, under guise of a political right, it was erected; the mountain of heroes who redeemed their error by the glorious tenacity with which they fought—it is all these things that the South seeks to salute in these current festivities, these cities bedecked for a holiday, these flag-lined streets, these pavements strewn with flowers, these scenes of defeat that make the eyes weep—and in the dying person of its former leader Jefferson Davis, who walks without bowing, before he dies.

Poor old man, there is more stubbornness in you than goodness! He must be very strong, for anyone who remains alive after his country has collapsed on top of him is strong. It is true that the light he now casts on the earth is rather dim; indeed, to judge by what he has said during these celebrations, he is now like an almost empty lamp that flickers back to life, its light magnified by the efforts of death, when the vision of his great cohorts or his fierce hope amid defeat stirs the air with its wings of gold or black!

What this country has calmly looked upon would, in another country, have been considered treason.

To erect a monument on the very days declared by the rebellion to be sacred to the dead rebels! To hold a great celebration in which disloyal soldiers jubilate in the cities that led the rebellion; to receive, not beneath the clear blue sky but beneath a sky crowded with treasonous flags, the man who first advocated the treason, and who presided over it, and who now amid the vapors of the tomb, raises himself upon his cane as upon a weapon of war, and with addled, senile words brandishes his treason on high as a glory!

But all of that has happened here, and the country has not been shaken by it, nor does anyone believe that the barbaric conflict will spring back to life.

Slavery was the essence of that war. And slavery no longer exists to be defended. A feeling for the South remains in those who thrilled to its victories and in their children, but the war and the reason for it are dead.

What greater punishment could there be for Jefferson Davis, who insisted upon his people's right to keep blacks in slavery, than to be received upon his arrival in Atlanta by two thousand black schoolchildren who walked along scattering flowers in front of his carriage, its wheels draped with the flags of the nation he wanted to destroy?

But this celebration was more than simply the generous tenderness of a people seeking to brighten the final days of an old man who inflamed it with his independent spirit, and has since spent his life grimly enveloped in his defeat like a standard-bearer who dies wrapped in his flag. The South's celebration has been like a rapture of many souls, like the tenderest of longings, like a great farewell, like a feast of love, in which those who are still alive wanted to see each other again, together as in their hour of glory, before leaving their uniforms behind in this world and going to join those who died for her.

"Who can think badly of us," they said, and rightly, "for honoring those who fought at our sides, in the name of an ideal that washed away with the blood from our wounds, to destroy a union that today we all uphold?"

And no one has thought badly of it. Some Republican politicians would like, in the next presidential campaign, to capitalize on the unanimous feeling with which a dignified people fearlessly honors those who died for it. For there are other nations—not as faithful or as worthy—that are ashamed to remember their dead out loud!

But not the South, and the North has bared its head in respect, and watched the bier of the war pass by, twenty-five years dead, as the honorable victor bares his head when the loser's corpse goes past. The greatest celebration was in Montgomery where Jefferson Davis, borne in triumph from his hotel to the capitol building, delivered without opposition his speech of gratitude and memory in the very spot—oh memorable moment!—where he swore, to be faithful to the constitution of the rebel states, as their president.

He was a sight to behold when he stood up to speak. The old man was trembling, as a steel blade trembles. His hair has not fallen out; its long, lank disheveled locks whip against his forehead like the shreds of a torn flag.

He looks like a man of stone, and all those around him seemed to want to make themselves small, in order to give him the consolation—which he was trying in vain to achieve on his own—of making this a great moment for himself.

He said not a word to regret his actions, acknowledge their illegitimacy, or sanction the North's victory.

He stubbornly defended the war. He vouched for the rebel movement and saluted it in the spirit of freedom he sees living on in the sons of the South.

"I will not say anything that will compromise anyone."

"Go on, old man, go on," a voice told him. "You're among friends here!"

And he spoke as if among friends, with rage and occasional outbursts of savage beauty, with a cry of love for the dead that drew tears of pity for the poor, broken man, and with sudden exclamations of invincible hatred, like a toothless and enfeebled mastiff who bares his gums at his enemy.

But he said all of this, leaning on a cane he seemed about to brandish, in the shadow of a large Federal flag beneath whose folds the rebel leaders were gathered, weaponless.

And General Gordon, who fought bravely and now wants to be governor, saluted the former days when he was a hero of the fallen Confederacy as one salutes a tomb, and proclaimed a new era of solid union in which the South loves the North, the side of Lincoln who—in answer to a man who told him, on the field of the dead at Gettysburg, "The Union that defended these heights will live on in history"—said, stretching out that hand of his which was like a blessing toward the place where the Confederate soldiers were buried, "And the Confederates who attacked them will live on in history, as well."

The emblems and colors of the Confederacy have waved in the open air, in peace.

The streets of Montgomery and Atlanta were bedlam. Parades by day; hotels by night. The entire South gathered in Montgomery.

A crippled man here, a one-armed man over there. Many gray beards and many weatherbeaten faces. Many men wore their uniforms from the war. They gathered in groups. Those who recognized each other embraced. Those who had served in the same regiment crowded, some of them weeping, beneath a window from which their regimental flag floated.

A secretary with only one leg was distributing red ribbons to the Confederate soldiers.

"I want my ribbon," said a thin old man. His voice startled the secretary, who raised his head.

"Doctor!"

"Davis!"

The brave soldier was reunited with the surgeon who amputated his leg.

One of them has an enormous mustache, because he swore never to trim it until the South won its victory, and it did not. Red ribbons are everywhere. In all the streets, not a man was alone. The ribbons seemed to whisper, agitated by the joyful emotion in those strong chests.

From the balconies of the houses Confederate flags fluttered next to national flags.

City Hall itself was bedecked; amid streamers and ensigns, banners and pennants, were the names and portraits of the Confederate heroes: "Robert E. Lee," "Stonewall Jackson," "Sidney Johnston." Large portraits of illustrious rebels lined the walls.

But atop its dome, as the last word and final standard beneath which all those in the building were united, the flag with the red stripes and white stars unfurled and waved majestically in the wind, with the air of a good mother smiling down.

—*La Nación* (Buenos Aires), July 15, 1886

THE CUTTING CASE

The following article deals with an incident along the U.S.–Mexico border that could have had serious consequences for relations between the two countries. In this account, written for a Mexico City newspaper, Martí is careful to present the actions of the American government and press in a favorable light that could allay the fears of the Mexican public. However, in an account of the same events written just three days later for La Nación, *in Buenos Aires, he was far more pessimistic: "But public opinion persists in a vague belief in the forthcoming reality of the possession of Mexico; in the public mind Mexico's current independence amounts to a mere concession that continues to be made because there hasn't yet been any need to interrupt it, but that will end as soon as is necessary. . . . Any pretext for conflict that arises between the two countries will find the border eager for war, the South prepared to assist it, the North convinced that the war must happen someday and might as well happen today, and the government obliged by diplomatic morality to seek peace but driven into war by the border's appetite for invasion, the bellicose spirit of the South, and the tacit consent of the rest of the nation. "*

The last two days have transformed the situation created by the Cutting[1] case, which now promises peace but only yesterday seemed, without the slightest exaggeration, to lead to war. Two days ago, the Republicans in the House of Representatives had not yet discovered what the whole country knows today: that the curt summary of events which the secretary of state attached to the documentation on the Cutting case that was submitted to Congress did not present the case fully and in its true light, but distorted it, and left out, as if purposely, the Mexican government's firm and prudent efforts to avoid conflict, efforts it has made without the slightest loss of dignity and without being compelled by fear of an untimely war to sacrifice the respectful relations between its federal authority and its states to the unjust demands of the United States.

Two days ago, it was believed, on the word of Secretary Bayard,[2] that the case was as he presented it, and that the entire matter stemmed exclusively from Mexico's insistence on judging by its laws and on its territory acts committed by an American citizen on U.S. territory. It seemed inexplicable, given the supreme discretion with which Mexican diplomacy has sidestepped every case of friction with the United States, that Mexico would have taken a controversy whose outcome was still pending to such an extreme that there was now virtually no way out; but no one dared doubt that this was the only point of conflict, for, in his summary of the case for the Congress, the secretary of state had said it was. This unexpected account of events poured oil on the flames kindled by the congressmen from Texas who have not yet managed to have their bellicose resolutions accepted by a Congress which this war took by surprise, and which is not, for the moment, in the mood for it. But when the secretary of state submitted to Congress the bare bones of the legal case, couched in the most inflammatory terms, from which it appeared that a foreign country was claiming to have jurisdiction over the actions of the United States on its own territory; when the wire services were transmitting the secretary's highly colored depiction of the sufferings and personal and legal violations that Cutting was enduring at Mexican hands; when, in that version of the events, it did not appear that Mexico had done all that it has in fact honorably and prudently done to resolve the conflict, nor was it clear that what the secretary was saying had not happened or had happened differently, a very serious reversal of opinion instantly occurred in the House of Representatives and in the press. Nothing could be seen but a legal case that questioned the exclusive jurisdiction of the United States over the acts of its sons within its own territory, and the Foreign Affairs Committee hastily drew up a resolution that called on the president to demand Cutting's freedom once more. And since the curt "no" that the secretary claimed was Mexico's only response seemed to indicate Mexico's decision not to heed that demand, there was unquestionably a resolute sentiment in favor of war.

But yesterday everything changed. It can be said, because it is true, that Mexico's vindication was accomplished entirely by the U.S. Congress itself. Today, the press unanimously and harshly criticized the secretary for having summed up the negotiations in a spirit that was different from the one in which they were conducted, concealing essential facts, and disregarding the legitimate reasons put forth by Mexico for not immediately attending to the petition for Cutting's freedom. And Congress, instead of approving the Foreign Relations Committee's resolution, as Congressman Belmont urged it to do on the pretext that it would please the secretary, has just declared a recess without taking it under consideration or pushing for any result or legitimizing the secretary's haste with any haste of its own. This in itself was a silent and energetic vote of censure. It seems incredible, after all the recent agitation and anger that from the first moment was vociferated in the House—which was preparing to call for Cutting's freedom—that the correspondence which was the cause of the Foreign Affairs Committee's aggressive draft resolution, on which a vote was requested, revealed precisely the opposite of what could be gathered from the secretary of state's summary of it, which was the only document known to the committee when it drew up its draft resolution. The House was surprised to hear this revelation from the mouth of one of the committee's own members. He said little and spoke sharply, like a man who has been deceived. He declared that there had been no arrogance on Mexico's part, only a constant spirit of forbearance. The case was not as the secretary described it: the issue was, rather, that Mexico, like the United States, has a federal system of government in which the federal government has limited power over the states. Thus did he depict to the representatives what had been described to them as defiance and audacity on Mexico's part. To fail to take a resolution in a case that the secretary of state depicted as so grave a question of the national honor was to send a silent message to the secretary that the Congress does not believe his allegations and is unconvinced that the nation's honor is at stake.

And it is only right to say that an important and active element in the appeasement of public opinion has been the calm and noble declarations made in Mexico to a member of the American press by the president of the Mexican Republic and Señor Romero Rubio.[3] Their words—the U.S. press declared—were suffused with a moving dignity at a time when the voice of Republican Congressman Hitt[4] still echoed, demonstrating that the federal power cannot summarily subject a state's judiciary to its will. The members of Congress gazed at each other in surprise. They left their chairs and formed groups. They stopped listening to those who were arguing that the declarations of the Republican Hitt, who wanted to discredit the secretary of state out of party loyalty, had to be met with a unanimous vote by the Democrats, as a party matter. The cloud of war was visibly dissipated by the voice of that simple man. And the sympathy for Mexico that awoke among the congressmen, who displayed the entirely natural vivacity of those who must hurry to repair the injustice they were about to commit, was reaffirmed when Hitt's statements, still warm from his lips, were corroborated by the clarity and restraint with which the case was explained in Mexico by the president and Sr. Romero Rubio. In this country, their language, which expressed neither fear nor defiance, was sincerely appreciated.

But nothing was as telling as Hitt's denunciation. "I voted for this resolution in the committee because I was assured that the causes for which it was drawn up were true: that Mexico was mistreating an American citizen, and that it refused to deliver him to us on the pretext that it had jurisdiction over our citizens on our territory. But these things are not true. Mexico has tried promptly and diligently to do what we asked it to do, and it has fully explained in these letters that it has no authority to compel a state court or a state in its proceedings. I was filled with surprise when, in this morning's newspapers, I saw the correspondence relating to these negotiations, which does not say what it has been reported to say and does say many things that have been silenced, for every word from the president and secretary of state of Mexico manifests a desire to attend to our claims. There has been no evasion on Mexico's part; there has been no defiance; it could even be said that there has been excessive forbearance."

"But, isn't Cutting in prison?" a congressman from Georgia asked him.

"Yes, he is," Hitt said quickly, "but because he wants to be, because he has disdainfully refused the freedom on bail that he was offered. That was the doing of the reckless individual who is our consul there and who goes about making speeches in the streets in vindication of our country's rights. The man we have placed in charge of our national interests there is the soul of indiscretion. He has insisted that a man who at every moment was free to leave his jail cell remain a prisoner."

Hitt faced down his other opponents with equal verve.

"Why such bravura in dealing with a country that is weaker and less populous than our own? Why so impetuous with Mexico, and so meek and compliant with England?" And the congressman who heard him conceded that he was right: because a year ago Spain was able to cast an American citizen it wanted as a soldier into a filthy provincial jail with impunity; and England, in particular, on the pretext that they are in violation of its fishing laws, captures boats and fishermen from the United States and denies them what the treaties promise them and expels them from its Canadian ports; and—what else!—to shake off its responsibility for the barbaric killings of Chinamen[5] in the Western states, whose courts do not dare punish the murderers, the United States has offered the government of China the very same explanation that the government of Mexico today gives the United States. "And we were not told that the Mexican government had given us this legitimate reason, as it now turns out that it had. Our belief that it is weaker than we are is no reason for us to treat Mexico as we dare not treat stronger nations. This case is no more than a common case of petitioning for the release of a prisoner between friendly governments. If there were truly an offense, we would certainly not deny the secretary our support. But it is in our interest, in our own nation's and that of all nations, that we preserve our peace with a country that has given us no reason to disturb it."

After this speech, which the congressmen listened to as they confirmed it by reading the correspondence it invoked, the unanimous sentiment arose that today censures the secretary for all he left out of his summary and recognizes the sincerity and skill with which Mexico handled this case. "The despatch of Mr. Mariscal, the Mexican minister of foreign affairs," says today's *Herald*, "ought to have made Mr. Bayard blush. In that despatch, which was in reply to Mr. Bayard's imperative demand for Cutting's immediate release, Mr. Mariscal, with the utmost courtesy and good temper, recites that the case is before a state tribunal; that the president has taken immediate and strong interest in it and exercised his influence that the trial shall be speedy and fair; that 'all has been done by the Mexican government that comes in the sphere of its facilities'; and he then goes on to remind Mr. Bayard that in Mexico, as in the United States, the federal power cannot give orders to a state court."

Thus does public sentiment on this matter stand today. The same sharp, revealing criticism can be read in newspapers of the most divergent views, which loudly proclaim that the president did not wish for such haste, or for any sort of violent solution, as he proved—he who is fond of sending specific messages to Congress—by remitting with only a few simple formulaic phrases the correspondence that he could have accompanied with indications and advice. The secretary is contradicted in sentences like this one: "In his unfortunate summary, Mr. Bayard dwelt strongly upon the point that Cutting was to be tried in Mexico for an offence committed in Texas. There is absolutely nothing in the despatches to prove this. It is plainly only a supposition by Mr. Bayard, which he has never, so far as the correspondence shows, taken a single step to verify." These criticisms are striking not only in their unanimity but because the newspapers and congressmen of the secretary's own party are as severe as those of the enemy party. The *Herald* is no enemy of the government, yet yesterday it said with ironic bitterness, "We advise the Texans to learn patience from our northern fishermen, many hundreds of whom have suffered graver and more galling provocations at the hands of England, without yet being assisted by a single word of advice from our State Department. The fishermen do not seem to be as favored with the friendship of Mr. Bayard as the brave Texans, but the latter's confidence in this predilection should not carry them too far, for unauthorized war has brought men to prison or the gallows before now in our country, and it would be sad were the haste of the Texans to take possession of the vineyards of

Naboth on the other side of the Río Grande to cast them into undertakings that would force the United States to use its troops against them, instead of sending them out against *those others* with whom they display such eagerness to quarrel."

Hour by hour, the telegraph has undoubtedly brought news to Mexico of the various aspects of this conflict, which seems already to have lost much of its initial seriousness. However, it is not only useful, but vital, indispensable, and of such importance that our eyes should not stray from it even for a moment, that we remain aware of every shift in United States public opinion regarding events in Mexico. By mere chance, the honor of a single man, and, perhaps, the gesture of a jealous party, a measure that was generally considered to be a precursor of war has, for now, been suspended. For in this country there exists a kind of constant preparation for war, promoted by a crude and traditional confidence; by the memory of the victory that strength and betrayal won in 1848[6] over justice and heroism; by the idleness of the warlike souls who can no longer remain at peace once they have taken up arms; by the penetrating and invasive nature of the character of man in the United States; and more than all of that, perhaps, by the ignorance in which the great majority of this country remains with respect to the originality, resilience, intelligence, hardships, strength, and hard work that make Mexico a country to be respected. Only these weapons can achieve a durable victory here; only these shields can, in the long run, protect against war. Intelligence must play its hand against strength. Because the education and practice of man in the laborious freedom of a republic cannot be entirely in vain, even amid the appetite for wealth and the corrupting egotism that mars this nation. Those who work learn to respect workers, and this country's general, offensive disdain for all that is ours arises principally from the fact that they think we are sugar-coated, vice-ridden peoples, devoid of the truly titanic force that, in enormous struggles, we have long manifested. In short, the battle that Mexico has just won was won not by intimidation or dangerous empowerments or agreements with foreign countries, but by the respect that its honor has inspired, and by the skill with which its representatives have expressed its justice.

—New York, August 6, 1886;
published in *El Partido Liberal* (Mexico City), August 20, 1886

THE POET WALT WHITMAN

"He seemed a god last night, seated in a red velvet chair, with his shock of white hair, his beard spread out on his chest, his eyebrows as thick as forests, his hand resting on his cane." This is what one of today's newspapers says of the poet Walt Whitman, now seventy years old, to whom the more profound critics—always the minority—assign an extraordinary place in the literature of his country and his time. Only the sacred books of antiquity offer a doctrine comparable in prophetic language and robust poetry to the one uttered in grandiose and priestly maxims, like sudden blasts of light, by this old poet whose staggering book is banned.[1]

And of course it was banned, for it is a book of nature. Universities and Latinists have so dislocated men that they no longer know each other: instead of throwing themselves in each other's arms, drawn by what is essential and eternal, they draw apart, heckling each other like fishwives over mere accidental differences. Like the pudding in its mold, man is formed by the book or forceful teacher that happened to come his way, or by the fashions of his time; schools, be they philosophical, religious, or literary, only straitjacket men as the livery does the lackey; men allow themselves to be branded, like horses and bulls, and go about proudly displaying their brands so that when they find themselves before a man who is naked, virginal, amorous, sincere, and powerful—a man who strides, loves, fights, rows, a man who does not let his misfortunes blind him but reads the promise of final joy in the grace and equilibrium of the world—when they find themselves before so sinewy and angelical a father as Walt Whitman, they flee as if from their own consciences and balk at recognizing the true nature of their dimmed, housebound, gimcrack species in his fragrant and superior humanity.

The newspaper says that yesterday, when that revered old man Gladstone[2] had just lectured his adversaries in Parliament on the justice of granting Ireland its own government, he looked like a bristling mastiff, upright and unrivaled amid the throng, and those at his feet were like a pack of curs. So stands Whitman, with his "natural person," his "nature without check with original energy," his "myriad youths, beautiful, gigantic," his belief that "the smallest sprout shows there is really no death," his tremendous tally of peoples and races in "Salut au Monde," his resolve that, "Knowing the perfect fitness and equanimity of things, while they discuss I am silent, and go and bathe and admire myself"; so stands Whitman who "does not say these things for a dollar," who writes, "I am satisfied—I see, dance, laugh, sing," who has "no chair, no church, no philosophy," in comparison to those scrawny philosophers and poets, philosophers of one detail or a single aspect, and book-poets, poets for hire, sugar-water poets—all the literary and philosophical dandies.

He must be studied because though he is not always in the best of taste, he is the most audacious, all-encompassing, and unencumbered poet of his time. In a window of his small wooden house, which is very humble, a portrait of Victor Hugo is on display, draped in mourning. Emerson, whose work purifies and exalts, threw an arm around his shoulder and called him his friend. Tennyson, one of those who sees the roots of things, sent tender messages to the "grand old man" from his oaken chair in England. Cries the outspoken Englishman Robert Buchanan to the North Americans, "What do you know of letters when you are letting the old age of your colossal Walt Whitman run its course without the high honors that he deserves?"

"The truth is that his poetry, though startling at first, leaves a delightful feeling of convalescence in the soul tormented by the diminishment of the universe. He creates his own grammar and logic. He reads the eye of an ox and the sap in the leaf." "That one who cleans the filth from your house, he is my brother." Whitman's apparent irregularity, initially disconcerting, soon turns out to be—but for brief moments of prodigious aberration—the same sublime order and composition as that of mountain peaks outlined against the sky.

He does not live in New York, his "beloved Manahatta," his "superb-faced . . . million-footed Manhattan," where he appears when he wants to sing "the song of what I behold, Libertad." His books and lectures barely earn him his daily bread, and he lives, watched over by "loving friends," in a little house tucked away in a pleasant corner of the countryside, from where the horses he loves take him in his old man's carriage to see the "athletic young men" at their virile diversions—the "comrades" who are not afraid to stand beside this iconoclast who wants to establish "the institution of the dear love of comrades"—and to see the flourishing fields, the friends who walk by arm in arm singing, the pairs of lovers, cheerful and lively as quail. He says in his "Calamus," the enormously strange book in which he sings the love of friends: "City of Orgies. . . . Not the pageants of you . . . Nor the processions in the streets, nor the bright windows with goods in them, Nor to converse with learned persons . . . Not those, but as I pass O Manhattan, your frequent and swift flash of eyes offering me love . . . Lovers, continual lovers, only repay me." He is like the old men he announces at the end of his forbidden *Leaves of Grass:* "I announce myriads of youths, beautiful, gigantic, sweet-blooded, I announce a race of splendid and savage old men."

He lives in the country, where the man of nature works the free earth alongside his peaceful horses and beneath the Sun that weathers him; but he does not live far from the gracious and ardent city, with its sounds of life, its mosaic of occupations, its collective epic, the dust from cart wheels, the smoke from gasping factories, the Sun that sees it all: the work-people at their meals, conversing atop piles of bricks, the swift-running ambulance that bears the hero fallen from a scaffold, the woman taken suddenly in the crowd by the august labor of maternity.[3] But yesterday, Whitman came from the country to recite, before a public of loyal friends, his prayer for that other man of nature, that great and sweet soul, the "powerful western fallen star," Abraham Lincoln. The New York literati listened in religious silence to that resplendent discourse, which, with its sudden silences, vibrant tones, hymnlike élan, and Olympian intimacy, seemed at times like the whisperings of the stars. Those raised on Latin, French, and the Academy may be unable to understand this heroic grace. The free and decorous life of mankind on a new continent has created a sane and robust philosophy that voyages out to the world in athletic stanzas. To the greatest number of free men and workers the Earth has ever seen corresponds a poetry of wholeness and faith, grave and soothing, that rises like the Sun from the sea, setting the clouds ablaze, edging the crests of the waves in fire, and rousing the nestlings and the drowsy flowers in the teeming jungles along the shore. Pollen floats on the air, beaks exchange kisses, branches unfold their leaves, which seek the Sun, and everything breathes out its own music. In a language of just such raw light did Whitman speak of Lincoln.

The mystical threnody that Whitman composed on the death of Lincoln is perhaps one of the most beautiful works of contemporary poetry. All of Nature accompanies the greatly lamented coffin as it travels to the grave. The stars foretold it. Black clouds appeared a month before. In a swamp, a gray bird sang a song of uttermost woe. Between the thought and the knowledge of death the poet journeys across the sorrowing fields, as if between two comrades. With musical art, he groups, conceals, and reproduces these sad elements into an all-encompassing crepuscular harmony. When the poem draws to a close, the whole Earth seems draped in black, covered with death from sea to sea, in the form of clouds, the drooping Moon that announces the catastrophe, and the broad wings of the gray bird. It is much more beautiful, strange, and profound than Poe's "The Raven." The poet carries a sprig of lilac to the coffin.

All of his work is embodied there.

No longer do willow trees keen over tombs: death is "the harvest," "the opener and usher to the heavenly mansion," the great revealer; what is, was, and shall be once more. All apparent oppositions and griefs are commingled in a grave and celestial spring: a bone is a flower. The sound of suns can be heard nearby, suns that with majestic movements seek their rightful place in the skies. Life is a hymn; death is a secret form of life; sweat is holy and the protozoa is holy; men should kiss one another's cheeks as they go by; all living things must join in an embrace of ineffable love; the grass, the animals, the air, the sea, sorrow, and death, all must love; suffering is attenuated when souls are possessed by love; life has no woes for he who understands its meaning in time; from the same seed spring honey, light, and kisses; in a darkness that sparkles placidly like a massive vault of stars, a vast and peaceable lilac tree rises in gentlest music above worlds that sleep like dogs at its feet.

Every society brings to literature its own form of expression, and the history of the nations can be told with greater truth by the stages of literature than by chronicles and decades. There can be no contradiction in Nature; the same human aspiration to find a perfect type of grace and beauty—in love during life, and in the unknown after death—demonstrates that the elements which seem contradictory and hostile in the portion of life we are currently passing through must, in the totality of life, join together in delight. Literature—which announces and propagates the final, joyous concordance of apparent contradictions; literature, which, as the spontaneous teaching and council of Nature, promulgates identity in a peace superior to the dogmas and rival passions that sunder the primitive nations and stain them with blood; literature, which inculcates men's fearful spirits with a conviction so rooted in definitive justice and beauty that the penuries and uglinesses of existence do not dishearten or embitter them—will not only reveal a form of society that is closer to perfection than any now known, but will also, by felicitously conjoining reason and grace, provide Humanity, ever eager for marvels and poetry, with the religion it has awaited in bewilderment since it became aware of the emptiness and insufficiency of its ancient creeds.

Who is the ignoramus who claims that poetry is not indispensable to a people? There are people whose mental sight is so poor that they take the peel for the whole fruit. Poetry, which brings together or separates, which fortifies or brings anguish, which shores up or demolishes souls, which gives or robs men of faith and vigor, is more necessary to a people than industry itself, for industry provides them with a means of subsistence, while literature gives them the desire and the strength for life. Where will a race of men go when they have lost the habit of thinking with faith about the scope and meaning of their actions? The best among them, those who consecrate Nature with their sacred desire for the future, will lose, in a sordid and painful annihilation, all stimulus to alleviate the uglinesses of humanity; and the masses, the vulgar people, the people of appetites, the common people, will profanely breed empty offspring, and will raise to the level of essential faculties those that should serve them as mere instruments, and will drown out with the loud noise of an always incomplete prosperity the irremediable affliction of the soul, which only finds pleasure in the great and the beautiful.

Liberty must be blessed, apart from all else because its enjoyment inspires modern man—deprived at its appearance of the calm, the elation, and the poetry of existence—with the supreme peace and religious well-being that the order of the world produces in those who live in the arrogance and serenity of their lineage. Look to the mountains, you poets who water the deserted altars with your puerile tears.

You thought religion lost because over your heads its form was changing. Stand up, because you are the priests. Liberty is the definitive religion, and the poetry of liberty the new form of worship. It soothes and beautifies the present, deduces and illuminates the future, and explains the ineffable purpose and seductive goodness of the Universe.

Listen to the song of this hardworking and satisfied nation; listen to Walt Whitman. The exercise of himself exalts him to majesty, tolerance exalts him to justice, and order to joy. He who lives under an autocratic creed is like an oyster in its shell, seeing only the prison that traps him and believing, in the darkness, that it is the world. Liberty gives wings to the oyster. And what seemed a prodigious battle when heard from within the shell turns out to be, in the light and open air, the natural movement of the vital fluids driven by the energetic pulse of the world.

The world, for Walt Whitman, was always as it is today. If a thing is, then it must have been, when it no longer must be it will not be. What no longer is, what cannot be seen, is proven by what is and can be seen; because everything is within everything, and one thing explains the other, and when what is now is no longer, it will be proven in its turn by what will then be. The infinitesimal collaborates toward the infinite, and all is in its place, the tortoise, the ox, and the birds—"wing'd purposes." It is just as fortunate to die as to be born, because the dead live: "No array of terms can say how much I am at peace about God and about death." He laughs at what others call disillusionment and knows the amplitude of time; he accepts time absolutely. All things are contained in him; and all of him is in everything: whoever degrades another degrades him; he is the tide, the ebb, and flow; why shouldn't he take pride in himself when he feels himself to be a living and intelligent part of Nature? Why should it bother him to return to the bosom from which he sprang and become, through the love of the humid earth, a useful vegetable, a beautiful flower? He will feed men, after having loved them. His duty is to create; the atom that creates is of divine essence; the act of creation is exquisite and sacred. Convinced of the oneness of the Universe, he sings the "Song of Myself." He weaves the song of himself from everything: the creeds that quarrel and pass away, man who labors and procreates, the animals that help him—ah! the animals, among whom "Not one is dissatisfied . . . Not one kneels to another." He sees himself as the inheritor of the Earth.

Nothing is alien to him; he considers everything: the trailing slug, the ox that gazes at him with mysterious eyes, the priest who defends a part of the truth as if it were the whole. Man must stretch out his arms and clasp all of it to his heart, virtue as well as crime, filth as well as cleanliness, ignorance as well as wisdom, all must merge in his heart as in a crucible; above all, he must let his white beard grow. But yes, "We have had ducking and deprecating about enough." Breed and add to the world instead of quarreling, he scolds the skeptics, sophists, and chatterers: believe with the ardor of the faithful who kiss the altar's steps.

He is of every cast, creed, and profession and finds justice and poetry in them all. He takes the measure of the religions without ire, but believes that the perfect religion is in Nature. Religion and life are in

Nature. If a man is sick, he tells the physician and the priest to "go home": I will embrace him, I will throw open the windows, love him, speak into his ear; you shall see how he grows well; you two are word and herb, but I can do more than you, for I am love.[4] The Creator is the "great Camerado, the lover true"; men are "comrades" and the more they believe and love the more they are worth, though everything in time and space is as good as everything else; but all must see the world for themselves, because he, Walt Whitman, who feels within himself the world from the beginning of its creation, knows, because the Sun and the open air teach him, that a sunrise shows him more than the best book. He thinks of the celestial spheres, lusts after women, feels himself possessed by universal, frenetic love, and hears, rising from the scenes of creation and the traffickings of mankind, a concert that inundates him with gladness. And when he leans over the river at the close of the workday, and the departing Sun sets fire to the water, he feels that he has an appointment with the Creator, he recognizes that man is definitively good, and sees, reflected on the swift current, fine centrifugal spokes of light radiating from his head.

But what can give you an idea of his vast and fiercely burning love? The man loves the world with the fire of Sappho. The world is, to him, a gigantic bed, and a bed, to him, is an altar: I will make illustrious, he says, the words and thoughts that men have prostituted with their secrecy and false shame: I sing and consecrate what Egypt consecrated. One of the sources of his originality is the Herculean force with which he kneels before ideas as if he were going to violate them, when he is only going to kiss them with the passion of a saint. Another is the material, brutal, and corporeal form in which he expresses his most delicate ideals. His language has struck those who are incapable of understanding its greatness as lascivious; there have been imbeciles who, with all the squeamishness of lewd schoolboys, believe they see a return to the vile lusts of Virgil for Cebes and of Horace for Gyges and Lysiscus[5] when in "Calamus" he celebrates the love of friends with the most ardent images in human language. And when he sings the divine sin, in "The Sons of Adam," in tableaux that make the most heated passages of the Song of Songs pale by comparison, he trembles, shrivels, overflows, and expands, mad with pride and sated virility; he is like the god of the Amazon who crossed forests and rivers scattering the seeds of life and saying "my duty is to create"! "I sing the body electric," he says in "Children of Adam"; and one must have read the patriarchal genealogies of Genesis in Hebrew or followed naked and carnivorous bands of primitive men through the untracked jungle to find anything resembling the ·Satanic force with which, like a ravenous hero licking his bleeding lips, he describes the attributes of the female body. And you say the man is brutal? Listen to "Beautiful Women," which, like many of his poems, has only two lines: "Women sit or move to and fro, some old, some young. The young are beautiful—but the old are more beautiful than the young." Another one is titled "Mother and Babe": He sees the child who sleeps nestling in its mother's lap. The mother is sleeping, and the child: Hush! He studies them long and long. He foresees that just as virility and tenderness are conjoined to a high degree in men of superior genius, the two energies that have had to be divided from each other in order to perpetuate the task of creation must come together with a jubilant solemnity worthy of the Universe.

If he goes into the grass, he says the grass caresses him, that he feels its soft patting. The most restless monastic novice could not find words as vehement as his to describe the happiness of his body, which he sees as a part of his soul, in the embrace of the sea. All that·lives loves him: the Earth, the night, and the sea love him: "You sea ... Dash me with amorous wet." He offers himself to the winds like a tremulous bridegroom. He wants to unscrew the locks from the doors, he wants bodies in their natural beauty; he believes he sanctifies all that he touches or that touches him and he finds virtue in all that is bodily; he is "Walt Whitman, a kosmos, of Manhattan the son, Turbulent, fleshy, sensual, eating, drinking and breeding, no stander above men and women or apart from them." He depicts truth as a frenetic mistress who invades his body in her eagerness to possess him and frees him of his clothes. But when, on the clear midnight, his soul, free of books and pursuits, emerges whole, silent, and contemplative from the nobly occupied day, it meditates on the subjects that most please it: the night, sleep, death, the song the Universe sings for the benefit of the common man, and on how "to die is different from what any one supposed, and luckier"—to fall at the foot of the primeval tree, ax in hand, bitten by the forest's last serpent.

Imagine the strange new effect produced by this language swollen with animal pride when he celebrates the passion that unites men. In one of the "Calamus" poems, he recalls the most vivid delights that he owes to Nature and to his patria, but finds only the waves of the sea worthy of chorusing his joy when in the moonlight he sees his friend lie sleeping by him. He loves the humble, the fallen, the wounded, even the wicked. He does not disdain the great, but for him only those who are useful are great. He throws his arm around the shoulder of trolley conductors, merchantmen, laborers. He hunts and fishes with them, and at harvest climbs with them to the top of the loaded wagon. More beautiful than a triumphant emperor to him is the vigorous Negro who, one leg poised on the stringpiece, riding behind his Percherons, guides his wagon serenely through the commotion of Broadway. He understands all virtues, receives all rewards, works at all trades, suffers from all pains. He feels a heroic pleasure when he pauses at the door of a blacksmith's and sees the youths, with their bare chests, rolling their hammers over their heads, each man hitting in his place. He is the slave, the prisoner, the one who fights, the one who falls, the beggar. When the slave arrives at his door, pursued and sweating, he fills the bathtub for him and seats him at the table, a loaded firelock in the corner to defend him with. If they come to attack him, he will kill the pursuer and sit back down at the table, as if he had killed a viper!

So, Walt Whitman is satisfied: what pride could prick him when he knows he will reach his end as grass or flower? What pride does a carnation have, a sage leaf, a honeysuckle? Why shouldn't he observe human suffering calmly, since he knows that beyond it is an endless being for whom a joyous immersion in Nature awaits? What haste can drive him on, when he believes that all is where it should be, and that the will of a man must not turn the world from its path? He suffers; yes, he suffers; but he looks upon that which suffers inside him as a minor and short-lived being, and feels, beyond the weariness and misery, another being who cannot suffer because he knows the greatness of the Universe. It is enough for him to be what he is, and impassive and content he watches the obscure or acclaimed course of his life. With a single gesture he tosses the romantic lament aside, as a useless excrescence: I need "Not ask . . . the sky to come down to my goodwill." And what majesty there is in his declaration of love for animals because "they do not sweat and whine about their condition." The truth is that there are too many instillers of cowardice: the world must be seen as it is, and ants must not be made into mountains. Give men strength, instead of robbing them with lamentations of the little strength sorrow has left them, for do the wounded go through the streets showing off their wounds? Neither doubt nor science troubles him. To scientists he says, "Gentlemen, to you the first honors always! Your facts are useful, and yet they are not my dwelling, I but enter by them to an area of my dwelling." "How beggarly appear arguments before a defiant deed!" "Lo! keen-eyed towering science . . . Yet again, lo! the soul, above all science." But where his philosophy has entirely overcome hatred, as the magi command, is in the line, not entirely free of the melancholy of defeat, which uproots any and all reason for envy: why would I be jealous, he asks, of one among my brothers who does what I cannot do? "He that by me spreads a wider breast than my own, proves the width of my own." "Let the Sun interpenetrate the Earth until it all be sweet and pure light, like my blood! Let the rejoicing be universal. I sing the eternity of existence, the happiness of our life and the beauty beyond change of the Universe. My signs are the calfskin shoe, the open collar and a staff cut from the woods."

And he says all of this in apocalyptic sentences. Rhyme? Meter? Oh, no! His rhythm lies in the linkage of his strophes, in the apparent chaos of convulsive phrases, superimposed into a skillful composition that distributes ideas into large musical groups—the natural poetic form of a people that does not build stone by stone, but with enormous blocks.

The language of Walt Whitman, entirely different from that which poets before him have used, corresponds in its strangeness and power to his cyclical poetry and to the new humanity which has congregated upon this fecund continent with such portents that in truth neither lyres nor dainty quatrains could contain them. This is no longer a matter of hidden loves, of ladies who choose one gallant over another, of cowardly discretion, or of the sterile complaint of one who lacks energy enough to master life. It is not a matter of trilling rhymes and bedchamber sighs, but of the birth of an era, the dawn of the definitive religion, the renewal of mankind, the faith that must replace that which has died and surge with radiant brightness from the arrogant peace of a redeemed mankind. It is a matter of writing the sacred books of a people that, at the fall of the old world, joins all the virgin forces of liberty to the great bosom and cyclopean splendors of savage Nature; a matter of finding the words to echo the sound of the settlement of great masses of people, the cities at their work, the tamed seas and the enslaved rivers. Will Walt Whitman yoke consonants together and in meek couplets harness these mountains of merchandise, forests of thorns, towns of ships, combats in which millions of men fall so that right may prevail, and the Sun that rules over all and streams in limpid fire across the vast landscape?

Oh, no! Walt Whitman speaks in verses that have no apparent music, though after listening for a while one can make out the sound of the surface of the Earth when triumphant armies are marching across it, barefoot and glorious. At times Whitman's language is like the entrance to a butcher's shop, hung with sides of beef; at other times it seems a song of patriarchs seated together in the soft sadness of the world at the hour when smoke curls up and is lost among the clouds; then again it sounds like a rough kiss, like a rape, like the snap of dry leather cracking in the Sun. But his lines never lose the rhythmic motion of the waves. He himself says he speaks in "prophetic screams"; these, he says, are "one or two indicative words for the future." His poetry is a pointing finger; a sense of universal things pervades the book and endows its superficial confusion with majestic regularity. His disjointed, lacerating, fragmented, drifting words do not express but emanate: "The white-topped mountains point up in the distance ... I fling out my fancies toward them"; "Earth! ... Say, old top-knot, what do you want?"; "I sound my barbaric yawp over the rooftops of the world."

No, he is not one of those who sends an impoverished thought tripping and dragging along beneath the ostentatious opulence of its regal garments. He does not inflate sparrows until they look like eagles; each time he opens his fist he casts forth forty eagles, like a sower sowing seeds. One line has five syllables, the following line forty, and the one after that ten. He does not force his comparisons, in fact he does not compare, but says what he sees or remembers graphically and incisively. Assured in his mastery of the impression of unity he sets out to create, he uses his artistry, which is entirely hidden, to reproduce the elements of his picture in the same disorder he observed in Nature. Though he raves, he never strikes a wrong note, because the mind does wander thus, without order or slavishness, from one matter to its analogies; but then, as if he had only let the reins go slack for a moment without letting go of them, he suddenly gathers them in and steadies the team of bucking horses with a horsebreaker's fist, and his lines go at a gallop as if they were swallowing up the Earth with every movement. At times they let out anxious whinnyings, like heavy-laden stallions; at other times, white and foaming, they set their hooves upon the clouds; or they plunge down into the Earth, black and daring, and the sound of them echoes long after. He sketches, but as if with fire. In five lines he gathers up all the horrors of war, like a bundle of recently gnawed bones. He needs only a single adverb to slow down or compress a sentence, and only one adjective to transfigure it. His method must be grand, for its effect is grand; but it may also be that he has no method, particularly in his selection of words, which he mixes with unheard-of audacity, placing august, almost divine words beside words thought inappropriate or indecent. Certain images are not painted in adjectives—which, in his work are always lively and profound—but in sounds, which he arranges and disperses with the utmost skill, thus using a change in technique to sustain the interest that might be lost by the monotony of a single mode. He uses repetition to summon up melancholy, like the savages. His unexpected, jolting caesura shifts constantly, not abiding by any rule whatsoever, though a knowing order can be discerned in its patterns, pauses, and breaks. Accumulation strikes him as the best sort of description, and instead of adopting the pedestrian form of argument or the high-sounding form of oratory, his reasonings emerge from the mystery of insinuation, the fervor of certainty, and the fiery whirlwind of prophecy. Certain words of our own language can be found on every page in his book: *viva, camarada, libertad, americanos.* And what better demonstration of his character than the French terms that, with evident bliss, he embeds in his lines, as if to expand their meaning: *ami, exalté, accoucheur, nonchalant, ensemble. Ensemble,* above all, seduces him because in it he sees the sky that looms above the life of nations and of worlds. From Italian he has taken one word: *bravura!*

In this celebration of muscle and audacity, inviting passersby to place their hands on him without fear, listening to the song of things, his palms outspread, discovering gigantic fecundities and proclaiming them in delight, gathering up seeds, battles, and orbs in epic verses, showing the astonished ages the radiant beehives of men that spread out over the American valleys and summits and brush the hem of vigilant Liberty's skirt with their bee-wings, shepherding the friendly centuries toward the final pasture of eternal calm, Walt Whitman—as his friends pour him champagne and serve him the first fish of spring on rustic tablecloths—having revealed to the world a sincere, loving, and resonant man, awaits the happy hour when material existence withdraws from him and, abandoned to the purifying air, he becomes blossom and fragrance on its swells: "disembodied, triumphant, dead."

—New York, April 19, 1887;
published in *La Nación* (Buenos Aires), June 26, 1887

CLASS WAR IN CHICAGO: A TERRIBLE DRAMA

On May 4, 1886, a dynamite bomb was thrown in Chicago's Haymarket Square and several policemen were killed. Eight anarchists were tried for the bombing, and seven were condemned to death, though the evidence linking them to it was scant and dubious. On November 11, 1887, four of them were executed.

In an article on the trial written for La Nación *in September 1886, Martí expressed little or no sympathy for the anarchists and no doubt at all about their guilt. He went so far as to claim that the death penalty itself was the most certain guarantor of that guilt, since the jury, allegedly threatened by anarchists still at large, imposed it at the risk of their own lives. ("If the evidence were not absolute, the jury would take advantage of that to avoid incurring the anarchists' wrath.") When he wrote this article a year later, his attitude, his account of the events, and his description of the anarchists had changed significantly.*

Neither fear of social justice nor blind sympathy for those who seek to achieve it should guide the nations through their crises or the narrator of those crises. Even at the risk of being taken for its enemy, the worthy servant of liberty preserves it steadfastly from those whose errors endanger it. No one who excuses its vices and crimes out of womanish fear of seeming halfhearted in its support deserves to be called a defender of liberty. Nor is forgiveness deserved by those who, unable to overcome the hatred and bitterness that any crime arouses, judge a class-motivated crime without knowing or weighing the historical causes it was born from or the generous impulses that gave rise to it.

In solemn procession, their coffins covered with flowers and the faces of their followers with grief, the four anarchists that Chicago sentenced to die by hanging have just been taken to their graves, along with the one who, to escape from the gallows, set off a dynamite bomb inside his own body, a bomb he had hidden in the thick, silken curls of his young golden-brown hair.

They were accused of having masterminded or been accomplices in the horrible death of one of the policemen who were breaking up an assembly gathered to protest the police's killing of six workmen during an attack on the only factory still in operation during a strike. They were accused of having manufactured and conspired to throw— though not of actually having thrown—the bomb the size of an orange that mowed down the front ranks of the police, leaving one dead on the spot and six more dead soon after, and doing serious injury to fifty others. The judge, in compliance with the jury's verdict, sentenced one of the defendants to fifteen years' imprisonment and the other seven to death by hanging.

Never since the South's war and the tragic days when John Brown died as a criminal for having attempted alone at Harpers Ferry what the whole nation, incited by his brave spirit, then attempted as its crown of glory, has a gallows awoken such clamorous interest in the United States.

The entire republic has fought with wolflike fury to ensure that the efforts of a benevolent lawyer, a young girl who is in love with one of the accused, and an Indian and Spanish mestiza who is the wife of an-other do not—alone against the wrathful nation—wrest from the gal-lows the seven human bodies deemed essential to its sustenance.

Alarmed by the growing power of the lower orders and the sudden accord among the working masses, which are held in check only by the rivalries between their leaders, on an impending demarcation of the na-tion's populace into the two classes—the privileged and the discon-tented—that convulse the societies of Europe, the republic resolved, in a tacit pact much resembling complicity, to take advantage of a crime that was born as much from its own transgressions as from the fanati-cism of the criminals, and to make an example of them that would strike fear not only into the wretched rabble that can never triumph in a country of reason but also into the tremendous nascent strata. In this trial that has been a battle, an ill-won and hypocritical battle, the free man's natural horror of crime along with the brute malevolence of the despotic Irishman, who sees this country as his own and the German and Slav as invaders, has placed on the side of the privileged classes the sympathies and almost inhuman assistance of those who endure the same woes, the same helplessness, the same brutal labor, and the same piercing misery that so inflamed the Chicago anarchists with eagerness to remedy it that their judgment was beclouded.

Not until the carpenter was assembling the gibbet did the petition-ers come, some out of shame and others fearful of some barbaric vengeance, to ask for clemency from the state's governor, a spiritless old man given over to the supplications and flattery of the rich who were begging him to save the society from this menace even at the risk of his own life.

Before that—except for those hired to defend them and their natural friends for whom, under the pretext of a single concrete accusation that was never proven and the additional pretext that they had attempted to establish a reign of terror, they died, the victims of class terror—only three voices had dared to intercede: Howells, the Boston novelist whose display of generosity cost him friends and reputation; Adler, a prudent and vigorous thinker who glimpses the new world in the pangs of our century; and Train, a crank who spends his life in the public squares giving bread to birds and talking to children.[1]

Already they have died, draped in white shrouds, revolving through the air in a horrible dance.

Already—though it has not meant that there is more fire in the stoves or bread in the cupboards or greater justice in the distribution of wealth or stronger safeguards to ensure that working people do not go hungry or more light and hope in the shanties or balm for all that seethes and suffers—a walnut coffin has taken in the ill-assorted fragments of a man who, in the belief that he was giving a sublime example of love to all humanity, blew his life away with the weapon he thought had been revealed to redeem it. This republic, in its excessive worship of wealth, has fallen, without any of the restraints of tradition, into the inequality, injustice, and violence of the monarchies.

In the United States, the European workers' revolutionary theories were like drops of blood washed away by the sea when, surrounded by a vast land and a republican way of life, the new arrival earned his bread and set something aside for his old age in his own home.

But then came the corrupting war, the habit of authority and domination that is its bitter aftertaste, the credit that precipitated the rise of colossal fortunes, the tumultuous wave of immigrants, and the idle former combatants who are always prepared, out of self-interest and the fatal rapacity of those who have had their first smell of blood, to serve the impure interests that the war begat.

From a wondrous, peaceful village, the republic was transformed into a monarchy in disguise.

With rekindled wrath, the European immigrants denounced the evils they thought they had left behind in their tyrannical birthplaces. The rancor of the native-born workers at seeing themselves victims of the avarice and inequality of the feudal nations also burst forth, but with a greater faith in liberty, which they hoped to see triumph in the social sphere as it triumphs in the political one.

Since the people of this country are accustomed to winning without bloodshed by the force of the vote, they neither understand nor excuse those born in regions where suffrage is an instrument of tyranny, who see in its slow workings only a new aspect of the abuse that their thinkers rail at, their heroes defy, and their poets curse. For a long while, essential differences in political practice and the discord and rivalry between the races that are battling each other for supremacy in this part of the continent hindered the formation of a powerful workers' party with unanimous methods and goals. But the identical nature of their afflictions was spurring those who endured them to concerted action, and now this horrendous act—however much it was a natural consequence of the passions that had been ignited—has been necessary to make those who spring with invincible impetus from the same wretchedness interrupt their task of uprooting and overhauling, while the bloody measures taken out of senseless love for justice by those who have lost their faith in liberty are condemned as ineffective.

In the newborn West, fewer restraints are placed on the new elements by the ruling influence of Eastern society, which, as its literature and habits reflect, is older. The more rudimentary way of life promotes intimate contact between men, who, in the larger, more cultured Eastern cities, are wearier and more dispersed. The West's astonishing rate of growth itself, accumulating palaces and factories on one side and the miserable multitude on the other, displays in broad daylight the iniquity of a system that punishes the hardest workers with hunger, the most generous with persecution, and the laboring father with the poverty of his children. In the West, where needy workers gather with their wives and offspring to read the books that teach the causes of and propose the remedies for their misfortunes; where, justified in their own eyes by the success of their majestic factories, the owners, poised on the precipice of their own prosperity, push the unjust methods and harsh treatment on which that prosperity is anchored to an extreme; where the working masses are kept in ferment by the German yeast that flees from the imperial country, intelligent and persecuted, disgorging Heine's three terrible curses over their wicked patria—in the West, and in Chicago, its metropolis, above all, the discontent of the working masses, the fiery admonitions of their friends, and the ire kindled by their masters' arrogant severity found vehement expression.

And since everything tends simultaneously toward the great and the small, as water changes from sea to mist and then from mist to sea, the problem of humanity, condensed in Chicago by the forbearance of its free institutions, was—even as it infused the republic and the world with fear or hope—transformed by events in the city and the passions of its men into a bitter and raging local problem.

Hatred of injustice became hatred of its representatives.

The fury of centuries, corrosive and consuming as lava, inherited by men who in the fervor of their compassion saw themselves as sacred beings, was focused—further stimulated by personal resentments—on those individuals who persisted in the abuses that engendered it. Once set in motion, the mind does not stop; once it has flared up, pain sears; once they have erupted, words can no longer be controlled; once put on display, vanity entrains all behind it; once set in action, hope ends in triumph or catastrophe. "For the revolutionary," said Saint-Just, "there is no rest but the tomb!"

Is there anyone who deals in ideas but does not know that the harmony among them all, in which love takes precedence over passion, hardly reveals itself even to the finest minds who sit at the summit of time and warm their hands over the sun while they watch the world seethe? Is there anyone who deals with men and does not know that there is more flesh in them than light and that they hardly know what they grope, hardly glimpse more than the surface of things, but see little more than what hurts them or what they want, barely conceiving of anything but the wind that gusts against their faces and the apparent but not always effective means of removing the obstacle currently barring the way to their hatred, pride, or appetite? Is there anyone who suffers from the woes of humankind and does not feel his reasoning mind grow incensed and lose its bearings, however much in check he keeps it, when he sees nearby—as if he were slapped or pelted with mud, as if his hands were stained with blood—one of those dire social miseries that may well drive those who must watch their wives and children rotting away within it to perpetual madness?

Once the disease is recognized, the generous spirit goes forth in search of a remedy; once all peaceful measures have been exhausted, the generous spirit, upon which the pain of others works like a worm in an open wound, turns to the remedy of violence.

Wasn't it Desmoulins who said, "As long as one embraces liberty, what matter if it be upon a mountain of corpses?"

Blinded by generosity, addled by vanity, drunk on their own popu-

larity, driven to dementia by constant offenses, by their apparent powerlessness in the electoral struggles, and by the hope of being able to
found their ideal nation in this newly settled territory, the keen minds
at the head of this angry mass, educated in lands where the vote is still
in its cradle, do not step back from the present moment, do not dare
appear weak to their followers, do not see that in this free country the
only obstacle to a sincerely desired social change is disunity among
those who demand it, do not believe—tired as they are of suffering,
and with a vision of the universal phalanstery in their heads—that justice can ever triumph in this world by peaceful means.

They reason like cornered animals. All that grows seems to them to
be growing against them. "My daughter works fifteen hours to earn fifteen cents." "I had no work this winter because I belong to the union."

The judge sentences them.

The police, in the pride of their broadcloth uniforms and their authority, which inspires fear in the ignorant, beat and murder them.

They are cold and hungry; they live in reeking shacks.

America, then, is the same as Europe!

They do not understand that they are only a wheel in the social
mechanism and that in order for them to change the whole mechanism
must be changed. The wild boar that is being hunted down does not
hear the music of the glad air or the song of the universe or the stately
dance of the cosmic scheme of things: the wild boar braces its
haunches against a dark tree trunk, sinks its tusk into its pursuer's
belly, and rips out his innards.

Where will the exhausted masses, whose sufferings increase daily,
find the divine state of greatness to which the thinker must ascend to
overcome the rage kindled by needless misery? All conceivable measures have already been attempted. It is the reign of terror depicted by
Carlyle, "Man's dismal and desperate battle against his condition and
all that surrounds him."

And just as human life is concentrated in the spinal cord and the life
of the earth in the volcanic masses, there arise from these multitudes
beings, standing tall and spewing fire, in whom all of their horror, despair, and tears seem to converge.

From hell they come: what language would they speak but the language of hell?

Their speeches, even when read in silence, send off sparks, billowing smoke, half-digested meals, reddish fumes.

This world is horrible: let us create another one! Amid thunder, as on Mount Sinai; from an ocean of blood, as in 1793. "Better to blow up ten men with dynamite than kill ten men by slow starvation as they do in the factories!"

Montezuma's decree is heard once more: "The gods are thirsty!"

A handsome youth, who had his portrait drawn with clouds behind his head and the sun on his shoulder, sits down at a table to write, surrounded by bombs, crosses his legs, lights a cigarette, and like a man fitting together the wooden parts of a dollhouse, explains the just world that will flourish upon the earth when the explosion of the class revolution in Chicago, symbol of the universal oppression, smashes it into atoms.

But it was all words, backstreet meetings, drilling with weapons in some cellar, three rival newspapers circulating among two thousand desperate readers and announcing the latest methods of killing—and those who permitted that, boastful of their liberty, are more guilty than those who, out of violent generosity, exercised their right!

Wherever the workers displayed the strongest will to improve their lot, their employers displayed the strongest resolve to resist them.

The worker believes he has the right to a certain degree of security for the future, a certain repose and cleanliness in his home, the right not to worry about feeding the children he fathers and to a fairer share in the profits from the work in which he is an indispensable part, the right to a place to live that is not a fetid and sickening slum like those in urban New York, and to an hour or two of sunlight in which to help his wife plant a rosebush in the yard. And every time the Chicago workers asked for these things in any way, the capitalists joined forces, punished them by denying them the work that is their meat, fire, and light, and called out the police, who are always eager to give their billy clubs free rein on the heads of ragged people. Sometimes the police would kill a child, or a man who dared to resist them by throwing a stone. And in the end hunger drove the workers back to work, their decency offended, their souls grim, their poverty festering, plotting revenge.

With only a few followers to listen to them, the anarchists went on meeting year after year, organized into groups, each of which had an armed wing. In their three newspapers of varying stripes, they publically advocated class war and declared war in the name of humanity on the existing society. They decided that no radical transformation could be achieved by peaceful means; they recommended the use of dynamite, holy weapon of the disinherited, and instructed their readers on how to make it.

Not in treacherous shadow but in the very faces of those they considered their enemies they proclaimed themselves free and rebellious; they acknowledged that they were at war to emancipate mankind; they blessed the discovery of a substance that by its singular power would be an instant equalizer of the opposing forces and thereby prevent bloodshed, and they promoted the study and manufacture of this new weapon with all the chilling horror and diabolical calm of an ordinary treatise on ballistics. When one reads these instructions, one sees bone white circles in a sea of billowing smoke; a fiend enters the darkening room and gnaws on a human rib and sharpens its fingernails. To measure the depth of man's despair, one must judge whether the terror that he usually plans out in tranquillity is greater than the other one against which, with the furor of centuries, he rises up in outrage—one must live in exile from one's patria or from humanity.

On Sundays, Albert Parsons, the American, whose socialist friends once nominated him for the presidency of the republic, and who believed in humanity as his only God, would gather his followers together to fire their souls with the valor they needed for their defense. He spoke in fits and starts, in whiplashes, in knife thrusts; his blazing oratory took him far from himself.

After him, his wife, the impassioned mestiza into whose heart the miseries of working people fell like daggers, would often burst forth into transports of discourse, and they say that never was the torment of the abject classes depicted with such flaming and rough-hewn eloquence, her eyes bolts of lightning, her words shrapnel, her two fists clenched, and then suddenly, in describing the woes of a poor mother, the sweetest of tones and long, trickling tears.

August Spies, the editor of the *Arbeiter-Zeitung*, wrote as if from his deathbed with a chill like that of the tomb: he set forth a rational basis for anarchy, depicting it as the desirable gateway to a life truly free. For seven years he explained its fundamentals in his daily newspaper, and then the need for revolution, and finally, like Parsons in *The Alarm*, the way of organizing to make it victorious.

Reading him is like stepping down onto empty space. What has happened to the revolving planet?

Spies walks in all serenity where a more solid intellect senses that he has no footing. He pares down his style as if he were cutting a diamond. This somber Narcissus is astonished and well pleased with his own greatness. Tomorrow, a poor girl will give him her life, a girl who clings to the bars of his prison cell as the Christian martyr clung to the cross, and he will let only a few cold words fall from his lips—for remember that Jesus, busy redeeming mankind, did not love Mary Magdalene.

When Spies stripped off the frock coat he wore so well to deliver a tirade to the workers, it was not a man who spoke but the howling of a storm, distant and foreboding. He was word without flesh. He bent his body toward his listeners like a tree doubled over in a hurricane and a cold wind seemed to rush from among branches and pass over his listeners' heads.

He thrust his hand into those rebellious, hirsute chests; he squeezed out, brandished before them and made them smell their own entrails. When the police had just killed a striker in a skirmish, he would clamber onto the wagon that is the shaky pulpit of revolutions with ashen face, and under that grim provocation his dry words would soon flash and give off heat like a quiver of flaming arrows. Then he would walk away alone down dark streets.

George Engel, ever envious of Spies, fought to place anarchism in a state of constant readiness for war, with himself at the head of a brigade, himself wherever men were being taught to load a rifle or aim for the heart, himself in the cellars during the nights of training "for when the great hour comes," himself, in his *Anarchist* and his conversations, accusing Spies of being lukewarm, jealous of Spies's mind: he alone was pure, immaculate, worthy to be heard. Anarchy, which without further ado gives all men equal ownership in everything, is the only good thing: the world is a spinning top and he—he is its handle. Of course the world would rise and stand tall, like the spinning top, "once the workers develop some shame"!

He went from group to group; he attended the Social Revolutionary Congress, made up of delegates from all the groups. He accused the Congress of cowardice and treachery because it did not, "with us, these eighty of us alone," proclaim the true revolution, the one Parsons wanted, the one that would call dynamite a "sublime substance" and tell the workers to "go and take whatever you need from the stores on State Street for the stores and everything in them are yours." Engels is a member of the "Lehr-und-Wehr-Verein," to which Spies also belongs, since a brutal police attack that felled many workers drove them, as brutal attacks always do, to take up arms and defend themselves, to exchange ideas and newspapers for Springfield rifles. Like his own rotund body, Engel was the sun: the "great rebel," the "autonomous one."

And Louis Lingg? He did not squander his virile beauty on the enervating love affairs that often drain a man during the glorious years of his youth. Instead, raised in a German city by an invalid father and a starving mother, he came to know life in a place where the generous soul is justified in hating it. His father was a longshoreman, his mother a laundress, and he was as beautiful as Tannhäuser or Lohengrin, a body of pure silver, eyes of love, a wealth of curling golden-brown hair. But what good was his beauty when the world was horrible? He found the history of the working class in his own history, and when the first peach fuzz sprouted on his upper lip he was already learning to make bombs. The infamy has spread to the very marrow of the globe so the explosion must reach to the sky!

He had just arrived from Germany and was about to turn twenty-two; what for other men were words, would, in him, be actions. He and he alone built bombs for—with the exception of individuals like him, driven by blind force—man is a creating being who only finds it natural to kill when he must save himself from death.

And while Michael Schwab, brought up reading the poets, helps Spies to write, and Samuel Fielden, the powerful orator, goes from town to town uplifting men's souls in the knowledge of the coming reform, while Adolphe Fischer gives encouragement and Oscar Neebe organizes, Lingg, in a secret room with four companions, one of whom would betray him, makes bombs, just as Johann Most[2] bids in his *Revolutionary War Science*. With a cloth tied over his mouth, as Spies recommended in *The Alarm*, he stuffs the deadly sphere with dynamite, covers the opening with a lid through which runs the fuse that ends at the detonator inside, and awaits the hour, his arms crossed.

Thus the forces of anarchy advanced in Chicago, with such sluggishness, envy, and internal discord, such conflicting opinions as to the right moment for the cherished rebellion and such a scant supply of their terrible devices of war and of the savage artisans prepared to manufacture them that anarchy was no more than the slatternly mistress of a few inflamed hearts, its only certain power the furor aroused by class disdain, at a moment of extremity, in the masses who reject anarchy. The worker, who is a man and has his aspirations, resists with all the wisdom of nature the idea of a world wherein man is annihilated. But when he and his companions are shot down in wholesale numbers for having asked for one hour of freedom in which to see their children by the light of day, and he rises from the fatal puddle and pushes his bloodied locks like two red curtains back from his forehead, then the dream of death spawned by a tragic group of compassionate madmen unfolds its smoking wings and wheels over the unhappy mob with a shrieking corpse in its claws, casting the light of a hellish dawn into their baleful hearts and enveloping their desperate souls in black billows of smoke.

The law protected them, didn't it? The press, inflaming them with its hatred instead of calming them with justice, was taking their story to the world, wasn't it? Their own newspapers, whose indignation was aggravated by contempt and whose daring grew with impunity, circulated freely, didn't they? Well then, since it was clear that they were living beneath an abject despotism, what else could they do but their duty, as set forth in the Declaration of Independence, and overthrow it to replace it with a free alliance of communities that exchange equivalent products among themselves, govern themselves without war by mutual agreement, and educate themselves by scientific methods without distinction of race, creed, or gender? Wasn't the whole nation rising up alongside them, like a herd of sleeping elephants, with the same pain, the same outcries? Wasn't the plausible threat of violence a likely if dangerous means of obtaining through intimidation what the law did not achieve? And those ideas of theirs, which always waned when the privileged classes showed them any cordiality, but were quickly exchanged for rifles and dynamite when they were provoked—weren't those ideas born out of the purest compassion, exalted into lunacy by the sight of irremediable misery and sanctified by the hope of just and sublime times to come? Hadn't Parsons, the evangelist of universal jubilation, been nominated for the presidency of the republic? Hadn't Spies been a candidate for Congress, running on their platform? Didn't the political parties solicit their votes by offering to respect the dissemination of their doctrines? How were they to believe that words and acts that the law permitted were criminal? And wasn't it the bloodfests of the police—drunk on the executioner's wine, like all plebeians vested with authority—that decided the bravest among them to take up arms?

Lingg, the recent arrival, hated Spies—the man of ideas, irresolute and morose—with all the obstinacy of a novice; Spies, the philosopher of systems, dominated him by that same superiority of mind. But the art and grandeur that culture requires even for its works of destruction aroused the ill will of the handful of irreconcilables who saw their proper leader in Engel, who, in turn, was enamored of Lingg. Engel, pleased to see himself at war with the universe, measured his own valor by his adversary's.

Parsons, jealous of Engel, whose passion was as great as his own, joins with Spies, the hero of words and friend of letters. Fielden, still attached to the patria that his system forbade him to love, believed—watching the mounting rage of the common man in London, his city—that by promoting anarchy in America he would be assisting the difficult triumph of the disinherited in England. Engel: "The hour has come!" Spies: "Has that terrible hour come?" Lingg, mixing clay and nitroglycerin with a stick: "When I'm done with my bombs, then you'll see whether the hour has come!" Fielden, who has watched the working class arising battered and fearsome from one coast of the United States to the other, determined to demand as proof of its power that the workday be reduced to eight hours, visits all the groups that until then had been united only in their hatred of industrial oppression and of the police who hunt them down and kill them, and repeats: "Yes, my friends, if they won't let us see our children by daylight, the hour has come."

Then came the spring, ever a friend to the poor. Without fear of the cold, in the strength born of sunlight, hoping to allay the first hunger pangs with their savings from the winter, a million workers across the republic resolved to demand that the factories comply with the routinely flouted law that the workday not exceed the eight legally permitted hours.[3] If you want to know whether the demand was fair, come here: watch them going back like flogged oxen to their squalid dwellings with the night already dark around them; watch them come from those distant slums, their shoulders shivering, the women unkempt and ashen, when the sun itself has not risen from its repose.

In Chicago, sore and quick-tempered, their guns at the ready, sure of the resistance that their arrogance provoked, the police, in the urgency of hatred rather than the measured calm of the law, summoned the workers to a duel.

The workers, determined to defend their rights by the legal measure of a strike, turned their backs on the macabre orators of anarchism and on those, bruised by billy clubs or pierced by police bullets, who decided, with their hands covering their wounds, to meet the next attack blow for blow.

March came. The factories threw out the workers who came to present their demand as if they were mangy dogs to be kicked into the street. As the Knights of Labor had ordained, the workers all left the factories together. Pork rotted without meat packers to wrap it; restless cattle lowed, neglected in their corrals; the grain elevators that stand guard over the river like a row of giants loomed mute, in terrible silence. But in that muffled calm, like the triumphant banner of the industrial power that wins every battle in the end, there rose from the McCormick Reaper plant, filled with workers whose poverty forced them to serve as weapons against their brothers, a trail of smoke, stretching, twisting, and coiling in on itself like a black snake against the blue sky.

After three days of rage, the road to the McCormick plant, Black Road, began to fill one gloomy afternoon with furious workers who strode up it, their jackets on their shoulders, shaking their clenched fists at the thread of smoke—for isn't it true that by some mysterious decree man always goes toward the place where danger awaits him and seems to delight in foraging for his own misery? "There stood the insolent factory that, to defeat the workers who are fighting against hunger and cold, is employing those who themselves are the desperate victims of hunger. Will this battle for bread and coal in which the worker's own brothers are raised up against him by the force of evil itself never end? Is it not the world's battle, in which those who build must triumph over those who exploit? We want to see which side these traitors are truly on!" And as many as eight thousand of them had come, while evening began to fall, sitting in groups on the bare rocks, walking in single file along the winding road, pointing angrily at the miserable shanties that stand out like the marks of leprosy against the harsh landscape.

The invective of the orators, speaking from atop the rocks, shakes these listeners who have sparks in their eyes and trembling chins. This orator is a teamster; that one a foundryman or a bricklayer. The smoke from the McCormick smokestacks spirals over the plant: the close of the workday is at hand. "Let's see how those traitors look at us!" "Get that speaker down, down: he's a socialist!"

And the speaker, who, from deep in those maddened hearts, is pulling forth, as if with his own hands, their most secret afflictions, exhorting these anxious parents to resist until they prevail, even if their children ask them for bread in vain, for the lasting benefit of all children—the speaker is Spies. First they walk away, then they surround him, then they look at each other, recognize themselves in that implacable portrait, give it their approval, and applaud him: "This one, he knows how to talk; let him talk to the factories in our name!" But the workers have already heard the bell that marks the end of the workday: what does it matter what Spies is saying? They pull all the paving stones up from the road and run to the factory: its windowpanes crash into shards! The policeman who stands in their way is pushed to the ground! "Those are the ones, pale as dead men, the ones who collaborate in the oppression of their brothers for a day's wages!" Stones! The workers inside the plant, huddled in a tower in fear, look like ghosts. A patrol wagon comes up the road vomiting gunfire under a frantic hail of stones; one policeman empties out his revolver from the footboard and another from the coach box, while those crouched inside fire their guns to open a path through the crowd of angry workmen, many of whom are thrown down and trampled by the horses. The police leap down from the wagon, assume battle formation, and charge, firing their guns into the throng, which defends itself with stones and a few wild shots. When the crowd hemmed in by the patrol wagons that descend upon it from across the city finally scatters to take refuge in its own neighborhoods—but not to sleep, for the wrath of the women rivals that of the men—the workers bury six corpses in secret, so that their enemy will not triumph once more.

Can't you see the emotion boiling in all those hearts? The gathering of the anarchists? Spies writing a burning account of the events in his *Arbeiter-Zeitung*? Engel demanding a proclamation that the hour has finally come? Lingg, who'd had his head clubbed by the police months earlier, placing his live bombs in a leather trunk? The hatred generated by police brutality mounting even higher with this new blind attack? "Workingmen to Arms!" says Spies in a scorching circular everyone reads with a shudder. "To arms against those who murder you for exercising your rights as men!" "We will meet tomorrow"—the anarchists agree—"and in a way and a place where it will cost them dearly if they attack us!" "Spies, put *ruhe* ('quiet') in your *Arbeiter; ruhe* means that all of us must go armed." And from the *Arbeiter* presses came a circular that invited the workers to gather in Haymarket Square, with the mayor's permission, to protest the killings by the police.

Fifty thousand workers gathered with their wives and children to hear those who offered to give voice to their pain. This time the speaker's platform was not in the open center of the square, but in a corner that branched into two narrow, dark streets. Spies, who had insisted that the words "Workingmen Arm Yourselves and Appear in Full Force" be removed from the poster announcing the event, spoke of the grave offense with caustic eloquence, not in a way that would make his listeners lose their senses, but trying instead, with remarkable mildness, to fortify their spirits for the necessary reforms. "Is this Germany or Russia or Spain?" asked Spies. During the minutes when the mayor put in an appearance at the meeting without interrupting it, Parsons—constrained by the gravity of the occasion and the vastness of the audience—read out one of the editorials he had published with impunity a hundred times. And just when Fielden, in a fierce outburst, was asking whether, since they are prepared to die, it is not just as well to fall defending themselves against the enemy as to die in brutal toil—turmoil breaks out in the crowd. A force of 180 policemen is coming up the street, guns drawn. They reach the platform and order the crowd to disperse. The workers are in no hurry to withdraw. "Why, Captain, this is a peaceable meeting. What have we done to disturb the peace?" asks Fielden, jumping off the speaker's wagon. The police open fire.

Then, arcing over their heads, a trail of red fire wound its way through the air. The earth shakes; the projectile makes a hole four feet deep; the policemen in the two front lines fall bellowing to the ground in a heap; the screams of a dying man rip the air. The police react with superhuman valor, they jump over their companions, aiming a running fire of bullets at the workers who resist them. "We fled without firing a shot!" say some. "We barely tried to resist," say others. "They were firing straight at us," say the police. A few seconds later there was nothing in that lugubrious corner but stretchers, gunpowder, and smoke. Once more the workers hid their dead in closets and cellars. As for the policemen, one dies at the square; another's wound is so big he has his whole hand inside it, and pulls it out only to send his last breath to his wife. Another, still standing, is lacerated from head to toe: the fragments of the dynamite bomb have sliced through his flesh like chisels.

How to portray the terror of Chicago and of the republic? Spies is seen as a Robespierre, Engel as Marat, Parsons as Danton. What? Even worse: these are the wild beasts, the Tinvilles, Henriots, and Chaumettes,[4] who want to pour the old world down a gutter of blood and fertilize the earth with living flesh. Their pursuers chase them with nooses, just as they chased a policeman yesterday. Wherever they appear they are met with gunfire, just as their wives met the "traitors" with rotten eggs yesterday! Isn't it said—though it isn't true—that their cellars are filled with bombs? Isn't it said—though this isn't true, either—that the workers' wives, real Furies, are melting down lead just as the women of Paris scraped walls to get the lime they needed to make gunpowder for their husbands? Destroy this worm that is eating away at us! There they are, like the rioters of the Terror, attacking the shop of a pharmacist who told the police where they were meeting, smashing his flasks and then dying in the street like dogs, poisoned by colchydium wine. Off with any head that appears! To the gibbet with all who speak and think!

Spies, Schwab, and Fischer are taken prisoner at the newspaper offices, where the police find a letter from Johann Most, the letter of a creeping, slobbering toad, in which he treats Spies as an intimate friend and mentions bombs—"the medicine"—and a rival of his, the great Paulus, "who goes to wallow in the bogs of Schevitsch's dog of a newspaper."[5] Fielden is dragged from his home, wounded. Engel and Neebe are taken from their homes as well, and Lingg from his cellar. He sees the police come in; a revolver is thrust against his chest and a policeman throws his arms around him; then the policeman and Lingg, who curses and swears, roll on the floor in their struggle, rising and falling in that wretched burrow full of nuts and bolts, carpenter's gouges and bombs, breaking the legs off the tables and the backs off the chairs. Lingg has almost strangled his adversary when another policeman falls on him and chokes him. And this youth who wants to eviscerate English law does not even speak English! Three hundred prisoners in a single day. The nation is aghast, the jails are full.

And the trial? All of the foregoing could be proved, but not that the eight anarchists accused of murdering Police Officer Degan had planned or even covered up a conspiracy that ended in his death. The witnesses were the police themselves and four anarchists who had been paid off, one of them a confessed perjurer. Lingg, whose bombs were similar to the Haymarket bomb, was found during the trial to have been far away at the time of the catastrophe. Parsons, happy with his speech, was watching the crowd from a neighboring house. It was the perjurer who claimed—though he later recanted—that he saw Spies strike the match that lit the bomb's fuse; that Lingg and another man had carried the leather trunk to a corner near the square; that on the night of the six deaths at the McCormick Reaper Works, the anarchists had agreed, at Engel's request, to take up arms and resist future attacks and to publish the word *ruhe* in the *Arbeiter;* that Spies was, for a minute, in the room where that agreement was made; that in his office there were bombs; and that in a house somewhere there were stacks of "handbooks of revolutionary warfare."

What was indeed proven beyond a doubt and agreed upon by all the contradictory witnesses was that the man who threw the bomb was a stranger. What did indeed take place was that Parsons, the beloved brother of a noble Southern general, presented himself in court one day of his own free will, to share in the fate of his companions. What is truly moving is the unhappiness of the loyal Nina Van Zandt who, captivated by Spies's handsome arrogance and humanitarian dogma, offered to be his bride at the threshold of death and, on the arm of her mother, whose family is a distinguished one, married the absent prisoner with her brother as his proxy, and then, day after day, brought books, flowers, and the consolation of her love to the bars of his cell, paid out of her own savings for her husband's short and haughty autobiography to be published in order to raise money for the defense, and went to beg on her knees at the governor's feet. What is undoubtedly awe-inspiring is the tempestuous eloquence of the mestiza Lucy Parsons, who crossed the United States, thrown out of one place, booed and hissed or jailed somewhere else, today followed by weeping workers, tomorrow by cruel packs of small boys or country people who chase her away as if she were a witch, all for the purpose of "picturing to the world the horrible conditions endured by the luckless members of society, a thousand times worse than the means proposed for putting an end to their sufferings."

And the trial? Under a special charge of conspiracy to commit homicide (which was by no means proven), seven of the anarchists were sentenced to death by hanging, and Neebe to imprisonment, for having explained, in print and in speech, doctrines whose dissemination is permitted by law. In New York, a case of direct incitement to rebellion was punished with twelve months in jail and a fine of $250.

When punishing a crime, even a proven crime, who could fail to take into account the circumstances that gave rise to it, the passions that mitigate it, and the motive for which it was committed? Nations, like doctors, should seek first to prevent the disease or cure its root causes, rather than allowing it to flourish with full-blown vigor, only then to combat by bloody and desperate means the sickness for whose progress they are to be blamed.

But these seven men must not die. The year passes. The State Supreme Court, in a ruling unworthy of the situation, upholds the death sentence. What happens then? For Chicago, out of remorse or fear, asks for clemency as ardently as it once demanded punishment. Workers' guilds from across the republic finally send their representatives to Chicago to intercede on behalf of those who are guilty of having loved the workers' cause to excess. The nation's clamorous hatred is equaled by the drive for compassion led by those who have witnessed the cruelty that provoked the crime.

Every newspaper from San Francisco to New York misrepresents the trial, depicting the seven accused men as noxious beasts, putting the image of the policemen ripped apart by the bomb on every breakfast table, describing their empty homes, their golden-haired children, their grieving widows. What is the old governor who does not confirm the sentence doing? If the police see that their enemies are pardoned and thus emboldened to carry out more crimes, then who will defend us when the working-class monster rises up tomorrow? What an act of ingratitude toward the police it would be not to kill these men! "No!" a police chief shouts at Nina Van Zandt, who goes with her mother to ask him for a signature for clemency, unable to speak for weeping. And not one hand takes from the poor, deathly pale creature the petition that she presents to them one by one!

Will the pleas of Felix Adler, the recommendations of the state judges, the magisterial speech in which Trumbull[6] demonstrated the cruel stupidity of the trial all be in vain? The jail is in ferment; packed trains come and go from the city; Spies, Fielden, and Schwab have, at their lawyers' behest, signed a letter to the governor in which they assure him they have never resorted to force. The others do not sign it; the others write bold letters to the governor: "Give me liberty or give me death, I am not afraid!" Will the cynical Spies, the implacable Engel, the diabolical Parsons be saved? Fielden and Schwab might be saved because the trial had little to say about them; they are old, and the governor, who is old, too, feels for them.

A long procession of defense lawyers, representatives of workers' guilds, and mothers, wives, and sisters of the prisoners goes to beg the governor, in audiences punctuated by sobs, for their lives. There, in that hour of truth, the hollowness of rhetorical eloquence was apparent! Sentences, in the face of death! "Sir," says one workman, "will you condemn seven anarchists to die because one anarchist threw a bomb at the police, when the courts have not wished to convict the Pinkertons because one of them shot and killed a working-class child without provocation?" Yes, the governor will condemn them: the entire republic demands that he condemn them as an example. Yesterday the guards found four pipe bombs in Lingg's cell; who put them there? Does that ferocious soul want to die amid the ruins of the jail, symbol, in his eyes, of all the world's evil? Whose life will Governor Oglesby spare in the end?

It won't be Lingg, from whose cell, shaken by a sudden explosion, winds a thread of blue smoke as if from a cigarette. Lingg is stretched out there, blown apart but still alive, his face a puddle of blood, his two eyes wide open amid a red pulp. He had hidden a capsule of dynamite in his luxuriant hair; he put it between his teeth and lit the fuse with a candle, and it blew off his jaw. They drag him brutally to hurl him into a bathtub; when the water washes away the coagulated blood, his shattered larynx can be seen between the shreds of dangling flesh, and rivulets of blood flow among the ringlets of his hair like the wellsprings of a fountain. And yet he wrote! He asked them to help him sit up! And he died within six hours. By that time Fielden and Schwab had received their pardons,[7] and now convinced of their men's unhappy fate, the women, the sublime women, were knocking for the last time at those barbaric doors, not with flowers and fruit as in the days of hope, but pale as ashes!

First comes Fischer's wife: death is visible on her white lips!

She waited for him without weeping, but will he emerge alive from that terrible embrace? Thus, thus does the soul leave the body! He murmurs lullingly to her, pouring sweetness into her ears, pulls her to his chest, kisses her mouth, her neck, her shoulder. "Good-bye!" He puts her away from him and moves off with firm steps, head lowered, arms crossed.

And Engel, how does he take his daughter's last visit? It left neither of them dead; does that mean they did not love each other? Oh yes, he loves her. Those who led Engel away by the arm tremble at the memory of the tearful light in his last gaze, as if he were suddenly growing tall in his shackles.

"Good-bye, my son!" says Spies's mother, stretching her arms toward him as she was dragged away from her choking son. "Oh, Nina, Nina!" Spies exclaims, holding for the first and last time his widow who was never his wife, and at the edge of death she seems to bloom, swaying like a flower, shedding her petals like a flower in the terrible joy of that revered kiss.

No, she cannot be said to swoon. Instead, in her sudden knowledge of the full force of life and the beauty of death, she passes like an Ophelia come back to her senses, a living hyacinth, between the prison guards who hold their hands out to her respectfully. And Lucy Parsons was not allowed to say good-bye to her husband because, her children in her arms, she demanded to see him with all the raging heat of a funeral pyre.

And now the night is well on its way; the greenish walls of the prison corridor are in darkness, and above the footsteps of the guards with their rifles on their shoulders, above the voices and laughter of the jailers and writers, mingled with the occasional jingling of keys, above the chatter of the telegraph that the *New York Sun* set up right there in the corridor—which meandered endlessly on, scolding and ranting, imitating with its skull's teeth all the inflections of a human voice—above the silence that overhung all these noises, the final taps of the carpenter's hammer on the gallows being erected at the end of that corridor could be heard. "Oh, the ropes are good, all right; the guard tested them!" "The executioner, hidden in a compartment down below, will pull the cord attached to a hinge on the trapdoor." "The trapdoor is solid, about ten feet off the ground." "No, the lumber used for the gallows isn't new: it's been given a fresh coat of tan paint so it will look good for the occasion; everything has to be done decently, very decently." "Yes, the militia is standing by; no one will be allowed to come near the jail." "Lingg certainly was handsome!" Laughter, tobacco, brandy, smoke that makes the unsleeping prisoners cough in their cells. In the dense, humid air, the electric lights sputter, balk, blink off. A cat sits motionless on the railing above the cellblock, watching the scaffold. . . . Then all at once a melodious voice full of strength and meaning, the voice of one of the men who are supposed to be wild beasts in human form, rose from Engel's cell, first tremulous, then vibrant and pure. In a transport of ecstasy, he was reciting Heinrich Heine's "The Weaver,"[8] his arms held high, as if offering his spirit to the skies.

Eyes dry, woeful and burning,
teeth clenched,
the weaver sits at his loom.
Old Germany, your mourning garb we craft!
Three curses into the cloth we weave.
Weave on, weave on, oh weaver!

A curse on the false God, beseeched in vain,
in wintry tyranny,
his worker's brawn consumed by hunger!
In vain the weeping and the hope!
War and vengeance upon this God who mocked us.
Weave on, weave on, oh weaver!

A curse on the false king of powerful men
whose haughty breast
our mortal anguish did not move.
He wrests from us our final cent
then makes us die like dogs!
Weave on, weave on, oh weaver!

A curse on the false State where public shame,
vast and measureless,
flourishes and spreads like ivy;
where the flower is battered by the storm,
and the worm feeds on rot!
Weave on, weave on, oh weaver!

Roll on, roll on, O my cloth, without fear!
Roll on, night and day,
accursed land, land without honor!
With firm hand we craft your mourning garb:
three times we weave the curse, three.
Weave on, weave on, oh weaver!

Bursting into sobs, Engel slumps down on his cot, plunging his aged face into the palms of his hands. The whole prison has listened, mute, some in an attitude of prayer, the prisoners leaning against the heavy bars, the writers and guards shaken to the core, the telegraph operator suspended over his machine, Spies half-sitting, Parsons upright in his cell with his arms wide open like a man about to take flight.

Daylight found Engel talking to his guards with all the volubility of a condemned man about curious incidents in his life as a conspirator; it found Spies strengthened by a long sleep and Fischer unhurriedly donning the clothes he had taken off at the beginning of the night in order to rest better, while Parsons, his lips ceaselessly moving, threw his clothes on after a short and hysterical sleep.

"Fischer, how can you be so calm when the sheriff who has to give the signal for your death is circling his office like a wild animal, red-faced from holding back the tears!"

"Because," Fischer answers, clamping a hand on the guard's trembling arm and looking him full in the eyes, "I believe my death will help the cause I espoused when my life began, and I love the cause of the working man more than my own life—and because my sentence is unfair, illegal, and unjust!"

"But Engel, it's eight in the morning now, with only two hours to go before you die, and it is clear in the kind look on every face, the affection in every greeting, the cat's mournful mewing, the faltering voices and feet, that they think your blood is turning to ice. How can you keep from trembling, Engel!"

"Tremble because I've been defeated by those I sought to defeat? This world does not seem just to me, and I have battled long to create a just world, and now go on battling with my death. What does it matter to me that my death is a judicial murder? Does it befit a man who has embraced a cause as glorious as ours to seek to live when he can die for it? No, Sheriff, I want no drugs: I want port wine!" And one after another he drains three glasses. . . .

Spies—his legs crossed just as they used to be when he was depicting for his *Arbeiter-Zeitung* the joyous flame- and bone-colored universe that would succeed this civilization of bailiffs and mastiffs—writes long letters, calmly rereads them, slowly places them in their envelopes, and from time to time puts down his pen, lies back in his chair, and blows great puffs and smoke rings into the air, like any German student: oh patria, root of life, like light and air you aid and comfort by a thousand subtle means even those who deny you out of a vaster love for humanity! "Yes, Sheriff," says Spies, "I will have a glass of Rhine wine!"

And when the silence grew anguished, in that moment when, at executions as at banquets, everyone stops talking at once as if before a solemn apparition, Fischer, Fischer the German, his face lit up with a glad smile, broke into the stanzas of "La Marseillaise," which he sang with his head raised toward the sky. . . . Parsons measures his cell in long strides: an enormous audience is before him, an audience of angels who rise in splendor out of the mists and offer him the fiery mantle of the prophet Elijah so that he can blaze across the world like a purifying star. He stretches out his hands as if to accept the gift, he turns toward the cell's bars as if to proclaim his victory to his killers, he gesticulates, argues, shakes his raised fist, and all the seething words die on his lips like waves that mingle and perish on the shifting sands.

The sun was pouring its fire into the cells of three of the prisoners who seemed, between those somber walls, like the men of the Bible who walked through flames unharmed, when a sudden noise, quick footsteps, an ominous mutter of voices, the appearance of the sheriff and his deputies on the other side of the bars, and the blood-red color that for no visible cause ignited the atmosphere, announce the news they hear impassively: the hour has come!

They emerge from their cells into the narrow corridor: All right? "All right!" They shake each other's hands, smile, grow taller. "Let's go." The prison physician had given them stimulants; new clothes were brought for Spies and Fischer; Engel doesn't want to take off his woolen slippers. The sentence is read aloud to each one in his cell, their hands are fastened behind their backs with silver-plated handcuffs, their arms are bound against their bodies with leather belts, white shrouds like the tunics of neophyte Christians are thrown over their heads, and all the while, down below, the audience sits in rows of chairs facing the gallows, as if in a theater. Now they are coming along the corridor from the cells, the gibbet looming at the end. The sheriff goes first, very pale; a deputy walks beside each prisoner. Spies paces with grave steps, his blue eyes lacerating, his hair carefully combed back, white as his shroud, his forehead magnificent. Fischer follows, robust and powerful, his vigorous blood throbbing in his throat, the strength of his limbs underscored by the graveclothes. Engel walks behind him, for all the world like a man going to a friend's house, kicking away the uncomfortable hangman's robes with his heels. Parsons, fierce and determined, as if not dying were what he feared, brings up the rear with energetic footsteps. The corridor ends and they step onto the trapdoor: the dangling nooses, the bristling heads, the four shrouds.

Spies's face is a prayer; Fischer's is steadfastness itself; Parsons's radiant pride; Engel ducks his head and makes his deputy laugh with a joke. Each one in turn has his legs bound with a strap. Then hoods are flung over the four heads like candlesnuffers putting out four flames: first Spies, then Fischer, then Engel, then Parsons. And while his companions' heads are being covered, Spies's voice rings out in a tone that strikes deep into the flesh of all who hear it: "The time will come when our silence will be more powerful than the voices you are throttling today." "This is the happiest moment of my life," Fischer says, while the deputy is attending to Engel. "Hurray for anarchy!" says Engel, who, beneath the graveclothes, was moving his bound hands toward the sheriff. "Will I be allowed to speak, O men of America . . ." Parsons begins. A signal, a sound, the trapdoor gives way, the four bodies drop simultaneously, circling and knocking against each other. Parsons has died in the fall; one quick turn, and he stops. Fischer swings, shuddering, tries to work his neck free of the knot, extends his legs, draws them in, and dies. Engel rocks in his floating hangman's robes, his chest rising and falling like the swell of the sea, and strangles. Spies dangles, twisting in a horrible dance like a sackful of grimaces, doubles up and heaves himself to one side, banging his knees against his forehead, lifts one leg, kicks out with both, shakes his arms, beating against the air, and finally expires, his broken neck bent forward, his head saluting the spectators.

And two days later—two days of terrible scenes in the executed men's homes, an endless procession of weeping friends filing past the grimly bruised corpses, mourning crepe hanging beneath a red silk flower in a thousand doorways, and crowds gathering respectfully to place wreaths and roses at the feet of the coffins—a stunned Chicago watched as, behind a band that played funeral marches with a mad soldier waving an American flag defiantly at its head, Spies's coffin went by, buried in garlands, and after it Parsons's, which was black, with fourteen artisans walking behind it carrying symbolic flowers, Fischer's, adorned with a colossal wreath of lilies and pinks, Engel's and Lingg's, draped with red flags, and the carriages of the widows who were swathed from head to toe in mourning veils, followed by workingmen's associations, guilds, *vereins,* singing societies, delegations, a company of three hundred women in black armbands, and six thousand bereaved workers with bared heads, wearing the scarlet rose on their chests.

Then, surrounded by twenty-five thousand sympathetic souls beneath the sunless sky that crowns those barren planes, Captain Black, the pale defense lawyer, spoke from the cemetery mound, dressed in black, his hand stretched over the corpses: "What is the truth?" he said amid a silence so absolute that the sobs of the grieving women and others in the crowd could be heard. "Since Jesus of Nazareth brought it to the world, what is the truth that a man cannot know it until he lifts it in his arms and pays for it with his death? These men are not despised felons, thirsty for disorder, blood, and violence, but men who have tried to bring peace, men of gracious tenderness of heart, loved by those who knew them, trusted by those who came to understand the loyalty and purity of their lives. Their anarchy was government by order, not by force, their dream a new world without misery or slavery, their sorrow the belief that selfishness will never yield to justice by peaceful means. Oh cross of Nazareth which for these corpses was a gibbet!"

From the gloom that enveloped the onlookers as the five executed men were lowered from the pine platform into their graves rose a voice that seemed to emerge from a heavy beard and a grave and bitter heart. "I have not come to accuse that hangman they call a sheriff, or the nation that has been thanking God in its churches today for these men's death on the gallows: I have come to accuse the workers of Chicago who have permitted five of their noblest friends to be executed!" Nightfall and the defense lawyer's hand on that unquiet shoulder dispersed the funeral-goers and their shouts of agreement; the flowers, the flags, the dead, and the grieving were all lost in the same darkness; the noise of the multitude going back to their homes came from afar like the sound of breaking waves. And the evening edition of the *Arbeiter-Zeitung*, which the eager crowd read on its return to the city, said, "We have lost a battle, unhappy friends, but we will see a just world order in the end; let us be wise as serpents, and harmless as doves!"

—November 13, 1887;
published in *La Nación* (Buenos Aires), January 1, 1888

A WALKING MARATHON

"Guerrero, the Mexican: Guerrero takes the lead!" No sooner do the newsboys utter the cry than *La Nación*, which loves those of its own blood, goes forth to ascertain whether it is true that in a test of physical endurance, a race whose participants have six days and nights to walk six hundred miles, the Scotsman, the Irishman, the Englishman, the German, the Austrian, and the Arab have all fallen behind a slender boy who laps up the miles at the pace of an Indian, or like a giant in seven-league boots: Guerrero the Mexican.

The race has just ended. Guerrero was not the victor, though he was in the lead for a while. Over the course of those six days, with blood gushing from his nose, he walked 574 miles; out of 67 competitors, the Mexican came in third.

Only Albert, the winner, brawny and agile as Peleus,[1] could stand up to his dauntless pace and heroic endurance. There go the two of them, shoulder to shoulder, moments before completing the final lap amid cheering and waving flags.

Albert, a Philadelphian, wears nothing but a knitted garment of the sort worn by gymnasts with a black velvet belt; he has walked 622 miles and could walk 622 more; his steps are short, quick, sure-footed; his complexion betrays no sign of fatigue; his hair is impeccably groomed by his wife, who looks after him, and as a talisman, he clutches an ebony rod, as Mercury clutched his caduceus; his eye sparkles.

And there goes Guerrero. He does not walk as Hercules did when he rushed out, wearing nothing but his own skin, to conquer the crown of olive leaves; nor does he wear a woolen shirt as Hipomenes did when he competed with mortal Atalanta for the prize of her hand in marriage; nor, like the swift Pan-Puk at the wedding of Hiawatha, does he wear a shirt and deerskin breeches trimmed with colorful wampum beads and a headdress of swan feathers; Guerrero is a dandy—though a dandy of the Bowery—and he is as careful of his good looks as of his speed: he wears a cloth hunting jacket, gaiters, knee breeches, and a jockey-style cap. His quick pace makes the luxuriant blue silk scarf—which a lady admirer untied from around her own neck to give him—trail floating behind him. That isn't a step, it's a glide: two of Albert's footsteps could fit into every one of Guerrero's. He seems not to set foot on the ground, but to fly: his mustache is black, his face broad and sensitive, and he is cross-eyed; one eye looks back as he walks forward, as though spies or serpents were pursuing him.

The music bursts forth! Which of the two will be first around the track? In his sculptural beauty, Albert is like the heroes of the ancient Olympic Games, and Guerrero is reminiscent of the Danes who slide over snowy fields like human ships, a candle upon their shoulders.

Now they're approaching, now they're here: Guerrero triumphs. Guerrero is the one going at the same mad dash that once beat a California horse, bounding rather than running over the sawdust, with two American flags at his shoulders like two wings!

Yes, but what of the wretches who, in bestial struggle for a percentage of the box office, push themselves on, hour after hour, mile after mile, unsteady, expiring, sick to their stomachs, the whites pale, the Negroes ashen, the mulatto greenish, one of them gnawing a rib as he walks, another groping at the air, another doubled over, spitting, almost licking the sawdust, another pitching headlong onto the track, unconscious.

The crowd that fills Madison Square Garden consists of ruffians who are there to place bets, slatternly women who are there to be seen and for love for whatever excites their impure flesh, one or two curious onlookers, attracted by the charm of tenacity in any type of victory, pickpockets and policemen; only people like these could, out of morbid curiosity or eagerness to see their favorite win, calmly watch these competitions, which are arranged by professional gamblers. The temptation of money or eagerness for fame, which is more necessary here than in any other country, attracts rude, ridiculous, or energetic people to participate in these odious exercises, which in no way enhance the utility, grace, or knowledge of mankind. But yes, Guerrero was beautiful, beautiful as a deer! And yes, Albert was beautiful, as a horse!

From one Saturday midnight to the following Saturday midnight the lights in the Garden stay on; in the afternoon or early evening, or after the theaters and balls are over, the curious come in for a few moments. Stretched out on the benches or sleeping sheltered by their hat brims, with their boots on the railing and their hands in their pockets, gamblers, tipplers, vagabonds who have no better bed, and imbeciles who have been drawn in by the terrible and monotonous competition spend the cold hours before dawn there while the wretched walkers make their way around the track.

That wan hour is when the scene can best be appreciated in all its nakedness. No luxuriously clad women of ill repute are showing off their hired lovers, sealskin coats, and gems in the front rows of the stands. No strutting masters of the art of gambling, clean-shaven and gleaming, are rivaling their rented beauties in the pomp of their overcoats and the size of their jewels. There is no music to enliven with its sparkle and crash the deathly footsteps of the hobbling walkers. None of the individuals who "put money down," as they would on a horse, are stimulating their man with the gift of a cane, a bouquet of flowers, a heart woven of hyacinths and carnations, a gold watch, a banknote, or the thing that seems most effective at reviving their flagging spirits: a letter from a woman who, truly or falsely, expresses her love for the man who evinces virile grace or extraordinary tenacity in this competition. Even the most unfortunate of them, those whom the music cannot reanimate and whose dragging footsteps and lumpen bodies are jeered by the crowd, break into a run with no thought for the gnawing in their bellies or their lacerated feet when they receive a letter or bouquet from a woman.

The only thing that the stench and iniquity of this dawn can properly be compared to is the substance left behind by a sick dog! The journalists from the daily papers, sleepy in their great cage, take note of how often the diabolically ugly Austrian—who is fast asleep as he walks—falls exhausted to the ground to rise again without the aid of a pitying hand; how one of the walkers is dragged unconscious to his box; how the sound of his retching announces the passage of the Scotsman, who is practically walking on his knees; how, with his arms over their shoulders so he won't slip to the ground, two solicitous relatives bear an agonized walker away. The scorekeepers, high on their platform, huddled up in their greatcoats and blowing on their stiff fingers, keep track of the number of laps with big, movable numbers made of white porcelain on black wood.

In the boxes, which are illuminated with clinical clarity by electric lights, Albert's wife, in diamonds and a sealskin coat, waits for her husband to take a cup of gelatin or a glass of iced tea from her hands as he goes by without stopping. The fiancée of Strokel, the Austrian, peers out from between the muslin drapes at her door to give an encouraging look to the poor ugly man who entered the competition in order to win a little money to start their home with. The trainers, egged on by the gamblers, pummel away at a poor walker who goes like a dog, his mouth foaming and his bones sticking out through his shirt, to seek the sleep that those barbarians would deny him. The police, alerted in time, arrest a rogue who had stolen into a deserted box to slip a powder into a walker's drink in order to make him fall ill and lose.

Full of rinds, cigarette butts, empty kegs, and red-shirted ruffians, the Garden reeks! The women stay up all night with their men. The walkers, eyes glassy or half-closed, cover lap after lap, slumping, drained, the skin of their bellies clinging to their breastbones, their white socks like two bones below their coats.

Let's go and have a look at the Garden on the last day of the competition. The air is rank with smoke from bad tobacco. Only with great difficulty can the spectator make his way through the crowd packed around the track, which is still of interest because, though the three victors have already walked five hundred and twenty-five miles, those who haven't yet collapsed—the ten men left standing out of the original field of sixty-seven—are still fighting to complete that distance, which will entitle them to a share of the box office. "Not one member of the New York underworld is missing," a policeman says. "That one there with curly hair and a cigar drooping from his mouth is the most successful pimp in New York; the gentleman going by over there, the one who's now drinking the cider that the vendor dressed as a clown gave him, is the greatest cardsharp in the nation and the king of swindlers; the one who looks like a church pastor is a bank robber, and the lady who's with him is another." Fashionable gentlemen, foreigners, and a few curious ladies stroll through the bluish, fetid air of the Garden, which is full of refreshment stands and advertisements, while, as the race draws to a close, the walkers, most of their entertainment value gone, take their final laps around the track—some looking as if these will be the last laps of their lives.

Let's be sure our coats are buttoned up tight and make our way through the crowd. That man there is Albert, who came in first: he's holding his head high and his triumphant face shows no sign of sleepiness or fatigue. He has slept three hours a day; gelatin has been his food and champagne his drink; he leaps like a buck: no sooner has he disappeared down one end of the track than he can be seen coming back around the other, waving a flag, or reading a telegram, or walking with the cane an admirer gave him, or picking out an Irish tango on the banjo his wife hangs around his neck as the ladies of old hung their colors on a triumphal knight.

The man in second place, dressed in red, is Herty, the Englishman, a groom: bowlegged, hirsute, and sweaty, with drooping shoulders and the murky gaze of an ox.

Guerrero follows, his steps so long and elastic that his two capitalist business partners—Brodie,[2] the news vendor who dived into the river from atop the Brooklyn Bridge, and Dillon, a famous boxer, who not long ago killed his opponent with a single punch—have to trot alongside while they converse with him.

Strokel, the Austrian, who has only a mile left to go, passes by, dead on his feet, his head turning on his shoulders like a doll's; he moves his hands the way a fish moves its fins and his rebelling tendons stand out from his neck; his legs have shriveled up beneath his pants; the muscles of his face are twitching in a mad dance; he is tortured with exhaustion, but at the door of his box is his fiancée, who has faithfully tended to him for six days!

Noremac, the Scotsman, still remarkably vigorous at the end of the competition, astonishes the audience by bursting out of his limping pace into a flat-out dash when, seeing him coming around the bend, the band breaks into a military march and the public into applause. His face has the sickly pink color of those whose hearts will no longer obey them; he has the halo of mortality that religious artists paint on crucifixes; he drags along his swollen feet as if they were nailed down.

Behind comes Moore, the Irishman: his enormous nose, dripping with sweat, towers between his fleshless cheeks and below his reddish eyes; he passes his hand over his shaven skull with the anguished gesture of a monkey.

Hart, the Haitian Negro, a great walker, has lost all the gallantry that made him famous and passes by humiliated, shrunken, deprecated, misshapen.

Stont, the Arab, comes after him, gigantic and impossible to miss, enveloped in his coat, his arms like wooden beams, his eyes like glowing embers, his colossal feet, which neither threats nor jeers can quicken to a more philosophical pace, wrapped in rags.

The man following Stont has to be, and is, a Yankee: Tailor, a weather-beaten old man with a Celtic head; his gray beard falls on his chest; he doesn't wear leather slippers like the others, but only socks; and instead of shorts he is wearing long pants held up by blue suspenders over a cotton shirt with red letters on it. He goes by like bad luck, like the night, like destiny; he does not lift his eyes from the ground and neither slows nor quickens his pace! Lanky and sad, he disappears around the curving track.

And the wretch who is coming along now is the last one, Filly, the parson; the public salutes his agony—his sagging head and half-drooping arms like the wings of a plucked chicken—with loud whistles and guffaws. He's been given a flag that is falling from his hand; he squeezes out his handkerchief, wet with sweat; he holds his head at an angle as if his very skeleton had been wrenched; he carries an advertisement on his back, like a horse's saddle. And yet he walks with a sway of his skinny body, like a man who wants to look good for the ladies.

While the winner, who still had the strength for it, took his leave of the spectators with a speech, in the boxes and the neighboring hotels, the wives of the losers were washing their husbands' black and stinking feet, the doctor was resetting a lean hip, and a journalist was probing in vain the hollow mind of a walker who lay stretched out on a portable cot amid withered flowers, sticky pots of jam, eggshells stained with wine, half-eaten mutton bones, brushes, tobacco, blood-stained rags, pounds of tea, and uncorked bottles of champagne.

—New York, February 12, 1888;
published in *La Nación* (Buenos Aires), April 15, 1888

NEW YORK UNDER SNOW

The most powerful blizzard ever to hit the eastern United States began on Monday, March 12, 1888. Over forty inches of snow fell on New York City within twenty-four hours, and the wind blew at up to forty-eight miles per hour, creating immense snowdrifts. The entire East Coast was paralyzed by the storm, and more than four hundred deaths were reported.

The first golden oriole had been glimpsed hanging its nest from a Chilean pine in Central Park, and the downy promise of spring was covering the bare poplars; the first leaves of the early-blooming chestnuts were appearing like a row of jabbering women poking their heads out after a storm, and, alerted by the chirping birds to its arrival, brooks were emerging from beneath layers of ice to watch the sun go by, for winter, vanquished by flowers, was fleeing in a huff, unleashing the March winds behind it to cover its flight; the first straw hats were just beginning to be seen on the streets of New York along with the glad, bright clothes of Easter, when the city opened its eyes one morning shaken by the roar of a storm, and found itself shrouded, mute, empty, buried in snow. Doughty Italians, facing down the blizzard, are already filling wagons with glittering, worthless snow and, amid whinnying, songs, jokes, and curses, taking it to be dumped in the river. The elevated train, encamped for two days in sinister vigil next to the corpse of an engineer who set out to defy the gale, is running again, creaking and shivering over the treacherous rails that gleam and flash. Sleigh bells jingle, newsboys shout, snowplows pulled by powerful Percherons spit out the snow they clear from the rails on both sides of the street, and with snow up to its chest the city makes its way to the trains—stuck in the middle of vast, white plains—the rivers, which are now bridges, and the silent docks.

The shriek of the combatants still echoes like a vault over the city. For two days, the snow had New York in its power, penned in and terrified like a champion prizefighter knocked to the ground by a punishing blow from an unknown gladiator. But as soon as the enemy's attack let up, as soon as the blizzard's initial fury was spent, New York, as if it had taken offense, resolved to throw off its graveclothes. Between the white mountains are leagues of men. Undone by its assailants, the snow is already running in murky rivers down the busiest streets. With ploughs, shovels, the horses' chests, and their own, men are pushing back the snow and forcing it to retreat to the rivers.

Great was man's defeat and great is his victory. The city is still white, the whole harbor white and frozen. There have been deaths, acts of cruelty and of kindness, exhaustion, brave rescues. Man, in this catastrophe, has shown himself to be good.

Never in this century has New York seen a storm like the one on March 13. The day before, a Sunday, had been rainy, and the insomniac writer, the ticket seller at the railway station, and the milkman on his cart making the rounds of the sleeping houses at dawn could hear the wind that had descended upon the city whipping in fury against the chimneys and in even greater fury against rooftops and walls, taking off the roofs, demolishing shutters and balconies in its path, clutching at trees, carrying them off, and pitching down the narrow streets with a howl, as if caught in a trap. The electrical wires snapped by its passage sputtered and died. The telegraph lines that had so often withstood it were wrenched from their posts. And when the sun was supposed to appear it was nowhere in sight for, as if a routed and panicking army were going by beyond the foggy windowpanes, with squadrons, heavy artillery, roughshod infantry, and unforgettable screams, the whirling snow went on for a whole day and night without stopping. Man did not allow himself to be cowed. He went out to defy it.

But the toppled, horseless streetcars lay beneath the storm; the elevated train, which paid for the first attempt with blood, let the steam die away in its useless engine; the trains that were scheduled to arrive from surrounding areas, derailed by the powerful wind or stopped by massive snowdrifts, tall as hills, toiled in vain to reach their stations. The streetcars would attempt to set out, but the horses reared, beating their hooves against the overpowering whirlwind. The elevated train took aboard a load of passengers, then got stuck midway through its journey, and after six hours of waiting, prisoners of the air, the men and women descended from the aerial track on ladders. The rich or those faced with an emergency found sturdy horse-drawn carriages that, for $25 or $50, carried them step-by-step over short distances. Lashing, pounding, throwing them to the ground, the turbulent wind, heavy with snowflakes, passed overhead.

Sidewalks and street corners were no longer visible. Twenty-third Street is one of the city's busiest, and a compassionate shopkeeper had to put up a sign on the corner that said "THIS IS 23RD STREET." The snow was knee-high; waist-high where the wind had heaped it up. The raging blizzard bit into the pedestrians' hands, pushed its way inside their collars, freezing their ears and noses, throwing fistfuls of snow into their eyes, leaving them sprawled on their backs on the slippery snow, pinning them down with new gusts, or throwing them hatless and dancing against the walls. Or it left them sleeping, sleeping forever, entombed! One man, a shopkeeper in the flower of youth, appeared today, sunk in a deep drift, his body noticed only because one hand was raised above the snow. Another, a messenger boy, blue as his uniform, emerged in the arms of his pitying companions from a cold, white tomb that was well suited to his childish soul. Another man sleeps, buried to the neck, with two red patches on his white face, his eyes purple.

And down Broadway and the avenues, falling and picking themselves up again, came old men, youths, children, and women—going to work!

Some of them, exhausted, sat down on a stoop, wanting only to die; other generous souls pulled them up by the arm, encouraging them, singing, and talking loudly; an elderly woman who had made a mask of her handkerchief, with two holes for the eyes, leaned against the wall and began weeping; the president of a bank, going to work on foot, carries her to a nearby pharmacy, which can only be made out beneath the snowdrift by its yellow and green lights. "I won't go on,"

says one man, "but what if I lose my job?" "I'm going on," says a
woman, "I need today's pay." The salesclerk takes the working woman
by the arm; the young factory girl supports her tired friend with an
arm around her waist. At the entrance to the Brooklyn Bridge, the secretary of a new bank implores the police officer with such anguish
that, though only death can cross the bridge just then, he lets him by,
"so he won't lose the position it has taken him three years to get!" and
the wind, at that formidable height, throws him down with one gust,
picks him up with another, tears off his hat, rips open his coat, makes
him bite the ground at every step; he doubles over against the wind,
grips the rail, moves ahead at a crawl; alerted by telegraph from
Brooklyn, the bridge police are waiting for him, and he falls into their
arms, inanimate, when he reaches the New York side.

But why such effort when hardly a store is open and the city has surrendered, cornered like a mole in its tunnel, and, arriving at the factories
and offices, they will find the iron doors barred? Only the compassion
of a neighbor, or the power of money, or the luck of living near the only
train line that, toiling bravely, drags itself up and down one side of the
city from hour to hour, will help all the faithful employees, all the magnificent old men, all the heroic working women on this terrible day.
From corner to corner they advance, stopping in doorways until someone opens up for them, knocking with panicked hands like sparrows
that knock against windowpanes with their beaks. Suddenly the gusting
becomes stronger, throwing the small group of people who were fleeing
in search of shelter against the wall like stones. The poor working girls
huddle against each other in the middle of the street until the gale's tormented tossing sends them fleeing once more. And women and men
walk backward up the city streets to brace themselves against the mighty
wind, rubbing the snow from their eyes, then cupping their hands over
them to try and find their way through the tempest. Hotels? The chairs
are being rented out as beds, and the bathrooms as bedrooms! Something to drink? Even the men will find no drink now in beer halls that
have already drunk up their supply; and the women, dragging their dead
feet uptown, have nothing to drink but their tears.

And at that hour, still recovering from the initial shock of dawn, the
men are already buttoning their clothes tightly so that the fury of the
blizzard will not bite as deep. At every step is an overturned wagon, a
shutter that bangs against the wall, suspended from its last hinge like
the wing of a dying bird, a torn awning, a half-fallen cornice, an eave
that has fallen. Walls, doorways, windows: everything is a solid mass

of snow. And without a minute of respite, the rush of snow blows on, whispering, moaning, whirling, devastating. And with snow up to their arms, men and women walk.

One man has made his umbrella into a silk mask with two holes for the eyes and another for the mouth; with his hands behind his back he moves forward into the wind. Others have wrapped their shoes in socks, bags of salt, wrapping paper, or strips of rubber tied on with twine. Others are bundled up in the leggings and caps worn by bicyclists; and one man is carried away, almost a corpse, wrapped in his buffalo-hide overcoat. Here's a man in riding boots, another is dressed as an actor, another as a hunter. "Sir," says the voice of a small boy who can hardly be seen for the snow, "get me out of here, I'm dying." He is a messenger boy, and some villainous company has allowed him to go out in this tempest to deliver a message. Many men are on horseback! One man goes out in a sleigh that is overturned by the first sally of the high-spirited wind, and he with it, and he dies not long after. A tenacious old lady goes out to buy a wreath of orange blossoms for her daughter who is getting married today, and the wreath is swept away. And when New York was like an Arctic plain and night was falling with nothing to light it up, and fear was everywhere; when the generous mailmen fell face down, numb and blind, defending the mail sacks with their bodies; when families, gripped by mortal terror, tried in vain to open blocked doors in their search for a way out of houses that had lost their roofs; when the fire hydrants, like the rest of the city, lay beneath five feet of snow, hidden to even the most faithful hand—a raging fire broke out, tinting its snowy surroundings with the colors of dawn, and bringing down three tenements in as many gulps. And the fire engine came! The firemen dug deep with their arms and found the hydrants! The walls and the snow-covered street were rose colored, and the sky as blue as eyes! And though the wind's fury threw the water they battled the flames with back in stinging droplets against their faces, though tongues of crimson fire snaked higher than the cross on a cathedral tower, though, whipped up by the wind, columns of smoke shot through with golden sparks singed their beards, they went on fighting the blaze with never a step backward and snow up to their chests until they had cut the fire off and had it under control. And then, with their arms, they opened a path for the fire engine through the heavy snow.

The city awoke this morning without milk, coal, mail, newspapers, streetcars, telephones, or telegraphs. How eagerly those who live uptown read the newspapers that, through the bold efforts of the poor newsboys, arrived from the presses downtown! And four theaters were open last night! All businesses are closed, and the elevated train, that false marvel, struggles in vain to take the angry crowds that pack the stations to work.

The trains and their human cargo are bogged down on the tracks. Nothing at all is known about the rest of the nation. The rivers are ice, which a few daredevils walk across; the ice suddenly breaks and its floes drift free with the men atop them; a tugboat sets out to save them, swings alongside the floe, pushes it toward the docks, brings it up to the nearest one, and they are saved: from both sides of the river an enormous "Hurray!" rings out. "Hurray," they shout in the streets to the fireman who goes by, the policeman, the brave mailman. What will happen to the trains that are still snowbound, to which the railway companies, with magnificent energy, are sending foodstuffs and coal, hauled by their most powerful engines? What will happen to those who are at sea? How many dead bodies lie beneath the snow?

The snow, like a retreating army that whirls back on its conqueror in an unexpected new attack, came again that night and covered the proud city with death.

No other society is as well suited to confront such ambushes of the unknown as these utilitarian peoples, in whom, as yesterday showed, the virtues promoted by hard work suffice, in moments of difficulty, to compensate for the absence of those other virtues that have been undermined by egotism. How brave the children were, how conscientious the workmen, how noble and unhappy the women, how generous the men! The whole city is speaking in loud voices today as if it were afraid of being alone. Those who would otherwise be jostling each other brutally are smiling today and telling each other about their mortal dangers, exchanging addresses and walking long distances beside their new friends. The parks are mountains of snow, and in the first rays of sunlight the icy lacework suspended from the branches of the trees sparkles like silver filigree.

Heaps of snow rise over the rooftops, and happy sparrows hollow out fragile nests in them. This city of snow dotted with brick-red houses is terrible and astonishing, as if flowers of blood were suddenly to bloom on a shroud. The telegraph poles broadcast and contemplate the mess, their lines lying in tangles on the ground like disheveled heads. The city is coming back to life, burying its dead, and pushing back the snow with the chests of horses and men, the ploughs of locomotives, and buckets of boiling water, sticks, planks, bonfires. And there is a feeling of immense humility and sudden goodness, as if the hand we all must fear had rested on all men at once.

—New York, March 15, 1888;
published in *La Nación* (Buenos Aires), April 27, 1888

BLAINE'S NIGHT

Republican politician James Gillespie Blaine (1830–93), whose oratorical style Martí—himself an orator of international renown—coolly assesses here, is a recurrent figure and something of a bête noire *in Martí's reports from the United States. First elected to Congress as a representative of Maine in 1863, Blaine was Speaker of the House from 1869 to 1875. His attempt to garner the Republican nomination for the presidency in 1876 was derailed by charges of influence-peddling, and his unsuccessful push for the nomination in 1880 was part of the web of events Martí alludes to in "The Trial of Guiteau."[1] He served as secretary of state under Garfield, but resigned when Garfield was assassinated. In 1884 he finally became the Republican nominee but lost the presidency to Grover Cleveland. In 1888 he declined to run for president but supported Benjamin Harrison, who made him secretary of state. In that office, he sought to boost commercial relations between the United States and Latin America by establishing reciprocal tariff treaties, but was ultimately prevented from doing so. He also organized the first Pan-American Conference, at which, as Martí puts it in the preface to Simple Verses, "out of ignorance, blind faith, fear, or mere politeness, the peoples of Latin America gathered in Washington beneath the fearsome eagle." He sought the Republican nomination again in 1892, but Harrison was renominated. Blaine died the next year.*

It was like the sea. Those sitting in back, in the covered part of the stands, which were like a mountain of grains of black corn, craned their necks. From afar, from the gates, the crowd slowly came in, as if astonished by the space and the night, surrounded by the empty seats of the enormous ballpark where Blaine is about to speak.

Facing the stands, at the center of their ellipse, a platform for the orators and distinguished guests has been improvised out of pine planks. From the stands to the platform, the human mass ripples like the surf. A row of policemen holds it in with their backs. A woman faints. Another is carried away in someone's arms, seized prematurely by the pangs of childbirth. An Italian assaults an Irishman. A wave surges from behind and throws the policemen face down against the boards. Hitting out without seeing whether their blows land on flesh or on bone, the white helmets force the throng back. The coal lamps hiss.

The electric lights, high atop their posts, occasionally cast a brightness like the tail of a comet over the multitude, and then withdraw it. A nebula of light floats overhead. Garlands of flags, their brightly colored diadem vivid against the gray sky, crown the top of the bleachers.

Blaine does not arrive. As if a town were being evacuated, lines of people continually stream through the gates, crossing the esplanade, joining the crowd. Outside are horns, fifes, tambourines, vendors of oranges, peanut stands, carriages that come and go, and messengers in uniforms and blue caps who fill the hands of passersby with speeches, newspapers, denunciations, programs, caricatures, statistics, paper flags, capsule histories, citations, portraits, circulars.

For blocks around, the ground is covered with trampled paper. Every train that stops pours thousands more souls down the steps: they come in pairs, shelling chestnuts; or in groups, all carrying canes of the same color; or alone, and those are the ones who walk fastest. And those who have no patria settle back to watch them go by in envy, swallowing down their tears.

All the Republicans? Oh no! In fact, it's apparent that the coalition is fraying at the seams and has far less weight than was believed. Many notable Republicans are deliberately absent. They said it would be a crowd of fifty thousand, but it will only be ten thousand.

Listen to the snatches of conversation among those who go by: "I want to see the man!" "I've come a hundred miles to see the man." "I already know the lies he's going to tell me, but I want to hear them from him." "In the West they like him, but they don't like him much around here." "Just let him tell us that the import tariff is making us rich—when I can't put on a single article of clothing that didn't cost me forty percent more than it should have, and the slippers I wear when I get up thirty-five percent more, and the towel I dry off with forty-five percent, and the plate I eat off fifty percent, and sugar eighty-two percent, and salt forty percent and the blanket I sleep under one hundred four percent, and my wife's suit made of poor-quality wool sixty percent, and the marble slab they'll set over me when I die fifty percent—if there's anything left in the house to buy it with after twenty-five years of fattening up monopolists and usurers and making industries produce more than they can sell and bringing millions of desperados in from outside to compete with our good workers, who are paid less for their labor than what the products of others' labor cost them!"

"With my bread—bread and wine—I'll take his speech right out of his mouth!" "Oh go on with you, you fool: as soon as you see him take off his hat, look at you as if he were skinning you alive, and throw his left shoulder forward, you won't be able to say a word." "No, he's no great orator, though he is articulate, a shameless spinner of sophistries and juggler of numbers, a nimble speaker who only points out the facts that suit him, and not the ones that negate his case; he can be solemn when he wants to be, and sarcastic, too, when he wants." "Run! Run! Don't you hear the cannon?" "Blaine is speaking already!"

The cannon booms, the bands erupt into music, fireworks stream across the sky: one gate is hung with colorful Bengal lights and the other is painted green. To the platform! To the platform! There is clamoring, cursing, shoving, insolence. The platform is full of generals, electioneers, well-dressed old men, privileged foreigners, women. But that isn't Blaine who is gesticulating, who turns around to ask that the lights behind him be put out because the crowd is shouting that they want to see the speaker's face, who throws fragmented words, like rags, out into that turbulence. The word *Cleveland!* is heard from him, and they whistle; the word *protectionism!* and they applaud. He is Foraker,[2] enemy of the South, who no longer dares attack it as he used to because among Cleveland's merits is that of having proven that the South could return to public life without harm to the national union, and even to its benefit, and that keeping the South out of government might have compromised the union, for it is only a step from disdain to wrath, and then only another one from wrath to rebellion. Foraker does not speak of the South, nor does he say anything at all worthwhile: his broken, choked, muffled, ignored, useless harangue inspires only pity as it is flung out by the fistful over the people's heads; it is as pathetic and revolting as the entrails of a horse that has been eviscerated in the bullring. Is this oratory, sacred oratory, or is it the harlot of Scripture who lieth in wait like a deep ditch? The quest for fame debases and the man who goes in pursuit of it is a piteous sight. If it is not to fall into discredit, the spoken word must preserve its majesty, as a woman preserves her honor.

Suddenly, everyone stirs. Those on the platform stand on top of their chairs. Foraker bites his lip and goes white. Scattered hurrahs, hoarse voices, a thousand paper flags fluttering overhead. Now Blaine arrives; two lines of policemen open up a path for his triumphal entry through the crowd. Now he is climbing the stairs. Now he is on the platform.

He is speaking to a nation of hats, not of men; of hats, flags, hands, and arms opened wide, particularly those of a certain journalist who seems to want to give Blaine his soul: a Democratic journalist who tosses off editorials for pay and then votes against what he writes in favor of—and his hand does not fall off! The veils must be stripped from politics. It is no use celebrating blindly or censuring for the sake of censuring; an objective study must be made, to ascertain where the festering sores are located on the public and the individual character. A writer must be a savior. That man should have been nailed to a cross, for there he was, in his overcoat and fur hat, acclaiming in the evening light what he would insult at dawn: "To hell with my newspaper!" he says to someone who challenges him on it: "I'm a Republican!"

But the uproar doesn't last long, like a fire fueled with straw. The band, which was playing "Hail to the Chief," stops. The light brown hat is handed to a friend of Blaine's; the yellow overcoat is shrugged off in a single gesture; with his two pale, knotted hands he seizes the railing and the flag draped over it wrinkles and shrinks beneath his fingers. He leans forward, as if beckoning for silence. He is obeyed. He straightens up.

And he speaks his mind with few gestures, one hand on the rail, his head thrown back, his right shoulder lowered, with an eye that does not see but only lets its gaze fall from on high. When he attacks a personal enemy, his body seems to fling the enemy away, as if that were the best of his oratory. He is seen in full profile, his forehead wide at the top and slightly rounded over the ears from the exercise of words; the nose is curving and fleshy, the mouth firm, and the chin evasive; a white goatee disguises the weakness of the jawbone. The hair is straight, naturally silky, and often falls over his forehead in the heat of argument, as if to help him fight. And the eye is defiant, aggressive, cold, viscous; more of a wall than a door, made to incite combat and enjoy it and see the enemy brought down, and not—like other eyes— to speak to men and allow them to enter the soul's palace as if it were their own home. It is an eye that stands and waits, that does not draw back, that does not close at nightfall, that has become hard and cynical during its voyage through souls, an enameled eye, a black diamond set in marble, a plundering eye.

The haughtiness of his heart can be read in that disdainful gaze. He is rumored to have gone down on his knees to beg the rival who had them for the letters that proved he had criminally profited from his legislative position for personal gain.[3] His eye will become all honey— as it is rumored to—for the magnates whom, under guise of protection for industry, he helps to maintain the monopolies that have plunged the country into King Midas's dilemma and that are breeding a terrible war, the war of the hungry masses who are already beating their drums: their belts are already tightened, and they roar in the shadows. For the wealthy, Blaine stands hat in hand, all smiles, favors, coquetry, eloquence, stories. But with his opponents and rivals, his eye bristles, he sows fear with his arts, suspecting other men of his own motives and methods. He shuts off in advance the paths on which his rivals might get ahead, treating them as conquered and inferior men who lack his sagacity, his cold-bloodedness, his agility, and his brilliant, supple power of speech, which does not weave majestuous fabrics like Webster's, or found, like Lincoln's, or set forth an entire issue with all the laborious ornamentation of a Hindu tower like Evarts's;[4] no, his is an oratory of battle. He feigns thunder, makes his rival put up his fists, and falls on him wherever he sees an opening, without giving him time to adjust his armor. Both the political and social spheres of this country are bedazzled by this versatile character, free of scruples and not overly attached to the truth—for the truth is offensive to those who are lacking in virtue—and full of stratagems and novelties when his desperate minions do not know what tactic to use next against the enemy. Lies? Well, then, he lies. False statistics? Well, then, let's falsify them, and say that it's the other side who are the falsifiers! And what if they call us on it? Well, then, what was the word *jackass* created for? Let's make people laugh, with a snappy anecdote, well worded and guaranteed to please, in which we'll call them jackasses! For what could be more necessary to political strength than participation in the defects of one's fellow men? Men will have their revenge on the one who dares to be unlike them.

And Blaine is well versed in the art of speaking to a crowd. Show up, bedazzle, go. Who is going to stop and think things out in a gathering of twenty thousand men? Who will hold their attention after they have, in half an hour, become habituated to the magic of the voice? How could these tightly packed, overwrought, impatient men, more curious than given to thought, and with the night already well advanced, have the spirit to follow the slow, serene flight of the eagle among mountain peaks that must be laboriously ascended? All of life is summed up in the world's cry to man: "Come down! Come down! Be like us! It wearies us to ascend!"

And therefore Blaine will do what he does tonight. He speaks for twenty minutes, with never a single pause, so that his listeners won't get away from him. He approaches a fact through the appearances that confirm it to the vulgar eye, and though it is so false that a man as educated as he is must see that clearly, he raises the fact above his head—the fact, in this case, that its experiments with free trade have been catastrophic to the country—and bundles together deceptive generalities with an archer's deftness. He claims the country is headed for ruin because the Democrats want to lower import tariffs to forty-five percent, and that the country lived happily under protectionism fifty years ago—when the fact is that the protectionist tariff of that time was seven percent, five times less than what the free traders call for now! And he doesn't say it with imperious gestures and a resounding voice, but as if it were a high decree issuing forth from a place where nothing can be discussed or disputed.

This is great, theatrical oratory, whose theatricality goes unseen. His very simplicity, in contrast with the strength of his persona, heightens that strength. In oratory, as in everything, the most consummate artistry is that which passes unnoticed. He arrives late, as he did tonight, throws his overcoat aside, strides toward the railing, stares out fixedly, speaks without a pause, summarizes his point in a sudden and dazzling sentence, and the public is left hanging on his words, almost without applauding, as he returns to his overcoat and vanishes.

—New York, October 20, 1888;
published in *La Nación* (Buenos Aires), December 10, 1888

A CHINESE FUNERAL

Martí took particular interest in the Chinese population of the United States, perhaps because since 1847, a significant number of Chinese "coolies"—who were supposedly indentured servants but in practice were often bought and sold as slaves—had been arriving in Cuba. By 1899, a census found 14,863 Chinese in Cuba: 14,814 men and 49 women. From the beginning, the Chinese proved far less "docile" than the promoters of their enslavement had claimed they would be; a number of them fought on the side of the Cuban rebels in the Ten Years War, the Little War, and the 1895 war of independence.

For a moment the furor of politics died down, and New York stepped aside to make way for the colorfully garbed Chinamen who, with highest honors, filed in the Asiatic manner behind the bier of Li-In-Du,[1] the illustrious general of the Black Flags,[2] who has died in their arms. The parades of the political parties, the mobile orators on their wagons, and the varied musics of the electoral process recede into the distance. Today there is a strange, new music, the music of Li-In-Du's funeral. Let us go with a curious New York to listen.

Li-In-Du was a man of valor: he drove France out of Tonkin and used his prestige to help the friends of liberty, but not even that prestige was of use against the harassment of the authorities who do not want China to be rid of its class hierarchy. He barely escaped with his life and was followed to San Francisco by a few loyal lieutenants. He did not wander in idleness, like the many swordsmen of our own race who think that the fact of having once been a man who defended the patria authorizes them to cease being a man and to live off of her instead. Liberty, too, has its scoundrels! And Li-In-Du did not want to be one of them, but instead busied himself with the trades of his land—that is, doing laundry and serving food—the two things the Chinese are allowed to do here. For if they work in mines or on railways, they are hunted down like wild beasts, chased from their shacks by gunshots and burned alive.[3]

In New York, Mott Street is theirs; that is the street where they have their banks, their stock market, their tailors and barbershops, their tav-

erns and their vices. On that street can be found the Chinaman friar, a
merry, mellifluous savant, well fleshed, with roses in his face, not much
in the way of cheekbones, an avid mouth, and a shrewd and lively eye.
There, too, is the shopkeeper Chinaman, with loose, spongy flesh the
color of earth, his billowing shirt and wide pants rolled up, his hair
short and dense, eyes bloodshot, hands meaty and long-nailed, a three-
layer chin falling to his chest like an udder, and, for a mustache, two
threads. There is the harsh and aloof Chinaman, the fenced-in nomad
who once wielded the sword or the pen and now makes his living as an
amanuensis and mediator, by turns mute or loquacious, kept in poverty
by the ignorant rich man who is pleased to avenge himself thus on one
whose head is fully inhabited. And there is the Chinaman of the laundries, who can sometimes be tall, youthful, naive, and gallant-faced,
with agate bracelets on his wrists, but more often is an ungainly runt,
meek and misshapen, without nobility in his mouth or gaze, or else a
man who does not walk but drags himself along, slumped and gloomy,
with two glass balls for eyes, drooling from opium.

But today the opium-smokers' daises are empty; the laundries are
closed; there is no entry to the houses that sell foodstuffs; and bands of
mourning adorn the lanterns that hang from balconies to advertise the
taverns. Mott and the surrounding streets are full of Asians, gathered
to bear their great man, Li-In-Du, to his grave; full of the Irishmen and
Italians who inhabit that muddy and odoriferous neighborhood
alongside them; and full, too, of the curious from all parts of the world
who by the thousands throng the streets along which the procession is
to pass. The yellow man lifts up his eyes, the eyes of a hunted animal;
he looks about as he walks along, as if to guard against an offense; he
swears under his breath as he walks, his eyes ablaze, or he walks with
his head low, as if to beg pardon for the sin of being alive. They go in
groups to the house where the funeral is held, walking along two by
two, in their flat black hats, their robes and dark blue pants, their
hands crossed on their chests, their feet in string slippers above which
their loose pants sway like petticoats; they enter the funeral parlor,
which is a stable, today lined in black, with two strips of cloth, one
black and one white, forming a cross on the ceiling; they go, two by
two, to prostrate themselves before the glowing altar at the body's
feet, beside two tables piled high with the goat, lambs, oranges, and
flower-wreathed cakes that will be served to the friends of the deceased three days hence at the funeral banquet, which will take place in
silence at the most silent hour of the night. Two by two they come,

taking from the altar, with its seven lamps, the cups of oil and holy rice given out by priests who wear white tunics with sashes and skullcaps of black. And they empty the cups, two by two, into the waiting basin that stands at the foot of the coffin, next to the tub where, on a bed of fresh earth, the candles of the soul are burning.

The dead man is in his coffin, with its rich fabrics and copious silverwork, exposed from the waist up; he has the head of a solid man, eyes set deep and close to the nose, nose with wide nostrils, lips slender and tight, the braid brought from behind to lie across the forehead like a crown, and one hand lying on his breast, which is covered with the paper money of Asia, to pay the toll of heaven. Around him, in bronze cups, the sacred perfumes give off their smoke and the candle of the soul its thick and waxy clouds; at the head of the coffin hangs a flag showing the sins of the deceased, surrounded by white circles, which he must overcome in order to ascend to the Elysian fields that crown them, represented by a black mark. The tables can no longer hold all the piles of fruit, baskets of nuts, platters of lemons, towers of funeral cake. There is no space for those who are arriving to make their way to the altar and prostrate themselves three times in quick succession and leave the oil in the basin and some flowers on the tables.

But they do not tear their hair or rend their garments; they do not bare their heads, cease their smoking, or evince any sorrow over the changed state of one who defended their land so well, beneath the great red banner. He who has done one thousand three hundred good deeds, is he not immortal in the heavens, according to the law of Tao?[4] The defeat of the Frenchman was more than three hundred good deeds, which is all that is required to be like a deputy of immortality, immortal on earth! Life is like the sides of a pitcher, which contain the useful emptiness that is then filled up with milk, wine, honey, or perfume; but the pitcher's emptiness is more valuable than its sides, just as eternity, joyful and unbounded, is worth more than this existence, in which man cannot lead freedom to victory. To die is to return to what one was at the beginning, is it not? Death is blue, white, opalescent; it is the return to a lost delight, a journey. And therefore he takes along provisions!

Hands buried in their loose winter shirts, they speak of how Li-In-Du was an awe-inspiring general, who looked, in battle, like a winged pillar, the type of pillar the Chinaman erects to ward off demons; of how he killed many a Frenchman, though Tao says one must not step on an insect or cut down a tree, because to do so is to destroy life; of how he was a great merchant, dealing in drugs and fabrics, teas and foodstuffs, though the law of Tao forbids the pursuit of vanity's false honors or the riches of this world.

That was the old Tao, whose beard is covered with ice in the heavens now. Li-In-Du? Fifty thousand dollars. And he has a son in China who inherits it all! The devils won't manage to carry him off; he has much gold in his hand to scatter when they ambush him along the way. Amid the smoke of incense and cigars a mourner appears dressed in blue, holding in upraised arms a stuffed pig garlanded with roses.

The priests in white tunics step aside to allow an old man wearing a yellow cape lined in black to reach the altar, advancing with solemn steps through the Freemasons in their gray tunics and red skullcaps. He is lost from sight amid all the smoke, and his salutation is drowned by the mad, shrieking clamor of the music: *Fom! Bang! Ba-tan-TAN! Piiii! Bon, son, son!* The shattered air crackles and squeals. The old man throws himself onto the glass part of the coffin, kisses it three times, and three times lets out a terrible cry, a cry that finally imposes silence and fear.

He returns to the altar, seizes a banner, and sings, in verse, of the feats of Li, and of how much the world will miss him, and of the feast that will now be held on the mountain of Tao. And others sing after him, one of them on his knees, forehead to the ground, another gesticulating like a man describing a battle, while at his feet, in a goblet with two serpents for handles, blaze the prayers that the celestial one burns, kneeling, rather than intoning them with his lips.

The room is full to the bursting now; the procession is beginning to form. We'll go outside to watch it so that we can see it all.

Is it an army or a funeral? Over the heads of the multitude move lanterns and flags. There are white horses. The horsemen are bareheaded; their braids are covered in black cloth and wrapped around their foreheads like a diadem. The great red banner, proud and graceful, waves above it all. Aggressive people charge toward it, laughing.

He looks as if he were about to die, the man who grips the flag with trembling gloves! The oriflammes and standards gather submissively around the flagpole like new shoots around a tree trunk, red and yellow, purple and sapphire, red and violet, amaranth and pink. The crests of the funeral coach can be glimpsed and the black heads of its four horses. The gold paper of the insignia glitters in the sunlight. But no idol can be seen, no image of Ts'ai-Shen,[5] the god of wealth, who now has more temples than any other god, in China and everywhere else; there is no image, either, of Kuan-Ti,[6] the god of battles, who has vipers for eyebrows and carries a huge whip. Li-In-Du does not believe in images or in any god but the pure creator Tao, who is all and one, and who engendered the two, and from the two the three, and from the three the world; he does not believe in any saint but the virtues themselves, without the dominions and hierarchies by which the priests have obscured religion, nor does he believe in Great Bears, Pearly Emperors, the mother of lightning, the king of the sea, the lord of the currents, the deity that protects man's every class and occupation, or the god of thunder whose thirty-six black and gray generals bring and bear away his orders as his restless feet mortify the plumage of nine beautiful birds. Li-In-Du is a mason, a freethinker, his own man, a venerable of Chinese freemasonry, who wore the leather apron edged in green. Everywhere the world is in turmoil and man suffers to assure the freedom of his will. That was why Li-In-Du's forehead was broad and level and his cheekbones were flattened: from banging his head against the despotic empire! He was a Taoist of the old school, who believed in the population of the air, the rest from struggle, the everlasting individual, transfiguration, and a final place on the mountain of Tao when duty has been fulfilled. But here below: liberty! And with his masonic hammer he went about softening up the Chinese emperor's head. They are touching to behold, these founding rebels. Such men rise like flames from the choking thicket. They appear clad in gold and fire, as Li-In-Du did in his coffin, wearing a tunic of yellow silk.

Now they are coming toward us in formation. The police go first, shoulder to shoulder, clearing the way, and after them a German band, in helmets and short jackets, playing a funeral hymn. The generals follow, the three generals who participated in the victory at Nanking:[7] they parade on white horses, riding like men more likely to charge headlong at the enemy than turn tail and run; their bodies are stringy and of medium height, and there is more muscle than dough in their faces; their plain helmets are encircled with a band of red linen, a black diadem on the front; they wear blue tunics, breeches and loose pants with a white sash at the waist in sign of mourning; their horses are well in check and move with high, slow steps. Tall flags jammed into sockets on their belts, three young Chinamen in mauve shirts and trousers pass by; on those flags are inscribed the glorious deeds of the departed, the nausea with which he left San Francisco where he saw the Chinaman contented with his base condition, the agony of his final days, when death was approaching on foot, like one who respects his victim, but the Congress in Washington, for internal political reasons, passed a law that would deport the celestial one,[8] and then death no longer came slowly, considerately, but galloped in on a horse and killed him with the news, ay! Li-In-Du, one of the men who devote their lives to the freedom of their people and the honor of their fellow citizens.

Next, heart-shaped and wreathed in flowers, came the yellow standard of Lun-Gee-Tong, the Masonic lodge he presided over, along with its members who wore blue tunics and skullcaps of black silk, and behind them the priests in white tunics, surrounding the old man in the black-lined cloak with their measured footsteps.

A low noise like a muffled clucking greets those who go by next, also wearing loose shirts, with knee breeches and puttees and wide white sashes at the waist and around the forehead: these are the twenty-five loyal soldiers who have followed Li-In-Du everywhere, and they seem taller than they really are as they move forward, proud and taut, a forest of banners over their heads, each a different color, and looming above them all a round canopy of mandarin orange and purple.

Behind two white lanterns, wearing tunics of various colors, with a sash around their chests and bows at their elbows and along their sides, come men who bear, on red poles, the eight pure insignia,[9] cut out of cardboard and decorated with gold and flowers: the commandments of the law of Tao that Tao himself gave to the chieftain Gwin-Li-Du on the bright mountain of Tien-San; the holy fruit that Tao ate on the mountain before his transfiguration; the sword with which Gwin defended the divine law; the celestial ax that falls wrathfully upon the world when evil prevails; the flute of peace; the lively *wooyin* with which the spirits of the redeemed accompany their happiness; the tea-scented celestial flowers that neither dry nor wither; and the white urn of life eternal.

And behind them, just ahead of the coffin, comes a white horse led by a groom with no rider in its bronze-trimmed leather saddle. Then comes the coach, with a beggar wearing an ash-colored tunic in the coachman's seat who drops imperial paper money on the multitude at intervals so that the dead man's way will be clear.

Then comes the mourner, the nephew Li-Yung, in a white cloak and black sash, his head bare. Then, in two black and yellow carriages, the Chinese musicians, their tones shrill and discordant, without notes or phrases, sounding more of triumph and joy than of mourning. And then the retinue of Chinese Freemasons, in greatcoats and fur hats, with the leather apron bearing the three letters, and then a thousand Chinamen more, two by two, arms crossed.

And this colorful swarm of people and the four white horses and the banners and the insignia of Tao gather in the cemetery around the grave, where they are jostled, amid laughter and cruel joking, by thousands of the curious: ruffianly idlers, sweethearts in the bloom of life, new mothers, fur-clad ladies, odoriferous Irishwomen. The trees have more urchins on them than leaves. On the ruined roof of a rambling house nearby, a group of actresses are peeling oranges.

Suddenly the crowd draws back; the banners fall to the ground, tunics and sashes fly through the air, and a wave of churning smoke rises from the sudden bonfire where all the funeral's garments and emblems are immolated, the cloaks and tunics, the black fabric that wrapped the braids, the mourning draperies of the horses, the oriflammes and pennants, the insignia of Tao, the great red banner, and the dead man's trunk.

As the crowd disperses, craning their necks, they can see the grave, arranged in the celestial manner: at the head is the Masonic heart, its pole plunged into the earth; then come two white lanterns, also stuck into the ground, and along the body are white and yellow roses in the shape of urns and cushions; to each side of the feet are the seven mystic candles, and near them are cups of rice, plates of cabbage, rolls, heaps of wine-drenched earth, cakes, buns, and two roast chickens: the banquet that the friends of Li-In-Du, on their haunches, have spread out to keep him from suffering the pangs of hunger during his difficult journey to the mansion of the spirits, where he will be a fortunate and immortal *djinn*, watching closely over those he loved in life, a pure spirit, interceding on behalf of mankind and the freedom of China, and assisting his friends and relatives with gifts and miracles.

—New York, October 29, 1888;
published in *La Nación* (Buenos Aires), December 16, 1888

INAUGURATION DAY

*** SELECTIONS ***

Grandson of William Henry Harrison (1773–1841), the ninth pres-
ident of the United States, who held office for only one month
(March 4–April 4, 1841) before he fell sick and died, Benjamin
Harrison (1833–1901), a lawyer who had been brigadier general of
an Indiana volunteer regiment in the Civil War, secured the Re-
publican nomination in 1888 and ran for president against Grover
Cleveland, the incumbent. Cleveland won a majority of the popu-
lar vote; Harrison won in the electoral college. Cleveland returned
to private life as a lawyer, then ran against Harrison again in 1892,
defeated him, and served a second term in office.

"Go on, Mr. Secretary, lend me your umbrella, this one isn't big
enough for two presidents. We'll give it back, you'll see—we're honorable men here in this coach." The four roans set off, the black coachman puts his whip back on its stand, and still under the impetus of its
departure, the carriage arrives at the Capitol, streaming with rain.
Harrison gets out first, then Cleveland.

This is how they change governments in the United States. We shall
tell of the enormous crowd, drenched to the bone, its hat brims drooping to its shoulders because the rain hasn't let up in six days; the inhuman night, marked by inclemency both of weather and of men, that
preceded the celebrated day; the courtesies, customs, and ceremonies
of a presidential inauguration, when one president takes his leave and
another takes office; the politics of the new government, which wants
protected industries, government-subsidized steamboats, a brake on
immigration, and more power on the Continent; the White House,
which is sad because its lovely mistress[1] is leaving it; the parade,
grandiose and ridiculous, with its heroes and its clowns; and the dance,
in a hall with columns that four men together could not stretch their
arms around, where, at five dollars a head, blacks and whites mingle
beneath the flag-draped ceiling, eager to see the new first lady in her
apricot silk gown.

Is anyone talking about Samoa and the naturalized Germans who
are siding, in Congress and in the press, with their adoptive country

against their native one, or about the pending conference on the disputes between Americans and Germans on that island, or about the half million dollars the House has voted for its naval base in Samoa?[2] Who takes the trouble to censure or applaud the endorsement of the Nicaragua canal company—a singular procedure that took place the same week Senator Edmunds requested an official declaration of the displeasure with which the United States government would see France endorse the Panama canal company?[3] Who gives a second thought to the now publicly acknowledged plan to purchase Cuba, though the blood is not yet dry which its astute neighbor—without lifting a finger, without stretching out an arm—watched it spill in defense of the same principles for which that neighbor once rebelled against its own masters? Who is thinking of Lincoln's birthday, which was yesterday, or of Washington's, celebrated with plays and parades, or of the four new states that were the bison's palace, virgin prairie with the stag alone for lord, when four thousand Federalists came here half a century ago to watch Harrison's grandfather assume the presidency, hefting his gold-handled cane, and today those states are the Dakotas, North and South, Montana, and Washington, with cathedrals made from the petrified wood of their forests, and a wealthy, avid population that has sent thousands of its citizens to march with a stalk of wheat in their buttonholes in the parade of fifty thousand men by which this nation, the home of forty-two free nations, celebrates the rise to power of Harrison the grandson, in his double-breasted frock coat and double-soled shoes?

Two hundred thousand outsiders have come to Washington for the inaugural ceremonies. Put off for tomorrow are the stories about Blaine and his rivals; the problems of the South with its blacks who are determined to stay alive; the review of New Mexico's request to become a state rather than a territory, though hardly a person there knows how to read the language in which they will have to make their laws. The trains arrive, a flag in every window, loaded with Californians in felt hats who've come all the way from the Pacific Coast; the Sioux people, who have left its cars littered with corn husks; Texan cowboys, dressed in leather shirts, fringed pants, and broad-brimmed hats; Arkansas mountain men in calico dusters, their hats adorned with deer tails. Where will this mass of fanatics, pugilists, politicians, job-seekers, gawkers, peddlers, vagabonds, and thieves find lodging? In chairs, because there are no more beds; on warped boards placed on top of bathtubs; against some counter with their heads on their arms, asleep over their whiskey with milk; on a visit to a house of ill repute, where the girls are showing off the new outfits they wear when a president takes office for the first time; or walking, walking across the sticky asphalt with mud up to their ankles, water in their hearts, their suitcases mauled, their notebooks destroyed . . .

But at the White House the lights have not gone out. Upstairs are women who cannot sleep. In his office, behaving as if he did not hear the insulting songs of the crowd outside, the hardworking president is studying the laws that await his signature of approval or his reasons for vetoing them, his faithful secretary at a nearby table.

It is a cold morning, and the logs in the fireplace seem to be speaking, saying good-bye. "I wholeheartedly approve the pension for Sheridan's widow."[4] "This plan to refund taxes to the states is an attempt to make the surplus[5] disappear artificially, when what we need to do is make its source disappear: the excess of import duties that has left us with no external trade and a social uprising at our doors: I veto the plan for a refund, even if the critics eat me alive!" The shouts grow louder. "In the soup! In the soup!" bands of men bellow just outside the White House windows. "Good-bye, Grover, sweet Grover!" And guffaws, growls, and shrill whistles are heard. They're dancing in the portico. They're knocking at the windows. He takes off his glasses, sets them down on the paper in front of him, which crackles as if something on top of it were trembling, and raises his head. "Sir! Sir!" says the secretary, half-rising from his seat to console him. "It's nothing, Lamont, my friend, nothing! If those men can insult me like that, I can endure it!" And he puts his glasses back on.

"I veto this draft that grants ten thousand dollars of public money to build a bridge where no river is known to exist." "I veto this unjust pension for the second cousin of a soldier who never actually fought in any of our battles."[6] At four in the morning he rose from the table, "Good-bye, Lamont. I'll be back at eight."

At eight o'clock, Washington was a solid, living mass. The streets filled up at dawn: the vendors of sausages and coffee hawked their wares; a lieutenant ran by at top speed, his feathered hat wrapped in a handkerchief; curious women peered out from between drawn curtains; and magnates went to the window in their nightshirts and stocking caps to watch the red-shirted firemen go by, and after them the Seventh Regiment of New York, wearing pearl gray, the delegation from Maryland, with raccoon skins on their chests like shields, the

Republicans of Indianapolis, Harrison's city, carrying tricolored umbrellas, and the people of Omaha behind a gigantic broom with green twigs and a blue and red handle. There is no way to cross the broad avenue; two wires have been strung along the sidewalks so people will not dash out into the parade. But the crowd, with water trickling down its necks, invades the bleachers along the avenue, wandering around the vacant platforms, taking shelter from the freezing wind beneath glistening umbrellas that shimmer, luminescent, in the mist through which the buildings loom, enormous and blurred, like monsters. Bursts of music explode through the air, crashing and flying. . . .

"Three cheers for Cleveland!" shouts a man with massive shoulders who's a head taller than everyone else in that Republican crowd. "We're going to make you pay for those cheers!" says a pipsqueak, sticking his head out from under his neighbor's sleeve. "Well then, come and make me pay!" "Beaver, that man over there is General Beaver, who's missing a leg!" "Look, they've arrested a cabbie who made a lady pay twenty dollars for a ride."

"Yes, Harrison visited Cleveland yesterday; he received him very cordially and they talked about the weather." "And Cleveland repaid the visit at four o'clock." "And what did they talk about?" "The weather!"

The crowds on the sidewalks go on swelling and the stands go on filling up; the militia is forming ranks; photographers are shooting groups of men; agile Negroes are bringing and taking away the city's wealthier visitors, or having their noses tweaked, or scattering sharp witticisms all around them; clubs of friends are there, with their insignia on their chests, those from the North fat, those from the South lean, and there are actresses in hoods and rubber overcoats.

A prizefighter, smelling of violets, strolls by, cigar hanging from the corner of his mouth, on the arm of a New York dandy in a short cape and pants that look more like petticoats; a leading Philadelphian, who contributed ten thousand dollars to the campaign and now has one job-seeker on his tail for every dollar he gave, goes past in a carriage; General Tracy, the wealthy Brooklyn lawyer who is now secretary of the Navy goes by, smiling and shaking hands, delight in his eyes; and other less cheerful men go by as well—the disappointed candidates, one of whom looks as if he'll soon be weeping like a child into his long white beard; other men, who've been drinking wine, go along strong and happy because "these fellows—may the Lord confound the Democrats—these fellows are going to give us subsidies for our steamboats!

Here's to Joe Chambertin, boys, and to good champagne!" With their heels in the air, holding their guns like clubs, some tardy militiamen race by, their cloaks fluttering in the wind.

A father, with a son at each shoulder, converses with a veteran, sitting on the base of a streetlight. One man says he knows Harrison. The other knows him better because he "fought beside the president." His son, he says, the one at the right shoulder, is taller than Harrison: "On horseback—that's how a man should be seen!" He adds that Harrison chews tobacco: "From Virginia!" And that Harrison is afraid of dying in the White House.

"Like his grandfather, poor old man, who didn't wear that hat more than six weeks!" This morning, he says, three ravens came cawing out of the Arlington, the hotel where Harrison is staying, "That's what the whiskey is for: to keep him alive!" Pursued by local police cadets, a group of Pennsylvania volunteers plow their way through the crowd with kicks and strong language, their eyes bloodshot, falling-down drunk. One of them collects rainwater in his helmet and tries to make a rustic fellow holding a cotton umbrella drink it. Another turns his face to the sky and opens his mouth wide because he's "very thirsty." The whole avenue is shouting; there is the sound of bugles and horses, and the furious rain adds its beat to the drums. A gentleman who's dressed to the nines jumps down from his coupé and goes into the Arlington carrying three bouquets of roses.

"Hip-hip hooray!" A hundred umbrellas open simultaneously. The daughters of the man who is about to be made president are coming. Their husbands are coming, with the children in their arms, the famous "government babies." His wife arrives with a bouquet in her hand and sparkling eyes. "Hooray again!" "God guide you, General!" "God bless my General," says a very hunched old black woman who suddenly emerges from among the tricornered hats and swords. Pale, with an anxious face and short legs, but strong from the waist up, an unsmiling Benjamin Harrison arrives. "To Willard," where he will join President Cleveland so the two can go to the Capitol together. There was a mistake about the time, and Harrison had lunch too early; he ate lunch standing up because "he can't sit down!" No, they won't wait, even if it isn't time yet. To the White House!

At the White House their visit was not expected quite so early, though flowers were already perfuming the Blue Room, full of palms and ferns, and the crystal chandeliers were blazing at full glory; the servants were coming and going in silence; the president's wife, already dressed to go out, was sitting in her bare room, closer to her mother than usual; trunks and baskets were being carried out the back door, and from one basket fell a worn copy of the Constitution; a black page hands the coachman a vase of lilies, so that he can carry it himself. Cleveland was signing the last of the laws with his deliberate hand, a full-length portrait of Harrison's grandfather behind him. "They're here already? I'll be right there." He stood up slowly, his hands resting on the briefcase that has seen so much work; he buttoned up his jacket, and he bade farewell to the servants who trooped in, the long and affectionate farewell of a friend. "One may well make a president wait to say farewell to a good servant!" And now, to the Capitol, in that open landau. The two presidents are met with lashing rain; laughing, they step into the carriage, which is filled with beaver skins, Harrison first. One of the two senators riding with them tries to open his umbrella and breaks one of its ribs. "Your umbrella, Mr. Secretary!" All hats rise, for in the window, leaning on her mother's shoulder, is Cleveland's wife, bidding him good-bye with a smile. She came back to the window with her hat on when the carriage was already far away. As her coach pulled out of the portico a wagonload of presents arrived for the new president's grandchildren.

Barely a whisper, like the soft humming of bees, could be heard in the Senate, where there is only a small space left for the presidents to walk through. Certain red faces and bald heads stand out above the black mass; holding a fanleaf palm, Ingalls,[7] he of the slanders, with his thatch of tousled white hair and his round eyes behind their lenses, raises his fearless head on the seat of honor; to the right, in their black robes, are the Supreme Court justices with their mettlesome chief, the poet Fuller;[8] to the left are the foreign ministers: the minister of Germany is wearing so much gold that it hides his clothes, while his retinue are adorned with shields and plumes; the minister of Siam wears a gaudy tunic and a pointed cap; the Chinese minister is dressed in yellow, with the skullcap reserved for great ceremonial occasions on his head; the Turk wears his fez; the Japanese, a dress coat.

Who are they applauding? Hannibal Hamlin,[9] who was Lincoln's vice president, and who enters with a youthful step, wearing a black silk tie and dress coat with squared tails. And now? It's Blaine,[10] and all eyes are upon him; some rush over to him and others—Senator Edmunds,[11] Senator Sherman[12]—turn their backs. And who is it now? The senior usher, who comes in with a pointer to turn back the hands of the clock, because the law dictates that the swearing-in must take place at noon; the usher turns back the clock so the ceremony will be on time.

And all of that applause is coming from the balconies, full of congressmen who have had to fight hard to force their way into their sister chamber, and of the senators' wives and lady friends. Harrison's wife is there, in a black-and-gold hat and a dark green dress, with her daughter, in green and white, and a vivid hat, and her daughter-in-law, in cardinal red edged with Russian fur; the wife of the vice president–elect is there, too, with her five daughters, in silver and light green. Blaine's wife is there, and his favorite son, who is going to act as his secretary. Ingalls's sons are there, as well; they see themselves in their father and read for him and skillfully summarize what they've read—a great help to a debating man.

Not a single noted beauty or politically inclined lady is missing from the balcony. Why didn't Cleveland's wife come? "Well, I know that this morning she herself arranged the lunch for the Harrisons!" "Oh, what furs, what magnificent furs Morton's wife is wearing!" "That woman's hat couldn't have cost less than a hundred dollars!" "The German foreign minister really is a fine-looking man!"

At a blow of the gavel the assembled men and women rise to their feet; Cleveland is entering on the arm of a senator amid great applause. The Democrats think he looks splendid; the Republicans find him peaked and sickly. Then the gavel sounds again and the assembly, on its feet once more, welcomes the president-elect; when he comes in on Senator Hoar's[13] arm the applause explodes. His face is pale but his steps are firm; he is short, famously short, but looks tall for the occasion because stature is, for the most part, in the gaze of the beholder. His nose sinks between his eyebrows, from where his rather pear-shaped forehead rises, high and spherical; he has cold, light-colored eyes, and his lips are pressed tightly together; his beard is long, but stringy. He sits down beside Cleveland, who says something to make him laugh; his eyes seek out his wife and children and grow calmer when he sees them.

At the third blow of the gavel another senator enters, Levi Morton,[14] the banker vice president, a man made to walk on fine carpets, clean-shaven and very well coiffed, with a laughing eye and fleshless lips, who strides to the seat of honor as if he owned it. In his grandiloquent voice, he swears what he is asked to swear by the supple Ingalls, who then thanks the Senate, which presented him with its compli-

ments yesterday on his fine manner of presiding over it, declares the
Fiftieth Congress to be at an end, and places the gavel in the vice president's hands. Morton makes his welcoming speech in the short, disjointed sentences of a man accustomed to paying others for his words,
and then opens the extraordinary session that has been convened so
that the executive power can change hands. The spectators glance at
the doors, already looking for the way out. The balcony begins putting its coats on, as if this were the final scene of the play. The new senators are sworn in, four by four, all except a Quaker, who only
promises. The hour has come, the hour when the new president swears
to the people—the people who are craning their necks, jammed
around the Capitol building as if they were going to tear it up by its
roots—that he will use the power he receives from them for their benefit. The entire Senate, the justices in their robes, the colorful diplo-
mats, and illustrious ladies all go out into the rain, which is pouring
down mercilessly, to the deserted stands. And when the cannon announces him and the crowd sees their hero appear, you might have
thought the rain had stopped because the tremendous roar was like a
canopy overhead that rippled and grew, as if a squadron of eagles were
stretching its wings over the city. The great hurrah came to an end, but
at every movement of the man who was about to be president—when
he spoke for a second with the patriarch Hamlin, present there at the
age of eighty, when he gestured away the scarf offered by an anxious
admirer, when he walked toward the chief justice, who held out the
Bible to him so that he could swear upon it to govern by God and by
the people, when he kissed the Bible with the timid kiss of a fervent
Protestant—from beneath that "ocean of umbrellas," and "from the
people beyond, whose high spirits could not be dampened," volley after volley of applause burst forth like artillery fire. The flags droop
miserably, plastered down by the rain; the banners are mere streamers,
licking their own poles; the senators peer out from the portico, their
coat collars turned up to their eyebrows, without daring to brave the
rain and make their way to the presidential group, while the wives of
Harrison and Morton walk outside, light and cheerful, as if the water
were sunlight. The seats are puddles and almost everyone stands: the
justices in their caps and gowns; a Japanese whose festive hat is
adorned with a feather that pokes the neck of a general who looks at
him angrily from under his tricornered hat; the ladies, who wish they
could hear better; Morton's eldest daughter, with her father's arm
around her waist; a mustachioed Virginian in a slouch hat who's there

to find out "what Harrison has to say about his South." Harrison drinks something that is served in a mug so it will look like hot broth, puts on his steel-rimmed spectacles, and without a single cry of impatience from the crowd, which stretches out and is lost in the mist, without a single man leaving his spot in the freezing multitude, the president reads his inaugural speech in fits and starts, beneath an umbrella held over his head by a handsome man who stands on a chair. , . .

The gist of his speech is that the Southern Democrats will have to allow the blacks, who are Republicans, to vote freely; that restrictions must be placed on immigration, which endangers us and brings us foreign ideas; that foreign products must not be sold more cheaply than American products in the United States; that American trade must be extended across the world; that whatever positions the law allows to be distributed freely will be given to Republicans; that the navy will be expanded as rapidly as is consistent with perfection in workmanship; and that we are prepared to place our flag wherever another nation aspires to place its own. He is distressed by what he sees in his own and the opposing party, the mortal enmities, the womanish hatreds, the blind jealousy that prefers anything to a rival's victory, the frantic self-interest. The military general who is fearful of politics can be glimpsed in the phrase "Let those who would die for the flag on the field of battle give a better proof of their patriotism and a higher glory to their country by promoting fraternity and justice." And the politician can be glimpsed in this one: "A party success that is achieved by unfair methods or by practices that partake of revolution is hurtful and evanescent even from a party standpoint."

And so ended the speech, which was greeted with hurrahs, music, and cannon fire, an affectionate smile from Cleveland, a hundred hands stretched out from beneath their umbrellas and battling to be the first to reach the new president, and hats waved by the crowd as it disbanded, eager to take part in the parade. "No other people have a government more worthy of their respect and love or a land so magnificent in extent, so pleasant to look upon, and so full of generous suggestion to enterprise and labor. God has placed upon our head a diadem and has laid at our feet power and wealth beyond definition or calculation. But we must not forget that we take these gifts upon the condition that justice and mercy shall hold the reins of power and that the upward avenues of hope shall be free to all people."

Between human walls that the policemen's shoulders are unable to hold back, Harrison and Cleveland, Morton and their companions walk to their landaus, one hitched to four roans and the other to four bays. Mounted guards gallop off to clear the way. The uproar is ceaseless, and every sidewalk, window, and railing is crammed with men, children, women who wave their umbrellas and handkerchiefs crying "God bless him!" and the battered hats of black men from the South and the brand-new homburgs of Northern Republicans. A man, hanging by both hands from a window, calls out, "Three cheers, three cheers and a tiger!" A job-seeker, carrying his petition in the sleeve of his overcoat, struggles with animal fury against the policemen who are trying to detach him from a coach. A sandwich, another sip of broth at the White House, and Cleveland, now in a coupé, like a free man, drives with his wife to the best presidency of all, which is the home of a friend. Harrison, in a silk hat and fur overcoat, goes with his retinue to the open stand to watch, through three hours of cheering and strong winds, the parade of regiments, "patriots" who have all asked for jobs, state militias, and fifty thousand men who, out of their own desire and their own pockets or that of their political party, have come to enhance—with all the ingenuity and abandon of the true people, the people that go astray and that hit the mark, the people that can do, the people that love—an event that raises all those who witness it in their own esteem because of the esteem they conceive for mankind. The cavalrymen who ride past are not standing in their stirrups but the spectator who watches them is! Few people other than his own family are around the president; in all the cold, muddy stand's long rows of empty seats there is no other group but those who are trying to shelter the proud general with their bodies. And with him his wife, whose dress, like his suit, is made of Yankee fabrics—his wife and his daughters, sitting impatiently, serving him tea, or serving it with their own hands to the generals. Oh, the stubborn rain, that lashes their faces and soaks through their coats, spoiling the great parade! . . .

From afar, as if emanating from an enormous stove, a hazy glow illuminates the wet sky. The troops scatter. Carriages come and go. Messengers pass by on horseback, and the glow of a streetlight reveals that they are carrying bouquets of flowers. For the colossal Pension Building, with its three rows of broad windows, its chimney that sends the smoke into the very clouds, and its eight columns that sustain a gigantic vaulted ceiling with a double gallery at their feet, is opening its doors to ten thousand eager partygoers who have come from across the country to see the wonder of its ballroom, which covers an entire acre, full of pennants, emblems, and wreaths; the presidential room, which is a mass of palms and roses; the hundred-piece orchestra to whose rhythm bald senators are dancing quadrilles, happy as if they were young again; the dining room, which serves no wine but pure milk and no champagne but water; and the triumphal entry of the president, with his wife, wearing a silk dress in the national colors, on his arm, and two athletes who make way for them with their shoulders through the throng, for "the president does not want policemen around him when he walks among his people." From the roof, thousands of streamers in the national colors fall to drape the emblems of the nation's allies, with an eagle above them all, and the balconies are covered with the same colors, which are also loosely wound around every pole, and brightly embellish the platform of honor, which is decorated with immortelle trees, and are worn by the men in satin ribbons on their lapels, and by the women in the corsages of white carnations, red roses, and violets on their breasts. Above it all, holding up the vaulted ceiling, stand the eight columns. At the same hour in New York, the engraver, who worked all night, was putting away his tools after adding a new name to the glass door of the office of Bangs, Tracy and MacVeargh: GROVER CLEVELAND, LAWYER.

—New York, March 5, 1889;
published in *La Nación* (Buenos Aires), April 16, 1889

POLITICAL CORRESPONDENCE

LETTER TO EMILIO NÚÑEZ

On May 7, 1880, General Calixto García[1] disembarked in Cuba to mount a new armed insurgency against Spain. As interim president of the New York Cuban Revolutionary Committee in García's absence, Martí issued a fervent proclamation announcing the general's presence on the island to all Cubans. But over the course of the summer the rebellion fizzled. No one knew what had become of García, and the committee had no funds to send the isolated pockets of revolutionaries who sporadically sent back increasingly dismal news. On August 1, after months of wandering barefoot through the wild with only six companions, Calixto García surrendered to Spanish troops. Before being deported to Spain, he wrote to the remaining generals in the field, urging them to lay down their arms. All but one did as he recommended. Emilio Núñez,[2] who disagreed strongly with the terms of the peace agreement, refused to cease fighting without the authorization of the Revolutionary Committee in New York. Martí sent him an official authorization and accompanied it with this letter.

Cuba's second war of independence, known as the Guerra Chiquita, *or "Little War," had failed, and the Cuban Revolutionary Committee of New York was, for the moment, disbanded.*

New York, October 13, 1880

Señor Emilio Núñez

My brave and noble friend:

I have your letter of September 20. What more repose could you seek for your soul—and what greater right to the esteem of even the severest critic—than to have written such a letter at such a time, from the encampment of Los Egidos?

You ask me for my advice—and I will not shirk the responsibility of giving it to you. I believe it would be futile—for you and for our land—were you and your companions to remain on the field of battle. Even if you had not asked me, I was already preparing—moved by wrath at the criminal solitude in which the country leaves its defenders, and by love and respect for your generous sacrifice—to beg all of you to spare your own lives, which today are absolutely unnecessary to the patria in whose honor they are offered up.

I do not tell you—despite the respect that your conduct in that letter has earned from me—all that is in my mind regarding our country's situation, because indiscreet and avid eyes might take advantage of it. But notwithstanding the resources we revolutionaries may still have at our disposal, and the importance of the excitement that still surrounds us, and the possibility of maintaining the Island in a state of permanent war, to the grave detriment of its current government, I do not think for my part that such a tenacious campaign would be legitimate, useful, or honorable.

Men such as you and I must seek for our land a radical and solemn redemption, imposed, if necessary and if possible, today, tomorrow, and always, by force, but inspired by magnificent purposes that will be sufficient to rebuild the country we are preparing to destroy. When, in the last two years, all the Revolution's leaders could not find a way of working vigorously together, nor was any such agreement achieved during a full-blown revolutionary movement and over the course of a year of war, it is unreasonable to suppose that it might now be achieved, with the war overcome once more and its finest leaders imprisoned or dead, and all of them isolated and impoverished. And so we would be bringing a new caudillo to the Island, and we would come to wage a petty, personal war, powerful enough to resist, but not to vanquish, and in all likelihood tainted by impure desires, encumbered by jealousies and, in short, unworthy of those who think and act as honest men.

What General Vicente García may be able to do today could have been done before now: and if out of jealousy, or lack of will, or remorse, or lack of means it was not done at that time, then it would be unreasonable for him to attempt to do it today. The war thus renewed would not answer to the urgent needs and the grave general problems that afflict Cuba. And that is why I do not refer to those problems, or advise you, as I could advise you, to wait until I have read your response.

Our honor itself, and our very cause, demand that we abandon the field of armed warfare. We do not deserve to be and must not be taken for professional revolutionaries, blind and turbulent spirits, obdurate, vulgar men, capable of sacrificing noble lives to uphold a goal—*the only honorable one in Cuba*—whose triumph is now improbable.

A handful of men, driven on by their people, can achieve what Bolívar achieved; what, with fortune on our sides, we ourselves will achieve against Spain. But a small band of heroes, abandoned by their people, can, to ignoble and indifferent eyes, appear to be no more than a gang of bandits. Others advise you, out of a disgraceful vanity, to detain on the field of battle men to whom, at the moment, we have neither the will nor the way of sending resources; they seek to spare themselves the criticism that might be levied if they were to advise you to withdraw. I, who have no apology to make to the Spanish government; who will look on serenely as my wife and son leave me, bound for Cuba;[3] who will venture forth into new lands or remain in this one, my chest sheltered by the last tattered shred of the flag of honor—I, who will never make it a merit, before the enemies of our patria, to have sent the last soldier away from combat, I advise you, as a revolutionary, as a man who admires and envies your energy, and as a loving friend, not to remain fruitlessly on a field of battle where those you are defending are powerless to send you their aid.

Having said this, what can I tell you now about how you should carry it out? If you alone were combating, I would tell you to find a way of leaving the Island—but you have not wanted to abandon those who fight with you so bravely. It is hard to say it, and all the ice in my soul rises to my lips as I say it, but so sterile is the struggle—unworthy today because the country is unworthy of its last soldiers—that it must be said: *Lay down your arms.*

Do not lay them down before Spain, but before the hazards of fortune. Do not surrender to the enemy government, but to the luck that was against you. Do not cease to be honorable: last among the vanquished, you will be first among men of honor.

José Martí

LETTER TO GENERAL MÁXIMO GÓMEZ

Antonio Maceo and Máximo Gómez were the two most distinguished military leaders of the Ten Years War; their participation in any future insurgency was key. In the summer of 1884, both generals arrived in New York to lay the groundwork for another war of independence. Martí met with them extensively throughout the summer and fall, and was beginning to be concerned by Gómez's growing authoritarianism; one of his greatest fears had always been that Cuba would achieve its freedom only to succumb to the military tyranny that plagued many Latin American countries. One day in October, during a meeting with the two, Martí was speaking of his plans and Gómez interrupted him curtly: "Look, Martí: You limit yourself to what you're instructed to do; for the rest, General Maceo will do what he must." Maceo attempted to soothe Martí after Gómez left the room, but Martí, fearing the worst, went home and wrote Gómez the following letter. He then withdrew from the Cuban revolutionary movement. Gómez and Maceo continued to pursue their plans, but by August of the following year, both men acknowledged that the independence movement had failed once more.

New York, October 20, 1884

General Máximo Gómez
New York

Distinguished General and friend:

I left your house early Saturday morning with an impression so painful that I have let it rest for two days, so that the decision that it, along with other, previous impressions, has moved me to make would not be the result of some passing agitation or excessive zeal in the defense of things I would never wish to see attacked, but the work of mature meditation. What sorrow it gives me to have to say these things to a man whom I believe to be sincere and good and in whom there exist qualities outstanding enough to make him truly great![1] However, there is one thing that lies beyond all the personal sympathy you may inspire in me, and beyond all argument, however opportune it may seem, and that is my determination not to contribute by one iota, out of blind love for the idea that is consuming my life, to bringing a regime of personal despotism to my land, a regime that would be even more shameful and calamitous than the political despotism it now endures, and more serious and difficult to eradicate, because it would be excused by certain virtues, and established upon an idea which it embodied, and legitimized by triumph.

A nation is not founded, General, as a military camp is commanded. When, in the preparations for a revolution more delicate and complex than any other, no sincere desire is manifested to know and reconcile all the various tasks, wills, and elements that make possible the armed struggle—which is merely one of the forms that the spirit of independence takes—but instead, at each step, a brusquely expressed or poorly concealed intention is evinced to make all the resources of faith and war raised by that spirit serve the furtive personal aims of the justly famous leaders who present themselves to captain the war, then what guarantee can there be that the civil liberties which are the only object worth plunging a country into battle over will be more fully respected tomorrow? What are we, General? Are we the heroic, modest servants of an idea that fires our hearts, the loyal friends of a nation in distress? Or are we bold and fortune-favored caudillos who with whip in hand and spurs on our heels prepare to bring war to a nation in order to take possession of it for ourselves? Both of you earned a reputation for valor, loyalty, and prudence in one undertaking: will you now lose that reputation in another? If the war, along with all the noble and legitimate prestige that arises from it, is possible, that is because of the prior existence of the spirit, tried by great suffering, that clamors for it and makes it necessary. This spirit must be heard, and the most profound respect must be demonstrated for it in every public and private act, because just as he who gives his life to serve a great idea is admirable, he who takes advantage of a great idea to serve his own personal hopes for glory or power is abominable, even if he risks his life for them. One has the right to give one's life only when one gives it without self-interest.

I can already see you in distress, for I understand that you are acting in good faith in all that you undertake, and that, feeling yourself to be inspired by pure motives, you truly believe that what you are doing is the only proper way of proceeding open to you. But the greatest mistakes can be committed with the greatest sincerity, and notwithstanding any secondary consideration, the austere truth, which knows no friend, must go out to confront all that it considers a danger, and set serious matters to right before they have progressed so far that there is no remedy. Control your distress, General, as on Saturday I controlled the amazement and disgust with which I listened to an unfortunate outburst from you, and the curious conversation General Maceo began with respect to it, in which he sought—oh utmost madness!—to make me understand that we should consider the war in Cuba as your exclusive property, and that no one else can put any thought or work into it without committing a profanation, and that anyone who wishes to assist it must do so by leaving it blindly and obediently in your hands. No, no, by God!—to seek to suffocate thought even before seeing yourselves, as you both will very soon, in front of an enthused and grateful people, wearing all the raiment of victory. The patria belongs to no one, and if it does it will belong—and then only in spirit—to he who serves it with the greatest selflessness and intelligence.

A war undertaken in compliance with the nation's mandate, in consultation with the representatives of its interests, in harmony with the largest number of friendly elements that can be achieved—it was such a war that I had believed—because I had depicted it to you in a letter three years ago, to which you sent me a beautiful response—you were now offering to lead, and to such a war I have given my whole soul because that war will save my people. But our conversation gave me to understand that this war was a personal adventure, cleverly undertaken at an opportune moment in which the particular aims of the caudillos could be merged with the glorious ideas that make them possible. And to a campaign such as that, waged as a private enterprise, without showing more respect for the patriotic spirit that makes it possible than that which cunning dictates as indispensable in order to attract the people and elements that can be useful in one way or another; to an armed struggle (however brilliant and magnificent it must be, and however much he who leads it shall be crowned with success and personally honored) that does not, from its first deed and earliest preparations, demonstrate that it is being attempted as a service to the country and not as a despotic invasion; to a military undertaking that is not publicly, openly, sincerely, and solely moved by the aim of placing, at its conclusion, civil liberties in the hands of the country, grateful in advance to its servants; to such a war of ignoble root and fearsome ends, whatever its magnitude and possibility of success might be—and I am aware that the possibility is now great—I would never lend my support—whatever it might be worth, and I know that because it arises from an invincible resolve to be absolutely honorable it is worth pure gold—I will never lend it.

How, General, could I undertake missions, attract affections, take advantage of the affections I already have, convince eminent men and set wills in motion, with such fears and doubts in my soul? I am desisting, therefore, from all the active labors that I had begun to take upon myself.

And do not take my having written you these reasons badly, General. I believe you to be a noble man, and you deserve to be made to think. You may become very great, and you may not. To respect a country that loves us and places its hopes in us is the utmost greatness. To use its sorrows and enthusiasms to our own advantage would be the greatest ignominy. In truth, General, ever since Honduras I had been told that intrigues were perhaps forming around you which were poisoning your simple heart without your feeling it, and taking advantage of your goodness, your impressions, and your habits to separate you from anyone you found along your way who would affectionately accompany you in your labors and help you free yourself from the obstacles that were presenting themselves on the path to an exaltation that is your natural right. But I confess that I have neither the will nor the patience to go about sniffing out intrigues or disentangling them. I am above all that. I serve nothing but duty, and that will always be power enough for me.

Has anyone approached you, General, with an affection warmer than that with which I held you in my arms on the first day I saw you? Have you felt in many men the fatal abundance of heart that would do me such harm if I needed to keep my aims hidden in order to promote today's womanish little ambitions or tomorrow's hopes?

Yet, after all I have written, and have carefully reread, and confirm, I still believe you are full of merit and I love you: but as for the war which right now it seems to me, perhaps by some misunderstanding, you represent,—no:—

Esteeming you, serving you, I remain

José Martí

A VINDICATION OF CUBA

In the late 1880s, the newly elected administration of Benjamin Harrison was bandying about the old idea of purchasing Cuba from Spain. At that point, the purchase was seen as a way of disposing of the surplus in the Treasury and postponing the looming and highly controversial issue of import tariff reduction, since Cuban sugar could be admitted free of tax if Cuba were part of the Union. On Thursday, March 21, 1889, the New York Evening Post *published a short article titled "A Protectionist View of Cuban Annexation," which noted the surprisingly anti-annexationist stance of the Philadelphia* Manufacturer, *which the* Post *called "the only professedly high-tariff organ in the country that is conducted with decent ability." The* Post *cited the following paragraph from an article recently published by the* Manufacturer:

The people of Cuba are divided into three classes, Spaniards, native Cubans of Spanish descent, and negroes. The men of Spanish birth are probably less fitted than men of any other white race to become American citizens. They have ruled Cuba for centuries. They rule it now upon almost precisely the same methods that they have always employed, methods which com-

bine bigotry with tyranny, and silly pride with fathomless corruption. The less we have of them the better. The native Cubans
are not much more desirable: To the faults of the men of the par-
ent race they add effeminacy and a distaste for exertion which
amounts really to disease. They are helpless, idle, of defective
morals, and unfitted by nature and experience for discharging
the obligations of citizenship in a great and free republic. Their
lack of manly force and of self-respect is demonstrated by the
supineness with which they have so long submitted to Spanish
oppression, and even their attempts at rebellion have been so
pitifully ineffective that they have risen little above the dignity
of farce. To clothe such men with the responsibilities of directing
this government, and to give them the same measure of power
that is wielded by the freemen of our Northern States, would be
to summon them to the performance of functions for which they
have not the smallest capacity.

The anonymous writer for the New York Evening Post then con-
curred:

All of this we emphatically endorse, and it may be added that if
we have now a Southern question which disturbs us more or less,
we should have it in a more aggravated form if Cuba were
added to the Union, with near a million blacks, much inferior to
our own in point of civilization, who must, of course, be armed
with the ballot and put on the same level politically with their
former masters. If Mr. Chandler and Gov. Foraker[1] can scarcely
endure the spectacle which they daily behold in the Southern
States, of negroes deprived of the elective franchise, what must
their sufferings be when the responsibility of Cuba is put upon
them also? Imagine a special Committee of the Senate going to
Cuba to take testimony on the disfranchisement of the freedmen.
In the first place, the difficulties of language would be insur-
mountable, for the Spanish tongue as spoken on the plantations
would be rather harder to learn than that of the Basque
provinces. The report of such a committee would either become a
laughing-stock, or would plunge Congress into dire confusion.
    Probably we shall be spared any such infliction as the annex-
ation of Cuba by the refusal of Spain to sell the island. A Madrid
despatch says that Minister Moret, in reply to a question in the
Senate yesterday, declared that Spain would not entertain any
offer from the United States for the purchase of the island, and,

*as if this statement were not sufficiently emphatic, he added that
there was not money enough in the whole world to buy the
smallest portion of Spanish territory.*

In response, Martí wrote the following letter, which the Evening
Post *published on March 25, 1889. It appears here exactly as it did
there. Martí subsequently published a pamphlet titled* "Cuba y los
Estados Unidos," *which contained Spanish translations of the articles from the* Manufacturer *and the* Post, *and of his response.*

To the editor of *The Evening Post:*

Sir: I beg to be allowed the privilege of referring in your columns to
the injurious criticism of the Cubans printed in the *Manufacturer* of
Philadelphia, and reproduced in your issue of yesterday.

This is not the occasion to discuss the question of the annexation of
Cuba. It is probable that no self-respecting Cuban would like to see
his country annexed to a nation where the leaders of opinion share
towards him the prejudices excusable only to vulgar jingoism or ram-
pant ignorance. No honest Cuban will stoop to be received as a moral
pest for the sake of the usefulness of his land in a community where
his ability is denied, his morality insulted, and his character despised.
There are some Cubans who, from honorable motives, from an ardent
admiration for progress and liberty, from a prescience of their own
powers under better political conditions, from an unhappy ignorance
of the history and tendency of annexation, would like to see the island
annexed to the United States. But those who have fought in war and
learned in exile, who have built, by the work of hands and mind, a virtuous home in the heart of an unfriendly community; who, by their
successful efforts as scientists and merchants, as railroad builders and
engineers, as teachers, artists, lawyers, journalists, orators and poets,
as men of alert intelligence and uncommon activity, are honored
wherever their powers have been called into action and the people are
just enough to understand them; those who have raised, with their less
prepared elements, a town of workingmen where the United States
had previously a few huts in a barren cliff; those, more numerous than
the others, do not desire the annexation of Cuba to the United States.
They do not need it. They admire this nation, the greatest ever built
by liberty, but they dislike the evil conditions that, like worms in the

heart, have begun in this mighty republic their work of destruction. They have made of the heroes of this country their own heroes, and look to the success of the American commonwealth as the crowning glory of mankind; but they cannot honestly believe that excessive individualism, reverence for wealth, and the protracted exultation of a terrible victory are preparing the United States to be the typical nation of liberty, where no opinion is to be based in greed, and no triumph or acquisition reached against charity and justice. We love the country of Lincoln as much as we fear the country of Cutting.[2]

We are not the people of destitute vagrants or immoral pigmies that the *Manufacturer* is pleased to picture; nor the country of petty talkers, incapable of action, hostile to hard work, that, in a mass with the other countries of Spanish America, we are by arrogant travellers and writers represented to be. We have suffered impatiently under tyranny; we have fought like men, sometimes like giants, to be freemen; we are passing that period of stormy repose, full of germs of revolt, that naturally follows a period of excessive and unsuccessful action; we have to fight like conquered men against an oppressor who denies us the means of living, and fosters—in the beautiful capital visited by the tourists, in the interior of the country, where the prey escapes his grasp—a reign of such corruption as may poison in our veins the strength to secure freedom; we deserve in our misfortune the respect of those who did not help us in our need.

But because our Government has systematically allowed after the war the triumph of criminals, the occupation of the cities by the scum of the people, the ostentation of ill-gotten riches by a myriad of Spanish office-holders and their Cuban accomplices, the conversion of the capital into a gambling-den, where the hero and the philosopher walk hungry by the lordly thief of the metropolis; because the healthier farmer, ruined by a war seemingly useless, turns in silence to the plough that he knew well how to exchange for the *machete;* because thousands of exiles, profiting by a period of calm that no human power can quicken until it is naturally exhausted, are practising in the battle of life in the free countries the art of governing themselves and of building a nation; because our half-breeds and city-bred young men are generally of delicate physique, of suave courtesy and ready words, hiding under the glove that polishes the poem the hand that fells the foe—are we to be considered, as the *Manufacturer* does consider us, an "effeminate" people? These city-bred young men and poorly built half-breeds knew in one day how to rise against a cruel government, to pay their passages to the seat of war with the product of their watches and trinkets, to work their way in exile while their vessels were being kept from them by the country of the free in the interest of the foes of freedom, to obey as soldiers, sleep in the mud, eat roots, fight ten years without salary, conquer foes with the branch of a tree, die—these men of eighteen, these heirs to wealthy estates, these dusky striplings—a death not to be spoken of without uncovering the head. They died like those other men of ours who, with a stroke of the *machete*, can send a head flying, or by a turn of the hands bring a bull to their feet. These "effeminate" Cubans had once courage enough, in the face of a hostile government, to carry on their left arms for a week the mourning for Lincoln.

The Cubans have, according to the *Manufacturer,* "a distaste for exertion"; they are "helpless," "idle." These "helpless," "idle" men came here twenty years ago empty-handed, with very few exceptions; fought against the climate; mastered the language; lived by their honest labor, some in affluence, a few in wealth, rarely in misery; they bought or built homes; they raised families and fortunes; they loved luxury and worked for it; they were not frequently seen in the dark roads of life; proud and self-sustaining, they never feared competition as to intelligence or diligence. Thousands have returned to die in their homes; thousands have remained where, during the hardships of life, they have triumphed, unaided by any help of kindred language, sympathy of race, or community of religion. A handful of Cuban toilers built Key West. The Cubans have made their mark in Panama by their ability as mechanics of the higher trades, as clerks, physicians, and contractors. A Cuban, Cisneros, has greatly advanced the development of railways and river navigation in Colombia. Marquez, another Cuban, gained, with many of his countrymen, the respect of the Peruvians as a merchant of eminent capacity. Cubans are found everywhere, working as farmers, surveyors, engineers, mechanics, teachers, journalists. In Philadelphia, the *Manufacturer* has a daily opportunity to see a hundred Cubans, some of them of heroic history and powerful build, who live by their work in easy comfort. In New York, the Cubans are directors of prominent banks, substantial merchants, popular brokers, clerks of recognized ability, physicians with a large practice, engineers of world-wide repute, electricians, journalists, tradesmen, cigarmakers. The poet of Niagara is a Cuban, our Heredia;[3] a Cuban, Menocal, is the projector of the canal of Nicaragua. In Philadelphia itself, as in New York, the college prizes have been more than once awarded to Cubans. The women of these "helpless," "idle" people, with "a distaste for exertion," arrived here from a life of luxury in the heart of the winter; their husbands were in the war, ruined, dead, imprisoned in Spain; the "Señora" went to work; from a slave-owner she became a slave, took a seat behind the counter, sang in the churches, worked button-holes by the hundred, sewed for a living, curled feathers, gave her soul to duty, withered in work her body. This is the people of "defective morals."

We are "unfitted by nature and experience to discharge the obligations of citizenship in a great and free country." This cannot be justly said of a people who possess, besides the energy that built the first railroad in Spanish dominions and established against the opposition of the Government all the agencies of civilization, a truly remarkable knowledge of the body politic, a tried readiness to adapt itself to its higher forms, and the power rare in tropical countries of nerving their thought and pruning their language. Their passion for liberty, the conscientious study of its best teachings, the nursing of individual character in exile and at home, the lessons of ten years of war and its manifold consequences, and the practical exercise of the duties of citizenship in the free countries of the world, have combined, in spite of all antecedents, to develop in the Cuban a capacity for free government so natural to him that he established it, even to the excess of its practices, in the midst of the war, vied with his elders in the effort to respect the laws of liberty, and snatched the sabre, without fear or consideration, from the hands of every military pretender, however glorious. There seems to be in the Cuban mind a happy faculty of uniting sense with earnestness and moderation with exuberance. Noble teachers have devoted themselves since the beginning of the century to explain by their words and exemplify by their lives the self-restraint and tolerance inseparable from liberty. Those who won the first seats ten years ago at the European universities by singular merit have been proclaimed, at their appearance in the Spanish Parliament, men of subtle thought and powerful speech. The political knowledge of the average Cuban compares well with that of the average American citizen. Absolute freedom from religious intolerance, the love of man for the work he creates by his industry, and theoretical and practical familiarity with the laws and processes of liberty, will enable the Cuban to rebuild his country from the ruins in which he will receive it from its oppressors. It is not to be expected, for the honor of mankind, that the nation that was rocked in freedom, and received for three centuries the best blood of liberty-loving men, will employ the power thus acquired in depriving a less fortunate neighbor of his liberty.

It is, finally, said that "our lack of manly force and of self-respect is demonstrated by the supineness with which we have so long submitted to Spanish oppression, and even our attempts at rebellion have been so pitifully ineffective that they have risen little above the dignity of farce." Never was ignorance of history and character more pitifully displayed than in this wanton assertion. We need to recollect, in order to answer without bitterness, that more than one American bled by our side,[4] in a war that another American was to call a farce. A farce! the war that has been by foreign observers compared to an epic, the upheaval of a whole country, the voluntary abandonment of wealth, the abolition of slavery in our first moment of freedom, the burning of our cities by our own hands, the erection of villages and factories in the wild forests, the dressing of our ladies of rank in the textures of the woods, the keeping at bay, in ten years of such a life, a powerful enemy, with a loss to him of 200,000 men, at the hands of a small army of patriots, with no help but nature! We had no Hessians and no Frenchmen, no Lafayette or Steuben, no monarchical rivals to help us; we had but one neighbor who confessedly "stretched the limits of his power, and acted against the will of the people" to help the foes of those who were fighting for the same Chart of Liberties on which he built his independence. We fell a victim to the very passions which could have caused the downfall of the thirteen States, had they not been cemented by success, while we were enfeebled by procrastination; a procrastination brought about, not from cowardice, but from an abhorrence of blood, which allowed the enemy in the first months of the war to acquire unconquerable advantage, and from a childlike confidence in the certain help of the United States: "They cannot see us dying for liberty at their own doors without raising a hand or saying a word to give to the world a new free country!" They "stretched the limits of their powers in deference to Spain." They did not raise the hand. They did not say the word.

The struggle has not ceased. The exiles do not want to return. The new generation is worthy of its sires. Hundreds of men have died in darkness since the war in the misery of prisons. With life only will this fight for liberty cease among us. And it is the melancholy truth that our efforts would have been, in all probability, successfully renewed, were it not, in some of us, for the unmanly hope of the annexationists of securing liberty without paying its price; and the just fears of others that our dead, our sacred memories, our ruins drenched in blood, would be but the fertilizers of the soil for the benefit of a foreign plant, or the occasion for a sneer from the *Manufacturer* of Philadelphia.

With sincere thanks for the space you have kindly allowed me, I am, sir, yours very respectfully,

José Martí
120 Front Street, New York, March 23

1891–1894

His fear of U.S. intervention in Cuba heightened by the public mood, the actions of the Harrison administration, and the Pan-American and International Monetary Conferences, Martí began divesting himself of all other duties, including his work as a foreign correspondent, to devote himself fully to Cuba's revolution of independence. Late in 1891, he traveled to Florida and delivered two stirring speeches to the Cuban communities in Tampa and Cayo Hueso (Key West), which generated a great deal of support and funding for the revolution. In 1892 he participated in the founding of the Cuban Revolutionary Party, was elected its delegate, and founded its official organ, Patria, *which was published in New York City. In the two years after that, he traveled ceaselessly up and down the East Coast of the United States and throughout the Caribbean, promoting, planning, and raising money for the war he knew to be imminent.*

The most notable of Martí's final "Letters from New York" (he stopped writing them after 1892) are stark accounts of horrendous acts of racism—acts that undoubtedly increased his concern about the U.S. threat to Cuban independence. Nevertheless, his overall depiction of the country did not lose its depth and nuance, and he continued to find much to appreciate and applaud; the articles from this period are as unstinting as ever in their praise of men like Lincoln, Peter Cooper, Charles A. Dana, and Walt Whitman, and of literary societies "where men learn to think on their feet," and churches "where the pastor stands up to address the country's vital issues." In one of the last of the "Letters," published in El Partido Liberal *(Mexico City) in May 1892, he described a lavish banquet given by the New York Chamber of Commerce; far more striking than the luxury of the decor and the fare, he wrote, was the sight of the head table, where men of fiercely opposing views—Democrats and Republicans, bitter political enemies, champions of rival candidates, men who hotly denounced the nation's growing imperialism and men who fostered it—sat next to each other and raised their glasses together "To the Star-Spangled Banner."*

POETRY

SIMPLE VERSES / *VERSOS SENCILLOS*

From October 1889 to April 1890, the First Pan-American Conference was held in Washington, with James G. Blaine presiding, to consider a variety of issues, including measures for preserving the peace, the formation of a customs union, the adoption of a common silver coin, and a uniform system of weights, measures, patent rights, copyrights, and trademarks. All of the independent Latin American republics except the Dominican Republic attended. The New York Tribune openly characterized the conference as an attempt by the United States to establish commercial supremacy in the hemisphere and exercise a direct and general influence on all matters within the American continent—a view shared by Martí. At the same time, a law authorizing the U.S. president to negotiate with Spain for the purchase of Cuba was being considered by the Senate, one of whose members urged the Department of the Navy to build a fleet "superior . . . to that of the nation which possesses the island of Cuba."

As the consul of Uruguay, Martí participated in the conference and, in December 1889, gave a memorable speech to its delegates on the divergence in history and temperament of the two Americas, a topic he would return to most significantly in "Our America." Finally, the First Pan-American Conference had few concrete results, but its aftermath gave rise to Martí's best-known collection of poems.

PROLOGUE

My friends know how these verses grew from my heart. It was during that anguished winter when, out of ignorance, blind faith, fear, or mere politeness, the peoples of Latin America gathered in Washington beneath the fearsome eagle. Who among us has forgotten that seal, on which the eagle of Monterrey and Chapultepec, López and Walker,[1] clutched all the flags of America in its talons? And the agony I lived through, until the caution and vitality of our peoples was proven to me; and the shame and horror into which I was plunged by my legitimate fear that we Cubans might with patricidal hands assist in the senseless project of separating Cuba, for the sole good of a new and covert master, from the patria that clamors for her and in her is complete, the patria of Latin America—all of it took away my strength, already worn down by unjust griefs. The doctor sent me off to the woods; streams flowed and clouds gathered; I wrote poems. Sometimes the sea roars in black night and waves crash against the rocks of the grim castle; at other times a bee hums as it roams among flowers.

Why publish these simple lines, written as if in play, and not my incensed *Free Verses*, those bristling hendecasyllables born of great fear and great hope, an invincible love of freedom and a sorrowful love of beauty, which are like a stream of natural gold running between turbulent waters, sand and roots, like red-hot iron that hisses and shoots off sparks, like incandescent fountains? And why not my *Cuban Verses*, so full of rage they are best left unseen? Or my many other secret sins, all those naive and rebellious attempts at literature? And why do I not deliver now, on the occasion of these wildflowers, a course in my poetics, and say why I deliberately repeat a consonant or balance and group them so they will reach through eye and ear to the emotions, or leap straight there when a tumultuous idea asks for no rhymes and will stand for no embellishment? These verses are being printed because the affection with which they were received by some good souls on a night of poetry and friendship has already made them public. And because I love simplicity and believe in the need to express emotion in plain and honest forms.

José Martí
New York: 1891

I

Yo soy un hombre sincero
De donde crece la palma,
Y antes de morirme quiero
Echar mis versos del alma.

Yo vengo de todas partes,
Y hacia todas partes voy:
Arte soy entre las artes,
En los montes, monte soy.

Yo sé los nombres extraños
De las yerbas y las flores,
Y de mortales engaños,
Y de sublimes dolores.

Yo he visto en la noche oscura
Llover sobre mi cabeza
Los rayos de lumbre pura
De la divina belleza.

Alas nacer vi en los hombros
De las mujeres hermosas:
Y salir de los escombros
Volando las mariposas.

He visto vivir a un hombre
Con el puñal al costado,
Sin decir jamás el nombre
De aquella que lo ha matado.

Rápida, como un reflejo,
Dos veces vi el alma, dos:
Cuando murió el pobre viejo,
Cuando ella me dijo adiós.

Temblé una vez,—en la reja,
A la entrada de la viña,—

I

I am an honest man
From where the palm tree grows,
And I want, before I die,
to cast these verses from my soul.[2]

I come from all places
and to all places go:
I am art among the arts
and mountain among mountains.

I know the strange names
of flowers and herbs
and of fatal deceptions
and magnificent griefs.

In night's darkness I've seen
raining down on my head
pure flames, flashing rays
of beauty divine.

Wings I saw springing
from fair women's shoulders,
and from beneath rubble
I've seen butterflies flutter.

I've seen a man live
with a knife in his side,
never speaking the name
of the woman who killed him.

Twice, quick as thinking,
I saw the soul, twice:
When the poor old man died,
and when she told me good-bye.

Once I trembled, at the bars
of the vineyard gate—

Cuando la bárbara abeja
Picó en la frente a mi niña.

Gocé una vez, de tal suerte
Que gocé cual nunca:—cuando
La sentencia de mi muerte
Leyó el alcaide llorando.

Oigo un suspiro, a través
De las tierras y la mar,
Y no es un suspiro,—es
Que mi hijo va a despertar.

Si dicen que del joyero
Tome la joya mejor,
Tomo a un amigo sincero
Y pongo a un lado el amor.

Yo he visto al águila herida
Volar al azul sereno,
Y morir en su guarida
La víbora del veneno.

Yo sé bien que cuando el mundo
Cede, lívido, al descanso,
Sobre el silencio profundo
Murmura el arroyo manso.

Yo he puesto la mano osada,
De horror y júbilo yerta,
Sobre la estrella apagada
Que cayó frente a mi puerta.

Oculto en mi pecho bravo
La pena que me lo hiere:
El hijo de un pueblo esclavo
Vive por él, calla, y muere.

Todo es hermoso y constante,
Todo es música y razón,

when a savage bee stung
the forehead of my little girl.

Once I reveled in a destiny
like no other joy I'd known:
when the warden—reading
my death sentence—wept.

I hear a sigh that passes
over lands and seas,
and is not a sigh—it is
my son, awakening from sleep.

If I'm told to choose
the jeweler's finest gem,
I'll leave love aside
and take an honest friend.

I've seen the wounded eagle
soar through serene azure;
I've watched the viper die
of venom in its lair.

I know that when the world
surrenders, pallid, to repose,
the murmur of a tranquil stream
through the deep silence flows.

I've set my daring hand
stiff with horror and exultation,
upon a fallen star
that lay lifeless at my door.

In my bold breast I hide
the pain that ever wounds it:
the son of a people enslaved
lives for them, falls silent, dies.

All is beautiful and unceasing,
all is music and reason,

Y todo, como el diamante,
Antes que luz es carbón.

Yo sé que el necio se entierra
Con gran lujo y con gran llanto,—
Y que no hay fruta en la tierra
Como la del camposanto.

Callo, y entiendo, y me quito
La pompa del rimador:
Cuelgo de un árbol marchito
Mi muceta de doctor.

III

Odio la máscara y vicio
Del corredor de mi hotel:
Me vuelvo al manso bullicio
De mi monte de laurel.

Con los pobres de la tierra
Quiero yo mi suerte echar:
El arroyo de la sierra
Me complace más que el mar.

Denle al vano el oro tierno
Que arde y brilla en el crisol:
A mí denme el bosque eterno
Cuando rompe en él el sol.

Yo he visto el oro hecho tierra
Barbullendo en la redoma:
Prefiero estar en la sierra
Cuando vuela una paloma.

Busca el obispo de España
Pilares para su altar;
¡En mi templo, en la montaña,
El álamo es el pilar!

and all, like the diamond,
is carbon first, then light.

I know that fools are buried
with much luxury and wailing—
and that no fruit on earth can rival
the cemetery's crop.

I fall silent, and understand,
and drop my rhymester's show:
Upon a barren tree I hang
my fine scholar's robes.

III

I hate the masks and vices
of the hallways of my hotel;
I turn to the gentle noises
of my woods of laurel.

With the wretched of the earth
I want to cast my lot:
A stream flowing over mountains
suits me better than the sea.

Let vain men have soft gold
that seethes and glitters in the crucible:
give me the eternal forest
when sunlight first breaks through.

I've seen gold transformed to earth
and burbling in the beaker;
I'm happier in the mountains
when a dove flies overhead.

The Bishop of Spain is seeking
pillars for his altar;
but in my forest temple
the pillars are all poplars.

Y la alfombra es puro helecho,
Y los muros abedul,
Y la luz viene del techo,
Del techo de cielo azul.

El obispo, por la noche,
Sale, despacio, a cantar:
Monta, callado, en su coche,
Que es la piña de un pinar.

Las jacas de su carroza
Son dos pájaros azules:
Y canta el aire y retoza,
Y cantan los abedules.

Duermo en mi cama de roca
Mi sueño dulce y profundo:
Roza una abeja mi boca
Y crece en mi cuerpo el mundo.

Brillan las grandes molduras
Al fuego de la mañana,
Que tiñe las colgaduras
De rosa, violeta y grana.

El clarín, solo en el monte,
Canta al primer arrebol:
La gasa del horizonte
Prende, de un aliento, el sol.

¡Díganle al obispo ciego,
Al viejo obispo de España
Que venga, que venga luego,
A mi templo, a la montaña!

XXVIII

Por la tumba del cortijo
Donde está el padre enterrado,

And the carpet is of ferns,
and birch trees are the walls,
and light falls from a ceiling
of pure blue sky.

In the night the bishop
goes sedately out to sing:
with a pinecone for a coach
he rides silent through the woods.

For ponies, his carriage has
two blue birds
and the air sings and frolics
and the birches sing along.

On my bed of rock I sleep
a sleep sweet and deep;
a bee skims past my lips,
and the world grows inside my body.

The great moldings flash
in the fire of morning,
that colors the vast draperies
pink, violet, and deep red.

The forest's lone bugle
rings in the first crimson glow:
and the sun, in one breath,
sets the horizon's gauze ablaze.

Tell that old, blind bishop,
the Bishop of Spain,
to come, and come soon,
to my temple, to the forest!

XXVIII

Past the manor with the tomb
where the father lies dead

Pasa el hijo, de soldado
Del invasor: pasa el hijo.

El padre, un bravo en la guerra,
Envuelto en su pabellón
Álzase: y de un bofetón
Lo tiende, muerto, por tierra.

El rayo reluce: zumba
El viento por el cortijo:
El padre recoge al hijo,
Y se lo lleva a la tumba.

XXX

El rayo surca, sangriento,
El lóbrego nubarrón:
Echa el barco, ciento a ciento,
Los negros por el portón.

El viento, fiero, quebraba
Los almácigos copudos:
Andaba la hilera, andaba,
De los esclavos desnudos.

El temporal sacudía
Los barracones henchidos:
Una madre con su cría
Pasaba, dando alaridos.

Rojo, como en el desierto,
Salió el sol al horizonte:
Y alumbró a un esclavo muerto,
Colgado a un seibo del monte.

Un niño lo vio: tembló
De pasión por los que gimen:
Y, al pie del muerto, juró
Lavar con su vida el crimen!

goes the son, a soldier now
for the invader: goes the son.

The father, valiant in the war,
rises up, swathed in his banner,
and with a single blow
lays his son dead upon the ground.

Lightning flashes, howling
winds engulf the manor:
the father gathers up the son
and brings him to the tomb.

XXX

Blood-hued lightning cleaves
the brooding storm cloud:
the boat's great door disgorges
Negroes by the hundreds.

The fierce wind was uprooting
the leafy mastic trees:
and the line marched on and on,
the line of naked slaves.

The sodden barracks
rattled in the storm:
a mother went past,
a shrieking baby in her arms.

Red as if it shone from a desert sky,
the sun came out on the horizon
and cast its light on a dead slave
hanging from a ceibo tree.

A child saw this and shuddered
with passion for those who groan;
he stood below the corpse and swore
to wash the crime away with his life.

XXXVI

Ya sé: de carne se puede
Hacer una flor: se puede,
Con el poder del cariño,
Hacer un cielo,—¡y un niño!

De carne se hace también
El alacrán; y también
El gusano de la rosa,
Y la lechuza espantosa.

XLV

Sueño con claustros de mármol
Donde en silencio divino
Los héroes, de pie, reposan:
¡De noche, a la luz del alma,
Hablo con ellos: de noche!
Están en fila: paseo
Entre las filas: las manos
De piedra les beso: abren
Los ojos de piedra: mueven
Los labios de piedra: tiemblan
Las barbas de piedra: empuñan
La espada de piedra: lloran:
¡Vibra la espada en la vaina!:
Mudo, les beso la mano.

Hablo con ellos, de noche!
Están en fila: paseo
Entre las filas: lloroso
Me abrazo a un mármol: «Oh mármol,
Dicen que beben tus hijos
Su propia sangre en las copas
Venenosas de sus dueños!
Que hablan la lengua podrida
De sus rufianes! que comen
Juntos el pan del oprobio,
En la mesa ensangrentada!

XXXVI

Yes, I know: flesh
can be shaped into a flower: by
love's power a heaven
can be made—and a child!

Flesh is the stuff
of the scorpion, too, and the worm,
that is in the rose,
and the dire bird of prey.

XLV

I dream of marble cloisters
where upright heroes
repose in divine silence:
at night, by the light of the soul,
I speak to them: at night.
They stand in rows: I stroll
among the rows: I kiss
their stony hands: they open
their stony eyes: move
their stony lips: their stony
beards tremble: they grip
their swords of stone: they weep:
the blade quivers in its scabbard:
silent, I kiss their hands.

I speak to them, at night!
They stand in rows: I stroll
among the rows, tearful
I embrace a marble statue: "Oh marble,
they say your sons drink
their own blood from the poisoned
cups of their masters!
And speak the rancid language
of their tormentors! And break
the bread of infamy together
at a table soaked in blood!

Que pierden en lengua inútil
El último fuego!: ¡dicen,
Oh mármol, mármol dormido,
Que ya se ha muerto tu raza!»

Échame en tierra de un bote
El héroe que abrazo: me ase
Del cuello: barre la tierra
Con mi cabeza: levanta
El brazo, ¡el brazo le luce
Lo mismo que un sol!: resuena
La piedra: buscan el cinto
Las manos blancas: del soclo
Saltan los hombres de mármol!

And that their useless tongues are losing
their last fire! They say,
oh marble, slumbering marble,
that your race is dead!"

    The hero I embrace throws me
to the ground: seizes
my neck: drags my head
across the floor: raises
an arm that flashes like a sun! The stone
reverberates: the white hands
seek their swordbelts: down from their pedestals
the men of marble leap!

from NOTEBOOK 18

Patriotism is (or has been until now), among the many known up to the present, the best (of all known) leavenings for all human virtues.

And I ask myself, with regard to Spain—(what we're worth now is inarguable)—was what existed in America when we expelled the conquistadores worth more than what was there when they came? In poetry, what colonial verses are worth the only known ode, or odes, of Netzahualcóyotl?[1] In architecture, what church wall, or celebrated facade, even that of the overwrought Sagrario in Mexico, is worth a wall of Mitla or the Governor's Palace?[2]

And Cuba must be free—of Spain and of the United States.

Honey corrodes iron. (The iron tanks for transporting honey on the boats of New Orleans.)

Those incapable of creation always accuse those who create of imitation.
    Frustrated talent is the implacable enemy of talent.

Who could photograph thought, as a horse is photographed in full gallop or a bird in flight?

It's grown wearisome to hear ignorant Hispanoamericans talk so much about the frequency of revolutions and the ineptitude of their governments. Let each one fulfill his duty as a man, and the governments, where they are bad, would have to improve. Let them stop living like revolting mollusks, cemented to the offices of the State.

Emerson anticipated Darwin. Poetry saw it first: it was anticipated in verse.

> And striving to be man, the worm
> Mounts through all the spires of form

Bryce and Noailles,[3] an Englishman and a Frenchman, think as I do, think as I do about the forceful, embryonic, and unsatisfactory state of the United States.

The phrase of the servant at the Murray Hill Hotel:
   "Do you know a South American gentleman, very tall, who has been dining here for a month now?"
   "I don't know. They come and go. *He has not made himself known to me.*" And the look of contempt, and the gesture of "leave the Emperor in peace!" with which he accompanied his answer! One lives in the United States as if under a hail of blows. These people speak as if they were brandishing their fists before your eyes.

"Héautontimoroumenos"
   (the executioner of himself)

My curiosities:
   How fire is produced. I believe in fire and in movement. Its generation and its phases may explain the whole of life in the universe.
   And my two problems—my three problems:
   What is to be done with a corpse? Burn it? Bury it?
   Should man eat other creatures who think and feel as he does, although to a lesser degree?
   And how does a father properly initiate his son into sexual knowledge—should he leave this matter on which all of life may depend to chance, or is there such a law within man that it alone guides him and is the only guide, or must be the indirect guide of the father, and no more? This problem, above all, in the city.
   That and suffrage are perhaps the only things that have left me uncertain.

When I close my eyes in the city, I see nothing but black. And when I close my eyes here, I see nothing but green.

from NOTEBOOK 20

Postrimerías[4]—I love this word in an extraordinary way. I love it as if it were a person: it made me a friend.

LETTERS FROM NEW YORK

OUR AMERICA

This essay is Martí's most frequently cited and anthologized work. It represents the culmination of a lifetime's reflection on Latin America, its essential unity, and its relationship to the United States, and it deliberately echoes and carries forward Latin American liberator Simón Bolívar's crucial 1815 "Letter to a Jamaican Gentleman," which also insisted on the importance of developing systems of government appropriate to a country, rather than importing them from outside.

The prideful villager thinks his hometown contains the whole world, and as long as he can stay on as mayor or humiliate the rival who stole his sweetheart or watch his nest egg accumulating in its strongbox he believes the universe to be in good order, unaware of the giants in seven-league boots who can crush him underfoot or the battling comets in the heavens that go through the air devouring the sleeping worlds. Whatever is left of that sleepy hometown in America must awaken. These are not times for going to bed in a sleeping cap, but rather, like Juan de Castellanos's[1] men, with our weapons for a pillow, weapons of the mind, which vanquish all others. Trenches of ideas are worth more than trenches of stone.

A cloud of ideas is a thing no armored prow can smash through. A vital idea set ablaze before the world at the right moment can, like the mystic banner of the last judgment, stop a fleet of battleships. Hometowns that are still strangers to one another must hurry to become acquainted, like men who are about to do battle together. Those who shake their fists at each other like jealous brothers quarreling over a piece of land or the owner of a small house who envies the man with a better one must join hands and interlace them until their two hands are as one. Those who, shielded by a criminal tradition, mutilate, with swords smeared in the same blood that flows through their own veins, the land of a conquered brother whose punishment far exceeds his crimes, must return that land to their brother if they do not wish to be known as a nation of plunderers. The honorable man does not collect his debts of honor in money, at so much per slap. We can no longer be

288

a nation of fluttering leaves, spending our lives in the air, our treetop crowned in flowers, humming or creaking, caressed by the caprices of sunlight or thrashed and felled by tempests. The trees must form ranks to block the seven-league giant! It is the hour of reckoning and of marching in unison, and we must move in lines as compact as the veins of silver that lie at the roots of the Andes.

Only runts whose growth was stunted will lack the necessary valor, for those who have no faith in their land are like men born prematurely. Having no valor themselves, they deny that other men do. Their puny arms, with bracelets and painted nails, the arms of Madrid or of Paris, cannot manage the lofty tree and so they say the tree cannot be climbed. We must load up the ships with these termites who gnaw away at the core of the patria that has nurtured them; if they are Parisians or Madrileños then let them stroll to the Prado by lamplight or go to Tortoni's for an ice. These sons of carpenters who are ashamed that their father was a carpenter! These men born in America who are ashamed of the mother that raised them because she wears an Indian apron, these delinquents who disown their sick mother and leave her alone in her sickbed! Which one is truly a man, he who stays with his mother to nurse her through her illness, or he who forces her to work somewhere out of sight, and lives off her sustenance in corrupted lands, with a worm for his insignia, cursing the bosom that bore him, sporting a sign that says "traitor" on the back of his paper dress-coat? These sons of our America, which must save herself through her Indians, and which is going from less to more, who desert her and take up arms in the armies of North America, which drowns its own Indians in blood and is going from more to less! These delicate creatures who are men but do not want to do men's work! Did Washington, who made that land for them, go and live with the English during the years when he saw the English marching against his own land? These *incroyables* who drag their honor across foreign soil, like the *incroyables* of the French Revolution, dancing, smacking their lips, and deliberately slurring their words!

And in what patria can a man take greater pride than in our long-suffering republics of America, erected among mute masses of Indians upon the bloodied arms of no more than a hundred apostles, to the sound of the book doing battle against the monk's tall candle? Never before have such advanced and consolidated nations been created from such disparate factors in less historical time. The haughty man thinks that because he wields a quick pen or a vivid phrase the earth was made to be his pedestal, and accuses his native republic of irredeemable incompetence because its virgin jungles do not continually provide him with the means of going about the world a famous plutocrat, driving Persian ponies and spilling champagne. The incapacity lies not in the emerging country, which demands forms that are appropriate to it and a grandeur that is useful, but in the leaders who try to rule unique nations, of a singular and violent composition, with laws inherited from four centuries of free practice in the United States and nineteen centuries of monarchy in France. A gaucho's pony cannot be stopped in midbolt by one of Alexander Hamilton's laws. The sluggish blood of the Indian race cannot be quickened by a phrase from Sieyès.[2] To govern well, one must attend closely to the reality of the place that is governed. In America, the good ruler does not need to know how the German or Frenchman is governed, but what elements his own country is composed of and how he can marshal them so as to reach, by means and institutions born from the country itself, the desirable state in which every man knows himself and is active, and all men enjoy the abundance that Nature, for the good of all, has bestowed on the country they make fruitful by their labor and defend with their lives. The government must be born from the country. The spirit of the government must be the spirit of the country. The form of the government must be in harmony with the country's natural constitution. The government is no more than an equilibrium among the country's natural elements.

In America the natural man has triumphed over the imported book. Natural men have triumphed over an artificial intelligentsia. The native mestizo has triumphed over the alien, pure-blooded criollo. The battle is not between civilization and barbarity, but between false erudition and nature. The natural man is good, and esteems and rewards a superior intelligence as long as that intelligence does not use his submission against him or offend him by ignoring him—for that the natural man deems unforgivable, and he is prepared to use force to regain the respect of anyone who wounds his sensibilities or harms his interests. The tyrants of America have come to power by acquiescing to these scorned natural elements and have fallen as soon as they betrayed them. The republics have purged the former tyrannies of their inability to know the true elements of the country, derive the form of government from them, and govern along with them. *Governor,* in a new country, means *Creator.*

In countries composed of educated and uneducated sectors, the uneducated will govern by their habit of attacking and resolving their doubts with their fists, unless the educated learn the art of governing. The uneducated masses are lazy and timid about matters of the intellect and want to be well-governed, but if the government injures them they shake it off and govern themselves. How can our governors emerge from the universities when there is not a university in America that teaches the most basic element of the art of governing, which is the analysis of all that is unique to the peoples of America? Our youth go out into the world wearing Yankee- or French-colored glasses and aspire to rule by guesswork a country they do not know. Those unacquainted with the rudiments of politics should not be allowed to embark on a career in politics. The literary prizes must not go to the best ode, but to the best study of the political factors in the student's country. In the newspapers, lecture halls, and academies, the study of the country's real factors must be carried forward. Simply knowing those factors without blindfolds or circumlocutions is enough—for anyone who deliberately or unknowingly sets aside a part of the truth will ultimately fail because of the truth he was lacking, which expands when neglected and brings down whatever is built without it. Solving the problem after knowing its elements is easier than solving it without knowing them. The natural man, strong and indignant, comes and overthrows the authority that is accumulated from books because it is not administered in keeping with the manifest needs of the country. To know is to solve. To know the country and govern it in accordance with that knowledge is the only way of freeing it from tyranny. The European university must yield to the American university. The history of America from the Incas to the present must be taught in its smallest detail, even if the Greek Archons go untaught. Our own Greece is preferable to the Greece that is not ours; we need it more. Statesmen who arise from the nation must replace statesmen who are alien to it. Let the world be grafted onto our republics, but we must be the trunk. And let the vanquished pedant hold his tongue, for there is no patria in which a man can take greater pride than in our long-suffering American republics.

Our feet upon a rosary, our heads white, and our bodies a motley of Indian and criollo we boldly entered the community of nations. Bearing the standard of the Virgin, we went out to conquer our liberty. A priest,[3] a few lieutenants, and a woman built a republic in Mexico upon the shoulders of the Indians. A Spanish cleric, under cover of his priestly cape, taught French liberty to a handful of magnificent students who chose a Spanish general to lead Central America against Spain. Still accustomed to monarchy, and with the sun on their chests, the Venezuelans in the north and the Argentines in the south set out to construct nations. When the two heroes clashed and the continent was about to be rocked, one of them, and not the lesser one, turned back.[4] But heroism is less glorious in peacetime than in war, and thus rarer, and it is easier for a man to die with honor than to think in an orderly way. Exalted and unanimous sentiments are more readily governed than the diverging, arrogant, alien, and ambitious ideas that emerge when the battle is over. The powers that were swept up in the epic struggle, along with the feline wariness of the species and the sheer weight of reality, undermined the edifice that had raised the flags of nations sustained by wise governance in the continual practice of reason and freedom over the crude and singular regions of our mestizo America with its towns of bare legs and Parisian dress-coats. The colonial hierarchy resisted the republic's democracy, and the capital city, wearing its elegant cravat, left the countryside, in its horsehide boots, waiting at the door; the redeemers born from books did not understand that a revolution that had triumphed when the soul of the earth was unleashed by a savior's voice had to govern with the soul of the earth and not against or without it. And for all these reasons, America began enduring and still endures the weary task of reconciling the discordant and hostile elements it inherited from its perverse, despotic colonizer with the imported forms and ideas that have, in their lack of local reality, delayed the advent of a logical form of government. The continent, deformed by three centuries of a rule that denied man the right to exercise his reason, embarked—overlooking or refusing to listen to the ignorant masses that had helped it redeem itself—upon a government based on reason, the reason of all directed toward the things that are of concern to all, and not the university-taught reason of the few imposed upon the rustic reason of others. The problem of independence was not the change in form, but the change in spirit.

Common cause had to be made with the oppressed in order to consolidate a system that was opposed to the interests and governmental habits of the oppressors. The tiger, frightened away by the flash of gunfire, creeps back in the night to find his prey. He will die with flames shooting from his eyes, his claws unsheathed, but now his step is inaudible for he comes on velvet paws. When the prey awakens, the tiger is upon him. The colony lives on in the republic, but our America is saving itself from its grave blunders—the arrogance of the capital cities, the blind triumph of the scorned campesinos, the excessive importation of foreign ideas and formulas, the wicked and impolitic disdain for the native race—through the superior virtue, confirmed by necessary bloodshed, of the republic that struggles against the colony. The tiger waits behind every tree, crouches in every corner. He will die, his claws unsheathed, flames shooting from his eyes.

But "these countries will be saved," in the words of the Argentine Rivadivia,[5] who erred on the side of urbanity during crude times; the machete is ill-suited to a silken scabbard, nor can the spear be abandoned in a country won by the spear, for it becomes enraged and stands in the doorway of Iturbide's Congress[6] demanding that "the fair-skinned man be made emperor." These countries will be saved because, with the genius of moderation that now seems, by nature's serene harmony, to prevail in the continent of light, and the influence of the critical reading that has, in Europe, replaced the fumbling ideas about phalansteries in which the previous generation was steeped, the real man is being born to America, in these real times.

What a vision we were: the chest of an athlete, the hands of a dandy, and the forehead of a child. We were a whole fancy dress ball, in English trousers, a Parisian waistcoat, a North American overcoat, and a Spanish bullfighter's hat. The Indian circled about us, mute, and went to the mountaintop to christen his children. The black, pursued from afar, alone and unknown, sang his heart's music in the night, between waves and wild beasts. The campesinos, the men of the land, the creators, rose up in blind indignation against the disdainful city, their own creation. We wore epaulets and judge's robes, in countries that came into the world wearing rope sandals and Indian headbands. The wise thing would have been to pair, with charitable hearts and the audacity of our founders, the Indian headband and the judicial robe, to undam the Indian, make a place for the able black, and tailor liberty to the bodies of those who rose up and triumphed in its name. What we had was the judge, the general, the man of letters, and the cleric. Our angelic youth, as if struggling from the arms of an octopus, cast their heads into the heavens and fell back with sterile glory, crowned with clouds. The natural people, driven by instinct, blind with triumph, overwhelmed their gilded rulers. No Yankee or European book could furnish the key to the Hispanoamerican enigma. So the people tried hatred instead, and our countries amounted to less and less each year. Weary of useless hatred, of the struggle of book against sword, reason against the monk's taper, city against countryside, the impossible empire of the quarreling urban castes against the tempestuous or inert natural nation, we are beginning, almost unknowingly, to try love. The nations arise and salute one another. "What are we like?" they ask, and begin telling each other what they are like. When a problem arises in Cojimar they no longer seek the solution in Dantzig. The frock-coats are still French, but the thinking begins to be American. The young men of America are rolling up their sleeves and plunging their hands into the dough, and making it rise with the leavening of their sweat. They understand that there is too much imitation, and that salvation lies in creating. *Create* is this generation's password. Make wine from plantains; it may be sour, but it is our wine! It is now understood that a country's form of government must adapt to its natural elements, that absolute ideas, in order not to collapse over an error of form, must be expressed in relative forms; that liberty, in order to be viable, must be sincere and full, that if the republic does not open its arms to all and include all in its progress, it dies. The tiger inside came in through the gap, and so will the tiger outside. The general holds the cavalry's speed to the pace of the infantry, for if he leaves the infantry far behind, the enemy will surround the cavalry. Politics is strategy. Nations must continually criticize themselves, for criticism is health, but with a single heart and a single mind. Lower yourselves to the unfortunate and raise them up in your arms! Let the heart's fires unfreeze all that is motionless in America, and let the country's natural blood surge and throb through its veins! Standing tall, the workmen's eyes full of joy, the new men of America are saluting each other from one country to another. Natural statesmen are emerging from the direct study of nature; they read in order to apply what they read, not copy it. Economists are studying problems at their origins. Orators are becoming more temperate. Dramatists are putting native characters onstage. Academies are discussing practical subjects. Poetry is snipping off its wild, Zorilla-esque[7] mane and hanging up its gaudy waistcoat on the glorious tree. Prose, polished and gleaming, is replete with ideas. The rulers of Indian republics are learning Indian languages.

America is saving herself from all her dangers. Over some republics the octopus sleeps still, but by the law of equilibrium, other republics are running into the sea to recover the lost centuries with mad and sublime swiftness. Others, forgetting that Juárez[8] traveled in a coach drawn by mules, hitch their coach to the wind and take a soap bubble for coachman—and poisonous luxury, enemy of liberty, corrupts the frivolous and opens the door to foreigners. The virile character of others is being perfected by the epic spirit of a threatened independence. And others, in rapacious wars against their neighbors, are nurturing an unruly soldier caste that may devour them. But our America may also face another danger, which comes not from within but from the differing origins, methods, and interests of the continent's two factions. The hour is near when she will be approached by an enterprising and forceful nation that will demand intimate relations with her, though it does not know her and disdains her. And virile nations self-made by the rifle and the law love other virile nations, and love only them. The hour of unbridled passion and ambition from which North America may escape by the ascendency of the purest element in its blood—or into which its vengeful and sordid masses, its tradition of conquest, and the self-interest of a cunning leader could plunge it—is not yet so close, even to the most apprehensive eye, that there is no time for it to be confronted and averted by the manifestation of a discreet and unswerving pride, for its dignity as a republic, in the eyes of the watchful nations of the Universe, places upon North America a brake that our America must not remove by puerile provocation, ostentatious arrogance, or patricidal discord. Therefore the urgent duty of our America is to show herself as she is, one in soul and intent, rapidly overcoming the crushing weight of her past and stained only by the fertile blood shed by hands that do battle against ruins and by veins that were punctured by our former masters. The disdain of the formidable neighbor who does not know her is our America's greatest danger, and it is urgent—for the day of the visit is near—that her neighbor come to know her, and quickly, so that he will not disdain her. Out of ignorance, he may perhaps begin to covet her. But when he knows her, he will remove his hands from her in respect. One must have faith in the best in man and distrust the worst. One must give the best every opportunity, so that the worst will be laid bare and overcome. If not, the worst will prevail. Nations should have one special pillory for those who incite them to futile hatreds, and another for those who do not tell them the truth until it is too late.

There is no racial hatred, because there are no races. Sickly, lamp-lit minds string together and rewarm the library-shelf races that the honest traveler and the cordial observer seek in vain in the justice of nature, where the universal identity of man leaps forth in victorious love and turbulent appetite. The soul, equal and eternal, emanates from bodies that are diverse in form and color. Anyone who promotes and disseminates opposition or hatred among races is committing a sin against humanity. But within that jumble of peoples which lives in close proximity to our peoples, certain peculiar and dynamic characteristics are condensed—ideas and habits of expansion, acquisition, vanity, and greed—that could, in a period of internal disorder or precipitation of a people's cumulative character, cease to be latent national preoccupations and become a serious threat to the neighboring, isolated and weak lands that the strong country declares to be perishable and inferior. To think is to serve. We must not, out of a villager's antipathy, impute some lethal congenital wickedness to the continent's light-skinned nation simply because it does not speak our language or share our view of what home life should be or resemble us in its political failings, which are different from ours, or because it does not think highly of quick-tempered, swarthy men or look with charity, from its still uncertain eminence, upon those less favored by history who, in heroic stages, are climbing the road that republics travel. But neither should we seek to conceal the obvious facts of the problem, which can, for the peace of the centuries, be resolved by timely study and the urgent, wordless union of the continental soul. For the unanimous hymn is already ringing forth, and the present generation is bearing industrious America along the road sanctioned by our sublime forefathers. From the Rio Bravo to the Straits of Magellan, the Great Cemi,[9] seated on a condor's back, has scattered the seeds of the new America across the romantic nations of the continent and the suffering islands of the sea!

—*El Partido Liberal* (Mexico City), January 20, 1891

THE LYNCHING OF THE ITALIANS

On March 14, 1891, a mob broke into the New Orleans jail and lynched eleven of the nineteen Sicilians who were being held there. The Italian government subsequently demanded that the lynchers be punished and entered claims for indemnity for the three Sicilians who had been Italian subjects. When it did not receive a prompt

answer, Italy withdrew its ambassador from Washington and there
was a brief war scare between the two nations, its flames fanned en-
ergetically by the sensationalistic U.S. press. In 1892, after a year-
long break in diplomatic relations, the United States paid Italy an
indemnity of $25,000.

From this day forward, no one who knows what pity is will set foot in
New Orleans without horror. Here and there, like the last gusts of a
storm, a group of murderers comes around a corner and disappears, rifles on their shoulders. Over there another group goes by, made up of
lawyers and businessmen, robust blue-eyed men with revolvers at
their hips and leaves on their lapels, leaves from the tree where they
have hung a dead man—a dead Italian—one of the nineteen Italians
who were in jail, accused of having taken part in the murder of Police
Chief Hennessy. A jury of North Americans had absolved four of the
nineteen, the proceedings against a few others had been declared a
mistrial, and others had not yet been tried.

And a few hours after that jury of North Americans absolved the
four Italians, a committee of leading citizens named by the mayor to
assist in punishing the murder, a committee led by the chief of one of
the city's political factions, convokes the citizens in printed and public
appeals to a riot to be held the next day, and presides over the crowd
that gathers at the foot of a statue of Henry Clay, then attacks the
parish jail with only the most minimal interference, meant only to preserve appearances, from the police, the militia, the mayor, or the governor; breaks down the compliant doors of the prison; rushes
bellowing through the corridors in pursuit of the fleeing Italians, and
with the butt-ends of its revolvers smashes in the heads of the Italian
political leader, the banker, and the consul—consul of Bolivia—who
are accused of having been the accomplices of a gang of murderers, a
secret gang of the Mafia. Three more of those who, like the banker,
had been absolved, along with seven others, are killed, against the wall,
in the corners, on the ground, at point-blank range. Returning from
this task, the citizens cheer the lawyer who presided over the massacre
and carry him through the streets on their shoulders.

Can these be the streets of blooming houses where tendrils of morning glory climb between white shutters, where mulattas in their turbans
and aprons bring in gaily colored Indian baskets from the wrought-

iron balconies and the Creole bride goes to the lake to lunch on pearly, golden fish, with a rosebud at her breast and an orange blossom in her black hair? Is this the city of oaks overgrown with a botanical filigree of Spanish moss, date palms that ooze honey, and weeping willows that contemplate their own portraits in the river? Is this the New Orleans of the merry Carnival, all torches and castanets, where King Momo's parade celebrates the romance of Mexico on a float festooned with lilies and pinks while other floats display the lovable heroes of the poem of *Lalla Rookh*[1] in bejeweled costumes, or a prince dressed in orange satin who awakens a Sleeping Beauty wearing a tunic of gold lamé?

Is this the New Orleans where they fish from dugout canoes, the city whose outskirts are enchanting and whose sunny marketplace is in perpetual commotion, the city whose beaux, their hats pulled over their eyebrows above gray goatees, gather to talk of duels and ladies in the Poetry Café? The shots ring out: the body of Bagnetto, the dead Italian, is strung from a branch; his face is pocked with more bullets; a policeman throws his hat in the air, and from the balconies and rooftops people watch the scene through their opera glasses.

The governor "is nowhere to be seen." The militia? "No one went for them." The mayor "isn't going to arrest a whole city." They saw off a branch, chop up another, shake off the leaves, which fall onto the throng below—so that they can have a souvenir to take away with them, a splinter of wood, a fresh leaf picked today at the foot of the oak from which the bloodied Italian hangs, slowly twisting.

The pleased or cowardly residents of the city of New Orleans, with their foremost men of letters and merchants in the lead, marched on the jail from which the prisoners the jury had just acquitted were to be released, and with the consent and aid of the municipal authorities attacked the municipal prison. The whole city, led by lawyers and journalists, bankers and judges, crushed to a pulp in the prison's corners and "shot to bits" the acquitted Italians—who consisted of a New Orleans resident originally from Italy, a rich man of the world who controlled the vote of the Italian community; the wealthy partner of a good firm and father of six; a high-spirited Sicilian at whom an Irishman had shot months before; a shoemaker who had some influence on the opinions of his neighborhood; a clothes mender accused of having killed one of his countrymen in a quarrel; and some fruit sellers.

The Italians quarrel among themselves like the bands of Kansas outlaws who in half a century have not left a single governor in peace, like the Southern whites who pass feuds between families down from generation to generation. Twenty years ago, because he had stuck his nose into the Italians' quarrels—or had wanted, on that pretext, to strip them of the municipal power they were acquiring with their votes—the father of the Hennessy who has recently died was felled by a man named Guerin. The same political trafficker who was a lieutenant in today's attack finished off the other Hennessy's killer with a gunshot. The gray-eyed politicians hated the black-eyed politicians. The Irish, who make their living primarily from politics, wanted to throw the Italians out of politics.

They were accused of being *dagos*—a word that makes Sicilian blood boil. Anyone who fell as a result of these rivalries was said to have been brought down "by the sentence of the Mafia." The terrible political executions of the Mafia, which conspired against the Bourbons[2] a century ago, were retold as if they were taking place right now, and were crimes committed for their own sake.

The contemporary Hennessy declared war without quarter on the Italians, though there once was a time when he had no better friend "for a turn around a club's green tables or a good plate of gumbo" than Macheca, the rich, elegant Italian whose head was smashed in by revolver butts. There were deaths in the Italian quarter. And the police stepped up their harassment until they found an Italian informer (who turned up dead one morning) and proclaimed that they now knew all there was to know about a society of murderers called the *Stiletto*, and another called the *Stoppaghiera*, and that they had in hand "full proof of the horrible Mafia, its death sentences, and its thousands of hit men." One night, at the door of his house, which has a rosebush on either side of it, Hennessy fell in a fight against a gang of assassins, his hand on his revolver.

Eleven bullets were found in his body. His death was declared to have been "the vengeance of the Mafia." The most incriminating evidence was promised. The mayor himself appointed a loose association of fifty citizens—politicians and businessmen, lawyers and journalists—to assist the normal forces of justice in their investigation. A jury without blemish was selected from among citizens with English surnames. A number of professional Sicilian fighting men were jailed, along with the two wealthiest Italians, who exerted the greatest influence over the Italian vote.

From the Gulf to the Pacific, the Italian population rose up on their behalf. Their press and their prominent men denied that there was a

Mafia, or a *Stiletto* or *Stoppaghiera* society, or any possible proof of so iniquitous an organization, and that there was any sense in arresting and imprisoning on charges of murder men of the stature of Macheca the banker and Caruso the businessman. They maintained that the cause of the persecution and the reason for its venom was politics, for it was designed to frighten the Italians, who refused to do the will of those who persecuted them, away from New Orleans and its voting boxes, and they declared that a nonexistent dark conspiracy had been trumped up for political reasons. The jury, after a trial that lasted months and was open to the public, amid charges that came and went, witnesses who went mad or committed perjury, and rumors of bribery and scandal, acquitted the accused. Yes, there were hostile gangs among the Sicilians of New Orleans; yes, *matrangas* and *provenzanos* hated each other here as they did in Italy; yes, the Italians often blood-ied the streets with Italian blood. But from the fact that they quarrel among themselves, the fact that *provenzanos* and *matrangas*, to satisfy their rancor, give false testimony against their enemies, the fact that the Sicilians have no qualms about pursuing their disputes in a city where every passerby has a revolver at his belt and there is no family that hasn't fought in the streets with another family, and the fact that a de-feated gang finally decided to end the life of the police chief who had taken sides with their rivals, it cannot be deduced that the Mafia, which was a rebellion against the Bourbon, reigns supreme in New Orleans, where there are no Bourbons, or that the anonymous letters that the police, in order to arouse hatred against the Italians, suspected of alluding to plotted conspiracies, were by Italian hands, or that all of the "dagos," who live as the fierce sun commands, loving and hating each other, giving their lives for a kiss and robbing another man of his over a hostile word, "are an organized school of assassins."

Moore, Irish Moore, who was for a time a New Orleans police lieu-tenant, said that "the murder of Hennessy, like his father's murder, arose from disputes over the votes—Hennessy's death was no more than another act in the dispute over a political booty that is now more abundant than ever."

New Orleans received the verdict with threats and wrath. New Or-leans alleged that "fraud occurred during the trial," that "Detective Malley paid a witness," that "there is evidence of the attempted bribery of a witness." But in Chicago, the red-shirted neighborhood put on all its lights; in the suburbs of Providence all work came to a halt for danc-ing and celebration; and New York's Little Italy, encamped along the

Bowery, covered its fruit stands with the latest papers, stuck a flag in the glossy boot by which the shoeshine man advertises his services, and left the house with a smoothly coiffed chignon and coral earrings—until the telegraph announced the terrible news that New Orleans was rioting, that the jail was surrounded, that they had hanged Bagnetto and were killing Macheca. Women came out of basements and alleyways screaming. They left their children on the sidewalks and sat down to weep. They unbraided their hair and tore at it. They called for their men to wake up and insulted them because they did not wake up at once. They ran with their hands on their heads. The square where the newspapers have their offices filled up with women and men. Their journalists, always at odds with each other, spoke to them, united for the first time, from a single portico. "We Italians are as one in this sorrow!" "Vengeance, Italians! Vengeance!" And they read the horrible telegrams, weeping. The women threw themselves on their knees in the streets. The men wiped away the tears with their callused hands.

It was true: New Orleans, with the law in its hands, had turned against its own law. The state's governor, who commanded the militia, abandoned the state capital to the riot. The leaders of the riot against the court's decision were officers of the court: magistrates, prosecutors, defenders. The captains of the massacre were delegated by the mayor, who sent no forces against the killers. There was not a single voice of pity, not a single supplicating woman, not a single plea from a priest, not one protest from the press: "Kill the dagos!" "To arms, good citizens!" "At one o'clock P.M., at Clay's statue, to take steps to remedy the failure of justice in the Hennessy case. Come prepared for action." The printed summons, signed by the city's powers that be and guiding minds, spread the word. "How could the mayor oppose us, when those summoning us are the very ones he appointed to help with the manhunt?" "Parkerson is our leader, the man who won the city elections at the head of the independent Democrats." "Linch, the commissioner of public works, which is such a powerful post, has signed it." At one o'clock the sloping intersection of old streets where Clay's statue stands was overflowing. They say the state militia is with them; that the militiamen are there without their uniforms; that there is a house filled with picks and axes; that yesterday a wagon unloaded a stack of beams to stave in the doors behind the jail; that in yesterday's meeting, the meeting of the fifty men, a plan was agreed upon, the leaders were appointed, and weapons were distributed. Some cheer for Wyckliffe, and everyone cheers for Parkerson: "Speech! Jump the rail and give us a speech!" An orator leaps up to the foot of the statue. It is Parkerson, a man of the law, a party leader, young; his jacket fits him snugly; he has a round head. Neither his tongue nor his hand falls off: he gesticulates, and gesticulates well, he throws his foot forward and raises his left arm over his head: "To arms, citizens! Crimes must be punished quickly, but when and where the courts fail, when jurors violate their oaths, when bribers appear, then the people must act and do what the courts and the jury failed to do!" "We're with you Parkerson!" "What resolution will we take, citizens? Will it be action?" "Action! Tell us what to do! We're with you!" "Are you ready?" "Ready!"

A certain Denegre, a lawyer and landowner, jumps up. "I'm a member of the Committee of Fifty; the mayor appointed me and I'm accountable to the public. We're on the dead man's side and we're going to get the murderers. The committee is powerless, the courts are powerless, but the citizens can do it!"

And then Wyckliffe, a lawyer and the owner of a newspaper, speaks. The throng's agitation is visible. Wyckliffe pushes his words forward with his arms: "We came to the foot of this statue for action! Down with the Mafia! Will we stand here with our hands in our pockets or will we cast this plague of heretics from the city?" "Let's go!" "Lead the way!" "Fetch the rifles!" Parkerson answers, "and on to the square, to Congo Square!"

To the square, to the prison! With light steps the column marches off. A Democrat, Parkerson, the ringleader, takes command. Honston, another ringleader who put the first Hennessy's killer to death twenty years ago, goes along. Their lieutenant is Wyckliffe, who prosecuted the Italians on the city's behalf. Ahead go three wagons with ropes and ladders; the noose for the gallows hangs from the shaft of one.

Behind go the riflemen at a military pace, with their two hundred rifles at their shoulders. The crowd follows and surrounds them; a few are carrying shotguns, the rest revolvers. There is a sound of marching feet. "They smile as they walk, as if they were on their way to a picnic." And when they reach the prison, which is built of stone and has balconies, a stake is thrown against each door, as if by prior order; the warden, amid shouts and hisses, refuses to give them the keys. They attack the door with sharp-pointed beams. Its panels sway, and a black man demolishes them with an ax. Fifty of them go in: they would all like to go in! "Here is the key to the cell," says the assistant warden. And the guards let them by.

The fifty men gather together. From an open cell, the prisoners can be heard moaning. Through the bars of another cell, a dying face can be seen. These aren't the ones; the guards obligingly point out that these are not the ones. They are upstairs in the women's section—and here is the other key. "Slowly, gentlemen, slowly," says Parkerson: "Who knows who they are? No one but the dagos!" They rush through the empty corridor; a pale, scaly hand, the hand of an African woman in her eighties, shows them the corner where the stairway goes up, along which rapid footsteps can be heard. "Hurrah, three cheers!" says one of the hunters, and the others, waving their hats, give three cheers with him and throw themselves up the stairs. "The medicine!" says one of them: the sound of a volley of shots rings out. The last of the men who were running from them spins through the air, dead from a shot to the brain. The sound of the shots drowns out the shouting and cheering from outside: "Hurrah for Parkerson!" "Hurrah for Wyckliffe!" The prisoners have no time to beg for mercy. Gerachi and Caruso are on the ground, full of holes. Romero is killed on his knees, his forehead against the flagstones, his hat in ribbons, and the back of his jacket in rags. The bullets fly. Macheca, cornered, falls from a blow to the head, and ends his life there among the feet of those men, the lawyers and the businessmen, ends his life without a single gunshot, only blows from revolver butts. The terrible wrath outside was clamoring for its share. "Bring them out here!" "Let us kill them out here!" The square was full and all the surrounding streets. Women and children were there. "Bring them to us!" "Out here!"

Through a door appears a squadron that pushes along Polozzi, the mad witness, as if he were drunk. He is collapsing from their arms to the ground. Two of them insult each other and come to blows because they each want to be the one to tighten the noose. A cluster of men hang on to the rope. And all those nearby empty their revolvers into him. The spurting blood splatters their chests.

Bagnetto is dragged out in their arms: there is no face left, only a wound. They throw a noose of fresh rope around his cold, dead neck and leave him hanging from the branch of a tree. Then they saw off the other branches: the women wear the leaves in their hats as an emblem, the men in their buttonholes. One of them takes out his watch: "Forty-eight minutes: we worked fast." From the rooftops and balconies people are watching through opera glasses.

—New York, March 26, 1891;
published in *La Nación* (Buenos Aires), May 20, 1891

THE MONETARY CONFERENCE OF THE
AMERICAN REPUBLICS

*** SELECTIONS ***

*The First Pan-American Conference was quickly followed by the
International Monetary Conference, which Martí attended as the
representative of Uruguay. He delivered a report to the delegates
on March 30, 1891, in which he opposed the bimetallism—the
equalization of gold and silver currency, at a fixed ratio—that was
being promoted by the United States in its drive for a single hemispheric currency. He participated very actively in other ways as
well, carrying on a voluminous correspondence with a number of
other delegates throughout the conference. He summarized his final reaction to it in the following account written for a Spanish
magazine published in New York.*

On May 24, 1888, the president of the United States sent the peoples
of America and the queen of Hawaii in the Pacific Ocean an invitation
in which the Senate and the House of Representatives summoned
them to an international conference in Washington, to study, among
other things, "the adoption by each of the governments of a common
silver coin . . . the same to be legal tender in all commercial transac-
tions between the citizens of all the American States."

On April 7, 1890, the Pan-American Conference, in which the
United States took part, recommended that an international monetary
union be established, that one or more international currencies, uniform in weight and law, be minted as the basis for that union, to be
used in all the countries represented at the conference, and that a commission meet in Washington to study the quantity, relationship, value,
and rate of exchange of the metals in which the international currency
was to be minted.

On March 23, 1891, after the United States delegation had requested a month's extension from the International Monetary Commission, "in order to have time to learn the pending opinion of the
House of Representatives on the free coinage of silver," that same delegation declared to the conference that the creation of a common silver coin as the compulsory legal tender in all the states of America was

a fascinating dream that could not be attempted without the agreement of the other powers of the globe. The delegation recommended the use of gold and silver currency, at a fixed rate of exchange. It desired that the peoples of America, and the queen of Hawaii, which participated in the conference, join together to invite the powers of the world to a Universal Monetary Congress.

What lesson can America learn from the International Monetary Conference, which, with the consent of Congress, the United States called for in 1888 to address the adoption of a common silver coin, and to which the United States says, in 1891, that a common silver coin is a fascinating dream?

It is not the form of things that must be attended to but their spirit. The real is what matters, not the apparent. In politics, reality is that which is unseen. Politics is the art of combining a nation's diverse or opposing factors to the benefit of its domestic well-being, and of saving the country from the open enmity or covetous friendship of other nations. Whenever an invitation is extended between nations, the hidden reasons for it must be sought. No nation does anything that goes against its own interests, from which we may deduce that what a nation does is in its own interest. If two nations do not have common interests, they cannot join together. If they do join together, they will clash. The lesser nations, which are still in the throes of gestation, cannot without danger unite with those that seek, in a union with lesser nations, a solution to the excess production of a compact, aggressive population, and a drain for their restless hordes. The political acts of real republics are a composite result of certain elements of the national character, economic necessities, the needs of the various political parties, and the needs of the political leaders. When a nation is invited to join in a union with another, the ignorant, bedazzled statesman might rush into it, young people enamored of beautiful ideas and lacking good sense might celebrate it, and venal or demented politicians might welcome it as a mercy and glorify it with servile words, but he who feels in his heart the anguish of the patria, he who watches and foresees, must investigate and must say what elements constitute the character of the nation that invites and the nation that is invited, and whether they are predisposed toward a common labor by common antecedents and habits, and whether or not it is probable that the fearsome elements of the inviting nation will, in the union it aspires to, be developed to the endangerment of the invited one. Some inquiry must be made into the political forces of the country that invites, and the interests of its parties, and the interests of its leading men at the moment of the invitation. And anyone who makes a decision without first investigating, or desires a union without knowing anything about it, or recommends it out of mere pleasure in words and bedazzlement, or defends it out of the pusillanimity of his villager's soul, will be doing harm to America. At what moment was the International Monetary Commission called for and convened? Can it or can it not be deduced from this conference that American international policy is no more than a banner waved by local politics and an instrument of party ambition? Hasn't the United States itself taught this lesson to Hispanoamerica? Which is best for Hispanoamerica: to allow this lesson to go unheeded, or to learn from it? . . .

No man who knows and sees can honorably say—for it is a thing said only by those who do not see or know, or do not want, for their own personal benefit, to see or know—that the predominant element in the United States today is that of the more humane and virile, though nevertheless egotistical and conquering, rebellious colonists, the younger sons of noble families or Puritan members of the bourgeoisie. That segment of the population, which devoured the Negro race, promoted and lived from its enslavement, and subjugated or robbed the neighboring countries, has been tempered, not softened, by the continual grafting onto it of a European rabble, the tyrannical offspring of political and religious despotism whose only common quality is a cumulative appetite for exerting over others the authority that was once exerted over them. They believe in necessity, in barbaric right, as their only right: "This will be ours, because we need it." They believe in the incontrovertible superiority of "the Anglo-Saxon race over the Latin race." They believe in the inferiority of the Negro race, which they enslaved yesterday and torment today, and of the Indian, whom they are exterminating. They believe that the nations of Hispanoamerica are primarily made up of Indians and Negroes. As long as the United States knows no more about Hispanoamerica than this, and respects it no more than it does now—though, by a ceaseless, urgent, multifaceted and sagacious explanation of our elements and resources the United States might come to respect us—can the United States invite Hispanoamerica to a union that will be sincere and useful to Hispanoamerica? Is a political and economic union with the United States to the benefit of Hispanoamerica?

To say economic union is to say political union. The nation that buys, commands. The nation that sells, serves. Trade must be balanced if liberty is to be ensured. Only a nation that wishes to die will sell to a single nation, for the nation that wants to save itself sells to more than one. The excessive influence of one nation on the commerce of another is quickly transformed into political influence. Politics is the work of men, who surrender their sentiments to their self-interest, or sacrifice one part of their sentiments to their self-interest. When a strong nation feeds another, it makes the other serve it. When a strong nation wants to make war on another, it compels the nations that are dependent on it into alliances and service. The first thing a nation does to achieve dominance over another is to separate it from all other nations. The nation that wishes to be free must be free in its business dealings. It must distribute its business among equally strong nations. If it must prefer one of them, it should prefer the one that needs it least and that disdains it least. There must be neither unions of America against Europe, nor unions with Europe against any nation in America. The geographical situation of our coexistence in America does not forcibly entrain, except to the mind of some degree candidate or recent graduate, a political union. Trade travels along the slopes of earth and sea in pursuit of any country that has something to give in exchange, be it a monarchy or a republic. Our union must be with the world, not with one part of it, and certainly not with one part of it against another. If the family of American republics has a task, that task is certainly not to be herded by one of those republics, like its own drove of beasts, against the republics of the future. . . .

When the host rises to his feet, the guests do not insist on remaining seated at the table. When the guests come from very far, out of courtesy more than appetite, only to find the host at the door telling them there is nothing to eat, the guests do not throw him to one side or enter his house by force, or shout that the dining room must be opened to them. The guests must speak of the courtesy out of which they came, and say that they did not come out of servitude or need, so that the host will not think their knees are permanently bent or that they are puppets that go wherever the puppetmaster sends them. And then: leave. There is a way of turning one's back and walking away that augments one's stature. A Hispanoamerican delegate, understanding that the Monetary Commission came only "to carry out what had been recommended" but not realizing that a recommendation must be discussed and confirmed before it is carried out, championed the opinion that wended its way among the delegates with no visible source: that the Monetary Commission had not come, as the United States, which promoted it, believed, to see if an international currency could be created, but to create one now, even if the United States itself acknowledged that no such currency could be created now. And the delegate proposed a minutely detailed plan for an American currency, which he called "Columbus," along the lines of the currency of the Latin Union, with an Overseeing Council to reside in Washington.

Hadn't the United States said that the obstacle to the creation of an international currency was not the House of Representatives' resistance to voting for the free coinage of silver, but the resistance of the vast world on the other side of the sea to accepting silver currency at a fixed and equal rate of exchange with gold currency? Yet a Hispano-american delegate asked this: "Would it not be more prudent, given the probability that the new House of Representatives votes the free coinage of silver before the end of the year, to suspend the sessions of the conference, for example, until the first day of January 1892, when this matter will have been decided by the government of the United States?" And when another delegation urged, for the sake of the guests' decorum, an easy and prudent acceptance of the United States' proposals, except for that of the Universal Congress, a Hispanoamerican delegate who does not speak Spanish[1] spoke up to request and obtain the suspension of the session. In whose interest might it be—for it was not in the Hispanoamericans' interest—that the commission promoted by the United States continue to function in opposition to the United States' own wish to terminate it? Who, in an assembly with a Hispanoamerican majority, was inciting opposition to the proposals of the United States? To whom but to those who have made the continental policy proposed by the United States their political standard was it harmful that the idea of a continental currency should be declared impossible by the commission gathered to study it in the United States itself? Why did the idea emerge—and how could such an idea naturally emerge in the Monetary Commission, with its Hispanoamerican majority—of opposing the closure of a commission that had gathered to study a plan that the Hispanoamerican delegates had expressly and almost unanimously declared unrealizable? If they were not serving themselves, what other interest, concealed in their very bosom, was taking advantage of their excessive goodwill and making them serve it? Or was it, as those who know politics from the inside said it was, that the interest of a political group or a single tenacious and daring U.S. politician,[2] was, by hidden levers and private influences, rousing an assembly of nations against the solemn opinion of the United States government? Was this assembly of Hispanoamerican peoples going to serve the interests of a man who is compelling them to make obscure, dangerous, and impossible alliances?[3] Was it going to disdain the advice of those who, out of local partisan interests or concern for international justice, are opening the doors for them so that they may save themselves?

There were meditations, there were fears, there was much urging, and there was a great risk of doing the wrong thing and leaving standing—because of the caprice of an alien, desperate, and unscrupulous politician—an assembly that, given the complexity and delicacy of the relations of many Hispanoamerican countries with the United States, could, in the hands of a pitiless office-seeker, yield to the United States more than would be beneficial to the self-respect and security of the Hispanoamerican peoples.

Showing themselves to be accommodating to the point of weakness would not be the best way for the Hispanoamerican countries to avoid the dangers that a reputation for weakness would expose them to in trade relations with a forceful, thronging nation. Prudence does not dictate that we confirm a reputation for weakness, but that we seize this opportunity to display our energy without risk. And a show of energy is the least dangerous move, when it is made at the right time and with restraint. Who can build a nation out of serpents? But there was a battle. However, if zeal for progress in republics that are not yet fully realized leads their sons, out of a singular mental lapse or a festering habit of servitude, to have greater confidence in the virtue of the progress of nations where they were not born than in that of the nation where they were born; if their eagerness to see their native country grow leads them into a blind hungering after methods and things that are the alien product of factors foreign or hostile to their own country, which must then develop in conformity with those factors and by the methods that result from them; if the natural caution of nations founded in the proximity of North America deemed inadvisable a course of action that, because of that very proximity, is more in their interest than in that of any other nation; if respectable local prudence, or fear, or private obligations made certain characters more tractable than they should be concerning matters of Hispanoamerican independence and creation, none of that was apparent in the Monetary Commission, for it agreed to a full adjournment of its sessions.

—*La Revista Ilustrada* (New York), May 1891

A TOWN SETS A BLACK MAN ON FIRE

Where do ten thousand souls gather, the men in broadcloth and the women in silk, to watch twenty human couples, twenty black couples, degrade themselves? From where do two hundred black men flee, without water and without bread, ruined and beggared? Where do five thousand souls gather to watch a woman set fire to the clothing of a bound black man—and see the black man burned alive? In New York, in the Garden built of porphyry, crystal, and cream-colored brick the ten thousand gathered to watch the dancing and walking of couples who were competing for the prize of a cake, the cake that goes each year to the most elegant cakewalker. From Indian territory, where the invidious white man has settled, the two hundred wretches are fleeing to Liberia, seeking "milk and honey." In Arkansas, Texans and Arkansans gathered, both women and men, and set fire to a Negro drenched in gasoline who was tied to a pine tree. "To Liberia!" "To Liberia!" the two hundred who were coming from Indian territory shouted in a chorus through the streets, with their bearded captain at their head, and in vain the men of their race who wear greatcoats and spectacles try to stop them. They do not want to listen to the lawyer or the pastor or the congressman or the senator; they want only to go "where they do not set fire to our men."

Nor did the prancing couples want to listen to the advice, pleas, and protests of the redeemed blacks who see the annual mockery of the "cakewalk" as an obstacle to the respect that their exemplary virtue and intelligence have succeeded in earning for their race. What good does it do for the family of a Brooklyn pastor, he with his white beard, she gray-haired and matriarchal in a sumptuous dress, the daughters arrayed in roses and lace, to listen to the firstborn son deliver the class speech at a law school? What good does it do for black historians to write and for their poets to win awards, for banquets to be held in their homes and for their doctors to drive out in their own carriages? These ignoble Judases, merely for a percentage of the clown show's take, will dress in elaborate getups with patent-leather shoes, the women in dancing pumps and the men in frilled shirts, so they can be mocked, ridiculed, whistled and shouted at, and have coins thrown at their heads by frenetic, curly-haired players from the gaming dens, by the gamblers on the stock market who are called brokers, and by students from the two great colleges, who throw their arms around each other and trumpet with delight, finding in their young souls neither pity nor any manliness that would make them—and the man who will be born from them—suffer from this degradation of mankind. These criminal couples, for a bottle of sour wine and a few dollars, will spin and strut around a cake, and will by their own baseness promote disdain for their own race!

"But there were a hundred couples two years ago," says a handsome, eloquent black man at the door, whose friends try in vain to restrain him—"and this year there are no more than seventeen of the shameless creatures! Upon the tower of this evil house I must say that the hearts of honorable black men bleed at the ignominy of these vile Negroes, and that in our homes Tchaikovsky is played on the piano and Draper and Littré are on the bookshelves. I must say that we abhor these dishwashers and hussies who want only to buy some pleasure for themselves with the money that this gambling-master collects at the door from those who come to jeer the black color of their faces!" And the handsome Negro could no longer hold back his sobs, and the gambling-master, spilling out of his dress-coat and opera hat, pulled aside the crimson velvet curtain, his fat face all smiles, to let in a petulant blond youth and the jingling lady friend, covered in silk and bracelets, who walked at his coattails. Behind the curtain was a glimpse of a crowd in a smoky room leaning against the railing, a gleaming dance floor, burnished by the procession, couples walking arm in arm, sashaying on tiptoe, competing to see who could put the best foot forward; and the lead drummer, in front of the cohort, in a waistcoat and cap, making the sticks fly. And then the whole crowd spills over into the ring and whirls around it.

In the basement of a mission, "pickaninnies," mothers, and grandparents greedily eat the charitable soup that the best black families in New York have sent to those who arrived from out in Indian territory, seeking the ship which the Liberia company agent offered them. Will the unfortunate race scatter, then? Those who have roots and a pillow to sleep on do not see their patria in the color of their skin or abjure the land where they were born, or promote a peregrination that would subtract from their race the weight its numbers can give it under the justice of the law. But those who have no pillow want to go to Liberia. And "George Washington" wants to take them there, with his yellow-ish, woolly beard and his eyes that command and caress and a hand that creases his hat when he takes it off in greeting. He wears a felt hat, a jacket, and boots; he fought in the war, and ever since then has been "wandering, wandering"; like those Indians out in the territory, he is no "lady's man"; he wants "to be a chief, a chief of somewhere before I die"; out of his own pocket he has paid something like half the fare for "all these children"; and with his arms on high he conducts the choir, which rises to its feet and sings, the grandparents leaning on their canes, the mothers with their heads wrapped in kerchiefs, the young men in their beggar's clothes, the "pickaninnies" with their arms around each other's shoulders. And all of them sway back and forth and chorus:

> No matter what they say,
> to turn us from our way
> While our legs do not fail
> We must set sail,
>   Set sail?
> To Liberia, to Liberia
> We must set sail!

And at the door, in a red shirt and knee boots, his refined face fringed with a short beard, a man from Louisiana perorates to the youths who listen to him, laughing, nudging each other, shuffling their feet and thrusting both hands deep into their pockets: "Are we cow-ards, then, because we don't stay here, here in these muddy waters, until the Messiah comes? Well, 'cowards live long lives,' they say. Is it back to Louisiana or Texas or Arkansas, then? 'Once bitten twice shy!' And don't we know where we're going? 'The pig knows what tree to scratch against!' For why would we stay here, to be like those who are never more than half gentlemen? 'Cutting the ears off a mule doesn't make it a horse.' And who cares if we don't have anything to eat? 'The monkey says it's nobody's business if his backside is bare!' They say we're going to have to wait a long time there before we'll have homes, but 'Little by little the bird makes its nest!'" So, resolute, grateful, huddled tightly against each other, they wait, sitting around their charity soup, for the boat that will take them to the biblical land of "milk and honey."

Down in Texarkana, on the border between Arkansas and Texas—those places that the man from Louisiana never wants to go back to—a whole town and the neighboring town piled out of wagons and carts at a stable door. The men, in small bands, were carrying rifles and pistols, and—eager to be the first with the news—running and leaping on the first horse they could find; the women were in hats, parasols, and triangular shawls. One of them was giving a speech, and her group applauded her. Young ladies were out strolling with their gentlemen. Strangers greeted each other in the streets. "Here he comes! Here he comes!" It's the black man who is coming out of the stable tightly bound: one man pushes him, another hits him in the face. He goes on walking, steady on his feet: "I offered Mrs. Jewell no offense! You're going to kill me, but I offered her no offense!" "We're going to kill you, Coy, you dog, kill you like the dog you are, before the mayor can sic the troops he asked the governor for on us!" And they take him up the street, surrounded by rifles, with the wagons and carts trailing behind, along with the crowd of men and women, five thousand souls in all. The town square seems suitable, but two townspeople are there demanding that the law be obeyed: "Get away, you orators who want law right now!" And the bound black man comes along at a trot—"out of town, in the open countryside where everyone can get a good view"—and behind him, as he trots along, the five thousand souls come running. He reached the only tree. One compassionate man wanted to climb it with a rope, asking that at least they hang him, but his compassion was diminished by the mouth of a rifle. Coy was trussed against the tree trunk with iron hoops. They threw buckets of petroleum over his head until his clothing was drenched. "Get back, everyone, get back, so the ladies can see me." And when Mrs. Jewell, in a triangular scarf and hat, came out from among the crowd, on the arms of two relatives, the crowd burst into a round of cheers: "Hurrah for Mrs. Jewell!" The ladies waved their handkerchiefs, the men waved their hats. Mrs. Jewell reached the tree, lit a match, twice touched the lit match to the jacket of the black man, who did not speak, and the black man went up in flames, in the presence of five thousand souls.

—New York, February 23, 1892;
published in *El Partido Liberal* (Mexico City), March 5, 1892

FROM *PATRIA*

After presiding over the founding of the Cuban Revolutionary Party in January of 1892, Martí returned to New York to found the newspaper that would be its official organ, Patria, whose name hearkened back to that other newspaper he had founded at the age of sixteen, La Patria Libre. It would be published weekly or semi-weekly from March 14, 1892, to December 31, 1898.

The first issue contained a manifesto titled "Our Ideas," which called for the independence not only of Cuba but of Puerto Rico as well. The pan-Antillian scope of the paper's ambition was under-scored by the appointment of Sotero Figueroa—a Puerto Rican of mixed race who is mentioned in the following article on the aboli-tion of slavery—as managing editor of Patria.

THE ABOLITION OF SLAVERY IN PUERTO RICO

March 22, 1873

On April 10, 1869, on the very first moment their independence was consecrated, the Cuban people gathered in Guáimaro and declared all slaves in Cuba to be free, without reparation or payment. And this le-gitimately glorious fact, the purest and most consequential fact of that revolution,[1] saved the Negro from servitude once and for all and saved Cuba from violence and upheavals that the freed slaves, grateful rather than injured, would never instigate in the republic. Four years later, at dawn, the representatives in the teeming amphitheater of the Cortes in Madrid were possessed by a strange agitation; beaming, loquacious groups were congratulating each other; a band of idlers fled as if they were being chased with sticks; an orator with a large head seemed to pluck his luminous paragraphs from the sky, and hurl them down, ra-diant, upon those gathered there, and an elderly general shouted *"¡Viva la república!"*[2] The president, who is pale, declares with the gesture of one who wrests a thorn from his mother's bosom, that "slavery is abolished forever in Puerto Rico." The freed slaves were to be under contract to their masters for three years; three administrators were to be placed in charge of the contracts; the owners were to be re-paid for their slaves "in cash," with a loan of 35 million pesetas against the island's annual revenue, or in bonds secured by the loan; a group of authorities and slaveowners "were to carry out the distribution"; and in five years the freed slaves would come into full possession of their political rights. In Cuba, the masters freed their servants with their own hands; they erased even the name of color from the republic's constitution and seated the slaves at their side on the very first day of their freedom. In Madrid, four years later—and with fifteen more years still to go before the Cortes would recognize the emancipation of the slaves of Cuba—the Congress of Labra, Vizcarrondo, Castelar and Gabriel Rodríguez, of Benot and Balart, voted for abolition in Puerto Rico, and the decree was signed by President Salmerón,[3] the Spaniard who once proclaimed to the Cortes the right of colonies to separate from the metropolis, "since, upon entering into their majority, its children have need and reason to leave the power that is their patria." At dawn on March 22, 1873, the thirty-five thousand slaves on the island of Puerto Rico were free.

The telegraph brought the yearned-for news to San Juan, whose population had had wind of it the day before, and hardly had the sun risen than all San Juan was in a state of fiesta. The *Gaceta* flew through the streets. The stores spread their wares on the sidewalks. Men came out of their houses wearing their Sunday best. The horses, braided and beribboned, proudly bore their riders. With speeches and embraces, ardent young men prepared for a demonstration. In the Plaza de Armas, one house had all its doors and windows barred, as if in mourning, like a livid fist shaken threateningly at the sky! But otherwise all of San Juan was flags, damask curtains, and blue hangings: one daring girl put a white rosette on one side of a blue drapery and a red one on the other. At noon, whispering, shouting, lining up, waving from the balconies, the town was already filling the Plaza de Santiago, with touching accord, as if it were an open-air church. The fort of San Cristóbal watched from afar, like an abandoned building, crouched against the sky, and a ray of sunlight falling on the barracks wall made the guards' bayonets sparkle. At the theater, no one could see the fort's old roof, or its frowning battlements and peeling walls, only the portal where the founding fathers of Puerto Rican liberty were organizing the demonstration, with orators and poets beside them. Julián Acosta,[4] with a soft voice, flaming eye, and the intensity of a man in love, listened to everyone and guided them all. Ramón Abad, as agile just then as his pen, held forth amid a chorus of young men. Félix Padial, his blond head upright as if in war, gathered, positioned, led, embraced the blacks, embraced the children: "And if anyone says that this greatness was not true, that these slaves have not entered into their freedom without hatred, I will tell you that he lies." From Julián Acosta's balcony, two young women of tempting beauty, whose gaze seemed a long-anticipated reward for the heroism of the struggle, were stripping flowers of their petals, which a campesino was collecting in his yarey hat. At last the demonstration, in which masters and slaves walked side by side, left for the Plaza de Armas, along the street that lead to the fortress.

The musicians, who lent their services to the fiesta as an honor, played beloved airs; the crowd passed between living masses; from windows and doors handkerchiefs fluttered. Arm in arm, at the head of the procession, as if they were the freed slaves, went all those who with their voices and pens, actions and words, had fought to overthrow slavery: lawyers and doctors, youths and elders, merchants and writers. Then the slaves went by, holding their children's hands, the men in shirts and trousers, the women in white tunics and madras kerchiefs, some with their hats off, one of them leading a blind man, all of them silent. One father bent down to kiss his son and continued on with the child in his arms. Another, a man with a tremendously powerful body, was holding his wife's hand tightly. Others walked in a row, all of them young men wearing resplendent clothing. One poor old woman fell to her knees in the middle of the march. Behind came the *jíbaros*, the campesinos who happened to be passing through the city, barefoot and with their shirts untucked, their yareys pushed back on their heads and their machetes at their belts.

They did not have to go all the way to the municipal palace, because Governor Primo de Rivera[5] was waiting for them on the balcony of City Hall. On one side of the plaza, those of the hostile house with the barred windows—the Spaniards of the Círculo Hispano Ultramarino—were crowded against a balcony rail. Primo de Rivera, wearing the costume of the country, spoke forth the whole republic of his heart: this was daylight, this was joy, this was the dawn of the new era, this was the just law by which he had come to govern. His hat off, he spoke to them as to a people at the moment of its birth, and the nobility and sincerity of his words made his magnificent stature seem even greater. The Spaniards of the Círculo hissed him, and the crowd wanted to go and tear down the balcony, but the governor asked them to grace that hour of glory with their forgiveness. There was a thunderous shout of

"¡*Viva Puerto Rico libre!*" and the musicians burst into "La Borin-queña"[6] while the crowd chorused along.

The whole afternoon was spent rejoicing as the demonstration spread across the city; no one walked alone for all San Juan was a single family. The tradesmen forgot about selling; every member of every household was out on the balcony, and the quickly improvised ball was open to anyone who passed by. From the outskirts of the city the frenetic drumming of the gatherings of Africa could be heard, and to the sound of the tiple and the bourdon, the high-pitched marimba and the restless maraca, the campesinos were dancing their merengues and seises in the clean-swept sugar mill. In the city, the chattering throng, accompanied by the overseer's violin, went from door to door singing the carols of freedom and asking for sweets and dances. To the master who told his Negro, "Now you are free!" the Negro replied, "I will never be free as long as my master exists." One slave said, "No! My *niña*, I'm staying with my *niña*!" Another slave, sitting in a doorway, was overcome by a great burst of weeping and cried without knowing why, gathering his sobs in the palms of his hands.

At night, the few proslavery homes that remained dark amid the city's luminous jubilation were like the silhouettes of owls outlined against a fire; and the thought of the day's beauty filled the small headquarters of the Círculo Artístico y Literario, which, over the course of the day, had arranged a celebration in honor of Primo de Rivera, with enthusiasm and valor, music and poetry, gratitude and eloquence. The facade of the Círculo was flooded with light, and transparent inscriptions in the windows praised the great day. Inside all was hubbub and glasses raised to the fathers of abolition, Ruiz Belvis,[7] Acosta, and Quiñones, the three commissioners who, face to face with Spain in Madrid at the 1866 Junta de Información, had, with the reasoning of deep-thinking statesmen, asked for the immediate abolition of slavery; the Indian Baldorioty, slow and certain creator of the new soul of Borinquen and the most beautiful and salient part of Moret's law of gradual abolition; and Betances,[8] who, after the commissioners' return, escaped from the fury of the proslavery forces on the ship that would then carry forth to the republics of the world, in search of aid for his land, the man who sacrificed his fortune and his own good health to the land where he was born: Ruiz Belvis. The fiesta springs from their overflowing souls more than from any program; first the stage was a podium where orators commemorated the great days of the abolition-

ists' martyrdom and poverty; then patriotic music sounded forth with
new meaning; and then Clotilde Tavares sang the valiant stanzas of a
hymn written to celebrate emancipation. A young man of audacious
forehead and indomitable gaze—Sotero Figueroa, the Círculo's secretary—strode forward with two beautiful young women on his arms
and the entire gathering behind him to present Primo de Rivera with
the tortoiseshell cane the Círculo gave him in honor of the great day.
The Spaniard listened, his hand on his chest, his eyes full of humanity;
the Puerto Rican, virtuous son of the two bloods, spoke to him with
simple loftiness of Captain Correa of Arecibo who was killed as, with
bare chest and machete, he swam against the invading Englishmen; of
the brave Amézquita who, during the time of the Dutchman Balduino
Enrico, challenged him to a singular duel in the Morro and gored Hol-
land in the course of it; the Puerto Rican spoke to the Spaniard of the
mettle and independence of his country and its aptness for liberty.
Primo de Rivera answered with nobility; from one pair of hands he received the cane and from others a fan where, with precious art, a
woman's hand had written on each leaf the names of the representatives in the emancipating Cortes. Many houses were still full of light
when, at the close of March 22, the people of the Círculo returned to
their homes, which were gladdened with a fleeting gladness by an hour
of justice—for there are still many slaves, black and white, in Puerto
Rico!

—April 1, 1893

MY RACE

"Racist" is becoming a confusing word, and it must be clarified. No man
has any special rights because he belongs to one race or another: say
"man" and all rights have been stated. The black man, as a black man,
is not inferior or superior to any other man; the white man who says
"my race" is being redundant, and the black man who says "my race"
is also redundant. Anything that divides men from each other, that
separates them, singles them out, or hems them in, is a sin against humanity. What sensible white man thinks he should be proud of being
white, and what do blacks think of a white man who is proud of being
white and believes he has special rights because he is? What must whites

think of a black man who grows conceited about his color? To insist upon the racial divisions and racial differences of a people naturally divided is to obstruct both individual and public happiness, which lies in greater closeness among the elements that must live in common. It is true that in the black man there is no original sin or virus that makes him incapable of developing his whole soul as a man, and this truth must be spoken and demonstrated, because the injustice of this world is great, as is the ignorance that passes for wisdom, and there are still those who believe in good faith that the black man is incapable of the intelligence and feelings of the white man. And what does it matter if this truth, this defense of nature, is called racism, because it is no more than natural respect, the voice that clamors from man's bosom for the life and the peace of the nation. To state that the condition of slavery does not indicate any inferiority in the enslaved race—for white Gauls with blue eyes and golden hair were sold as slaves with fetters around their necks in the markets of Rome—is good racism, because it is pure justice and helps the ignorant white shed his prejudices. But that is the limit of just racism, which is the right of the black man to maintain and demonstrate that his color does not deprive him of any of the capacities and rights of the human race.

And what right does the white racist, who believes his race has superior rights, have to complain of the black racist, who also believes that his race has special traits? What right does the black racist who sees a special character in his race have to complain of the white racist? The white man who, by reason of his race, believes himself superior to the black man acknowledges the idea of race and thus authorizes and provokes the black racist. The black man who trumpets his race—when what he is perhaps trumpeting instead is only the spiritual identity of all races—authorizes and provokes the white racist. Peace demands the shared rights of nature; differing rights go against nature and are the enemies of peace. The white who isolates himself isolates the Negro. The Negro who isolates himself drives the white to isolate himself.

In Cuba there is no fear whatsoever of a race war. "Man" means more than white, more than mulatto, more than Negro. "Cuban" means more than white, more than mulatto, more than Negro. On the battlefields, the souls of whites and blacks who died for Cuba have risen together through the air. In that daily life of defense, loyalty, brotherhood, and shrewdness, there was always a black man at the side of every white. Blacks, like whites, can be grouped according to their character—timid or brave, self-abnegating or egotistical—into the diverse parties of mankind. Political parties are aggregates of concerns, aspirations, interests, and characters. An essential likeness is sought and found beyond all differences of detail, and what is fundamental in analogous characters merges in parties, even if their incidental characteristics or motives differ. In short, it is the similarity of character—a source of unity far superior to the internal relations of the varying colors of men, whose different shades are sometimes in opposition to each other—that commands and prevails in the formation of parties. An affinity of character is more powerful than an affinity of color. Blacks, distributed among the diverse or hostile specialties of the human spirit, will never want or be able to band together against whites, who are distributed among the same specialties. Blacks are too tired of slavery to enter voluntarily into the slavery of color. Men of pomp and self-interest, black and white, will be on one side, and generous and impartial men will be on the other. True men, black or white, will treat each other with loyalty and tenderness, taking pleasure in merit and pride in anyone, black or white, who honors the land where we were born. The word "racist" will be gone from the lips of the blacks who use it today in good faith, once they understand that that word is the only apparently valid argument—valid among sincere, apprehensive men—for denying the Negro the fullness of his rights as a man. The white racist and the Negro racist will be equally guilty of being racists. Many whites have already forgotten their color, and many blacks have, too. Together they work, black and white, for the cultivation of the mind, the dissemination of virtue, and the triumph of creative work and sublime charity.

There will never be a race war in Cuba. The Republic cannot retreat and the Republic, from the extraordinary day of the emancipation of blacks in Cuba and from its first independent constitution of April 10, in Guáimaro, never spoke of whites or blacks. The rights already conceded out of pure cunning by the Spanish government, and which have become habitual even before the Island's independence, can no longer be denied now, either by the Spaniard, who will maintain them as long as he draws breath in Cuba—in order to continue dividing Cuban blacks from Cuban whites—or by the independent nation, which will not, in liberty, be able to deny the rights that the Spaniard recognized in servitude.

As for the rest, each individual will be free within the sacred confines of his home. Merit, the clear and continual manifestation of culture and inexorable trade will end by uniting all men. There is much greatness in Cuba, in blacks and in whites.

—April 16, 1893

TO CUBA!

In January 1894, the tobacco workers in Cayo Hueso (Key West), Florida, who were a major source of financial and political support for the Cuban revolution, went on strike. They were outraged because the tobacco factories, newly reopened after a period of economic crisis, had replaced many of them with Spanish workers brought directly from Cuba. While doing what he could from New York to bring an end to the strike, Martí also used the strike and the events leading up to it as final, culminating proof of the absolute need for Cuban independence. He considered the following article so important that he had a rather illegible English translation of it published as a supplement to Patria *(it has been retranslated for publication here).*

In November 1894, a "Cubans only" community that had been growing on the outskirts of the north Florida town of Ocala for several years, populated by Cubans seeking respite from the persistent unrest in Tampa and Cayo Hueso, was at last legally incorporated. Its name was Martí City.

When has the cry "To Cuba!" burst from the Cuban heart with greater reason—and greater anguish and love—than today, after the events in Key West and the loathsome spectacle of a town built by its adoptive sons that is straying from its own soil and laws to bring the enemies of those sons in from outside?

The city of Key West emerged triumphant from its early trials. In Yankee hands it was no more than sand and shacks, but now it can point proudly to factories that in their continual thought and study are like academies of learning; schools where the hand that rolls the tobacco leaf by day lifts a book and teaches by night; societies of art and recreation from which only those unfaithful to their patria are, for reasons of moral hygiene, excluded; homes whose great virtue makes their poverty scarcely noticeable. Key West was built by the poorest, neediest Cubans, along with a wealthy criollo or two, led there by his love of the sun, and later by a handful of fervent souls, both moneyed and destitute, drawn there by that loyal town's reputation for being like a single family. From this hybrid mixture—into which a corrupted Havana poured its crimes by the boatload—from this Cuban core, where all the sublimity of hope sprang from all the miseries of life; and where the humble worker's quota for Cuban honor was, year after year, the primary support of the proud,[1] from this everyday mingling of dethroned master and emancipated slave, eating the same bread together at the workingman's productive table, arose, with no counsel or teaching but that of our island soul, a virtuous and orderly industrial city that then spilled over and gave life to the gray state, animating its moribund coast with Tampa's industries, creating and sustaining railroads and steamers throughout that region of Florida, and transforming the Yankee village of small farmers and fishermen into a city of free academies and schools and generous gentlemen of industry: the principal port of the State of Florida. Those who silence this fact or deny it are paper men, with a magazine covering one eye and the other one blinded by preoccupation, for this is a fact acknowledged by men of truth, who work themselves and admire workingmen and know that the hands of masons, who assemble and construct, must be hardened by stone and stained by lime. We must cast into the fire—for its impurity and uselessness—the silken hand that, by way of greeting, licks the bloodied, debased hand of its country's corrupter, and instead beckon the rough hand that works the rifle which must drive the insolent to the sea, and the saintly hand, sometimes bony from hunger, that caresses and constructs in darkness, with the hope of the humble, the just and warmhearted patria that will rise from sea to sky with arms open to all mankind.

Excessive gratitude and trust were the principal and perhaps the only errors of that budding community: trust in the Washington of legend, who was more the offspring of his people than their father, and in the love of Lincoln, for whom we Cubans wore mourning, and who showed ineffable goodness in everything, except in consenting to make Cuba the dumping ground for all his nation's aggravations. Because of that blind admiration for North American liberties, which is just another form, natural in any progressive man, of the hatred of Spanish injury, blood-rule, and un-Americanism, and because of the forthright nature of the Cuban, who has been deeply marked by a long-rooted affection for the land in which he could at last think freely and work without dishonor, the Cubans of Key West came to love this harboring republic so well and to be so thoroughly taken in by the liberty it wears as a mask for the conquest it nurtures in its bosom that with their very hands they delivered to the few native settlers the government of the town that, before the Cubans arrived, had never been built. The grateful Cuban, already converted into an enthusiastic American citizen, carried this love for his adopted country into his domestic life: one quarreled with his friends for the sake of an American vote-hunter; another, though devoted to his mother island, spent his whole savings on building a house, as the monument of his affection, by the hospitable sea; another blessed every morning, from under the trees he had planted, the land where his family, persecuted and impoverished in Cuba, had brightened again into hope and prosperity; a daughter was born to another and he called her by the name of a state of the Union; many had Blaine's picture on the mantelpiece, believing that crafty manipulator of national prejudices to be the friend of Cuba; many had Cleveland's picture in their parlor, honoring him as steely foe of the republic of privileges and unjust monopolies that must everywhere be stamped out.

American industry had been living off of the future, assuming that when the domestic market was replete it would be ever so easy to empty their excess products into the torpid lands of the American continent: this and this alone was the purpose of their farcical reciprocity treaties and the shamelessness, averted in time, of the Pan-American Congress. The Hispanic republics did not lack forethought or clear-eyed sentinels and the plan failed, so the North has lived since then with its hands tugging at its purse strings, unable to pay for the production of its surplus manufactures and still less able to sell them. The sumptuary industries such as cigar-making were naturally the first to suffer from the stringency and alarm that greeted the sudden and unexpected imbalance in the nation's accounts. But the Cubans of Key West did not much mind their penury. Hadn't the city's founders lived there for twenty-five years? Hadn't the workingman, by his own sweat, bought his home there? Weren't the poor aged mother, the wife with her callused hands, and the firstborn son buried there, in that white sand? Hadn't the former slave, the oppressed campesino, and the urchin of the city streets learned all the delights of liberty there and all the arrogance of men? Work was scarce or slack, there was only one meal a day, and shoes were only for Sunday; but there they remained, hundreds and thousands of them, unemployed but faithful to the family tombs and the beloved town, faithful to Key West.

Suddenly one of the city's factories, which had been closing and reopening for some time and had recently been shored up by two new Spanish partners, began negotiating with the rival city of Tampa, which offered manufacturers land and privileges that Key West unwisely refused them. The North Americans in Key West asked why Seidenberg[2] wanted to go to Tampa, only to hear that it was because he could not bring Spanish workers to Key West. Subterranean forces, which buy and keep watch, stirred up the unbridled greed of the English-speaking population. And that city, built by Cuban effort, those merchants whose every dollar was increased a hundredfold by the Cuban Saturday, those judges placed on their benches by Cuban votes, those drunkards cured of their deliria by Cuban doctors, those sons of emancipated colonies who cannot, without denying their own history, wonder at the natural fact that the Cubans wish to rid Cuba of its masters, just as they themselves wished to be rid of the English tax on tea—those very men whom the Cubans upheld in true friendship filled the public square in anger, calling the Cubans ruffians, expressing a foul wish "to hang some Cubans," and deserting the positions they owe to the trust and prosperity of the Cuban community and the patriotism and labor of the sons of the Cuban revolution. They left the city created by the Cuban revolution to beg a foreign monarchy for soldiers known to be the rabid enemies of the American-born men who built the town for them; they began bringing new workmen, simply because those workmen were Europeans and sworn enemies of the Cuban community, to the city where hundreds of the workmen who built it had been unemployed for a year.

It was not a blow to their income; it was a blow to the heart. Those men were loved like brothers, and they had turned against their brothers. Those men were seen as the embodiment of the liberty for which the Cubans yearned, the freedom and republicanism, the justness and prestige of the law, the progress and emancipation of America—and they filled our homes with terror, took the bread from our workingmen's mouths, sent innocent men to jail, locked a messenger who was taking a note to the jail in a cell, asked for a gallows to be put up for the Cubans, and bore on their breasts as a badge of honor the colors that are in America the emblem of tyranny and that have waved, stained with blood, over the ruins of our households and the corpses of our brothers. The republicans of America were wearing the emblem of murder upon their bosoms! The men of a free people were knocking at the door of a hypocritical foreign despot to ask him for workers and soldiers with whom to impoverish and humiliate those whose only guilt is to seek, as the North Americans once sought, freedom for their country! No greater shock could have stricken the Cubans had they seen those they love most killed by a knife in their beds. Was this blue sea a sea of blood, too, like the one back in Cuba? Were they, too, to be ousted, like the *zorros* of California or the last *tejanos*, from the town they had built by the product of their industry, and, more important, by their earnest and uncompromising patriotism!

One Cuban wanted to uproot his new house and throw it into the bay; another wanted to take his nine children and leave to seek justice somewhere in the world; another wanted to change his daughter's name. There is no greater and more irreparable horror than seeing that which we loved become contemptible or infamous. Is the whole universe thus? Can no merit or virtue, no persecution or misfortune, ever move a stranger's heart? Is it futile, then, to have raised, before the eyes of a nation that the world supposes to be judicious and manly, stone by stone, out of the defective remnants of a tyrannical civilization, a city where the disorder and crime of despotism have been compressed and ordered into honest industry and the frank and diverse life of liberty? Can it be, then, that the world's leading republic is a nation without love, without charity, without friendship, without gratitude, without laws? Even in the leading republic of the world there is no harbor for a people seeking refuge from ignominious slavery! What right does a man without patria have to the security of a patria. Let he who wants a safe patria conquer one. He who does not will live in exile, under the lash, hunted down like a wild animal, cast from one country to another with a beggar's smile on his face to hide the death in his soul from the disdain of free men. There is no solid ground but the ground on which one was born. "To Cuba!" says our whole soul, after this deceit in Key West, this brutal wound to our love and our illusions: to the only country in the world from which we shall not be chased away like the *zorros* from California and the *tejanos* from Texas!

Had there been some provocation, some relation between a Cuban offense and the action of the North Americans, had in fact the Cubans violated the right of free transit, until recently conceded to all men with no exception by the United States Constitution, it could never have been a sufficient pretext for the North Americans to go forth—in patent violation of international law and the labor laws of their own country—and ask a foreign government for workers to import into a market glutted with labor, and for enemies to provoke a conflict in the city whose peace they should be preserving. However, in stark justice, which is the only sort of justice to which a sensible and dignified man must appeal, the Key West authorities would be right to uphold the law against any abusive, untenable resistance by the Cubans. If the Cubans want a land of special privilege, where they can command, they must win their own land, as the Yankee won his from the Englishman. A Yankee who has conquered his land is not equal but superior to a Cuban who has not conquered his, just as the Yankees who fought the Englishman for their freedom are superior to the Yankees who are going to ask a foreign power for help in impoverishing and humiliating the sons of America who are fighting for their own freedom! And while the Cuban revolutionaries who populated and enriched Key West out of their love for Cuban independence believe they have a moral, though not a legal, right to keep their city free of Spanish persecution, it is also true that the history and spirit of the American nation gave them some right to hope that it would show for the sons of an American nation who are fighting for emancipation from a European monarchy the same sacred indulgence that the Irish who fight to emancipate themselves from Great Britain enjoy here. But that indulgence is up to the North Americans, and it falls to the Cubans to abide by the law of the country.

Cubans have no right whatever to forbid a Spaniard, because he is a Spaniard, to disembark on United States territory. The United States can and must punish whoever breaks this law or any other. But before a violation is punished, the law must have been violated and proof of the violation must be established in accordance with the law and the guarantees that the law furnishes to the accused. Years ago, a passion for independence may have driven a handful of fanatical Cubans, who can fight as well on a Key West pier as when they face the Spaniard's artillery, to brandish punitive clubs, and one Cuban or another might have waited on the pier, club in hand, for the Spaniards who, not content with driving the Cuban away from all of his own worktables, pursue him to a foreign country to rob him of the industry that the Spaniard learned from the Cuban. Have the Spaniards no heart, that they do not see the injustice of this? Have the North Americans no heart, that they can assist in this injustice? For on the basis of something that a handful of Cubans may have attempted in the past, when the disorderly life of Key West had not yet been gathered into the superior social order of today—and which, even in the past, because of the Cuban's natural nobility, never was nor could have been anything like the South's barbaric lynchings or the continual murders perpetrated by men in white masks in the Northeast—a law-abiding people, a people of sensible, honorable, just, and friendly men, cannot presume, against truth and all appearances, that the law has been violated in a much later case, and with rabid rage and wicked vengeance turn against an entire city of men who have done it only good, to punish in advance a crime no one has committed.

Did not a friendship of so many years' standing at least demand a proper investigation of the idiotic conspiracy that a few Spanish-speaking rogues groundlessly charged the Cubans with? Do not the moral grounds for the Cubans' unhappiness at seeing the city they have peopled and where they live today without work occupied by workers who despoil them in their own country at least deserve the respectful affection and generous courtesy of right-thinking North Americans, rather than their frenzied hatred? What mysterious hand was at work there? What North American scoundrel took money from the government of Spain to incite the greed and discredit the republicanism of his compatriots? What vengeful losing candidate or base and venomous heart inflamed the unjust suspicions of those of the North against the Cubans, whose labor of twenty-five years was forgotten in an hour? Why does the city that owes us its commerce, its industry, its renown, and the intimate love we once had for it, rise up unquestioningly against us, and organize, with cries of terror, a resistance that is completely out of proportion to the vague rumor that seems to have given rise to it? Who prepared this resistance, which was so well prepared? For how long had it been planned, to have sprung up so fully formed? Who paid for it, and was so well served? Why did the good men of Key West yield, out of passion, ignorance, or a false idea of their true interests, to what was obviously a coalition of the private interests of demagogues who make their living catering to public prejudices, and pedants who are unable to understand a people they disdain and who, in one hour of revolt, vented the wrath they had suppressed for years at having lived from their favor and their votes? Or is the entire North American nation incapable of justice, and the respect that is virtue's due, and the gratitude that is an obligation of friendship? Is the entire North American nation so ferocious and ungrateful? Is there in the soul of that race such a hatred of the Hispanic criollo, so false an idea of his moral and political capacities, that the most despicable men of the North dare to disdain the Cuban's most admirable virtues simply because the Cuban has maintained them amid impoverishment and slavery? Are there no honorable men there who feel ashamed of what they have helped to do, and are turning against those who, with wicked deceit, forced them to violate the laws of their nation, of all nations, and of humanity? And as for rights, did the North Americans have any right whatsoever to commit such acts, to hold the accusatory meeting in the public square, and distribute the inexcusable printed protest, to go and negotiate, without permission from their country, with a foreign and despotic monarch, to request military aid from a foreign government by which to injure and provoke their fellow citizens, to bring more workers from abroad, against the law of the country and the natural generosity of mankind, to a country where hundreds of workers are unemployed? All of this was done because it was said that nineteen Cuban conspirators had decided to oppose the landing of the Spaniards. But when the most highly respected men in the city, heroes of antique lineage in the Cuban revolution, justly venerated apostles of the rights of citizens, and former mayors of Cuban cities, asked in the name of their people for some evidence of the conspiracy, and volunteered their help in punishing it, no one presented them with any evidence, and no one could give them an answer. And when a lawyer, alone in that unfriendly and terror-stricken city, demanded the immediate release of the two Cubans unlawfully imprisoned as the heads of the conspiracy, the court released both men immediately, because no charges had been brought against them.

Why, O Spanish tyranny, did we fly from you only to find all your horrors in an American republic? Why did we trust and love this inhuman and ungrateful land? There is no patria, Cubans, but the one we shall win with our own efforts. The foreign sea, too, is a sea of blood. No one loves or forgives except our own country. The only solid ground in the universe is the ground on which we were born. We will be brave, or we will wander. We will finally put our efforts to the test, or we will be outcasts, roaming the world from one country to another. The very ones we love shall bite us in the heart like rabid dogs. Cubans, there is no man without a patria, and no patria without freedom. This insult has made us all the stronger, has further united us, and has taught us, better than books and diplomas, that we are all of one soul: Spain is our only enemy, in Cuba we are trapped and corrupted, and outside of Cuba we are harassed, wherever there is a man of honor or a table with bread on it. We have no other friend or source of help than ourselves. Once more, Cubans, with our homes at our backs, abandoning our dead, we must make our way across the sea! Cubans: to Cuba!

—January 27, 1894

THE TRUTH ABOUT THE UNITED STATES

It is urgent that our America learn the truth about the United States. Its faults should not be deliberately exaggerated out of an urge to deny that it has any virtues, nor should they be concealed, or praised as virtues. There are no races: there is nothing more than mankind's various modifications of habit and form in response to the conditions of climate and history in which he lives, which do not affect that which is identical and essential. The entertainment of locating any substantial distinction between the Saxon egotist and the Latin egotist, the generous Saxon and the generous Latin, the Saxon bureaucrat and the Latin bureaucrat—for Latins and Saxons have an equal capacity for virtues and defects—is only for men of prologue and surface, men who have not sunk their arms into human entrails, men who do not, from an impartial height, watch the nations all boiling on the same stove, men who do not find, in their very germ and fabric, the same permanent duel between constructive selflessness and wicked hatred.

What varies are the particular consequences of the distinct historical grouping. Whatever potentially fatal disturbances are entrained by the original divorce between lordliness and simplicity, which simultaneously founded it, and by the inevitable hostility, native to the human species, between the greed and vanity that aristocracies create and the fairness and self-denial that reveals them, a people of like-minded Englishmen, Dutchmen, and Germans cannot experience the confusion of political habits that arises in nations where the needs of the conquistador left the natural population alive, terrified, and multiple, and where the way is still barred, with patricidal blindness, by the privileged caste that the European engendered. A nation of strapping Northern youths, accustomed for centuries to sea and snow and to the manliness promoted by the perennial defense of their local liberties,

cannot be like a tropical island, easy and smiling, where, beneath a pi-
ratical government, labor the famished excrescences of a warlike and
backward European people; the descendants of that harsh and uncul-
tured tribe, divided from each other by the hatred of accommodating
docility for rebellious virtue; and the forceful and simple, or debased
and rancorous, Africans, who through a horrific enslavement and a
sublime war have become the fellow citizens of those who once
bought and sold them and, by virtue of those who died in the sublime
war, today greet as equals those who made them dance with the lashes
of their whips yesterday. The only way to find out whether Saxons
and Latins are different, or to compare them, is by seeing how they
have reacted under comparable conditions; and it is a fact that in the
Southern states of the American Union, where there were black slaves,
the predominant character of the people is as haughty, as idle, as tempestuous, and as helpless as the character of the sons of Cuba may be,
as a result of slavery. It is a mark of supine ignorance and childish,
punishable light-mindedness to speak of the United States, and of the
real or apparent achievements of one of its regions or a group of them,
as a total and equal nation of unanimous liberty and definitive achievements: such a United States is an illusion or a fraud. The hills of the
Dakotas, and the barbarous, virile nation that is arising there, are
worlds away from the leisured, privileged, class-bound, lustful, and
unjust cities of the East. There is a whole world between the North of
Schenectady, with its brick houses and lordly freedom, and the South
of St. Petersburg, between the clean, self-interested town of the
North, and the loafers sitting on cracker barrels at the country store in
the angry, impoverished, ramshackle, bitter, gray towns of the South.
An honorable man cannot help but observe that not only have the elements of diverse origin and tendency from which the United States
was created failed, in three centuries of shared life and one century of
political control, to merge, but their forced coexistence is exacerbating
and accentuating their primary differences and transforming the unnatural federation into a harsh state of violent conquest. Only the
petty, or those plagued with futile, gnawing envy, would seek to find
fault with evident greatness or roundly deny it because of one or another mole on its face, or raise themselves above it as an oracle, like
one who would take a speck of dust off the sun. But anyone who ob-
serves the way the bonds of union are loosening rather than tightening
in the United States is not prophesying but attesting. Rather than being resolved, the problems of humanity are being reproduced here.

Rather than amalgamating within national politics, local politics divides and inflames it; instead of growing stronger and saving itself from the hatred and misery of the monarchies, democracy is corrupted and diminished, and hatred and misery are menacingly reborn. And the one who silences this is not doing his duty, while the one who says it aloud is. For silence would be a failure of one's duty as a man to know the truth and disseminate it, and of one's duty as a good American, who sees that the continent's glory and peace can only be ensured by the honest and free development of its different natural entities, and of one's duty as a son of our America to keep the American peoples of Spanish descent from falling, out of ignorance, bedazzlement or impatience, and on the advice of cowardly greed and the pompous toga, into an immoral, enfeebling servitude to a damaged and alien civilization. The truth about the United States must be made known to our America.

Wickedness must be abhorred, even when it is our own wickedness, and even when it is not. We must not fail to love what is good only because it is not ours. But it is a barren and irrational aspiration, the cowardly aspiration of secondary and inadequate people, to seek to achieve the stability of a foreign nation by paths that differ from those that led the envied nation to security and order by its own efforts and by the adaptation of human liberty to the forms required by the particular makeup of the country. In some, an excessive love for the North is the imprudent and understandable expression of a desire for progress so powerful and ardent that they fail to see that ideas, like trees, must grow from deep roots, and must be adapted to the soil in which they are planted in order to grow and prosper, and that the newborn is not fed the strong spices of adulthood only because the mustache and sideburns of adulthood are playfully hung on his soft face. Monsters are created thus, not nations: we must live our own lives and sweat out our own fevers. In others, Yankeemania is the innocent fruit of some small burst of pleasure, like one who judges the essence of a house and of the souls that pray or perish within it by the smiling luxury of the parlor, or the champagne and carnations on the table set for guests. For you must suffer, do without, work, love in vain, study with all your courage and freedom, keep vigil with the poor, weep with the miserable, hate the brutality of wealth, live in the palace and in the tenement, in the classroom and on the front steps of the school, in the private box at the theater, decorated with gold and jasper, and in the cold, bare wings; and only then can you, with some glimmering of accuracy, give an opinion on this greedy, authoritarian republic, and the growing lustfulness of the United States. Others, the feeble after-thoughts of the Second Empire's literary dandyism, or the phony skeptics beneath whose mask of indifference there generally beats a heart of gold, think it fashionable to express the utmost disdain for all that is native, for it seems to them that there is no greater elegance than drinking up both the cut of the foreigner's pants and his ideas, and go-ing about the world like petted lapdogs with the pompoms of their tails sticking up. In others it is a kind of subtle aristocracy whereby, pub-licly loving all that is fair-skinned as if that were natural and proper, they try to cover over their own origin, which they see as mestizo and humble, without seeing that it was always a sign of bastardy in men to go about branding others as bastards, and that there is no more certain betrayal of sin in a woman than a great display of contempt for other women who have sinned. Whatever the cause might be, whether im-patience for freedom or fear of it, moral laziness or laughable aristoc-racy, political idealism or the parvenu's ingenuousness, what is certain is the desirability and urgency of placing the whole American truth before our America, about the Saxon and about the Latin, so that an excessive faith in the virtue of others does not weaken us, in our period of foundation, with an unfounded and catastrophic distrust of what is ours. In a single war, the war of secession, which was more about the struggle between North and South for predominance in the republic than about the abolition of slavery, the United States—after three cen-turies of republican practice in a country whose elements are less hos-tile than any other—lost more men than were lost in the same amount of time, and with the same number of inhabitants, by all the Spanish republics of America together in the naturally slow work, which tri-umphed from Mexico to Chile, of bringing into being in the new world, without other impetus than the apostolic rhetoric of a glorious minority and the popular instinct, remote nations with distant centers and adverse races, in regions where the command of Spain had left be-hind all the rage and hypocrisy of a theocracy and the indolence and suspicion of a prolonged servitude. And it is a matter of simple justice and legitimate social science to recognize that in relation to the facili-ties of the one and the obstacles of the other, the North American character has declined since its independence, and is less humane and virile today, while the Hispanoamerican, from any point of view, is su-perior today, despite his confusion and weariness, than he was when a few wily clerics, untutored ideologues and ignorant or wild Indians began to emerge from the restless masses. And to foster greater knowledge of the political reality of America, as a counterpart or corrective with the supreme force of fact to the unsupported—and, in its excess, pernicious—acclaim for North American political life and character, *Patria* is inaugurating today a permanent column of "Notes on the United States," where we will publish, rigorously translated from the country's leading newspapers and without commentary or editorial intervention, not crimes or accidental errors, which are possible in all countries, and in which only the pettiest mind finds fodder and contentment, but those events that reveal the fundamental qualities that in their constancy and authority demonstrate the two truths that are useful to our America: the crude, unequal, and decadent character of the United States, and the continual existence within it of all the violences, discords, immoralities, and disorders of which the Hispanoamerican peoples are accused.

—March 23, 1894

1895

This was the year Martí had spent his entire life preparing for, and it began with a disaster. A secret expedition to Cuba, which was to leave from Fernandina Beach, Florida, on three ships that had been purchased and stocked with supplies and weapons at great expense, was betrayed, and the ships and all their cargo were seized by the United States government on January 10. When he heard the news, Martí raced from New York to Florida, where, at a meeting with other Cuban insurgents in a Jacksonville hotel, he could do little more than choke, "It's not my fault. It's not my fault."

History did not give him much time to recover. On February 24, the third Cuban war of independence began with the Grito de Baire; Martí was already in the Dominican Republic, trying to find a way to get to Cuba with little money and only a small handful of companions. Finally, after an absence of fifteen and a half years he set foot on the island once more. The fact of his presence there was of enormous political significance, yet it was clear that Martí, a slight middle-aged writer in failing health with no prior military experience, could do far more for the revolution in New York, organizing, raising funds, and promoting the cause. But only three years earlier, Enrique Collazo had written, in an open letter to Martí that appeared in a Cuban newspaper, "If the hour of sacrifice comes again, we may not be able to shake your hand in the Cuban manigua— undoubtedly not, because you will still be giving the Cuban emigrants lessons in patriotism under the shadow of the American flag."

"I called for this war, and my responsibility does not end with its onset, but begins," Martí wrote in March 1895. In a lifetime of organizing and advocating a war of independence, he had never actually fought in battle. When the opportunity arose, he took it.

POLITICS

Before disembarking in Cuba, Martí and General Máximo Gómez drew up the following manifesto in the Dominican town of Montecristi, to announce the goals and intentions of the rebel forces and lay the cornerstone of the government the rebellion was intended to achieve.

By this point, Martí had come to see Cuban independence as not only of hemispheric but of global importance. In a letter written the same day as the manifesto, he said, "The freedom of the Antilles will preserve the independence and honor of our America, and the already dubious and much-injured honor of English America, and will perhaps accelerate and stabilize the equilibrium of the world."

THE MONTECRISTI MANIFESTO

The Cuban Revolutionary Party Addresses Cuba

Cuba's revolution of independence, initiated in Yara, has now, after a glorious and bloody preparation, entered a new period of war, by virtue of the order and agreements of the Revolutionary Party both in and outside the Island, and of the exemplary presence within that party of all elements consecrated to the betterment and emancipation of the country, for the good of America and of the world. Without usurping the accent and declarations that are appropriate only to the majesty of a fully constituted republic, the elected representatives of the revolution that is reaffirmed today recognize and respect their duty to repeat before the patria, which must not be bloodied without reason or without just hope of triumph, the precise aims, born of good judgment and foreign to all thought of vengeance, for which the inextinguishable war that today in moving and prudent democracy leads all elements of Cuban society into combat was initiated and will reach its rational victory.

In the serene minds of those who represent it today and the responsible public revolution that elected them, this war is not the insane triumph of one Cuban party over another, or even the humiliation of a group of mistaken Cubans, but the solemn demonstration of the will of a country that endured far too much in the previous war to plunge lightly into a conflict that can end only in victory or the grave, without causes sufficiently profound to overcome human cowardice and its several disguises, and without a determination so estimable—for it is certified by death—that it must silence those less fortunate Cubans who do not have equal faith in the capacities of their nation or equal valor by which to emancipate it from its servitude.

This war is not a capricious attempt at an independence that would be more fearsome than useful—which only those who manifest the virtuous aim of conducting it to a more viable and certain independence can stave off or do away with, and which must not in truth tempt a people that cannot endure it—but the disciplined product of the resolve of solid men, who in the repose of experience have decided to face once more the dangers they well know, and of a cordial assembly of Cubans of the most diverse origins, all convinced that the virtues necessary for the maintenance of liberty are better acquired in the conquest of liberty than in abject dispiritedness.

This is not a war against the Spaniard, who, secure among his own children and in his deference to the patria they win for themselves, will enjoy, respected and even beloved, the liberty that will sweep away only those imprudent individuals who seek to block its path. This war will not be a cradle of tyranny or of disorder, which is alien to the proven moderation of the Cuban spirit. Those who promoted it, and who can still raise their voices and speak, affirm in its name, before the patria, their freedom from all hatred, their fraternal indulgence toward timid or mistaken Cubans, their radical respect for the dignity of man, which is the catalyst of combat and the cement of the republic, and their certainty that this war can be conducted in a way that contains the redemption that inspires it, and the ongoing relations in which a people must live among others, alongside the reality of what war is. They must express, as well, their categorical determination to respect, and to ensure that all respect, the neutral and honorable Spaniard during and after the war, and to be merciful toward the repentant, and inflexible only toward vice, crime, and inhumanity. In the war that has just begun again in Cuba the revolution does not see cause for a jubilation that could commandeer an unreflecting heroism, but only the responsibilities that must preoccupy the founders of nations.

Cuba is embarking upon this war in the full certainty, unacceptable only to halfhearted, sedentary Cubans, of the ability of its sons to win a victory through the energy of the thoughtful and magnanimous revolution, and the ability of the Cuban people, developed during those ten early years of sublime fusion and in the modern practices of work and government, to save the patria at its origin from the trials and troubles that were necessary at the beginning of the century in the feudal or theoretical republics of Hispano-America, which were without communication and without preparation. Inexcusable ignorance or perfidy it would be to remain unaware of the often glorious and now generally remedied causes for those American upheavals, which arose from the error of trying to adapt foreign models of uncertain dogma, related only to their place of origin, to the ingenuous reality of countries that knew nothing of liberty except their own eagerness to attain it and the pride that they won while fighting for it. The concentration of a merely literary culture in the capitals, the erroneous adherence of the republics to the lordly habits of the colony, the creation of rival caudillos as a consequence of the distrustful and inadequate treatment of remote areas, the rudimentary state of the only industry, which was farming or cattle herding, and the abandonment and disdain of the fertile indigenous race amid the disputes between creeds or locales that these causes for the upheavals in the nations of America carried on—these are in no way the problems of Cuban society. Cuba returns to war with a democratic and educated people, zealously aware of its own rights and those of others, and with even the humblest of its populace far more educated than the masses of plainsmen or Indians by whom, at the voice of the supreme heroes of emancipation, the silent colonies of America were transformed from herds of cattle into nations. At the crossroads of the world, in the service of war and the foundation of a nationality, there come to Cuba, from their creating and conserving labor in the most capable nations of the globe and from their own efforts on behalf of the country's persecution and misery, the lucid sons, magnates or servants, who after the first era of compromise between the heterogeneous components of the Cuban nation, which is now past, went forth to prepare, or on the Island itself continued preparing, by their own self-improvement, for the enhancement of the nationality to which today they bring the soundness of their industrious persons and the certainty of their republican education. The civic-mindedness of Cuba's warriors, the skill and benevolence of her craftsmen, the real and modern employment of a vast number of her minds and fortunes, the peculiar moderation of the campesino seasoned by exile and war, the intimate and daily contact and rapid and inevitable unification of the diverse sectors of the country, the reciprocal admiration for the virtues equally distributed among Cubans who passed directly from the differences of slavery to the brotherhood of sacrifice, and the benevolence and growing capability of the freed slave, far more common than the rare examples of his deviation or rancor, all ensure Cuba, without unwarranted illusions, a future in which the conditions of stability and immediate labor for a fruitful people in a just republic will exceed those of dissociation and partiality stemming from the laziness or arrogance that war sometimes breeds, from the offensive rancor of a minority of masters stripped for their privileges, from the censurable haste with which a still invisible minority of discontented freed slaves might aspire, in disastrous violation of free will and human nature, to the social respect that solely and surely must come to them by their proven equality of talent and virtue, or from the sudden and widespread loss by the literate inhabitants of the cities of the relative sumptuousness or abundance that they derive today from the colony's immoral and facile sinecures and the positions that liberty will cause to disappear. A free nation, where work is open to all, positioned at the very mouth of the rich and industrial universe, will without obstacle and with some advantage replace, after a war inspired by the purest self-sacrifice and carried out in keeping with it, the shameful nation where well-being is obtained only in exchange for an express or tacit complicity with the tyranny of the grasping foreigners who bleed and corrupt it. We have no doubts about Cuba or its ability to obtain and govern its independence, we who, in the heroism of death and the silent foundation of the patria, see continually shining forth among the great and the humble its gifts of harmony and wisdom, which are only imperceptible to those who, living outside the real soul of their country, judge it, in their own arrogant concept of themselves, to possess no greater power of rebellion and creation than that which it timidly displays in the servitude of its colonial tasks.

And there is another fear from which cowardice, disguised as prudence, may wish to profit just now: the senseless and, in Cuba, always unjustified fear of the black race. The revolution, with all its martyrs and generous subordinate warriors, denies indignantly, as the long experience of those in exile and those on the island during the truce denies, the slanderous notion of a threat by the Negro race, which has been wickedly employed to the benefit of those who profit from the Spanish regime to stir up fear of the revolution. There are already Cubans in Cuba, of one color or another, who have forgotten forever—through the emancipating war and the work they carry on together—the hatred by which slavery may have divided them. The novelty and asperity of social relations following the sudden transformation of the man who belonged to another into his own man are less important than the sincere esteem of the white Cuban for the equal soul, painstaking education, freeman's fervor, and lovable character of his black compatriot. And if vile demagogues are born to the race, or avid souls whose own impatience incites that of their race, or in whom pity for their own people is transformed into injustice toward others, then out of their gratitude and prudence and love for the patria, out of their conviction of the need to disprove by a manifest demonstration of the intelligence and virtue of the black Cuban the still prevailing opinion of his incapacity for those two qualities, and in their possession of all the reality of human rights and the consolation and strength of their esteem for whatever element of justice and generosity there is in the white Cubans, the black race itself will extirpate the black menace in Cuba without a single white hand having to be raised to the task. The revolution knows this and proclaims it; those in exile proclaim it as well. The Cuban black has no schools of wrath there, and in the war not a single black was punished for arrogance or insubordination. Upon the shoulders of the black man, the republic, which he has never attacked, moved in safety. Only those who hate the black see hatred in the black, and those who traffic in such unjust fears do so in order to subjugate the hands that could be raised to expel the corrupting occupier from Cuban soil.

From the Spanish inhabitants of Cuba, the revolution, which neither flatters nor fears, hopes to receive, instead of the dishonorable wrath of the first war, such affectionate neutrality or truthful assistance as to make the war shorter, its disasters lesser, and the peace in which fathers and sons must live together easier and friendlier. We Cubans are starting the war, and Cubans and Spaniards will finish it together. If they do not mistreat us, we will not mistreat them. If they show respect, we will respect them. The blade is answered with the blade, and friendship is answered with friendship. There is no hatred in the Antillian bosom, and in death the Cuban salutes the brave Spaniard who was torn by the cruelty of forced military service from his home and his land to come and murder in manly breasts the liberty that he himself yearns for. More than saluting him in death, the revolution would like to welcome him in life, and the republic will be a tranquil homeland for however many hardworking and honorable Spaniards wish to enjoy the liberty and well-being within it that they will not find for a long time to come in the torpor, apathy, and political vices of their own land. This is the heart of Cuba, and in this way will the war be carried out. What Spanish enemy will the revolution truly have? Will it be the army, republican for the most part, which has learned to respect our valor as we respect theirs, and sometimes feels a greater impulse to join us than to do battle with us? Will it be the conscripts, already versed in the ideals of humanity and opposed to spilling the blood of their equals for the benefit of a useless scepter or a greedy patria, the conscripts who were cut down in the flower of their youth to come and defend—against a people that would happily welcome them as free citizens—an unstable throne that presides over a nation sold by its leaders? Will it be the mass of craftsmen and clerks, now, after their years in Cuba, humane and educated, who, on the pretext of defending the patria, were dragged yesterday into ferocity and crime by the interests of the wealthy Spaniards who now, with most of their fortunes safe in Spain, evince less zeal than when they bloodied the land of their riches after war found them with all their fortune there? Or will it be the founders of Cuban families and industries, vexed and oppressed like the Cubans and weary by now of the deceptions of Spain and its misrule, who, ungrateful and imprudent, with no thought for the peace of their homes and the preservation of a wealth that the Spanish regime threatens more than any revolution, turn against the land that has transformed them from sad peasants into happy husbands and fathers of an offspring capable of dying without hatred to ensure for their bloody father a free land at the end of the permanent discord between the criollo and those born on the Peninsula, a land where an honorable fortune can be maintained without bribery and amassed without anxiety and where the son does not see, between his kiss and his father's hand, the abhorrent shadow of the oppressor? What fate will the Spaniards choose: relentless war, open or concealed, that threatens and further disturbs the country's perennially turbulent and violent relations, or definitive peace, which will never be achieved in Cuba except by independence? Will the Spaniards who have roots in Cuba provoke a war in which they may be vanquished? And by what right would the Spaniards hate us, when we Cubans do not hate them? The revolution makes use of this language

without fear because the mandate to emancipate Cuba once and for all
from the irremediable ineptitude and corruption of the Spanish government, and to open it forthrightly to all men of the new world, is as
absolute as our will to welcome to Cuban citizenship, without faint
hearts or bitter memories, the Spaniards who in their passion for liberty help us to victory in Cuba, as well as those other Spaniards who
by their respect for today's war redeem the blood that in yesterday's
war coursed, under their blows, from the chests of their sons.

The forms the revolution takes will provide no pretext for reproach
to the vigilant cowards, fully aware of its selflessness, who in the formal errors or scant republicanism of the nascent country might have
found some reason for which to deny it the blood they owe it. Pure
patriotism will have no cause to fear for the dignity and future fate of
the patria. The difficulty of America's wars of independence and of its
first nationalities has not lain primarily in any discord among its heroes or the emulation and mistrust inherent in mankind, but rather in
the lack of a form that could contain both the spirit of redemption
which, supported by lesser incentives, promotes and nourishes the
war, and the practices necessary to war, which the war must sustain
and not encumber. In its initiatory war, a country must find a manner
of government that can satisfy both the mature and cautious intelligence of its literate sons and the necessary conditions for the assistance
and respect of its other peoples, and that does not hinder but enables
the full development and rapid conclusion of the war that was calami-
tously necessary to the public happiness. From its origin, the patria
must be constituted in viable forms, forms born of itself, so that a government without reality or sanction does not lead it into biases or
tyranny. Without impinging by an unrestrained concept of its duty
upon the integral faculties of constitution by which, in their peculiar
responsibility before the liberal and impatient contemporary world,
the country's educated and uneducated elements are ordered and rec-
onciled—both equally moved by executive impetus and ideal purity,
and with identical nobility and the unassailable title of their blood, to
hurl themselves after the guiding soul of the first heroes and open an
industrious republic to humanity—the Cuban Revolutionary Party
can do no more than legitimately declare its faith that the revolution
will find forms that will guarantee it, in the unity and vigor indispensable to a civilized war, the enthusiasm of the Cuban people, the trust
of the Spaniards, and the friendship of the world. To know and establish reality, to form in a natural mold the reality of the ideas that pro-

duce or extinguish deeds and the reality of the deeds that are born from ideas, to organize the revolution with dignity, sacrifice, and culture so that no man's dignity is harmed, and the sacrifice does not strike a single Cuban as futile, to ensure that no Cuban sees the revolution as inferior to the country's own culture or to the foreign, unauthorized culture that has alienated the respect of virile men by the inefficacy of its results and the doleful contrast between the current pusillanimity of its sterile possessors and their arrogance, but that all Cubans perceive it, rather, as based in a profound knowledge of man's endeavor to rescue and maintain his dignity—these are the duties and intentions of the revolution. It will be governed to ensure that a powerful and effective war will quickly establish a stable home for the new republic.

The war, healthy and vigorous from the start, which Cuba begins again today, with all the advantages of its experience and victory at last guaranteed to the unyielding resolve and lofty efforts of its unfading heroes, whose memory is always blessed, is not merely a pious longing to give full life to the nation that, beneath the immoral occupation of an inept master, is crumbling and losing its great strength both within the suffocating patria and scattered abroad in exile. This war is not an inadequate drive to conquer Cuba, for political independence would have no right to ask Cubans for their help if it did not bring with it the hope of creating one patria more for freedom of thought, equality of treatment, and peaceful labor. The war of independence in Cuba, the knot that binds the sheaf of islands where shortly the commerce of the continents must pass through, is a far-reaching human event and a timely service that the judicious heroism of the Antilles lends to the stability and just interaction of the American nations and to the still unsteady equilibrium of the world. It honors and moves us to think that when a warrior for independence falls on Cuban soil, perhaps abandoned by the heedless or indifferent peoples for whom he sacrifices himself, he falls for the greater good of mankind, for the confirmation of a moral republicanism in America, and for the creation of a free archipelago through which the respectful nations will pour a wealth that must, at its passage, spill over into the crossroads of the world. Hardly can it be believed that with such martyrs and such a future there could be Cubans who would bind Cuba to the corrupt and provincial monarchy of Spain and its sluggish, vice-ridden wretchedness! Tomorrow the revolution will have to explain anew to its country and to the nations the local causes, universal in concept and interest, by which for the progress and service of humanity the emancipating nation of Yara and Guáimaro begins again a war that, in its unswerving idea of the rights of man and its abhorrence of sterile vengeance and futile devastation, deserves the respect of its enemies and the support of the nations. Today, as we proclaim from the threshold of the earth, in veneration of the spirit and doctrines that produce and animate the wholehearted and humanitarian war for which the people of Cuba unite once more, invincible and indivisible, it is fitting that we evoke, as guides and helpers to our people, the magnanimous founders whose labor the grateful country takes up once again, and the honor that must prevent Cubans from wounding by word or deed those who gave their lives for them. And thus, making this declaration in the name of the patria and deposing before her and her free faculty of constitution the identical labor of two generations, the Delegate of the Cuban Revolutionary Party, created to organize and support the current war, and the Commander in Chief elected by all the active members of the Liberating Army, in their shared responsibility to those they represent and in demonstration of the unity and solidity of the Cuban revolution, sign this declaration together.

—José Martí, Máximo Gómez
Montecristi (Dominican Republic), March 25, 1895

FINAL CORRESPONDENCE

LETTER TO HIS MOTHER

Montecristi, March 25, 1895

Madre mía,

Today, March 25, on the eve of a long journey, I am thinking of you. I think of you ceaselessly. In the wrath of your love you are pained by the sacrifice of my life—but then why was I born from you with a life that loves sacrifice? Words—I cannot. The duty of a man lies where he is most useful. But in my growing and necessary agony the memory of my mother is with me always.

Embrace my sisters, and your friends. Would that I might one day see them all around me, contented with me! And then I will take care of you with tenderness and with pride. Now give me your blessing and believe that no work that is not charitable and pure will ever emerge from my heart. The blessing.

Your
José Martí

I have good reason to set off more contented and certain than you can imagine. Truth and tenderness are not useless. Do not suffer.

LETTER TO MANUEL MERCADO

On the day before his death, Martí began a letter to Manuel Mercado (1838–1909), then the Mexican undersecretary of the interior, who had been one of his dearest friends since 1875, when Martí arrived in Mexico to live with his parents, whose house was next door to Mercado's.

The letter breaks off suddenly in the middle of a sentence. Martí must have been interrupted, and his death made the interruption definitive.

Camp at Dos Ríos, May 18, 1895

Señor Manuel Mercado,

My dearest brother: now I can write: now I can tell you with what tenderness and gratitude and respect I love you, and your home that is my own—and with what pride and commitment. Every day now I am in danger of giving my life for my country and my duty—since I understand it and have the spirit to carry it out—in order to prevent, by the timely independence of Cuba, the United States from extending its hold across the Antilles and falling with all the greater force on the lands of our America. All I have done up to now and all I will do is for that. It has had to be done in silence, and indirectly, for there are things that must be concealed in order to be attained: proclaiming them for what they are would give rise to obstacles too formidable to be overcome. The nations such as your own and mine, which have the most vital interest in keeping Cuba from becoming, through an annexation accomplished by those imperialists and the Spaniards, the doorway—which must be blocked and which, with our blood, we are blocking—to the annexation of the peoples of our America by the turbulent and brutal North that holds them in contempt, are kept by secondary, public obligations from any open allegiance and manifest aid to the sacrifice being made for their immediate benefit. I lived in the monster, and I know its entrails—and my sling is the sling of David. Even now, a few days ago, in the wake of the triumph with which the Cuban people greeted our free descent from the mountains where we six expeditionaries walked for fourteen days, a correspondent from the *New York Herald* took me from my hammock and hut and told me about the activities aimed at annexation—which is less fearsome because of the scant realism of those who aspire to it—by men of the legal ilk who, having no discipline or creative power of their own, and as a convenient disguise for their complacency and subjugation to Spain, request Cuba's autonomy without conviction, content that there be a master, Yankee or Spaniard, to maintain them and grant them, in reward for their services as intermediaries, positions as leaders, scornful of the vigorous masses, the skilled and inspiring mestizo masses of this country—the intelligent, creative masses of whites and blacks.

And did the *Herald* correspondent, Eugene Bryson, tell me about anything else? About a Yankee syndicate, backed by the Customs Office, in which rapacious white Spaniards have a deep hand, and that may become a toehold in Cuba for those from the North, whose complex and entrammeled political constitution fortunately leaves them unable to undertake or support this plan as the project of their government. And Bryson told me something else, though the truth of the conversation he reported to me can only be understood by one who has seen at close hand the vigor with which we have launched the revolution, and the disorder, reluctance, and poor pay of the raw Spanish army—and the inability of Spain to muster, either in or out of Cuba, the resources with which to fight this war, resources that, during the last war, it extracted from Cuba alone. Bryson told me about a conversation he had with Martínez Campos[1] at the end of which he was given to understand that no doubt, when the time came, Spain would prefer to reach an agreement with the United States than to hand the Island over to the Cuban people. And Bryson told me still more: about an acquaintance of ours who is being groomed in the North as the United States' candidate for the presidency of Mexico, once the current President has disappeared. I am doing my duty here. The Cuban war—a reality that is superior to the vague and disparate desires of the annexationist Cubans and Spaniards whose alliance with the government of Spain would give them only relative power—has come at the right hour in America to prevent, even against the open deployment of all these forces, the annexation of Cuba to the United States, which would never accept the annexation of a country that is at war, and which, since the revolution will not accept annexation, cannot enter into a hateful and absurd commitment to crush, for its own benefit and with its own weapons, an American war of independence.

—And Mexico? Will it not find a wise, effective, and immediate way of supplying aid, in time, to those who are defending it? Yes, it will, or I will find one on Mexico's behalf. This is life or death; there is no room for error. Discretion is the only option. I would have found and proposed a way already, but I must have more authority myself, or know who does have it, before acting or advising. I have just arrived. The constitution of a simple, practical government may take two more months, if it is to be real and stable. Our soul is one, I know that, and so is the will of the country: but these things are always a labor of connections, timeliness, and compromise. I represent a certain constituency, and I do not want to do anything that might appear to be a capricious expansion of it.

I arrived in a boat with General Máximo Gómez and four other men, taking the lead oar through a storm to land on an unknown, rocky stretch of one of our beaches. For fourteen days I carried my rucksack and rifle on foot across brambles and high places—rousing the people to take up arms as we passed through. I feel, in the benevolence of these souls, the root of my attachment to the pain of mankind and to the justice that will alleviate it. The countryside is undisputedly ours, to such a degree that in a month I've heard gunfire only once; at the gates of the cities we either win a victory or pass three thousand armed men in review, to an enthusiasm akin to religious fervor. We are going on now to the center of the Island where, in the presence of the revolution that I have given rise to, I will lay aside the authority given me by the Cubans off the island, which has been respected on the island, and which an assembly of delegates of the visible Cuban people, the revolutionaries now in arms, must renew in accordance with their new state. The revolution desires full liberty for the army, without the trammels once imposed on it by a Chamber of Deputies with no real authorization, or by the suspicions of a younger generation that is zealous in its republicanism, or by jealousy and fear of the excessive future prominence of some painstaking and farsighted caudillo. However, at the same time, the revolution wants concise and respectable republican representation—the same spirit of humanity and decency, full of yearning for individual dignity, in the republic's representatives as is driving the revolutionaries on and keeping them at war. For myself, I understand that a nation cannot be made to go against the spirit that moves it, or to do without that spirit, and I know how to set hearts on fire and how to use the ardent and gratified state of those hearts for incessant agitation and attack. But where forms are concerned, there is room for many ideas, and the things of men are made by men. You know me. For myself, I will defend only that which I believe will guarantee or serve the revolution. I know how to disappear. But my ideas would not disappear, nor would my own obscurity embitter me. —And as long as we have a form, we will work, whether the fulfilment of it falls to me or to others.

And now that matters of the public interest have gone first, I'll tell you about myself. Only the emotion of this duty was able to raise from coveted death the man who knows you best—now that Nájera[2] no longer lives where he can be seen—and who cherishes the friendship with which you distinguish him like a treasure in his heart. I know how you have been scolding me, silently, since my journey began: We give him all our soul, and he is silent! What a disappointment! How callused his soul must be if the tribute and honor of our affection has not been enough to make him write one letter more, among all the pages of letters and newspaper articles he writes each day!

There are affections of such delicate honesty,

WAR DIARIES

From Montecristi, Dominican Republic, to Dos Ríos, Cuba, February 14–May 17, 1895

On the brink of war, pursued by Spanish spies, and with a strong premonition that he was going toward his death, Martí began, for the first time in his life, to keep a diary. Initially intended as a link to two beloved young girls back in Brooklyn, the first part of the diary, which says little about Martí's plans and the purpose of his journeys, is full of lighthearted character sketches and sensual appreciations that belie the constant peril through which he was moving.

The second half—whose first few pages were initially scribbled in the back of a copy of Thompson's Pocket Speller—*is more explicitly political; Martí's personal diary had become a record of history in the making. Though most of his time was given over to far more pressing activities, he worked at the diary with his usual obsessive care, going back over his writing, rephrasing sentences, substituting a better word here and there, searching for the precise name of a plant. José Lezama Lima, Cuba's greatest twentieth-century poet, considered the diary "the greatest poem ever written by a Cuban."*

PART I

From Montecristi to Cap-Haïtien, February 14–April 8, 1895

MY GIRLS:[1]

Organize these notes, which I wrote for you, by date, along with the ones I sent you earlier. They were written for no reason but to show that day by day, on horseback and on the sea, and in the greatest anguish a man could endure, I was thinking of you.—

February 14

Six-thirty in the morning it must have been when we left Montecristi, the General, Collazo,[2] and I, on horseback for Santiago: Santiago de los Caballeros, the old city dating from 1507. As I write this now, while my companions have a siesta here in the pure home of Nicolás Ramírez, all that stands out in my memory from the journey are a few trees, a few characters, men and women, and a few phrases, phrases that have come down through time, picturesque, concise, suggestive: a kind of natural philosophy. Ordinary language is based in the study of the world, passed down from fathers to sons in subtle maxims and childish first impressions. A single phrase explains this country's crude, needless arrogance: "When I'm given (gifts, gifts from friends and relatives to the home of newlyweds) it depresses me, because I'm the one receiving." To give is a manly thing; to receive, no. Out of sheer ferocity, they deny themselves the pleasure of gratitude. But the wisdom of the campesino is in the rest of the phrase: "And if no one gives me anything then I have to kill the young hens I'm just starting to raise for my wife." The speaker is a handsome youth with long, agile legs, bare feet, machete ever in hand, and a good knife at his belt; his eyes, in his earthen, fevered face, are healthy and distressed. He is Arturo, newly married, whose wife left to give birth among her own people in Santiago. From Arturo comes this question: "Why do they say, when my wife has a child, that my wife parió [dropped], but when Jiménez's[3] wife has hers, they say she has dado a luz [given to light]?" And phrases like that are collected along the road. To a girl who goes past, her waist swaying freely, not much in the way of breasts, her yellow kerchief loosely knotted, and a campeachy flower in her black hair: "There's a nice little frying pan for my cracklings!" To a country matron on a big Arab horse, wearing a ring over her glove, earrings, and a parasol, who in evil hour married her daughter off to a musié[4]— an orator of the Castelarian school and a Zorilla-esque poet,[5] full of useless learning, "inchoate light," and an "unquenchable thirst for the ideal"—her husband, in leather shoes and a manaca hat, who is holding the stirrup for her, says, "What did I tell you, but you didn't want to listen: 'To every fish its own water.'" We spur the horses on so a good run can refresh them, and while we're drinking water from the Yaque River at Eusebio's house, the General utters this phrase, which constitutes a whole theory of the healthiness and necessity of human effort: "The horse bathes in its own sweat." Eusebio is alive out of pure manliness; his old head is protected by a blue-checked handkerchief, not because of the harsh sun, but because a blow from the butt of a revolver left him with a hole in the back of it that half a hen's egg can fit into, and the edge of his hand fits into the two sword cuts that stretch across his ear and half his forehead: they left him for dead.

"And Don Jacinto, is he here?" Our three horses are resting, their muzzles at the fence. A door is pried open and there's Don Jacinto, sprawled in a straw chair with one skinny arm resting on a cushion tied to a chairback, and the other in the air, held up by two loops of new rope suspended from the ceiling: the frame of a camp bed is leaning against the window: the dried mud of the floor is fissured with cracks. Resting on their sides in a row from the table to the door are two glazed gin jugs and an empty flagon corked with a corncob: the table, teetering and dusty, is strewn with jars, an inhaler, an atomizer, asthma powders. Don Jacinto has a rapacious profile and wears a green velvet cap that pushes his stiff ears forward; there are sticking-plasters at his temples; the two heavy, curving tips of his mustache meet at the small tuft of hair under his lip, his drowning eyes bulge out of his face, pained and fierce; his socks are made of flesh-colored wool, and his faded wool slippers are frayed. He was a leader among men, a firebrand general: once, when fleeing, he left his wife in the care of a close friend and she gave herself to the friend. He came back, found out, and at the door of his own house closed the unfaithful friend's eyes forever with a shot from his carbine. "And to you, *adiós!* I won't kill you because you're a woman." He wandered across Haiti into new territory, a local midwife's fresh young daughter became attached to him, and now his own lovely daughter, eight years old, comes in shyly to kiss us, wearing slippers with no socks. From the store next door, a bottle of rum and some glasses are brought in. Don Jacinto is embroiled in disputes: he owns some land, and a friend—the friend who took him in when he was on the run after the carbine shot—wants to graze his animals on that land. "And the world must know that if I'm killed, it was José Ramón Pérez who killed me. And you can't tell me he doesn't hire killers, because he came to me once to ask if I'd find him a good peón who'd put a bullet into Señor So-and-So for one Spanish doubloon; and another time he had to kill someone else, and he told me he'd paid out another doubloon." "And the man who comes to visit you, Don Jacinto, does he still have to eat a scorpion?" That is: does he find himself facing a valiant man: does he meet with some return fire? Don Jacinto's eyes bulge out further, and the sickly pink of his cheeks rises. "Yes," he says, gentle and smiling. And his head sinks onto his chest.

Across the comfortable, dry savanna covered with huisache and prickly pear we come, with the sun already setting, to the heights of Villalobos and the house of Nené, big mama of the town, with twenty or more offspring who all come running at the news and kiss her hand. "Y'all please forgive me," she says, sitting down at the table where we're eating white rice and fried eggs with rum and coffee, "but I bin takin' a machete to the cornfield the whole day." Her tunic is black and she's wearing a kerchief on her head. The whole hamlet of Peña respects her. At the first light of dawn we leave the hilltop and make our way through fields of plantains and corn, tobacco and yerba, and then down a footpath to Laguna Salada and the General's hacienda. In one angle of the courtyard is a dense planting of banana trees, in another, a plot of sweet potatoes; behind the house, with four rooms facing it, and palm trees and spikes of cacti, is the garden of orange trees and amaranthus, with the high, naked cross of a tomb surrounded by lilies. Mercedes, a Dominican mulatta, fine and pure in her old age, cooks for us with wood that her Haitian husband, Albonó, breaks across his knees, a lunch of white rice, chicken with arrowroot, sweet potato, and squash; I prefer cassava to bread, and the coffee is sweetened with honey. In the thick of the day we converse about war and men, and later in the afternoon we visit the home of Jesús Domínguez, father of many daughters, one of whom has green eyes, finely curving brows, and a commanding head, her dress of crimson muslin all unkempt, her shoes dusty and misshapen, holding a silk umbrella, with a flower in her hair; and another daughter comes in smoking, plump and piquant, with a sock on one foot and a slipper on the other, her seventeen-year-old bosom bursting out of her red bodice, and a rose in the curls at her forehead. Don Jesús comes in from the field where he was burning off tobacco worms, "a tough job," and lying at the door of his good house he talks about his crops and his sons, who've come in with him from working, because he wants "my sons to be like me" and he's been rich and then rich no more, and when his fortune runs out he still holds his head high and no one knows anything about his ruin, and he goes back to the earth to ask for the gold he lost, and the earth gives it to him: because the miner has to crush stones to extract gold from them, but the earth gives Don Jesús "gold ready-made, and pesos ready-made." And there is a remedy for everything in the world, even for a balking mule, because the mule balks only when its driver sets out without the remedy, which is a lemon or two, squeezed and rubbed vigorously into the mule's hooves, "and it goes on walking." On the table are chicken and beans, and rice and *viandas,* which is meat and vegetables stewed with garlic, and cheese from the North, and chocolate. The following morning, before we ride off to Santiago, Don Jesús shows us a corroded pick that he says dates from Columbus's time and was dug up in La Esperanza [Hope] "from the Indian excavations," in the days of the Bulla [Racket] mine, which was already known as "Bulla" in Columbus's time because at dawn the sound of all the Indians getting up for work could be heard from afar. Then Don Jesús brings out a fine, basket-hilted sword, an old Castilian sword, with which the General, standing in profile, shields his entire body from bullets, except the elbow, which is the only thing the stance the General's fencing master taught him leaves exposed. The youngest girl offers to have six flowering shrubs planted for me, for my return. She does not plant flowers, and her brothers, magnificent lads with brawny chests and eyes like honey, do not know how to read.

La Esperanza, made famous by Columbus's route, is a hamlet of palms and yaguas on a wholesome stretch of level ground encircled by mountains. La Providencia [Providence] was the name of the first general store, back in Guayubin, the one that belonged to a Puerto Rican husband, who had some yellowing antique medical books and a fresh young Indian girl with a marble profile, an uneasy smile, and flaming eyes, who approached our stirrups to hand cigars up to us. The other store, Don Jacinto's, is called La Fe [Faith]. Another one nearby bore the name—written in inky letters on a strip of yagua palm—La Fantasía de París [Parisian Fantasy]. And in La Esperanza we dismounted in front of La Delicia [Delight]. From within, General Candelario Lozano, his hair too long and his pants too short, comes to open the gate—"la pueita" is how he says *la puerta*—for our mounts. He isn't wearing socks and his shoes are made of leather. He hangs up his hammock, talks about the local padre, now in town "to pocket the money for the confirmations"; he shows us his office, glued together out of cardboard, from the days when he was a brigadier general under Báez; he listens, his legs dangling from his tilted perch, to Ana Vitalina, his literate girl, who with great aplomb and without pause reads the letter in which the Minister exhorts General Candelario Lozana to continue "keeping the peace" and offers to bring him the saddle he is requesting—but "later." He sells beer, and has three half-barrels of it on hand, *"poique no se vende má que cuando viene ei padre"* ['cause it only sells when the padre comes]. He goes off to buy rum for us. There, some way away, where the town drops off, are the ruins of the fort of La Esperanza, from Columbus's time, and of the first chapel.

From La Esperanza, walking and galloping with few stops to rest, we reach Santiago in five hours. The road is dark now and goes through tall trees. It follows the course of the Yaque, on the left, through a luxuriant palm grove. Powerful ceibas form arches above it. One of them is pocked with bullet marks, from roots to foliage. The open plain can be seen in quick glimpses, like a spark shooting up or the temptation of serene beauty and, in the distance, the blue of the mountains. When we reach the city, we look back from the top of a slope and see the dense valley and the road slipping away into the depths to dive straight for the plains and the low, rolling mountains beyond, and the long line of lush green that marks the course of the Yaque.

February 15

This is Santiago de los Caballeros, and the house made of palm and yagua that belongs to Nicolás Ramírez, who transformed himself from a rebel *guajiro*[6] into a doctor and a good apothecary; across the way is a house almost in the style of Pompeii, but without the color: a single continuous floor, raised well above the ground, with five doors whose wide carved frames give out onto a spacious porch, and the entrance in one corner, through a sumptuous wrought-iron fence that leads up the stairway on one side, across the front, and at the rear through a graceful half-door, into the garden, full of roses and *cayucos:* the *cayuco* is a cactus. The portal's slender white columns support a curving, elegant frieze. Soldiers wearing blue twill and kepis pass by resplendent on their way to mass at the new church, bearing the silk flag of the Yaque Battalion. The foot soldiers are black; the officers, mestizo and black. The architect of the church, Onofre de Lora, is from Santiago; its front door was made by the Cuban hand of Manuel Boitel.

Manuel Boitel lives on the other side of the river. Paquito Borrero, whose fine, saintly head resembles the *San Francisco* painted by Alonso Cano, looks for a place to ford the river on his white horse, with Collazo behind him on Gómez's roan. Gómez and I await the raft, which is coming now, and is named *La Progresista*. We go back uphill to Manuel Boitel's neat sugar-mill compound. From there, the other bank can be seen, all cabins and footpaths as it rises from the river, the summit a dark green with the two towers and cupola of the pink-and-white church emerging from it, and in the distance, through rooftops and hills, the crenellated wall and bonneted tower of the "patriotic redoubt" of the fortress of San Luis.

Everything in that little house bears the mark of hardworking hands: here is a toy wagon that will soon come up from the river loaded with beams, over there is a yellow-and-black phaeton made entirely, down to the last nut and bolt, by the skilled Boitel, and farther off is a silky dog, chained up and lying on the ground, guarding the doorway of the immaculate house. On the parlor table, among old books, are the Protestant Bible and a treatise on beekeeping. Sitting in chairs and armchairs all made by Boitel, we look out onto the serene landscape while Collazo sketches it. The mother brings us meringue. The father is at the sawmill. The eldest daughter goes past, driving an ox that is pulling beams. The garden is full of basil, poinciana, cotton, and rose of Sharon. We pick some flowers for Rafaela, Ramírez's wife, her hands callused from work, her whole noble soul in her luminous face. Nothing less than noble: she is loyal, modest, and loving. The sun sets fire to the sky above the dark forest. The Yaque runs clear and wide.

They take me, still in my travel clothes, to the Centro de Recreo, the young people's society. I begged them to give up on the public, ceremonious festivities they had wanted to welcome me with; the house is decorated for a gala occasion, but an intimate and simple one. Fine young people are waiting, sitting around tables. A crowd throngs at the doors. The shelves are full of new books. A band greets me with a local waltz, flowing and almost hushed, for piano and flute with guiro and tambourine. The *mamarrachos* enter, bringing their own music with them: those are the masked figures that come out at night here at the approach of carnival: the Corpus Christi dragon comes out, too, swallowing up little boys, and accompanied by some enormous giants. One giant was wearing gloves, and Máximo, Ramírez's two-and-a-half-year-old son, says that "the giant is wearing his necktie on his hands."

Conversation at the Centro was abundant and kind: about the country's newest books, about the free reading room I would like the society to open for impoverished youths, about the traveling teachers who instruct the country people, an idea I suggested in an article many years ago,[7] and that was put into law, with a solid grounding and much applause, by the Dominican government in the days of José Joaquín Pérez, during Billini's presidency.[8] We speak of the deficiency, and regional renewal, of Spanish thought: of the force and beauty of the local arts: of a book that would depict the customs and collect the legends of the epic and industrious city of Santiago. We speak of the city's new houses and the rightness of their construction, full of air and light.

I hear this song:

> El soldado que no bebe
> y no sabe enarmorar,
> ¿Qué se puede esperar de él
> Si lo mandan avanzar?

> If a soldier never takes a drink
> and can't make a girl's heart dance,
> what's he going to do, you think,
> when he's ordered to advance?

February 14[9]

—Day broke upon us on the way from Santiago de los Caballeros to La Vega, and its clarity was a property of the soul, deep and mellow. In the uncertain light on both sides of the wide road was all of American nature: the horses moved more spiritedly across that flowering landscape, bordered with distant mountains, where dense canebrakes grow at the foot of the leafy mango: the mango trees were in bloom and there were full-grown orange trees, and a fallen palm tree, with many threading roots still attaching it to the earth, and the coconut with its rugged fronds, sagging under its own weight, and the ceiba, whose strong arms open out high in the sky, and the royal palm. Tobacco pokes out through a fence, and star apple and guanabana trees bend over a stream. The chest swells steadily with authority and faith. Our conversation is measured and affectionate. We stop off at a small inn to have our *cafecito* and an *amargo*.[10] A ragged old Haitian with ardent gray eyes, sitting on a tree trunk, a grubby bundle at his feet and his sandals in shreds, is surrounded by listeners. I speak to him in a long burst of French that startles him, and he gazes at me with something between gloom and mockery: who is this pilgrim who has dropped out of nowhere and drawn the crowd's attention with his incoherent sing-song? People are laughing: so, then, another man speaks the saint's language, does he, and even faster than the saint? "Look at him, there he was like God on a banana plantation!" "We were the yucca, and he was the tall guayo tree." The old man shoulders his bundle and starts walking, chewing on his lips: walking to the sacred hill. The lady who keeps the local inn is very pleased with the walls of her house because of the clumsy figures her son has made on them with colored paint. Sitting in a corner, I draw, on the back of a useless letter, two heads, which he gazes at covetously. The man of the house is in jail: he's *a politician*.

February 15

I dreamed that there were two lances: on the rusting lance the sun did not shine while the polished lance was a huge bloom of light, a flaming star. No fire can be drawn from a lethargic soul.—And from the sugar mill, I admired, with a son's love, the eloquent calm of the illuminated night and a group of palm trees that seemed to be resting on top of one another, and the stars that shone above them. It was like a sudden, immaculate cleanliness, the revelation of the universal nature of man. Later, at noon, I was sitting next to Manuelico in the shade of the sugar mill. His wife and a serving woman were hulling rice at the door of the house, and a rooster was picking at the grains that spilled. "Careful, don't let that rooster eat rice, it's very bad for his stomach." Manuelico is a cock-fighter and has many of them, tied to pickets in the shade or in the sun. He "suns" them so they'll "know heat," so they "won't choke up during the fight," so they will "be seasoned," "knowing heat, even if it doesn't make them run." "I never talk up the fame of any rooster, good as it may be: on a good day, any rooster is good. And when it isn't good, then forget it, not even with beef. Beef gives roosters great strength. The only liquid I give them is milk, and they eat corn, fine ground. The best way to take care of a rooster is to get it crowing and put it somewhere where it can scrabble around: there's not a rooster that will end up lame like that." Manuelico goes off to move a picket to the next spot, and the rooster turns on him, its neck feathers puffing out, and challenges him to a fight. From the house, they bring us coffee flavored with anise and nutmeg.

February 19

Everyone in the district talks about Ceferina Chaves: her house is the gracious one, with a commodious sugar mill and garden and a guesthouse in back where she invites respectable travelers to sit in her fine chairs and serves them sweet wine from her daughter's hand. She buys what the district produces at a good price, sells it at a profit, and sends her daughters away to fine schools so they can later come back and live as she does in the well-being of the country, in the house that, with its luxuries and hospitality, presides over the whole pale-skinned region: Ceferina has fame and power throughout the area. We stop at a fence and she comes up from her distant field among the men who pick tobacco for her. She sets her elbows on the fence, holding some leaves in her elegant, dry hand, and speaks with ease and intellect as if the open countryside were a salon and she its natural mistress. Her husband doesn't often show himself, or is busy with tasks of his own: Ceferina, who puts on gloves and jewels when she rides into town, is the one who, as her own mistress, and by sheer energy of will, began planting the fallow land, putting in beds of sweet potatoes, getting the tobacco to grow, fattening up a pig. She'll marry her daughter to an educated man, but she won't forsake her productive labor or the pride she takes in it. The rocking chair next to the mortar. Porcelain in the parlor, and out to the fields every morning. "Something must be given to the poor, so let the poor have all the divi-divi[11] on my land." Her conversation has a natural authority; it flows and sparkles. Her gentle daughter, wearing a thimble, brings us cool wine: she has a frank smile and speaks loftily of hopes and injustices: she slips me the portrait of her mother I ask her for, as her mother is saying, with a rock of her chair: "We must see whether we are rearing good men."

February 18

And we converse as we go along, about honey of lemon, which is lemon juice, boiled down, and cures lingering ulcers: about the Moorish way, unknown in Cuba, of stanching a wound with fistfuls of earth; about the *guacaica*, which is a good-tasting bird that lives on worms and yields a broth that stimulates the appetite; about honey, "perfect for coffee, better than sugar." "If you want food enough for a day, squeeze a honeycomb that has larvae in it, so that all the milk comes out of the honeycomb along with the larvae, mixed in with the honey. It's a day's living, and a cure for excesses." "I once saw Carlos Manuel—Carlos Manuel de Céspedes[12]—do a thing that showed how much of a man he was: it's easy to pick up a live wasps' nest because the wasps have a good sense of smell, so as long as you rub your hand on your sweaty armpit first the wasps quiet down from the smell it gives off and let the nest be moved without coming out to sting you. I wanted to pass myself off as a sorcerer in Carlos Manuel's room and offered to take care of the wasps' nest, but he cut me off: 'Let's see how it's done, friend.' But the wasps didn't seem to find the medicine strong enough, and I saw two of them stab right into his hand, and with the two wasps there, he took the nest to the door without saying a word about the pain, and without anyone but me knowing about the stings on his hand."

February 18

We go to dinner at Don Jesús's house, the house where I saw the basket-hilted sword dating back to the time of Columbus, and the old pickax that was found in the mines, the house with the buxom young ladies whom I scolded because they don't plant flowers even though they have sunny ground, women's hands, and long hours of leisure. That day, a traveler accused them of being indelicate, of having souls that were not like flowers. And now, what do we see? They knew we were coming back, and Joaquina, brimming over with her eighteen years, comes to the doorway holding her lighted *túbano* between two fingers, her head covered in flowers: a carnation falls across her forehead, a rose peeps out from behind her ear: above her bangs she has a chignon of jasmine, and at the back of her neck a bunch of geraniums and purple guayacán flowers. Her sister stands beside her with a plume of yellow roses in her hair, which is done up like a flowerpot, and two green eyes beneath the fine arch of her brows. We get off our horses, and can see the table in a corner of the parlor, drowning in flowers, flowers in vases and cups, in bottles and basins; and up above, as if wreathing a saint, in two olive jars, two long, thick, green sansevieria leaves, slashed open here and there, and in every slash a geranium.

March 2

We leave Dajabón, sad Dajabón, the last Dominican town guarding the border in the north. There I have my man Montesinos, the volcanic Canary Islander, still a Guanche[13] in his skeletal structure and rebelliousness; ever since he was imprisoned, at the same time I was, he will accept neither warmth nor favor from any Spanish hand. There lives "Toño" Calderón, widely renowned for his good looks, who, when I first came through during his tenure as Comandante de Armas, had exchanged no more than a few words with me before he made me get off the rented nag I was riding to Montecristi and gave me his roan, the horse he had never allowed anyone else to ride, "the horse that man loves more than his wife." Toño, with his mysterious, threatening gray eyes, his anxious, yearning smile, his light step and straight, disheveled hair. There, too, is where Salcedo, a Cuban, practices, as if swimming to nowhere; a doctor without a diploma—a *mediquín*, as we say in Cuba—bewildered in his moral solitude, beaten down in his futile tenacity, his gentle soul overwhelmed in these hinterlands of the charlatan and the fist. Life, like a child, behaves badly toward those who fear it, and respects and obeys those who stand up to it. Hearing me say that the pants I've come in are torn, Salcedo, without complaint or flattery, brings me his best pair, made of fine blue twill, honorably patched: with his own hand he slowly mixes a dose of antipyrine for me: and when he embraces me, he clings to my heart. There, Pancho and Adolfo between them—Adolfo, Montesinos's loyal son, who accompanies his father in his humble labor—bundle my cloak and trousers into an improvised saddlebag, and add the rum the group will drink, some hard bread, a good, salubrious, bracing Piedmont wine, and two coconuts. Then to horse, in Montesinos's saddle, on a colt he rented from a "compadre" of "General Corona." "The General is here now, he's a friend already," "judging by the look he gave us": he has a broad-brimmed panama, a three-piece linen suit, a bone-handled umbrella, and is a fine, swarthy fellow with the mustache and sideburns of a *guajiro*. To horse, and on to the nearest Haitian town, which is visible from Dajabón: Ouanaminthe.

Across the Massacre River the land blooms. Behind are tumble-down houses, a few scattered gardens, dry ground, and the tight cluster of trees around the Bel Air fort, from where, at the moment of Dominican independence, the famous shot was fired that plugged the mouth of the Haitian cannon.[14] Here, on the Negro side, suddenly there are mango, guanabana, custard apple, palm, and banana trees everywhere, and people coming and going. In a patch of shade at the edge of the ford, Haitians and Dominicans are talking among their flocks of animals; people from Ouanaminthe arrive, coming down the hill on good horses, along with a man from farther away and a horse trader from Cap-Haïtien. Going up the hill, her rounded torso wrapped in a cloth, is a girl of about fifteen: her wrapper covers her breasts beneath her arms, and goes no lower than the thigh: from her delicate, nappy head, two knots of hair stick out at the back of the neck: she walks along singing. *"Bonjour, conmère. Bonjour, compère."* A barefoot old woman in a black robe cinched very tight around her waist and a wide-brimmed sun hat goes along behind her burro. A strapping girl with a predatory walk has on a purple gown with a train, her breasts high and compact, a black shawl around her shoulders, and on her head a white lace kerchief. The houses are no longer built of palm leaves and yagua, leprous and dusty; instead, the sugar-mill compound is clean and full of fruit trees, with a good fence, and the houses are plastered with unpainted mud, its natural dark color a pleasure to the eyes, with roofs of dried, blackish straw and doors and windows of planed wood, with solid latches—or else they're painted yellow, with a wide border of white around windows and doors. Soldiers go by on their afternoon drill, squat or lanky, neat or torn, blue or faded, in sandals or boots, their kepis at their noses, their bayonets at the ready; they march and laugh: a swamp scatters them and they get back into formation uproariously. The top brass looks on from a balcony. The Dominican consul notes his authorization on the passport, "to continue on, after presenting yourself to the local authorities," and gives me a cup of grenache wine. Corona arrives, prancing, and after a mutual tip of hat and consular cap we leave in the gold of late afternoon.

March 2

Ouana Minthe, the animated border town, is full of cheer because it's a Saturday afternoon. I saw it once before when I first set foot in Santo Domingo: rushed along in the blackness of a storm by the Haitian guide who, as we went, told me about his new cabin and how he would soon be entering into matrimony with his beloved, and that he was going to put white curtains on the two parlor windows: and I offered him the ribbons. Seeing nothing in all the rain and the evening darkness, we rode into Ouanaminthe, our horses streaming with water, me out in the rain, and my Haitian fellow beneath Dellundé's[15] parasol. We went to the guardhouse, looking for the Comandante de Armas so he could countersign our passports. And that was all I saw of Ouanaminthe then, the guardhouse, smoky and mud-smeared, lit by torches stuck into cracks in the wall, an old revolver leaning across the door, and grimy, barefoot men who came and went, taking puffs of the sentinel's only tobacco, and the broken chair they gave me as a special favor, with listeners crowded around it. They spoke the rural Creole, which is not the same as the city's, but easier and more French, though crude, and with Indian and African nouns. I spoke to them of war, and of our war, and their mistrust slowly diminished, and their affection was fired. Finally, one of them exclaimed this very sad phrase: "*Ah! gardez-ça: blanc, soldat aussi.*"[16]—I saw the guardhouse, and then the Comandante, at the home of some women friends: a dim lamp on a pine table, all of them seated in rickety chairs, kerchiefs on their heads, and he, skinny and polite. That was how I passed through then.

This time the plaza is full of military exercises, and the lieutenants, on white or dun horses, wearing epaulets on their coats and tricornered hats with a feather in the crown, move to and fro at the head of the lines. Horses that are to be sold go prancing past. Viennese chairs can be seen in the big houses. The church is almost pompous, in the middle of a such a backwater, with its sturdy brickwork and square towers. There are tall houses with narrow, cheerful hanging balconies. It is the first Haitian settlement we come to, and there is life and faith here now. We leave the town, saluting the Dominican consul in Fort Liberté, an exuberant mulatto in a blue suit and panama hat who handles his white horse well, sitting on his varnished saddle. Droves of mules go by, and smugglers. When tariffs are unjust, or border justice is vengeful, smuggling is the people's right of insurrection. The smuggler is the brave man who takes risks, the cunning man who deceives the powerful, and the rebel in whom others see and admire themselves. Smuggling comes to be loved and defended, as the true justice. A Haitian goes past on his way to Dajabón to sell his coffee; a Dominican comes up the road toward him, on his way to Haiti to sell his chewing tobacco, his famous *andullo:* "*Saludo.*" "*Saludo.*"

March 2

Corona, "General Corona," rides beside me, talking. "Friendship among men," according to Corona, "is a very great thing." And with his "dimpués" for *después,* and his "inorancia" for *ignorancia,* he goes along depicting in luxuriant, flowery paragraphs the consolation and strength it is for the heart "crushed down from all the wickedness and double-dealing as there is in this world," to know that "in a field over yonder is a brother you can give your life for." "I can tell you that, at my age now, I've fought more than eighty battles." He wants "decency in mankind," and does not want a man who thinks a certain way to have to give it up for money or surrender out of fear "to anyone who wants to keep him from thinking." "I don't want to be, not even Comandante de Aimas, or any of what they want me to be; the governor offers it to me because he sees me upright, in order to bring me dishonor, or give me to fear his revenge, so I did not accept." "But I go on living with my honor and my canefields." And he tells me about the country's political parties: and of how he set out with two friends to make the party that killed his father pay for his death: and how with only a few men, because the others failed him, he defended the fortress of Santiago, "the redoubt of San Luis," when Tilo Patiño, "who's now working for the government," took up arms with him against Lilí.[17] "I don't revolt for this man or the other one, but out of great rage, and because it bothers me to see low-down men obeying or serving tyranny." "When I see injustice, my two hands get to dancing and I go for my rifle, and I want no more knives or forks. Because I don't know much about high politics, but to me, in my own way of feeling it, I think I know that politics is a kind of duty of dignity." "Because for me, *ó todo, ó náda,* everything or nothing." "Thirteen children I have, friend, but not from the same woman, because when I look around and see I'm going to have to be in a place for longer than a month or two, right away

I go in search of my greater comfort"—and then, when it's time to say good-bye, "she sees there's no other way, and I leave her with her cabin and some coins: because for nothing in the world will I be unfaithful to my legitimate wife." He always goes back to her, she kept his hacienda for him when he was in exile, paid his debts, helps him in all his labors, and "she has my dignity in her hands, and if I have to go out whoring to get work, I know I leave my little ones well taken care of, and that that woman doesn't hold it against me if I act like a man." —Suddenly, with night already upon us, a runaway mule from Corona's drove goes by, dragging its harness, which breaks between two tree trunks. He takes off with his two men to look for the mule in the forest, and will spend the whole night at it. I'll find myself a Haitian guide in that cabin up there where a light is showing. I must reach Fort Liberté tonight. Corona comes back, pained for me.—"You won't find the man you're looking for." He speaks to them, and they don't come. But I found him.

March 2

My poor Haitian Negro goes ahead of me. He's a man in his fifties, long-legged, with a mustache and goatee, a battered hat, the shreds of his shirtsleeves hanging around his elbows, and a flintlock musket with a long bayonet at his back. He goes down the path in long strides, and I, in Creole and French, pay him his two *gourdes,* which are the Haitian pesos, and offer not to make him pass through the town gate, which is what he fears, because the night watch are under orders to take anyone who comes into town after nightfall prisoner. *"Mosié blanc pringarde: li metté mosié prison."*[18] He warns me of each and every branch. At every bump or puddle he turns his head back. He holds a branch aside for me so I won't run into it. The night is overcast with patches of moonlight, and my colt is jumpy and skittish. As we leave a clearing, I show the man my Colt revolver, gleaming in the moonlight, and right away, as if he were sucking in his voice, he says: *"Bon, papá!"*

March 2

It's already after ten when I enter Fort Liberté, alone. From far off I could hear the evening's military parade, the barking of dogs, the hubbub. From the locked house of a woman named Feliciana, who speaks to me through the door and has no room to let, I go looking for the home of Nephtalí, who may have one. My horse recoils at the strip of light shining through the half-closed door and I rein him in.—"Is Nephtalí here?"—I hear a noise, and a young woman comes to the door. We speak, and she goes back inside. . . . ". . . *Bien sellé, bien bridé: pas commun . . .*"[19] That's what they have to say about me in there.

Yes, I can go in, and the girl, with her broken Spanish, comes to open the gate for me. In the darkness I unsaddle my horse and tie him to a Palma Christi. The henhouse is full of hammocks where people who came for Saturday's cockfights are sleeping. And inside "for charity's sake," would there be somewhere for a respectful passerby to sleep and something for him to eat? A slender, pallid young fellow comes to talk to me, wearing a black shirt and pants, with a chin beard, a thin mustache, and boils, speaking a pretentious, blue-blooded French. I rifle through some old books on the dusty table: textbooks that have lost their bindings, catalogs, a Bible, some Masonic reviews. From the next room comes laughter—and then the young woman, the daughter of the house, to arrange the Viennese chairs in facing rows, and bring out a mattress, which I throw on the floor, pushing the chairs aside. Who in there has given me his mattress? A black head peers out through the door, a big lad in a nightshirt who laughs. Dinner is a kind of peanut candy, and cassava, and the Piedmont wine that Montesinos packed for me, which I share with the daughter, who is confident and smiling.

The blue blood withdrew early. "*Le chemin est voiturable*": the road to Fort Liberté: "*Oh, monsieur: l'aristocratie est toujours bien reçue!*";[20] adding that nothing can be expected of Haiti, and that there is great superstition here, and that he hasn't been to Europe "yet," and that if "the ladies next door would like, I'll go and help them." I caress the good girl's delicate hand, and sleep stretched out beneath that kind roof. —At six, Nephtalí is standing at the head of my bed: may the guest be welcome: the guest has caused no trouble: the guest must forgive him for not having been there last night at his arrival. His whole being smiles, with his clean twill clothes and muttonchop whiskers; in the course of the conversation some well-known names come up: Montesinos, Montecristi, Jimenez. He doesn't ask who sent me. A fragrant breakfast is for me; the slight young fellow, enormously cravatted, sits down to enjoy it with me, and Nephtalí and his daughter serve me. Breakfast is good cheese and soft bread from the house's own ovens, and special small empanadas in my honor, made from the lightest flour, with a very large egg: the coffee is golden, with the best milk. "Madame Nephtalí" shows herself, tall and smartly dressed, carrying

her missal and wearing a hat and a long cloak, and Nephtalí ceremoni-
ously introduces her to me. In the yard, the rosebushes are sunning
themselves, and trays of dough are carried in and out of the bakery,
and the henhouse is so clean and well swept it's like a jewel, and Nephtalí tells the blue blood that there is and is not superstition in Haiti,
and anyone who wants to see it sees it, and anyone who doesn't never
does, and that he himself, a Haitian, has seen little superstition in
Haiti. And to what does Monsieur Lespinasse, the blue blood, friend
of a musician he has come to see, devote himself? Ah! He writes a few
articles for *L'Investigateur: "on est journaliste"; "l'aristocratie n'a pas
d'avenir dans ce pays-ci."*[21] For the road, Nephtalí packs me some
good cheese and the small empanadas and sponge cake. And when that
good man takes me over to a corner and I ask apprehensively what I
owe him, he grips both my arms and gives me a look of reproach:
"Comment, frère? On ne parle pas d'argent, avec un frère."[22] And he
held my stirrup for me, and followed me on foot with his friends, to
set me on the highway.

March 3 ·

Petit Trou was like a great basket of light that Sunday, as loose knots
of people, starched and radiant, watched the troops drilling.

The sunlight is a celebration; it seems clearer and calmer somehow,
washing everything with a gold that is almost orange, all the bright,
freshly pressed clothes, the people sitting in doorways, having a cold
drink, or an absinthe with anise, or sprawling under a guanabana tree,
within earshot of the gusts of laughter that greet a doddering old man's
attempts to woo an old woman, and young men dressed in white cotton twill who throw their arms around the waists of girls in purple
gowns. A mother comes up to my horse to show me her jolly little
mulatto baby, in a cotton chemise adorned with ribbons, a pink cap,
and yellow-and-white knitted shoes.

His eyes devour me and he starts to giggle while I cuddle and kiss
him. I turn back toward the blue general store so the colt can have a
few minutes' rest and I can spread out my empanada and cheese on a
table, along with the beer I don't drink. His cane raised high, an octo-
genarian in a fine striped suit and button-up boots appeared. The wife,
lovely and sad, gazes at me, half-hidden behind a door frame, a story
and a plea in her eyes as she plays distractedly with her daughter. The
owner, his back turned, spies on me with his round eyes from his arm-

chair, wearing half boots and a black jacket, with a good silver watch, his conversation edgy and tedious. Carrying books from the church, the ends of her kerchief tied under her neck, a woman friend enters, speaking good French. At a glance I take in the parlor, daubed green, with soft yellow stenciling and a pink stripe around the border. At the windows, the air is moving the curtains. Good-bye. The owner smiles, standing solicitously beside my stirrup.

March 3

I forded a stream, with a grove of sandbox trees on the other side, and through their high, airy fronds, ripping off leaves and breaking branches, a ripe fruit comes falling down and bursts open. Not far from there, I stop to mend the broken cords of my cloak strings, at the edge of the river, near a campesino, all buttoned up in his Sunday best, who is going along on his agile burro, his pipe at his bearded lips and the tip of his machete sticking out through a rip in his white cotton jacket. He jumps down, at my service. *"Ah, compère! ne vous dérangez pas. Pas ça, pas ça, l'ami. En chemin, garçon aide garçon. Tous sommes haïtiens ici."* And he bites, and separates, and fastens the cords: and we go on, conversing about his house and his wife and the three children with whom *"Dieu m'a favorisé,"* and of the well-being a man feels when he meets up with a friendly soul and the stranger suddenly seems like a part of himself, and stays in his soul, strong and deep, like a root. *"Ah oui!"* with the Haitian *oui,* low and drawn out: *"Quand vous parlez de chez un ami, vous parlez de chez Dieu."*[23]

March 3

Going through the marshlands, which were extensive, I thought I'd lost my way. The sun is scorching and the colt strains to make its way through the thick mud. The jungle casts long shadows on both sides. I see a house in a clearing, and knock. Slowly a grandmother peers out, then the girl with a child in her arms, and then a big lad, in pants that are barely there, a rag for a hat, and a blue shirt hanging loose. This is the right direction. The saucy mother is sixteen years old. In order to leave them some small thing in payment for their goodness, I ask for a little water, which the big lad brings me. And when I go to give him a few coins, *"Non: argent non: petit livre, oui."* A book is sticking out of my jacket pocket, Paul Bert's second scientific handbook.—Of mud and straw, atop a mountain of corn, is the *"habitation de Mamenette," chemin du Cap.*[24] Swampland and solitary jungle all around. On tiptoe, over the ramshackle fence, a pair of luminous eyes: *Auguste Etienne.*

March 2

At a crossroads, next to where the road opens out with the river down below, a wooden Christ stands beneath a zinc canopy, a French Christ, rosy and delicate on his green cross, with a fence made of wire. Across the way, within the jagged ruins of a spacious brick house, is a mud hut; a sentinel in a blue cap is standing at the door and presents arms to me. And the officer salutes. I go through an arbor into an inn to sprinkle my water with some anise-flavored rum, but no one has change for a peso. Shall I leave the whole peso, then, since I've partaken of something here? *"Pas ça, pas ça, mosié."* They don't want my peso. I shake hands all around. *"Bon blanc! Bon blanc!"* At eight, Nephtalí calls me his brother, in Fort Liberté: at five, circling the rim of the conch-shaped bay, I come across the salty sand into Cap-Haïtien. I set my feet back on the ground at the generous doorway of Ulpiano Dellundé.[25]

March 2

The alert spirit sleeps badly. When something remains to be done, sleep is a fault, a desertion. I leaf through some old books: *Origines des Découvertes attribuées aux Modernes,* by Dutens, London, 1776, when the French were irritated with Franklin's fame, and Dutens says that "a trustworthy person has assured him that a Latin medal was recently found with the inscription *Jupiter Elicius,* or Electric, representing Jupiter on high, thunderbolt in hand, with a man below flying a kite, by which means a cloud can be electrified and fire extracted from it"—to which I could add what I was told in Belize by the wife of Le Plongeon,[26] the man who wanted to remove the Mayan ruins from Yucatán, where a painted rock, part of a frieze, shows a seated man with a thunderbolt coming out of his Indian mouth and aimed into the mouth of another man in front of him. Another of the books is a Goethe in French. In Goethe, and much earlier, in the Greek Anthology and the poetry of Oceania—the pantuns,[27] for example—are all the ritornellos, aphorisms, and eccentricities that novelty-seekers and people whose culture is pinned on take to be so contemporary: a prophecy and condemnation of all of today's hairsplitting and hollow elegance can be found in Goethe's lines on "A Chinaman in Rome."

March 3

I find, in a pile of books forgotten under a console table, one that I was not acquainted with: *Les Mères Chrétiennes des Contemporains Illustres* [The Christian Mothers of Illustrious Contemporaries]. I leaf through and discover its spirit: it is a book written by the author of *L'Académie Française au XIXme Siècle* [The French Academy in the Nineteenth Century], in order to make artful use of biography to promote practical devoutness, which it views as the supreme and creative virtue, in the home: confession, the "good priest," the "holy abbot," and prayer. And the book is lavish, with large pages, gilt edges, and a red-and-gold cover.

The index, even more than the book, belongs to the hollow society that is coming to an end: "The highest social spheres," "The world of letters." "The clergy." "The liberal professions."—Profession: the open, easy channel, the great temptation, the satisfaction of needs without the original effort that releases and develops a man, and makes him grow, through respect for those who suffer and produce as he does, in the only lasting equality, for the professions are a form of arrogance and egotism that ensure nations of peace, which is only truly attainable when the sum of inequalities reaches the minimum limit at which human nature itself keeps them.

The man who enjoys a well-being that is not of his own creation is useless and generally pernicious, a supporter of injustice or a timid friend to reason who, in the undeserved enjoyment of a degree of comfort and pleasure that bears no relation to his individual effort and service, has lost the habit of creating and all respect for those who create. The professions, as they are currently understood, are odious and harmful, a residue of the weft of complicities by which, turned by self-interest away from its initial and just unifying power, authoritarian society was and is still maintained—an authoritarian society being, of course, one based on the concept, feigned or sincere, of human inequality, in which persons to whom all rights are denied are forced to carry out social duties to serve the power and pleasure of those who deny them those rights: merely the remains of the barbaric state. All this with regard to the index of *Les Mères Chrétiennes:* "The highest spheres of society." "The world of letters." "The clergy." "The liberal professions."

I open the book where it says "Madame Moore." Madame Moore, mother of Thomas Moore,[28] whose poem "Betsy" I admire: loyal and lighthearted, always faithful, and a true mother to her vain and giddy husband. The book presents Moore's mother as very saintly, and her saintliness is borne out by her son's life. But it does not give another fact: that the Christian son began his career with a highly spiced and felicitous translation of the odes of Anacreon.—It has much to say about Marguerite Bosco, the mother of a cardinal who is very reminiscent of the spoiled priest in *La Regenta* by Alas[29]—that ruddy priest whose astute mother made his bed and set his table for him. I know a man who is Prince Bosco's son: his father was the lover of the Queen of Naples, the last queen; the son had once been a captain in the Texas Rangers, and in Brooklyn he was a horsebreaker. Another mother is "Madame Rio," of A. del Rio, "the illustrious author of *L'Art Chrétien.*" Another, "Madame Pie," is the mother of the Bishop of Poitiers. "Madame Osmond" is another, mother of the count who wrote *Reliques et Impressions.* Another is the mother of Ozanam, the eloquent, active Catholic. And yet another one is the mother of Gerando, he whose metaphysics were carefully perused by Michelet,[30] when, wearing a dress-coat and shoes with buckles, he gave history lessons to princesses.

March 3

I go to lose some hair at Martínez's miserable barbershop on calle de la Playa: he is glowing clean, diminutive, and irreverent, in the barbershop which has wallpaper in some places and grime or old chromolithographs in others, and, high up on the ceiling, hanging from strips of cloth, six paper roses.—"And you, Martínez, would you be a married man?" "Man like me, traveling man, can't marry."—"Where'd you learn your Spanish?"—"In San Tómas: I was a *santomeño,* from San Tómas." "But you aren't anymore?"—"No, now I'm Haitian. I'm descended from a Dane, but that's worthless; I'm descended from an Englishman, but that's worthless; I'm descended from a Spaniard, even worse: Spain is the world's wickedest nation. For a man of color, nothing is worth anything."—"So you don't want to be a Spaniard?"—"I don't want to be Cuban, Puerto Rican, or Spaniard. A smart, white Spaniard, yes, because I'd get me the governorship of Puerto Rico with $500 a month: but a son of Puerto Rico, no. The worst in the world, Spaniard."—To the beggarwoman who comes to the door: "I have yet to earn the first copper penny."

March 4[31]

And I opened my eyes on the boat, to the song of the sea. The sea was singing. We left Cap-Haïtien at ten P.M., with looming storm clouds and a strong wind, and now in the wee hours of the morning the sea is singing. The skipper straightens up and listens, erect, with one hand on the planking and the other on his heart; the helmsman slackens his hold on the tiller: "Beautiful, that." "It's the most beautiful thing I've heard in this world." "Twice in my life, no more, have I heard such beauty." And then he laughs: the *voudous,* the Haitian sorcerers, will know what it is: today is the day of the *voudou* dance at the bottom of the sea, and now the men on land will know that there, down below, the sorcerers are working their enchantments.[32] The music, long, broad, and sweet, is like the sound of a tumultuous orchestra of platinum bells. Steady and strong, its vibrant echo pulses. The body feels as if it were clothed in music. The sea sang for an hour, more than an hour:—The boat gives an impatient lunge and goes down toward Monte-Cristi.

March 6

Ah, the eternal barber, with his straw hat pushed to the back of his neck, the perfumed curls on his forehead, and his slippers with their stars and roses! The barbershop has only two mirrors, with wooden frames, and a shelf of empty flasks, a grimy comb, and some old pomades. On the wall, in a display case, are panama hats with fine bands, books without bindings, and papers in an untidy heap. In the middle of the shop's main room, with its great damp stains, is the chair where the barber's boy powders anyone who presents himself to be shaved.—"Look, you, boy with the tickets: come over here."—"Buy a ticket from him: give him a peso."

March 6

I hear a sound out in the street flooded with Sunday sunlight, a sound of waves, and I think I know what it is. It is. It is the starched white petticoat of a black woman who passes by in triumph, her eyes on fire, in her clean gown of dark purple calico with her shawl around her shoulders.—The Haitian woman has the legs of a deer. The natural, supple figure of the Dominican woman endows even the most wretched ugliness with rhythm and power. The form of woman is conjugal and melodious.

March 29

Over our meal we spoke of animals: of black ravens that are capable of talking and drink milk; of how the rat saves itself from fleas, and licks its own tail after sticking it into butter; of the toad, which eats wasps; of the bat, which eats the firefly, but not its fire. A rascally raven saw that a slave woman milked the cows every morning and put the milk in bottles, and he, with his hard beak, sipped the milk at the top, and when he had emptied the neck of the bottle, dropped pebbles into it so the milk would rise. The rat goes into the water with a piece of cotton between his teeth where the fleas rush to keep from drowning; and when the rat sees that the cotton is black with fleas he lets go of it. The toad plunges its front leg into a honeycomb, and then, sitting very still, puts the sweet leg in the air so the greedy wasp will come: and the toad swallows it. The bat snaps up the firefly in the air, letting its luminous head fall to the ground.

March 29

We were coming from the beach, from clusters of campeachy trees and dense mangroves: we were coming through prickly pears and huisache. And a barefoot man came along singing from far away, in a big, rasping voice, first a ballad that wasn't quite audible, and then this one:

> Te quisiera retratar
> En una concha de nacle,
> Para cuando no te vea
> Alzar la concha, y mirarte.

I'd like to make your picture
In a seashell's mother-of-pearl
And whenever I don't see you,
I'd pick it up and look at you.

March 30

César Salas, who let his rich companions go off to Cuba, refusing to return there himself except "as a good Cuban must return," is a creating man, a sower of seeds, and diligent, with a hand that deftly wields the machete and the paintbrush, and an equal capacity for sacrifice, work, and art. He comes now from the caves of San Lorenzo, over in Samana, and he speaks of the caves.[33] The largest is a good example of all the caves there, with its walls and ceiling of distilled stone dangling toward the earth like fine lace, or squeezing out, drop by drop, "a water that is hardening into stone." It is very cool, and the floor is covered with fine white guano that is not displeasing to the mouth, and dissolves. In places, the passageway, which lacks elbow room, begets a vault, and in one of those—both in the same one—are two faces, part of designs painted on the wall a little above a man's height, which are like imperfect circles whose center is a great human face at the vertex of a triangle with decorated edges and two lesser faces at the sides, surrounded by hieroglyphic drawings of homunculi with hoes in their hands, or without them, and horses or mules, and hens.—This may be the conquest, and the barbaric mines, offered up to the country's religion on the altars of its caves of refuge.—There, César Salas has found innumerable seashells that the Indians must have lived off of, and some large flint axes with necks or shafts. There are mountains of seashells at the cave's entrances. The cave can be entered through four mouths. The sea comes in through one of them, foaming and sonorous. Another leads up through lianas to a green clearing.

April 1

At an anxious pace, stabbed by thorns, we crossed marshes and sand in the midnight darkness. Hitting out with our elbows, we break through the tangles of mesquite. The sand is bald in stretches, but covered with patches of the prickly trees. The bare sand sends a light like a shroud's into the starless sky, and all green is blackness. The waves of the sea can be heard exhaling on the beach, and there is a smell of salt. Suddenly we emerge from the last of the mesquite thickets onto the seashore, which is frothy and overcast—as if restless and trapped—with damp flurries of wind. Standing there, pants rolled to the knee, shirt flapping around his thighs and open at the chest, arms held out in a high cross, his aquiline head, with its mustache and goatee, topped with a yaray hat, is an impassive black Haitian, with the sea at the soles of his feet and the sky behind him. Man ascends to his full beauty in the silence of nature.

April 3[34]

Ingratitude is a bottomless pit—and generous attempts to make amends for it are like the dribble of water that only revives a fire. There is no greater insult to a man than the virtue he himself does not possess. The pretentious ignoramus is like the coward who shouts out in the night to hide his fear. Indulgence is the most certain mark of superiority. Authority exercised without cause or object only betrays a lack of true authority.

April 3

Black-winged flamingos with rosy breasts fly overhead like great crosses high in the sky. They go in lines, at equal spaces from each other; the lines move apart toward the rear. A short row of them serves as the rudder. The squadron advances, rippling.

April 3

In the middle of the sea, I remember these lines:

> Un rosal cria una rosa
> Y una maceta un clavel,
> Y un padre cria una hija
> Sin saber para quien es.

> A rosebush raises up a rose,
> A flowerpot a carnation,
> And a father raises up a daughter,
> Not knowing who she's for.

April 4

Stretched out on the deck of the schooner *Brothers*, I see, as the light opens out, a corner of Inagua, its bristling trees emerging tall and green from amid its ruins and salt marshes. Flamenco pink and blackish crimson are the colors of the clouds rising from the few houses into the pearly sky. I jump down to the beach, off to catch scoundrels, master them, and get their triumphal hats into their hands. I manage to do it. In the comings and goings, I have a look at the town: deserted, decapitated mansions, walls crumbling from abandonment and fire, white houses with green windows, small, thorny trees, and poisonous flowers. There are no buyers for the island's abundant salt; the train never moves; anyone in possession of a boat sells it; the sisal industry is in dire straits; the reading room has fifteen members, at a cost of one real per month; the most glittering of the merchants enjoys a tender friendship with one of the leading smugglers; the captain of the port—a paunchy young fellow—has a noble soul, so he is polite, and wears white linen; the salty sunlight is blinding. Against a broken wall sleeps a pile of lignum vitae, the "wood of life," which "burns like a torch" with its hard heart; two shaggy burros are pulling a wagon clumsily heaped with cracked, warping rosewood; next to a pillar is a sack of local potatoes; from a wretched store, an enfeebled old white woman comes out, in spectacles, a picture hat and apron, to offer us bread, fishhooks, eggs, chicken, thread; the Negress, her belly to her nose and coral earrings hanging down to her shoulders, leaning against the counter of her empty store, says that her "guesthouse is not here" where three scorched men are taking a moment's repose to let their bloody sweat dry, sitting on the boxes that serve as chairs. In order to sit down, they buy from the shopkeeper, with her marble teeth and eyes, all the bread and sweets in the house—three shillings' worth—and she covers the floor with her wide smiles. Hopkins comes by, a man in his forties with an English torso and copper-colored skin, selling "his great heart," his valiant chest, "which is worth two chests," his groveling half-boots, which he takes off his feet, a torn overcoat. He will go "anywhere, if I'm paid," because he is "a family man with two wives"; he is "a loyal soul"; he glues himself to the other sailors and slowly poisons their will so they won't accept the job that was not given to him; he resells a chicken that a policeman in a cork helmet, mutton-chop whiskers, and blue cashmere with red buttonholes carries to him by its legs. The man from Guadeloupe comes by, with his chocolate-colored torso and the curly gray hair of his seventy-four years; he goes bare-chested and barefoot and his hat is woven of leaves; he neither drank nor smoked nor loved anywhere but at home and he doesn't need glasses to read at night: he is a bricklayer and a contractor and a fisherman.—The boss of the smugglers comes by holding his stubby walking stick with its New York handle, a thick ring on his finger, an expensive panama hat on his well-respected head.—The blandishing skipper comes by, with his patriarchal speech and fox's deeds—a man who at the death of his son "didn't weep the pain, but sweated it"— and, stammering, gives back the money he robbed. But he is "a gentleman and knows gentlemen," and, hat in hand, he gives me a jug of gin.

April 5

Beyond the beach's cerulean sea, the cargo ship unloads its wood from Mobile, Alabama, onto the raft that floats beside it, from stem to stern, on the turquoise swell. The wood is lowered, and the workmen haul it and sing to it. The steamship pushes diagonally to move the raft toward the shore, and the towboats take it away, with the row of blacks above, hauling and singing.

April 5

David, from Turks and Caicos, attached himself to us the moment we pushed off from Montecristi. In half-words he said that he understood us, and without hope of any greater payment, or agreement upon it, or coddling from us, he grew larger and larger for us, after the others fled, and he alone was the schooner, with his pants in shreds, his worn-out feet, the greatcoat that hung around his flesh, his yaray with its brim to the sky. He would cook *locrio* of rice and salt pork, or *sancocho* of chicken and a few stewed vegetables, or white fish, good "muttonfish," with a sauce of butter and bitter orange juice: he brought and carried, by pure *gudilla*, the only boat—with an oar for a rudder; on the wretched deck, he spread out, as a pillow for us, his greatcoat, his overcoat, the garment that was his own pillow and mattress; lean and agile, he was already polishing up the pots at dawn. He never asked for anything and he gave himself entirely. His weathered head was supported by a slender, graceful neck; his eyes, large and sincere, were full of laughter, and his cheekbones opened out, jocular and strong . . . two curls of mustache grew at the corners of his thin, toothless mouth, and on his honest, flat nose the light played. When he said good-bye to us, his face and chest fell and, weeping, he threw himself headlong against the sail tied to the boom.—David, from Turks and Caicos.

April 6

It has good mahogany posts, the captain's bunk onboard the steamship,[35] the German cargo ship that is taking us to Cap-Haïtien. The bunk lies over drawers full of maps. On the shelf above the desk, amid gazetteers and navigators, is all of Goethe and a novel by Gaudy. Presiding over the bunk is a portrait of the captain's candid, bony wife. In a corner is the arsenal: a fowling piece, two daggers, a small pistol fit for a dogcatcher, and two pairs of handcuffs, "which I occasionally use on the sailors." And next to it is a framed piece of embroidery, "made from my wife's yarn," that says, in Gothic letters:

> In allen Stürmen,
> In allen Noth,
> Mög er dich berschirmen
> Der treue Gott.

> In every storm,
> In every tribulation,
> May you be sheltered
> By steadfast God.

April 7

A Cap-Haïtien Sunday reaches me through the shutters of my concealed room. The coffee was "clear, hot, and strong." The sunlight is soft and fresh. The neighboring marketplace chatters and squabbles. From my writing chair, my back to the door, I hear a petticoat going by, the shuffle of slippered feet, the name of the Haitian poet Tertulien Guilbaud, the great and polished author of *Patrie*—and the cry of a fruit vendor hawking *"Caïmite!"* Drums and trumpets sound in the distance. Ponies stumble on the stones that yesterday's rain dislodged from the street. I hear *"le bon Dieu"*—and the progress of a cane, pushing off from the sidewalk. At an intersection, an eloquent old man is preaching religion to the empty streetcorners. I hear him: "We must force out of this strong black nation those merchants of savage divinity who demand of the poor peasants, as the angel demanded of Abraham, the sacrifice of their children in exchange for God's favor. The government of this black nation of hardworking women and virgin men must not put to death the wretched woman who killed her daughter yesterday, as Abraham was about to kill Isaac, without doing away, 'like a bolt of lightning,' with the *papá-boco*, the false priest who enters their hearts by the prestige of medicine and the sacred power of the language of their fathers. Until civilization has learned Creole, and speaks in Creole, it will not be civilized." And the old man went on talking in proud French, punctuating his speech by hitting his cane against the rocks. Now they're listening to him: a drummer, two laughing boys, a young man in a pink tie and pearl-gray pants, with a marble-topped cane. Through the shutters I see the old man in his dark suit, fluting and unctuous. At his feet run silent, muddy waters. A desiccated mulatta of about fifty fords them with a jump, wearing fine half-boots, a short cloak, and a hat, and carrying a book of hours and a parasol: her green eyes probe her surroundings. From the book on my writing desk, to which I return, two cards fall to the floor, tied together with a piece of white string: the smaller one, hers, says "*M'elle, Elise Etíenne*, Cap-Haïtien"; and his, the big one, says "*Mr. Edmond Férère:*—Frenchman." Today is Palm Sunday.

April 8

From the Indian's power of *resistance* can be gauged his potential power of *originality* and therefore of *initiation* as soon as he is treated with affection and inspired with a valid faith, and his nature is emancipated and unfrozen. —I'm reading about Indians.

April 8

I've just been reading about irresolute Moctezuma, and the uselessness of timidity and intrigue. I read with great love about Cacama, and Cuitlahuac, who blocked the mouths of Cortés's cannons with heroic corpses.[36] I read with anger about the infamous and unhappy Tecuichpo, who defended the Aztec eagle with Cuauhtémoc in the royal canoe and with feathers upon her breast threw herself against the Spaniards' matchlock guns, but then—she who had slept beneath that martyr's Indian kisses, lay down, a Spaniard's woman, to sleep in the bed of Alonso de Grado, and Pedro Callejo, and Juan Cano.[37] Searing lines of poetry leap from my pen. The things I hold in are spilling out. Everything in me is speaking, all that I don't want to say—about the patria or about womankind. For the patria, more than mere words! And for woman, either praise, or silence. The baseness of our woman hurts, and humiliates, and pierces, more than that of our man.[38]—Tom enters my concealed room, Tom the loyal Negro from San Thomas, who with a century behind him serves and loves the house of Dellundé. I give him a folded note that asks the corner bookshop, the Haitian bookshop, for some books to choose among, and a two-peso bill along with it, as a hostage, while I choose.—And the bookseller, the black gentleman of Haiti, sends me the books—and the two pesos.

PART II

From Cap-Haïtien to Dos Ríos,
April 9–May 17, 1895

April 9[39]

Lola, *jolongo,* sobbing on the balcony. We're off.

April 10–11[40]

We leave Cabo. Greet the dawn at Inagua. Hoist the boat aboard. Leave at 11. Skirt past Maisí and see the beacon. I'm on the bridge. At 7:30, darkness. Activity onboard. Captain deeply moved. The boat is lowered. Hard rain as we push off. Wrong direction. Opinions on boat varied and turbulent. More squalls. Lose rudder. We set course. I take the forward oar. Salas rows next. Paquito Borrero and the General help out in the stern. We strap on our revolvers. Making for the cove. A red moon peers from under a cloud. We put in at a rocky beach, La Playita (at the foot of Cajobabo). I'm the last one in the boat, emptying it. Jump ashore. Great joy. We turn the boat over, and the water jug. Drink Málaga. Up through rocks, thorns, and marshland. Hear noise and get ready, near a fence. Bypassing a farm, we come to a house. We sleep close together, on the ground.

April 12

At 3 we make up our minds to call Blas, Gonzalo, and the "Niña."[41]
José Gabriel, smart fellow, goes to call Silvestre. Silvestre ready. We set
out over hills, loaded down, looking for Mesón and the Tacre
(Záguere) River. We wait in the bright forest from 9 to 2. I convince
Silvestre to take us to Imía. We follow the course of the Tacre. The
General decides to write Fernando Leyva, and Silvestre goes. We set-
tle into a cave, an old campsite, under a crag to the right of the river.
We sleep: dry leaves: Marcos knocks down: S. brings me leaves.

April 13

Abraham Leyva arrives, with Silvestre loaded down with pork, sugar-
cane, sweet potatoes, and chicken sent by the Niña. Fernando has
gone for the guide. Abraham, rosary at his neck. Alarm, and we get
ready, when Abraham comes striding up. Silvestre was following with
his load, at 11. That morning we'd moved to the edge of the river—
swollen during the night, with a clatter of stones that sounded like
gunfire. Guide will come. Lunch. Silvestre leaves. José comes at one
with his mare. We'll go on with him. Whistles and whinnying: we
jump: take aim: without Abraham. And Blas. From a conversation
with Blas, Ruenes[42] learned we'd arrived, and is sending to see, join up
with us. We decide to meet up with Ruenes at Sao del Nejesial. We'll
leave in the morning. I gather dry leaves for my bed. We roast sweet
potatoes.

April 14

A *mambí* day.[43] We leave at five. Up to our waists, we cross the river,
then cross back again: high on the bank are clams. Then, in new shoes,
with heavy loads, we climb the very steep hillside, through the delicate
leaves of the yaya tree, the Cuban majagua, and the copey with its star-
shaped cones. We see our first jutía, curled in a milkwood. Marcos
takes off his shoes and goes up. Cuts its throat with the first swipe of
his machete: "She's stunned." "Her throat's cut." We eat bitter oranges
José gathers, twisting them off with a pole: "Such sweetness!" Uphill
again. *Subir lomas hermana hombres.* Climbing hills together makes
men brothers. Over the hills we reach Sao del Nejesial: a pretty spot, a

clearing in the forest, with old palm, mango, and orange trees. José leaves. Marcos comes, his handkerchief full of coconuts. I'm given a rose apple. Guerra and P. stand guard. I rest in the camp. César sews my shoulder belt. The first step was to gather royal palms and lay them on the ground. With a machete, Gómez cuts and brings fronds, for him and for me. Guerra makes his hut; four forked stakes: hanging branches: royal palms on top. All of them: some are grating coconut; Marcos, helped by the General, skins the jutia. They bathe it in bitter orange and salt it. The pig gets the orange rinds and the jutia's skin. Now the jutia is in the improvised frying pan over a wood fire. Suddenly, men: "Ah, brothers!" I leap toward the guard. It's Ruenes's guerrillas, Félix Ruenes, Galano, Rubio, all 10 of them. Resplendent eyes. Embraces. Each has a rifle, machete, revolver. They came straight over the hills. The sick men felt better. We load up. The jutia is wrapped in palm fronds. They argue with us over who'll carry it. With my rifle and my 100 bullets I go on down the hill to Tibisial. A patrol. Another. Now we're at Tavera's ranch, where the guerrillas are encamped. They're waiting for us all in a row. Their clothes váry, some are in undershirts, others in shirts and pants, others in loose jackets and rough trousers; peaked yaray palm hats; blacks, mulattoes, two Spaniards—Galano, white. Ruenes introduces us. The General speaks, standing very erect. I speak. March-past, joy, cooking, groups.—At the new outpost: we speak again. Night falls, wax candles, Lima cooks the jutia and roasts plantains, argument over guard duty, the General hangs my hammock under the entrance to Tavera's palm frond hut. Ah! and before we fall asleep, José comes, a candle in his hand, carrying two yagua boxes, one of fresh meat, one of honey. Greedily, we set to work on the honey. Good honey, in combs. And all day long, what light, what air, how full the chest is, how light the anguished body! I look out from the hut and see, at the top of the peak that looms behind, a dove and a star. The place is called Vega de la . . .

April 15

We awaken amid orders. One detachment will be sent to las Veguitas, to buy at the Spanish store. Another, to the supplies left along the way. Another, to find a guide. The detachment returns with salt, hemp sandals, a cone of sweets, three bottles of liquor, chocolate, rum, and honey. José comes with hogs. Lunch—stewed pork with plantains and malanga. In the morning, *frangollo*, the sweet made of plantains and cheese, and water with cinnamon and anise, hot. Chinito Colombié arrives in Veguitas, a hunter, bad eyes: he tugs his yellow dog along behind him. In late afternoon, with the men lined up, the General goes off to a ravine with Paquito, Guerra, and Ruenes. Will you let the three of us go alone? I resign myself, peeved. Is there some danger? Ángel Guerra comes up, calling me and Captain Cardoso. Gómez, splendid and tender, at the foot of the mountain, on a path shaded by banana trees, with the gully below, tells me that apart from recognizing me as the Delegate, the Army of Liberation, through him, its Commander, elected in a council of commanders, names me Major General. I embrace him. They all embrace me. At night: pork with coconut oil, and it is good.

April 16

Each one with his offering: sweet potatoes, sausages, rose-petal liqueur, plantain broth. At noon, uphill march, river to the thigh, beautiful dappled forest of rose apples, oranges, and caimitos. Through gorges, thickets, and mango groves without fruit we come to a place of palm trees in the depths of a basin of joyous mountains. There we encamp. The woman, a copper-colored Indian with burning eyes, surrounded by seven children, wearing a ragged black gown, her kerchief tied up by her braids for a headdress, is hulling coffee. People hang up their hammocks, run to the cane field, get a fire together, bring cane to the sugar mill to make cane juice for the coffee. She puts the cane in, barefoot. Earlier, at the first stop, in the house with the mother and the big, scared daughter, the General gave me honey to drink, to show me that drinking it staves off thirst. Rum is being made from rose apples. All the correspondence for New York is written, and all the correspondence for Baracoa.

April 17

Morning in the camp. Yesterday a cow was slaughtered and as the sun comes up, groups are already standing around the cauldrons. Domitila, agile and good, in her Egyptian kerchief, springs up the mountain and brings back the kerchief full of tomatoes, cilantro, and oregano. Someone gives me a piece of malanga. Someone else, a cup of hot cane juice and leaves. A bundle of cane is milled. At the back of the house is the slope facing the river, with its houses and banana trees, cotton and

wild tobacco; below, along the river, a cluster of palms; in the clearings, orange trees; and all around are mountains, rounded and peaceable; and the blue sky above, with its white clouds, and a palm tree,
half in cloud—half in the blue.—Impatience makes me sad. We'll leave
tomorrow. I tuck the *Life of Cicero* into the same pocket where I'm
carrying 50 bullets. I write letters. The General makes a sweet of coconut shavings with honey. Tomorrow's departure is arranged. We
buy honey from a rancher with a short beard and alarm in his eyes. At
first it's four reales a gallon, but then, after the sermon, he gives away
two gallons. "Jaragüita" comes, Juan Telesforo Rodríguez, who doesn't
want to go by Rodríguez anymore because he used that name as a
guide for the Spaniards, and now he's leaving with us. He has a wife
now. When he goes, he slips away. The villainous El Pájaro plays with
the machete; his foot is tremendous; his eye shines like marble where
the sun hits the ebony black spot. Tomorrow we leave the home of
José Pineda: Goya, his wife. (Toward Jojó Arriba.)

April 18

At nine-thirty we leave. Farewell, the men lined up. G. reads the pro-
motions. The sergeant, "Puerto Rico," says: "I die where General Martí
dies." A rousing good-bye to all, Ruenes and Galano, Captain Cardoso, Rubio, Dannery, José Martínez, Ricardo Rodríguez. Over high
hills we pass the Jobo [Jojó] River six times. We go up the steep hill of
Pavano, with El Pomalito up above and a glimpse of Chinese orange
trees on the summit. We mount along the crest, light air striped with
manaca palms floating on all sides. High above, dense, and hanging
from plant to plant like a drapery was a delicate vine with small, lance-
olate leaves. On the hills, cimarron coffee. A grove of rose apples.
Around us, the river valley, and beyond, the blue mountains crested
with clouds. On the road to Los Calderos—Angel Castro's village—
we decide to sleep on the hillside. With our machetes we make a clearing. We string up our hammocks from trunk to trunk: Guerra and
Paquito on the ground. The night is too beautiful for sleep. A cricket
chirps; a lizard says "quee-quee-quee-a" and is answered by its chorus; even in the darkness I can see that the mountain is covered with
copeys and *paguás*—short, spiny palms—with lightning bugs hover-
ing around them. Through the shrill noises I hear the music of the forest, soft and complex, as if made by the most delicate violins; the music
undulates, entwines, and unravels, opens its wings and alights, flutters,

and ascends, always subtle and faint, a myriad of fluid sounds. What wings are brushing past the leaves? What diminutive violin, and waves of violins, are extracting sound and soul from the leaves? What dance of the souls of leaves is this? We forgot about our meal, so we ate sausage and chocolate and a slice of roasted malanga.—Our clothes dried out by the fire.

April 19

Two in the morning. Ramón Rodríguez, the guide, arrives with Ángel; they bring torches, and coffee. At five we set out over rugged slopes. To Los Calderos, high up. The ranch is new, and a *mambisa*'s voice comes from inside: "Come in without pain, you need feel no pain here." Then coffee is sweetened with her own honey: she, serious, in her loose sandals, recounts her history of the great war, one hand on her waist and the other waving in the air: her husband died, he was skinning his hogs for the rebels one night when they came and took him away; and she wandered the mountainside dragging her three children behind her, "until this good Christian took me in, and even if I serve him on my knees I'll never repay him." She comes and goes lightly; her face sparkles; each time she brings something else, more coffee, Castilian coriander—"so that when you get a bellyache along those trails you can chew one of the seeds and take some water on top of it"—lemons. She is Caridad Pérez y Piñó.—Her daughter Modesta, sixteen years old, puts on a new tunic and shoes in our honor, and sits with us, calmly conversing, on the palm benches in the little parlor. Ramón brings her a *flor de muerto,* a marigold, from near the garden wall, and she puts it in her hair. She sews for us. The General tells the story of "Caridad Estrada in Camagüey, hacked with a machete."[44] Her husband killed the Chinamen who betrayed their ranch, and another; Caridad was wounded in the shoulder; the husband fell dead; the guerrillas fled. Caridad picked up her child in her arms and went after them, her blood gushing out: "if she'd had a rifle!" She comes back, calls her people, they bury the husband, and she sends for Boza: "Look what they've done to me!" The troop leaps up: "We want to go find this captain!" The camp couldn't sit down. Caridad displayed her wound. And she went on living, preaching, and instilling the whole camp with her enthusiasm.—Pedro Gómez, a nervous neighbor, comes with coffee and a hen, as an offering.—We're winning souls.— Valentín, the Spaniard who's been assigned to be Gómez's assistant, is busy in the kitchen. Ruenes's six men make their *sancocho* in the open air. Isidro arrives, a hefty lad with azure eyes, all dressed up, in clownish leather shoes: he was the one who showed up at Pineda's place with his finger just severed. He can't go to war: "he has to look after three first cousins." At two-thirty, after the downpour, we're off over hills and the Guayabo River to the mango grove a league from Imía. Felipe Domínguez is there; Imía's mayor, Juan Rodríguez, takes us on a rough nighttime march, skirting the locals, to near the top of the Yaya, a march by candlelight at 3 in the morning of the 19th.

April 20

Teodoro Delgado leads us from there to El Palenque: a rocky mountain, palo amargo and bitter orange trees: the surrounding countryside is almost grandiose; as we go we're encircled with mountains, jagged, bosomy, peaked: folds of mountain all around, and to the south, the sea. Up high, we stop beneath some palm trees. People arrive loaded with cane. The locals: Estévez, Fromita. Antonio Pérez, of noble bearing, leaves for San Antonio. From a house they send us coffee, then chicken with rice. Jaragüita deserts. Did they threaten him? Will he go looking for the [Spanish] troops? A hunter brings word from Imía that they've set off after us along the Jobo. We'll wait here, as planned, for tomorrow's guide. Jaragua: cone-shaped head; just a moment ago he was telling me he wanted to stay with us to the end. He went to do sentry duty and slipped away. Barefoot forest scoundrel, Spanish guide; his face full of anguish, his speech lisping and shrill, sparse mustache, dry lips, loose, wrinkled skin, glassy eyes, cone-shaped head. He hunts mockingbirds and young pigeons, with birdlime made from the sap of the *lechugo*. Now he has animals and a wife. He went down through the forest. They don't find him; the locals fear him. In a group, they're talking about remedies for cloudy eyesight: salt water, the milky juice of the spurge, "which once gave a rooster its sight back," the spiny leaf of the *rosetilla*, thoroughly crushed, "a drop of blood from the first one that saw the cloud." Then they talk about remedies for ulcers: the yellow pebbles of the Jojo River, ground to a fine powder, the white, furred dung of a dog, honey of lemon:—sifted dung and mallow. We sleep on the mountain under yagua palms. Jaragua, big stick.

April 21

At six we set out with Antonio, heading for San Antonio. Along the way we stop to watch a palm tree being cut down, hacked by a machete at the base, to get at a beehive, which is brought to us, dry, the cells full of white offspring. Gómez sends for honey, squeezes the larvae into it, and it makes a delicious milk. Soon after, Luis González, an old man, black and beautiful, comes down the path, with his brothers, his son Magdaleno, and his nephew Eufemio. He had already sent word to Perico Pérez, and we'll wait with him, near San Antonio, for the troops. Luis picks me up in his embrace. But what sad news! Can it be true that Flor, daring Flor, has died? That Maceo was treacherously wounded by Garrido's Indians? That José Maceo slashed Garrido with his machete?[45] We were having sweet potato and roast pork for lunch when Luis arrived; cassava from his house is set out on a white cloth on the ground. We go bucking through thickets of sea grape again, and from above we catch a glimpse of the wide river of Sabanalamar; we wade across its stones, pass through its reeds, camp on the other side. Luis's embrace was beautiful, his eyes smiling as much as his mouth, his beard close-cropped and gray, and his spacious, serene face a pure black color. He is the father of the whole area and wears good pepper-and-salt cloth; his free home is the one closest to the forest. The peace of his soul gives absolute beauty to his majestic, agile body. We ate his jerked beef and plantains while he went to town, and he came back through the forest at night, without light, loaded down with new provisions, his hammock on one side, and in his hand a yagua box of honey, full of larvae. Today I saw the *yamagua*, the carbolic leaf that stanches blood, and whose very shade is beneficial to the wounded: "mash up the leaves and put them in the wound to make the blood dry up." Birds seek out its shade. Luis told me how to keep a wax candle from going out as you walk: wrap a piece of damp cloth around it, and with that the candle stays lit as it goes and uses up less wax. The doctor taken prisoner in the betrayal of Maceo, could it be poor Frank?[46] Ah, Flor!

April 22

Day of waiting impatiently. A bath in the river, with waterfalls, eddies, and boulders, and clusters of reeds along the bank. My blue clothes are washed for me, my jacket. At noon Luis's brothers arrive, proud of the home-cooked lunch they bring us: fried eggs, fried pork, and a big loaf of corn bread. We eat beneath a downpour; after some work with the machetes a tent is put up, roofed with our rubber rain capes. Troubling news all afternoon: a deserter from the Escuadras de Guantánamo[47] arrives, a nephew of Luis, who's gone off to get weapons, and he says that troops are coming down; someone else says that from Baitiquirí—where lame Luis Bertot, traitor at Bayamo, is a lieutenant—two scouts have reached San Antonio to search the forest. The Escuadras, made up of paid criollos, with a ferocious rogue at headquarters, fight Spain's battle, the only battle to fear in these regions. Luis, who came at sunset, received a letter from his wife: that the scouts—and her own brother is one of them—have been summoned by Garrido, the rogue lieutenant, to meet up with him at La Caridad and search all of Cajuerí; that at Vega Grande and Los Quemados and many other passes they've set up ambushes for us. We slept where we were, within sight of the path. Today we're talking about Céspedes, and Gómez describes the house with the grand entryway where he met him in Las Tunas, when he went from Oriente, wearing his worst clothes, with fifteen riflemen, to tell him how the war was escalating dangerously. Immaculate aides, in gaiters. Céspedes: kepi and cigarette holder. The war, abandoned to the commanding officers who asked for guidance in vain, in contrast with the festivity of the retinue in Las Tunas. Soon the government had to flee to Oriente. "There was nothing, Martí": no campaign plan, no set or constant objective. Someone says that creeping juniper, with a scent like cedar, gives flavor and medicinal value to aguardiente. That a tea made from trumpetwood, the large leaves of the trumpetwood tree, is good for asthma. Juan arrived, the one from the Escuadras, he saw Flor dead, dead, his beautiful head no longer warm, his lips torn and two gunshots in his chest; the 10 killed him. Patricio Corona, who wandered hungry for eleven days, turned himself in to the Voluntarios.[48] Maceo and two others met up with Moncada. Luis's sons and nephews are coming home: Ramón, Eufemio's son, with his smooth chocolaty skin, like rosy bronze, his elegant, perfect head, and agile pubescent body,—Magdaleno, magnificently made, firm-footed, with lean shanks, swelling calves, long thighs, full torso, graceful arms, and, on a slender neck, a pure head, with its downy upper lip and curling beard, a machete at his belt and his yaray hat wide-brimmed and pointed. Luis sleeps beside us.

April 23

Ready at dawn, but still no Eufemio, who was supposed to watch the
scouts set out; and still no answer from the troops. Luis goes to see,
and comes back with Eufemio. The scouts have left. We set out behind
them. From our campsite of two days in El Monte de la Vieja we go
down the mountain. From a hill in a clearing the palm grove of San
Antonio is visible to the south, surrounded by *jatía* trees and sea grape
in the fertile depths of the gulches, with mountains to one side and the
other and the sea in between. The mountain on the right, with what
looks like a bleeding gash near its peak, is Doña Mariana; that one, to
the south, rising above many others, is the Sugar Loaf. From eight to
two we walk through the thorny *jatía* trees, with good grass and the
low, red flower of the *guisaso de tres puyas;* prickly pears, some free-
ranging animals. We talk about Gómez's squadrons during the other
war. Gómez praised the bravery of Miguel Pérez: "He made a false
step, he was forgiven, and he was always loyal to the government."
"His body was retrieved from a yagua palm; they just about made
mincemeat out of him." "Some Spaniard did that to Santos Pérez."
And, says Luis, Policarpo put the other Pérez's balls on his face like a
pair of glasses. "I'm going to cut your balls off," he shouted at Policarpo in battle. "And I'm going to cut yours off." And Policarpo made
him wear them.[49] "But why do these Cubans fight against Cubans?
I've seen that it isn't a matter of opinion or some impossible affection
for Spain." "They fight, the pigs, they fight like that for the peso
they're paid, one peso a day, less the lodging that's deducted. They're
the bad seed of the little villages, or men who have a crime to pay for,
or tramps who don't want to work, and a handful of Indians from
Baitiquirí and Cajuerí." We talked about coffee and the other grains
that can be substituted for it: *platanillo* and *boruca.* Suddenly we go
down into a tall, pleasant forest, fallen trees serve as a bridge over the
first pool, and we walk over soft leaves and cool stones, in pleasant
shade, to the place where we'll rest: water runs by, the ground is white
with trumpetwood leaves, enormous leaves are dragged from the
creek, to protect us from rain, I go toward the sound and see pure water running among rocks and ferns, through pebbled pools and glad
cascades. By night Luis's 17 men arrive, and so does he, 63 years old,
alone, an hour before them: all of them off to war: and with Luis goes
his son.

April 24

Across the wide gulch, over the Monte de Acosta, across crumbling stone, with pools of clear water where the mockingbird drinks, and a bed of dry leaves, we haul ourselves along the exhausting path from sunup to sundown. The danger is palpable. Since El Palenque they've been following our tracks closely. Garrido's Indians could fall on us here. We take shelter on the porch of Valentín, overseer of the Santa Cecilia sugar plantation. Strong Juan, with good teeth, comes out to give us his warm hand, and his uncle Luis calls him over: "And you, why aren't you coming?" "But don't you see how the bugs are eating me up?" The bugs, the family. Ah, rented men, corrupting salary! The man who is his own man, who belongs to himself, is different. And these people? What does he have to leave behind? The house of yagua palms, which the land gives them and they make with their own hands? The pigs, which they can raise on the mountainside? Food the earth gives; shoes, the yagua and the majagua; medicine, herbs, and bark; sweets, honey. Farther along, digging holes for fence posts, is an old man, bearded and big-bellied, in a dirty shirt and pants that reach his ankles, his skin earth-colored, his eyes viperish and shrunken: "And what are you men doing?" "Well, we're here to build these fences." Luis swears and raises his long arm into the air. He strides away, his chin quivering.

April 25

Day of war. Through virgin forest, we're drawing closer—now in the very claws of Guantánamo, hostile during the first war—to Arroyo Hondo. We lost our way. Thorns slashed us. Reeds whipped and choked us. We passed through a forest of calabash trees, the green fruit sticking out from a bare trunk or a thin branch. The men clean out the calabashes as they go and smooth down the openings. At eleven, a round of gunfire. Running fire that booms out against a scatter of muffled shots. The combat seems to be at our feet: three heavy bullets come in and hit the tree trunks. "Distant gunfire—what a fine sound!" says the big handsome young fellow from San Antonio, just a boy. "It's even better up close," says the old man. Following the path we go up along the bank of a stream. The gunfire intensifies; Magdaleno, seated against a tree trunk, carves decorations into his new calabash. We lunch on raw eggs, a sip of honey, and chocolate from La Imperial in Santiago de Cuba. Soon, news reaches us from the town. They've seen a dead body come in, and 25 wounded. Maceo has come to find us, and is waiting nearby: away to Maceo, happily. I said in a letter to Carmita:[50] "Along the very road where the battle took place the triumphant Cubans were waiting for us; they threw themselves off their horses, the horses they took from the *guardia civil,* they embrace each other and cheer for us; bundle us onto the horses and put spurs on us." How is it that the patch of blood I saw on the road doesn't fill me with horror? Nor even the half-dried blood, from a head that is buried now, laid to rest in a satchel by one of our horsemen? In the afternoon sunlight we started on our victory march back to camp.

At midnight they went out, across rivers and cane fields and brier patches, to save us: they had just arrived, close now, when the Spaniards fell on them: with no breakfast they fought for two hours and staved off the hunger of their triumph with crackers: and then they set out on a journey of eight leagues, first through a glad, bright afternoon, and then under vaults of thorns in the dark of night. In single file the long column proceeded. The aides go past, running and shouting. On horseback and on foot, we wind through the giddy heights. We march through a cane field and every soldier emerges with his own piece of cane. (We cross the wide railway tracks: we hear the whistles that announce nightfall in the sugar mills: we see electric lights across the plain.) "Halt the column, there's a wounded man back there." A man drags along a leg with a bullet hole in it, and Gómez sets him on his horse's croup. Another wounded man won't have it: "No, friend: I'm not dead," and keeps on walking with a bullet in his shoulder. The poor feet are so tired! They sit, rifles at their sides, at the edge of the path, and smile at us, glorious. An occasional "Ay!" is heard and then more laughter and contented chatting. "Make way!" and strong Cartagena, a lieutenant colonel who earned his rank in the Ten Years War, arrives on horseback with a burning torch of cardona cactus stuck like a lance into his leather stirrup. And other torches clustered here and there. Or they set fire to dead trees that sputter and shoot out sparks and send shafts of flame and plumes of smoke into the sky. The river cuts us off. We wait for the weary. Now they are all around us, their yaray hats in the darkness. This is the last water, and on the other side, sleep. Hammocks, candles, steaming pots, the camp is asleep now: later I'll sleep at the foot of a tall tree with my rubber rain cape for a pillow and my machete and revolver beside me; now I rummage through my *jolongo* and take out medicine for the wounded. The stars look down fondly, at 3 in the morning. At 5, eyes open, Colt on hip, machete at belt, spurs on, and to horse!

Brave Alcil Duvergié died—every flash of gunpowder takes its man—death went in through his forehead; another man, a rifleman, had a whole volley fired into him; another fell as he was boldly crossing the bridge. And where, when we make camp, are the wounded? Laboriously I gathered them together at the foot of the worst case, who is believed to be shell-shocked, and was carried in on a hammock slung from a stick. The juice of the tobacco tucked into one corner of his mouth has made his teeth fall out. Unhappily he takes a sip of cordial. And the water, which doesn't come, the water for the wounds, which is finally brought in a muddy bucket—? Fresh water is fetched by the obliging Evaristo Zayas from Ti Arriba. And the medic, where is the medic, why doesn't he attend to his wounded? The other three are complaining, in their rubber rain capes. Finally he comes, huddled in a quilt, alleging fever. And between us all, with the gentle assistance of Paquito Borrero, we treat the wounded man in the hammock, a wound that goes through the shoulder. A thimble would fit into it on one side, and a chestnut on the other: we wash it, apply iodoform, phenolated cotton. On to the next, on the upper thigh: it went in and came out. On to the next, who turns over onto his stomach, the bullet didn't come out of his back: there it is, it emerges from the patch of red, swollen skin: syphilis has eaten away at the man's nose and mouth. The last one has both entry and exit wounds, also in the back: they were firing knee to the ground and the low shots went right through their muscular backs. Antonio Suárez, from Colombia, a cousin of Merchan's wife, Lucía Cortés, has the same wound. And he lost his way, on foot, and found us later.

April 26

We form ranks at sunrise. To horse, still sleepy. The men are shaky, haven't yet recovered. They barely ate last night. About 10, we rest along both sides of the path. From a small house they send a hen, as a gift to "General Matías," and honey. In the afternoon and at night I write, to New York, to Antonio Maceo who is nearby and unaware of our arrival, and the letter for Manuel Fuentes, to the *World*,[51] which I finished, pencil in hand, at dawn. Yesterday I cast an occasional glance over the calm, happy camp: the sound of a bugle; loads of plantains carried on shoulders; the bellow of the seized cattle when their throats are slit. From his hammock, Victoriano Garzón, a sensible black man with a mustache and goatee and fiery eyes, tells me, humble and fervent, about his triumphant attack on Ramón de las Yaguas: his words are restless and intense, his soul is generous, and he has a natural authority: he pampers his white aides, Mariano Sánchez and Rafael Portuondo, and if they err on a point of discipline, he lets them off. Stringy, sweetly smiling, in a blue shirt and black pants, he watches over each and every one of his soldiers. The formidable José Maceo parades his tall body past: his hands are still raw from the brambles in the pine forest and on the mountainside, when the expedition from Costa Rica was pursued and took flight, and Flor was killed, and Antonio took two men with him, and José was left all alone, sinking beneath his load, dying from cold amid the damp pines, his feet swollen and cracked: and he arrived, and now he triumphs.

April 27

Camp at last, at the Filipinas ranch. I attend at once to the duties under my jurisdiction; next to me, in his hammock, Gómez writes. In the afternoon, Pedro Perez, the leading insurgent of Guantánamo, who, after 18 months of hiding, finally came out, with 37 men, death following behind them, and today he has 200. His wife is out in the countryside, with the 17 members of the household, and she sends us the first flag. And he served Spain in the Escuadras, during the Ten Years War! Family loyalty to Miguel Perez.—Leaning on his cane, short in stature, with a silver watch fob, his wispy sideburns trailing along the sides of his thin, benevolent face, he and his brave men went searching for Maceo in vain across all Baracoa, in the teeth of the Indians. His jipijapa is dyed purple; its hatband, embroidered by a woman's hand, is the same color, the ends trailing down his back.—He wants no mounted men and doesn't ride himself, and has a low opinion of rubber capes, preferring the pure rain, suffered in silence.

April 28

Dawn finds me at work. At 9, the men form ranks, and Gómez, sincere and concise, exhorts them. I speak, beneath the sun. And back to work. To bind this force together in the spirit of union: to establish and organize an energetic, magnanimous war: to open up channels to the North, and supply lines: to check any spurious attempt to disrupt the war with promises. I write a circular to the commanders; they must punish any spurious attempt with the penalty for betrayal—another circular to the landowners—a note from Gómez to the plantations—letters to probable friends—letters to establish mail service and supply lines—letters to make an appointment with Brooks—a note to the British Government, for the consul at Guantánamo, including José Maceo's declaration concerning the accidental death, from a shot unintentionally fired by Corona, of a sailor on the schooner *Honour* on board which the expedition came from Fortune Island—instructions to José Maceo, whom Gómez is promoting to Major General—a note to Ruenes, inviting him to send a representative from Baracoa to the Assembly of Delegates of the revolutionary Cuban people, to elect the government that the revolution must create for itself—letter to Masó. Luis Bonne came, so wise and benevolent that Gómez sent for him to create a guard for me. As his aide he brings Ramón Garriga y Cuevas, whom I used to make a fuss over when he was a little boy back in New York and I would see him acting mischievous or helpless; he is mild, affectionate, lucid, and brave.

April 29

Work. Ramón stays at my side. In the attack on Arroyo Hondo, a flank of ours, in which the brother of a criollo lieutenant was fighting, killed the criollo lieutenant, who was fighting on the other side. Luis González left me, with his goddaughter. "That face will stay engraved here." He said that to me with a celestial face.

April 30

Work. Antonio Suárez, the Colombian, talks, unruly and full of complaints: what carelessness, what kind of colonel is that. Maceo, claiming an urgent operation, won't wait for us. We leave tomorrow.

May 1

We leave the camp of Vuelta Corta. That was where Policarpo Pineda, alias the *Rustan*, or the Moth, had Francisco Pérez, the one from the Escuadras, hacked to pieces. One day the Moth executed Jesus Christ himself: he was wearing a big crucifix on his chest and a bullet sent an arm of the cross into his flesh, so later he fired four shots into the cross.

We were talking about this during the morning, when the path, now in the blooming region of the coffee plantations, among plantains and cacao, emerged into a magical hollow called the Tontina; from the depths of the vast greenness its roof of palm trees can hardly be seen and on all sides are mahogany trees with their purple flowers. Not much farther was the Kentucky, Pezuela's coffee farm, the large brick driers in front of the house, which is cheerful, spacious, and white, with balconies, and a low area nearby where the machines are. At the door is Nazario Soncourt, a slender mulatto, with rum and a pitcher of water on a small table, and glasses. The Thoreau brothers come out to see us from their vivid coffee farm, with its little houses of brick and tile: the youngest one, red with effort, his eyes anxious and misty, stammers: "But we can work here, right? We can go on working." And he says nothing but that, like a madman.—We reach the forest. Estanislao Cruzat, a good mountaineer, Gómez's groom, cuts a slash near the base of two trees, pounds two forked sticks in front of each one, and others to support the trunk, and some crosspieces, and sticks laid lengthwise: and there's a bench. After a short rest, we continue along an overgrown footpath in the fertile region of Ti Arriba. Sunlight glitters on the cool rain: oranges dangle from airy trees: high grass covers the wet ground. Slender white tree trunks weave through the green forest, from their roots to the blue sky; liana twists around delicate bushes in spirals of even rings that look man-made, and copey trees grow down into the earth from above, swaying in the air. I drank clear water from a bromeliad clinging to a hog plum tree: crickets were chirping in broad daylight.—To sleep, in the house of the "bad Spaniard": he fled to Santiago de Cuba: the house has a zinc roof and a filthy floor: the men devour the bunches of plantains hanging from poles along the roof, two pigs, doves and ducks, a heap of cassava in a corner. This is La Demajagua.

May 2

Onward to Jaragüeta. Among the sugar mills. Through the vast and abandoned cane field of Sabanilla: Rafael Portuondo goes home to bring back 5 head of cattle: they come yoked together. The poor men, out in the rain! We reach Leonor and, rejecting the thought of a late dinner, had already settled in our hammocks with bread and cheese, when, with cavalrymen sent by Zefí, George Eugene Bryson arrived, the correspondent from the *Herald*.[52] I work with him until 3 in the morning.

May 3

At 5, we go with Colonel Perié, who came last night, to his coffee farm high up in Jaragüeta, with a parlor like a stage set, and below, as if in a vast painting, the lazy mill, for cacao and coffee. The vast landscape spreads out, descending, on both sides, and two nearby streams go flowing down over a deep bed of stones, with a scattering of palm trees, and a background of very distant mountains. I work all day on the manifesto for the *Herald* and other things for Bryson. At 1, when I go in search of my hammock, I see a number of them on the ground and think they've forgotten to put it up. I use my hat for a pillow and stretch out on a bench. Then the cold sends me into the lighted kitchen; they give me an empty hammock; a soldier throws an old cloak over me: and at 4, reveille.

May 4

Bryson leaves. Soon after that: the court-martial of Masabó. He raped and robbed. Rafael presides and Mariano reads the charges. Somber, Masabó denies them, his face brutal. His defender invokes our arrival and asks for mercy. Death. As the sentence was read out, a man was peeling a piece of sugarcane at the back of the crowd. Gómez holds forth: "This man is not our comrade: he is a *vil gusano,* a vile worm." Masabó, who hasn't sat down, lifts his eyes toward him with hatred. The troops, in great silence, hear and applaud: *"¡Que viva!"* And as the march gets in order, Masabó remains standing; his eyes do not fall nor can any fear be seen in his body: his pants, wide and light, flap constantly, as if in a fast wind. At last they go, the horses, the prisoner, the entire force, to a nearby hollow, in the sun. A weighty moment: the troops silent, standing on tiptoe. The shots ring out, and then one more, and another to finish him off. Masabó died a valiant man. "How do I stand, Colonel? Front or back?" "Front." He was brave in battle.

May 5

Maceo had told us to meet him in Bocuey, which we cannot reach by 12, the hour when he was to meet us. Last night the messenger set out: he was to wait for us at his camp. We go, with the whole force. Suddenly, horsemen. Maceo, on a golden horse, in a gray cambric suit: his graceful saddle, with stars, has silver on it now. He came to find us because he has his men on a march. Maspon goes to Mejorana, the nearby mill, to have them start making lunch for a hundred. The mill greets us as if it were a holiday: the delight and admiration of the servants and workers is visible: the boss, a ruddy old man with sideburns, a jipijapa on his head, and small feet, brings vermouth, tobacco, rum, and malmsey wine. "Kill three, five, ten, fourteen hens." A woman with bared breasts, wearing slippers, comes to offer us a green aguardiente made from herbs: another brings pure rum. People come and go. Castro Palomino, an adjutant to Maceo, fetches and carries, supple and verbose. Maceo and G. are speaking in low voices, near me: soon they call me over to them on the porch. Maceo has changed his thinking on the government: a junta of generals in command, through their representatives, and a Secretary-General: in other words, the patria and all its occupations, which creates and gives power to the army, as Secretary to the Army. We go to a room to talk. I cannot make heads or tails of Maceo's conversation: "but are you staying with me or going with Gómez?" And he speaks to me, cutting off my words as if I were the continuation of the pettifogging government, its representative. I see that he is wounded: "I love you"—he tells me—"less than I used to" because Flor replaced him as the one in charge of the expedition and the handling of its money.[53] I insist on making a statement to the representatives who are meeting to elect a government. He does not want each chief of operations to have his own command, born from his own force: he will command the four in Oriente: "Within fifteen days they will be with you gentlemen, and these will be men that Doctor Martí won't be able to confuse." At dinner, opulent and awkward, with chicken and suckling pig, the matter comes up again: he wounds and repels me. I understand that I must shake off the role I am to be marked with, as the civilian defender of shackles hostile to the military movement. I hold out, roughly: the Army, free—and the country, as a country, with its full dignity represented.[54] I show my displeasure at so indiscreet and forced a conversation, before the whole table, and with Maceo's haste to leave. For night is about to fall on Cuba and he has a six-hour journey ahead of him. His troops are nearby but he doesn't take us to see them: the combined forces of Oriente: Rabí of Jiguaní, Busto of Santiago de Cuba, and José's, which we brought. In the saddle, a quick good-bye. "You leave by that way over there," and we follow, our guards fretful, now late in the afternoon, without the aides, who stayed with José, uncertain of the way, to a slave hut along the path where we don't unsaddle the horses. The aides

are sent for: we go on to another muddy shack outside the encampments, open to attack. G. sends to José's camp for meat: the aides bring
it. And so, like outcasts, and with sad thoughts, we sleep.[55]

May 7

We leave Jagua and its old and loyal *mambises* for the Mijial. At the
Mijial, the horses eat wild piñon; lids for gallon jugs are made from it
and cedar. César is given a tea of guanábana leaves, a good pectoral and
a pleasant tisane. Along the way, Prudencio Bravo, guardian of the
wounded, came out to tell us good-bye. We saw Nicolás Cedeño's
daughter, who speaks contentedly and is going with her five sons to
her forest in Holguín. Along the road to Barajagua—"there was a lot
of fighting here," "all of this was ours in the end"—we talk about the
last war. There, from the dense forest of the slopes, or from the heights
and hillside bends of the road, they harassed the [Spanish] columns,
which finally stopped coming: the road leads to Palma and Holguín.
Zefí says he brought Martínez Campos[56] along here, when he went to
his first meeting with Maceo. "The man came out of there red as a
tomato, so enraged he threw his hat on the ground and went off to
wait for me half a league away." We're close to Baraguá. We go off the
road onto the brief flatlands of Pinalito, which descend to the stream
of Las Piedras and, beyond it, the hill called La Risueña, its red, rocky
soil curving like an egg against a background of graceful mountaintops
in strange contours: a small woods, then a saddle-shaped hilltop, and a
stairway of hills. We're heading straight for the plain of Vio, a green
shell with forest all around, and palm trees in it, and in the open areas,
a couple of little islands of forest, like rosettes, and a lone hawthorne,
which is good wood for burning. Black paths run across green grass,
dotted with purple and white flowers. To the right, in the heights of
the mountain range, a crest of pines. Hard rain. The advance guard
moves forward, one with a yagua on his head, another with a piece of
cane on his saddle, or a palm frond resting there, or his shotgun. A
telegraph wire twists in the dirt. Pedro goes by, with a bare flagpole,
made of   .[57] Zefí, his lead spoon sticking out between his bandoliers, has a cockade sewn on to the back of his jacket. Chacón is
barefoot, but the bluing on his rifle butt glitters from his waist to his
knees. Zambrana plods along, a cooking pot dangling from his hip.
Another man is wearing a black frock coat over his jacket. I look back
to where the tail of the march is coming, the mules and oxen, and the

short carbines of the rear guard, and against the gray sky I see, moving ponderously, three   ,[58] and one has a yagua on its head, like a poncho. Across the next plain, Hato del Medio, famous during the war, we continue on, the grass drowning under the cloudburst, to the campsite, over there behind those few cows. "Here," Gómez tells me, "is where the cholera broke out, when I came with two hundred weapons and 4,000 freed slaves, so that the Spaniards wouldn't take them from us; all this was dark with cattle, and they killed so many that people began to die of the stench, and I was scattering corpses along our march: I left 500 corpses along the way to Tacajó." And then he tells me about Tacajó, the agreement between Céspedes and Donato Mármol.[59] After Bayamo was taken, Céspedes disappeared. Eduardo Mármol, a cultured, baleful man, recommended dictatorship to Donato. Félix Figueredo asked Gómez to support Donato and join those who favored dictatorship, to which Gómez responded that he already had a mind to do so, and would do so not because Félix advised it, but in order to be on the inside and better able to prevent it from there: "Yes," said Félix, "because the revolution has given birth to a viper." "And he was the same thing," G. told me. From Tacajó, Céspedes sent a message to Donato inviting him to a meeting, once G. was with him, and G. wanted to go first and then send a message. Upon reaching Céspedes, as G. was coming with the guard he met about a quarter of a league away, he thought he saw confusion and agitation in the camp, until Marcano came out to meet Gómez, who told him: "Come here and embrace me." And when the Mármol brothers arrived, at the table set for fifty where the differences of opinion were discussed, it was clear from the start that, like Gómez, the rest were in favor of deferring to Céspedes's authority. "Eduardo turned black." "I'll never forget Eduardo Arteaga's speech: 'The sun,' he said, 'in all its splendor, is sometimes darkened by a sudden eclipse; but then it shines again with renewed brilliance, all the brighter for its transitory darkness: that is what has happened to the Céspedes sun.'" José Joaquín Palma spoke up. "Eduardo? He was having a siesta one day, and the blacks were making noise in the sugar mill. He called for silence, and they went on talking. 'Ah, so they don't want to listen?' He took out his revolver— he was a very good shot—and a man went down with a bullet in his chest. Then he went back to sleep." Now we're arriving, to the sound of the bugle, among huts, and Quintín Banderas's troops are standing in formation under the rain. Narciso Moncada,[60] Guillermo's brother, very black, with a mustache and chin beard, wearing boots, a cape, and a jipijapa, embraces us. "Ah, but one number is missing!" Quintín, around sixty, his head sunk between his shoulders, a heavy torso, a low gaze and few words, greets us at the door of the hut, burning up with fever; he buries himself in his hammock; his small, yellow eyes look as if they came from deep inside him, and we have to stoop over him; at the head of his hammock is a small drum. Deodato Carvajal is his lieutenant, with a slim body and a mind bent on promotion, capable and orderly; his words grow muddled in their quest for refinement, but there is method and command in him, and he shows spirit on his own behalf and on behalf of others; he tells me he made sure Moncada received my letters. Narciso Moncada, verbose and robust, is a man of goodness and ostentation: "I spend nothing on liquor." His brother is buried "lower than a man's height, with engineer's maps, in a place known only to a few of us, and if I die, another man knows, and if he dies, another man, and the grave will always be preserved." "And our mother, who has treated us as if she were the mother of the patria?" Dominga Moncada has been in El Morro⁶¹ three times: and all because a certain general, who later died, sent for her to tell her she had to go recruit her sons, and she told him: Look, General, if I see my sons coming along a path and I see you coming the other way, I'll shout: "Flee, my sons: that man is the Spanish general."—We enter the hut on horseback, because of all the mud outside, so as to be able to dismount, and there is a stench in the earth and the air from the many cattle that have died nearby; the hut sags, dense with hammocks. Pots boil on a big stove in the corner. We're served coffee, ginger, a tisane of guanábana leaves. Moncada, coming and going, alludes to Quintín's abandonment of Guillermo. Quintín speaks to me like this: "And then there was the business that came up with Moncada, or that he had with me, when he wanted to send me off with Masó, and I asked to be discharged." Carvajal had spoken of "the disappointments" Bandera suffered. From his hammock, Ricardo Sartorius speaks to me of Purnio, when the forged telegram from Cienfuegos arrived telling them to take up arms: he speaks to me of the perfidy toward his brother Manuel, whose forces Miró made off with and who was then "forced to present himself": "this was at stake for him"—pointing to his throat. "Calunga" came from Masó, with letters for Maceo: he won't reach his rendezvous with M. very soon because he is protecting an expedition from the south that has just arrived. There's heavy fighting in Bayamo. Camagüey is up in arms. The Marqués has joined the uprising and so has Agramonte's son. It stinks in here.

May 8

Off to work, on a nearby hilltop where the new encampment is being
built: huts made of tree trunks tied together with reeds and roofed
with palm fronds. They clean up a tree for us and we write at its foot.
Letters to Miró: from G., addressing him as Colonel, certain he will
help "Brigadier Ángel Guerra, named Chief of Operations"—and
mine, to make sure, though without exposing my thoughts, that he
sees the advisability and justice of accepting and helping Guerra. Miró,
as colonel, is in control of the region. Guerra fought in the Ten Years
War, and would not obey him.[62] Letters to prominent people in Holguín, and circulars: to Guadalupe Pérez, a rich man, Rafael Manduley,
a solicitor, Francisco Freixas, a lawyer. At a table, the court-martial of
Isidro Tejera and Onofre and José de la O. Rodríguez muddles along:
some civilians attested to the terror into which they plunged the region: Captain Juan Peña y Jiménez—Juan the Lame, who served "in
the three wars,"[63] has only a stump left of one leg, and mounts his
horse with a bound—saw the abandoned houses and listened to the locals' fear, and testifies that the three of them refused him their weapons
and made death threats. The court, its confusion cleared up, sentences
them to death. We go to the new hut, with low eaves and no walls.—
José Gutierrez, the affable bugler that Paquito is taking with him, sig-
nals the men to fall in. The prisoners are brought up through the silent
ranks; Ramón Garriga reads the sentence, and the pardon. Gómez
speaks of a flag's need for honor: "this criminal has stained our flag."
Isidro, who wept as he came, asks permission to speak: moaning, with
no idea what to do, he says he will die innocent, that he can't be allowed to die, that it's impossible that all these brothers won't ask for
him to be pardoned. The bugler sounds the march. No one speaks. He
moans and twists in his rope; he doesn't want to walk. The march is
sounded again, and the ranks move on, marching two abreast. With
the imploring prisoner, Chacón and four riflemen bring up the rear.
Behind, alone, in his gaiters, blue jacket, and small hat, Gómez. A few
others after that, and Moncada, who doesn't go to the prisoner, who is
now at the place of death, crying out in desolation, taking off his
watch which Chacón snatches from him and throws onto the grass.
Gómez commands, clutching his revolver, his face contorted, a few
steps from the prisoner. They set the terrified man on his knees,
though for all their haste he still has time to turn his face back two or
three times, hat in hand. A couple of yards from him, the lowered ri-

fles. Aim! says Gómez: Fire! And he falls onto the grass, dead. Of the two who were pardoned—whose pardon I recommended and obtained—one, his mulatto color changing only slightly, evinces no dismay, only a cold sweat: the other, in ropes up to his elbows, stands as if he were still recoiling, as if his body were fleeing, turned aside like his face, twisted and emaciated. When the sentence was read to them, in the wind and clouds of the afternoon, the three of them seated on the ground, their feet in stocks made of branches, he pressed his fingers into his temples. The other man, Onofre, listened as if he didn't understand and was only turning his head toward some noises. While he was waiting for the verdict, "El Brujito," the dead man, would stoop down and scrabble in the dust, or suddenly raise his black face with small eyes and a sunken nose with a wide bridge. The stocks were made in an instant: a sturdy branch stuck in the earth with another, slenderer one beside it, tied together above and pounded in below, leaving a narrow space for the imprisoned foot. "El Brujito," they said later, was a bandit from before the war: "I can swear to you," said Moncada, "that he leaves fourteen thousand pesos buried somewhere."—Sitting on a trunk in the hut, around a candle, Moncada recounts the dying Guillermo's last march on his way to his appointed meeting with Masó. Guillermo went into prison healthy and came out thin and feeble, spitting up clots of blood at every cough. One day during the march he sat down on the path with his hand on his forehead—"my brain hurts"—and gushed up blood, in red gobs. "These here are from the pneumonia," Guillermo said, stirring them; "and these here, the black ones, are from the back." Zefí speaks, and Gómez, too, of Moncada's fortitude. "One day," he says, "he was wounded in the knee, and one bone was on top of the other, like this" and he put one arm over the other on his chest: "the bones couldn't be set right, and so we hung him up from under his arms, in that hut that was higher than this one, and I grabbed hold of his leg and pulled down on it with all my strength, and the bone went back into place, and the man did not utter a word." Zefí is very tall and wiry: "and I'll stay in the forest and be a bandit if they want to end this thing in infamy again." "A thing as well launched as this one," says Moncada, "and then go wheeling and dealing with it." He complains bitterly of Urbano Sánchez's abandonment and deception of Guillermo: Guillermo, always eager for white company; "I'm telling you, in Cuba today there is a horrible division."[64] And the rancor of his memories is apparent in his violent condemnation of Mariano Sánchez and the time in Ramón de las Yaguas when he argued that the promise to respect the surrendered Lieutenant's weapons should be kept, and M. and others, who had nothing but old hunting guns, wanted to seize the sixty rifles. "And who are you"—Narciso says Mariano Sánchez said to him—"to have a vote in this?" And G. expresses the thought that M. "doesn't have the face of a Cuban, whatever you want to tell me, and forgive me for saying so." And that the father is on the outside, and sends his son inside, to be in both camps at once. We talk a lot about the need to harass the bewildered enemy, and tirelessly force them out to battle, to harden the unoccupied revolutionary army with battle and transform camps like this one, with four hundred men, and more every day, who eat in peace and tend three hundred horses, into a more orderly and active force. "With my hunting gun and my two precision weapons, I know how to arm myself," says Bandera: Bandera, who spent the day in his solitary hammock down there in the stinking hut.

May 9

Adiós to Bandera, to Moncada, to fine Carvajal who would like to go with us, and to the huts that the men lean out of waving their yaray hats at us. "May God guide you well, my brothers!" Not a single man turns his eyes toward it as we go past the grave. And shortly we emerge from the muddy cattle ranch out onto the plain and some mango trees in the distance. This is Baraguá, and the mango trees, two trunks with a single crown, are where Martínez Campos met with Maceo. A man from Mayarí who was there is acting as our guide: "Martínez Campos went to embrace him, and Maceo put his arm in front of him, like this: that was when he threw his hat on the ground. And when he told him that García was with them already! You should have seen the man when Antonio told him: 'Do you want me to introduce you to García?' García was there, in that forest, the whole forest was only Cubans, no one else. And over there was another force, in case they tried any treachery." From the plains of the Protest of Baraguá[65] we came out onto the high ridge of an abandoned ranch, from where we see an arm of the Cauto River, still dry now, the whole riverbed full of grass and fallen tree trunks, covered with reeds, and blue and yellow flowers, and beyond a bend, a sudden drop. "Ah, Cauto"—says Gómez—"it's been such a long time since I've seen you!" The high and fertile gullies, broken up in places, thrust down toward the riverbed, still narrow here, through which the first rains flow, muddy and turbulent.

The chest swells with quiet reverence and powerful affection before the vast landscape of the beloved river. We go across it near a ceiba, and after greeting a *mambí* family who are overjoyed to see us, we enter the bright woods, with gentle sunlight, widely spaced trees, dripping leaves. The grass is so thick the horses move as if on a carpet. The bromeliads above us look up into the blue sky, and the young palm, and the dagame, which has the finest flowers, beloved of bees, and the gaucimo, and the *jatía*. All is festoon and frond and through the clearings to the right a pure green can be seen on the other side, sheltered and dense. Here I see the *ateje*, its high, sparse crown full of parasites and bromeliads, the courbaril, "the strongest wood in Cuba," the stout *júcaro*, the gumbo-limbo with its silken skin, the broad-leafed genipap, the sagging calabash tree, the hard sabicu, with its black core for making canes and its bark for tanning, the *jubabán*, or ax handle tree, with its light foliage whose leaves, layer upon layer, "make tobacco smooth," the rough-barked mahogany, the break-ax, its striated trunk opening out into strong branches near the roots, and caimitillo, copey, canella, and the *yamagua*, which stanches blood. We found Cosme Pereira along the path, and with him one of Eusebio Venero's sons, who turns back to announce our presence to Altagracia. Still to be found in Altagracia is Manuel Venero, progenitor of patriots, whose beautiful daughter Panchita was killed by the machete of Federicón, the Asturian, for refusing to yield to him. Gómez was very close to the Veneros; he made a fearsome guerrilla leader of their daring Manuel and had a deep friendship with Panchita, which rumor called love. The Asturian carried off the whole house one day and on the march he gradually made Panchita fall behind, propositioning her while she resisted. "You don't want to because you're Gómez's querida?" She stood straight and proud, and with his own hand he finished her off. Her house welcomes us with joy and good coffee in today's gloomy rain. Along with his men from Holguín, Miró is staying there, and came to meet us on the road: ahead of him he sent Pancho Díaz, a youth who, after causing a death, fled to take refuge in Montecristi, and is a river guide, who fords the highest waters, and a roper and slaughterer of hogs, which he kills with the machete. Miró arrives, polite on his fine horse: I see his affection when he greets me; his way of speaking is very Catalán; his looks are refined, a bald head and pointed beard, lively eyes. He sent his troops to Guerra, and came up to meet us with a retinue of brawny young men. "Rafael, come here." And Rafael Manduley, the Holguín solicitor who has just come out to the countryside, walks over in his jacket of Manila hemp cloth and his white waistcoat, a narrow-brimmed jipijapa covering his ears. The men, all well mounted, are of very good stock: Jaime Muñoz, hair parted in the middle, who is a good administrator, José González, Bartolo Rocaval, Pablo García, the sagacious guide, Rafael Ramírez, the war's first sergeant, a gaunt fellow with a small black mustache, Juan Oro, Augusto Feria, tall and good, from the town, a literate man, a typesetter, Teodorico Torres, Nolasco Peña, Rafael Peña, Luis Pérez, Francisco Díaz, Inocencio Sosa, Rafael Rodríguez—and Plutarco Artigas, camp boss, blond and one-eyed, pure and obliging: he left his big house, his well-being, and "nine children of the ten I have, because I brought the oldest one with me." His hammock is large, its pillow made by loving hands; his horse is solid, one of the best in the region; he is going somewhere far away, to another jurisdiction, so that he "won't be tied down by his family" close by: "my little ones bunched together around me and went to sleep with me." And here come Miró and Manduley, both bursting with local politics: "No one said anything about the war" to Manduley, who has a reputation as an insurgent and some moral authority; he has saddle sores; he went to see Masó: "and to think I was feeding my children a scientific diet; who knows what they must be eating now." With animated gestures and overflowing speech, Miró describes his seven-year campaign in the Holguín paper *La Doctrina*, and then in Manzanillo's *El Liberal*, funded by Calvar and Beattie, where he rooted out all the "oblongs," the "Asturians," the "fundamentalist armor." He left his wife and daughter behind and has taken his good cavalrymen across the region without much fighting. He tells me about the efforts of Gálvez, in Havana, to subdue the revolution: of the great hatred with which Gálvez speaks of me and of Juan Gualberto: "you, you are the one they fear": "they were muttering that you wouldn't come, and that's what's going to confound them now."—I'm surprised, here as everywhere, by the affection I'm treated with, and the unity of soul, *which will be diluted and ignored and dispensed with only to the detriment of the revolution, at the very least the detriment of delay, in the momentum of its first year.* The spirit I sowed is the spirit that has taken hold, the spirit of the Island, and with it, guided by it, we will triumph quickly, for a better victory, and for a better peace. I foresee that, for at least a certain time, the revolution will be divorced, by force, from this spirit, deprived of the charm, pleasure, and prevailing power of this natural consortium, robbed of the benefit of this conjunction between the activity of these revolutionary forces and the spirit that moves them.— One detail: *Presidente*, I've been called, from my first appearance in camp, by all the troops, despite my public rejection of the term, and in every camp I arrive at this mark of respect is reborn, along with the gentle enthusiasm of the general affection, and demonstrations of the men's joy in my presence and simplicity. A man approached me today saying *presidente*, and then it was my turn to smile: "Don't let me hear you calling Martí *presidente:* call him general. He is here as a general: don't let me hear you call him president." "And who can hold back the men's impulse, General?" Miró says: "It springs straight from the hearts of all of them." "Fine: but he is not yet president: he is the *delegado*." I fell silent and noted embarrassment and displeasure in all of them, and some seemed offended. Miró is returning to Holguín as a colonel; he will not oppose Guerra; he will defer to him. We speak of the need for active pursuit, driving the enemy from the cities, harassing them across the countryside, cutting off their supply lines, following their convoys. Manduley is going back, as well, none too happily, to influence the region that knows him, to serve as a good adviser to Guerra, to unite the Holguín troops and prevent clashes among them, to maintain harmony between Guerra, Miró, and Feria.—We sleep crowded together, between curtains of rainwater. The dogs, sated from the afternoon's massive slaughter, vomit up beef. That's how we slept in Altagracia.—On the road, the only settlement was Arroyo-Blanco: the empty store, the cluster of shacks, the potbellied rancher, white and egotistical, the tip of his nose drooping over the wings of his skimpy black mustache; his black wife. An old blind woman stuck her head out the door, leaning to one side, her arm propped on her yellow walking stick, she's clean, with a kerchief on her head: "So the *patipeludos* are killing people now?"[66] The Cubans never did a single thing to me, no, señor.

May 10

From Altagracia we go to La Travesía. Arriving there I suddenly caught sight of the Cauto again, swollen now, its wide bed deep underwater, and the steeply sloping ravines on both sides. In the face of such beauty I suddenly thought of the base, fierce passions of man. As we were arriving, Pablo chased after a young heifer, her horns just beginning to grow; she was thrown against a tree where, in slow turns, they short-ened her rope. The horses snort, heads raised; their eyes gleam. Gómez takes a machete from a guardsman's belt and opens a red slit in the heifer's thigh. "You men: hamstring this heifer!" A man hamstrings her with a single blow and the animal kneels, bellowing; Pancho, hearing the order to kill, thrusts his machete awkwardly into her chest, again and again: another man, with a surer hand, pierces to the heart, and the cow totters and falls, blood gushing from her mouth. They drag her away. Francisco Pérez arrives, round-faced and energetic, with good bearing, a natural captain to his few good horsemen, a healthy, steadfast man. Captain Pacheco arrives; a small body and tenacious, encumbered speech, with his talent and decency beneath it: he took a drove of pack animals, his own Cuban men damaged his house and broke his comal, "I haven't come for any purpose but to serve the patria!" but he talks without pause and as if by halves, of those who do things and those who do nothing and of how those who do less generally attain more than he who does more, "but he has come only to serve the *patria*!" "These are my gaiters!": the calves bare; the pants to the knee, leather half-boots; the yellow and purple yaray hat. Bellito arrives, Colonel Bellito of Jiguaní, who had stayed behind here because he was sick. I sense him to be loyal, his eye is clear and combative, he is brave in word and deed. He likes to speak a confused language of his own, in which his thoughts must be captured on the run among words of his own in-vention. "The revolution died for the infamy of overthrowing its caudillo." "That filled the men's hearts with sadness." "From then on, the revolution began to turn back." "They were the ones who gave us the example," they, the men of the Chamber[67]—at which point Gómez bitterly condemns the rebellions of García and his cohort of advisers: Belisario Peralta, Barreto the Venezuelan, Bravo y Senties, Fonseca, Limbano Sánchez, and then Collado. Bellito speaks, pacing back and forth like a man who's looking out for the enemy, or catches sight of him, or falls on him, or leaps away from him. "That's what the men want: good character in the command." "No, señor, we shouldn't be spoken to like that, because no man born can take that." "I've suffered for my patria just as much as the best General would've suffered." He faces off with Gómez who berates him because the officers allowed some cattle through to Jiguaní under a safe pass signed by Rabí. "What's more, that's the order of the commander and we have to obey our commander." "I already know that it's bad and the cattle shouldn't come in; but the lesser has to obey the greater." And at that point

Gómez says, "Well, he's certainly gotten to you with all this about being president. Martí will not be president as long as I am alive"—and
then, "because I don't know what happens to presidents: as soon as
they get there they start going bad, except Juárez, and him, too, a little,
and Washington." Bellito, irate, stands up and gives two or three jumps
and his machete dances at his waist: "That will be up to the will of the
people," and he goes on muttering. "Because we"—he told me another
time, elbows on my table with Pacheco—"we've come to the revolution in order to be men, so that no one can offend us in our dignity as
men." Night falls amid rain, mugs of coffee, and talk about Holguín
and Jiguaní. We're waiting for news of Masó. Has he gone to the summit with Maceo? Miró, in the darkness, gnaws at the bones of a fantail
dove. Tomorrow we'll move to a different house.

May 11

Farther on, still in Travesía, to a less muddy house. Miró leaves with
his men. We get there quickly. Gómez harshly berates Rosalío
Pacheco, who served through the whole war and was deported to
Spain in the Guerra Chiquita, and married an Andalusian woman
there. Pacheco suffers, sitting on a cot at the foot of my hammock.
Notes, continual conversation on the need to expedite the war and the
blockade of the cities.

May 12

From La Travesía to La Jatía, through the pastures, still rich in cattle,
of La Travesía, Guayacanes, and La Vuelta. The grass is thick now
with the continual rain. Excellent grazing, and fields, for cavalry. The
wire fences must come down to open the forest to the cattle or the
Spaniards will take them when they make camp in La Vuelta, at the
crossing of all these roads. The Contramaestre River emerges, with
ravines like the Cauto, but narrower and clearer, and we cross it and
drink. We speak of sons: Teodosio Rodríguez, of Holguín, is with his
three; Artigas is bringing his; Bellito came with his two, aged 21 and
18. A cow goes past in a hurry, sorrowful and mooing, and jumps the
fence: slowly the lost calf, who doesn't seem to see much, goes to her;
and suddenly, as if recognizing her, he arches his back, leans in close,
tail in the air, and applies himself to the udder; the mother goes on
mooing. La Jatía is a good house, made of cedar with a zinc gallery,

abandoned by Agustín Maysana, a rich Spaniard; the floors are covered with letters and papers. Outdoors, I write, to Camagüey, all the letters Calunga will take, saying what I've seen, announcing the journey, to the Marqués, to Mola, to Montejo. I write the circular prohibiting all safe passes for cattle, and the letter to Rabí.[68] Masó is crossing the Sabana de Bio with Maceo, and we write him: we have to stay here a week, waiting for him. Three veterans of Las Villas arrive; one of them was shot three times during the imprudent attack on Arimao, under Mariano Torres—and his brother, trying to save him, was shot once: they're going to Jiguaní for supplies and news: Jiguaní has a fort, a good one, outside the town, and in the town plaza two rubble-work tambours, and another two that are unfinished, because the carpenters disappeared; and so they say, "See what these countrymen of ours are like, they don't want to be on our side even when they're paid." When we lie down after the plantains and cheese, all the writing done, from our hammocks we talk about Rosalío's house where we went that morning for coffee and he was waiting for us, his arms on the fence. The man is large and virile, a hard worker and fine-looking, his white face now lined, his black beard flowing. "Here you have my señora," says the faithful husband with pride: and there she is in a purple tunic, her feet in flowered slippers with no socks, the lovely Andalusian woman, hulling coffee on a stone bench. She wears her hair gathered up tightly in back, and from there it flows down like the train of a bishop's robe: we see her smiling and in pain. She doesn't want to go to Guantánamo with Rosalío's brothers; she wants to be "wherever Rosalío is." The oldest daughter, white, her face a pure oval, her luxuriant short hair parted and tangled, quiets down a bony little creature with a stringy neck, his drooping head in a little lace cap: the latest delivery. Rosalío built the finca; he has cows, presses cheese; we're eating slices of his cheese that weigh a pound each, soaked in coffee. With a nursing bottle, Rosalío, on his stool, feeds milk to a big naked angel of a son who bites his brothers when they try to get close to their father. On tiptoe, Emilia takes a cup down from the cupboard she made out of boxes, against the wall of the shanty. She sits and listens to us with her sorrowful smile, her children hanging off of her on all sides.

May 13

We'll wait for Masó in a less exposed place, near Rosalío, at his brother's house. I'm calming Bellito and Pacheco down, while keeping them from showing me too much affection. We go back across yesterday's pastures, follow the Cauto upstream, and Bellito digs in his spurs to show me the beautiful stirrup-shaped channel, with its lush greenery, where, with a wide bend in front, the two rivers meet: the Contramaestre enters the Cauto. There, within that stirrup, the lower part of which looks out on the pastures of La Travesía, Bellito once had a camp, a good camp: a dense grove of trees there, and a great ceiba. We cross the Contramaestre and soon we're dismounting among Pacheco's abandoned huts. Here, when all this was forest, was the camp of Los Ríos, where O'Kelly[69] first came upon the rebels, before going to Céspedes. And we speak of the three Altagracias: Altagracia la Cubana, where we were, Altagracia de Manduley, and Altagracia la Bayamesa. Of hats: "there are so many weavers in Holguín!" Of Holguín, where the earth is dry and drinks up the rain, with its houses and its ample courtyards, "there are a thousand cows in Holguín that just gave birth." They gather false sandalwood and tomato leaves for me, to smear with grease and place over my boils. Artigas cuts a fringe on the halter Bellito brought me. And the hut is swept out: hammocks; writing; reading; rain; unquiet sleep.

May 14

A guerrilla band leaves for La Venta, the hamlet with Rebentosos's store and the fort with 25 men. Hours later they send for the Mayor, José González, a Galician, married in this country, who says he was forced to be Mayor, and waits at the ranch owned by Miguel Pérez, the mulatto who is the healer and barber here. I write, little and badly, because my thoughts are uneasy and bitter. Up to what point will my stepping down be useful to my country? And I must step down, as soon as the right moment arrives, in order to have the freedom to advise, and the moral power to resist the danger I've foreseen for years, which, in the solitude I'm moving in now, may prevail, through the disorder and lack of communication that in my isolation I cannot overcome—though, free of constraint, the revolution would, by its own unity of soul, enter naturally into the forms that would assure and accelerate its triumph. Rosalío comes and goes, bringing messages, milk, silverware, plates: he is now the prefect of Dos Ríos. His Andalusian wife prepares a castor-oil purge for a sick man, makes him a hammock from a camp bed, provides him with a suit of clothes; the sick man is José Gómez, from Granada, a cheerful man with honest teeth: "And you, Gómez, how did you come to us here? Tell me about what's happened since you came to Cuba." "Well, I came two years ago, and they discharged me, and I stayed on in Camagüey, working. They discharged all of us like that, in order to collect our salary themselves, and we lived off our work. I didn't see anyone but criollos, who treated me very well: I always dressed well, and earned money, and had friends: in two years I collected only twelve pesos of my pay.— And now they called me to the barracks, and I didn't suffer as much as others did because they put me in charge: but there was mistreatment of the men, which I couldn't endure, and when an officer hit me twice in the head I held my peace and and told myself he wouldn't hit me again and picked up my gun and bullets and here I am" on horseback, with his jipijapa and brown jacket, his rifle across the pommel of his filly's saddle, always smiling.—The rafters, arriving from the Sabana and from Hato del Medio, who went to ask permission to transport wood, crowd into the ranch: they're returning to Cauto del Embarcadero, but not to transport wood: whatever work might directly or indirectly benefit the enemy is prohibited. They don't grumble: they wanted to know: they're prepared to go with Commandante Coutiño. I see, riding calmly toward us under the rain, a magnificent man, black in color, wearing a big hat with an upturned brim, who stands behind the group, listening, with his head above it. He is Casiano Leyva, Rosalío's neighbor and a guide around Guamo, first among woodcutters with his powerful ax: and when he takes his hat off I see the noble face, the forehead high and receding, bulging out in the middle, the eyes firm and gentle in their large sockets, the pure line of the nose between the wide cheekbones, and along the sharp chin the grizzled goatee. The trunk of the body is heroic, raised upon slender legs, a bullet in one of them; he has a permit to give meat to the surrounding area so they won't kill too many head of cattle. He speaks gently and there is intelligence and majesty in all he does. Later, he'll go back to Guamo. I write the general instructions to the commanders and officers.

May 15

Rain during the night, mud, a bath in the Contramaestre: caress of flowing water: silk of the water. In the afternoon the guerrilla band comes, saying Masó is on the Sabana and they're going to find him for us: they bring a convoy, picked up in La Ratonera. They empty it at the door: Bellito distributes it. There are fabrics, which Bellito measures off with his arm; so much for the guardsmen, so much for Pacheco, captain of the convoy, and Bellito's men, so much for the staff officers: candles, a piece of cloth for Rosalío's wife, onions and garlic, potatoes and olives for Valentín.

When the convoy arrived, the first one there was Valentín, at its foot, as if he were sniffing, eager. Then the men were all around him. For them, a gallon of "blended wine for tobacco," and also sweet wine. Let the convoy for Bayamo go peacefully on to Baire, distributing rations. It has eleven guides, Francisco Diéguez among them: "But he will come: he's written me: what's happening is that among our troops we had bandits that he had hunted, and so he doesn't want to come—the bandits of El Brujito, the man put to death at Hato del Medio." And there are no forces around with which to attack the convoy, which is accompanied by 500 men. Rabí, they say, attacked the train to Santiago de Cuba in San Luis, and stayed there. We speak of Limbano over our meal; and his death is remembered, as it was told by the guide from Mayarí who had hurried to save him and arrived too late. Limbano, already far gone, was with Mongo, and reached the home of Gabriel Reyes, who has a bad wife, and for whom Limbano had done many favors; he gave him all the coins he had: half for his son, Limbano's, and the other half for Gabriel, so that he would go to Santiago de Cuba to arrange a way out for him, and Gabriel came back with the promise of $2,000, which he earned by poisoning Limbano. Gabriel went to the post of the *guardia civil* who came and fired a shot into the corpse so it would look as if he had died from it. Gabriel lives on in Santiago de Cuba, accused by all of his own; his godson told him, "Godfather, I'm leaving your side because you are despicable."[70] When we go to bed, Artigas puts unsalted lard on a tomato leaf and covers the mouth of my boil with it.

May 16

Gómez goes out to visit the surrounding area. First, a search of the bags of Lieutenant Chacón, Officer Díaz, and Sergeant P. Rico—who grumble—to find a stolen half-bottle of lard. Conversation with Pacheco, the captain: the Cuban people want affection and not despotism; because of despotism many Cubans went over to the government and they'll do it again; what exists in the countryside is a people that has gone out in search of someone to treat it better than the Spaniard, and that thinks it only fair for its sacrifice to be acknowledged. I soothe—and deflect his demonstrations of affection toward me, as well as everyone else's. Marcos, the Dominican: "Even your footprints!" Gómez returns from Rosalío's house. The mayor of La Venta is going free: the soldiers in La Venta, Andalusians, want to come over to our side. Rain, writing, reading.

May 17

Gómez goes with 40 horsemen to give the Bayamo convoy some trouble.[71] I stay behind, writing, with Garriga and Feria, who are copying the *General Instructions* to the commanders and officers, twelve men with me under Lieutenant Chacón, with three guards at the three roads, and next to me, Graciano Pérez. Rosalío, riding his lead pack mule, mud up to his knees, brings me, in his own basket, a fond lunch: "for you, I give my life." The two Chacón brothers arrive, just come from Santiago, one of them the owner of the herd that was seized day before yesterday, and his blond brother, an educated, comical man, and José Cabrera, a shoemaker from Jiguaní, sturdy and frank, and Duane, a young Negro like a carving, in shirt, pants, and a wide belt, and [72] Avalos, shy, and Rafael Vasquez, and Desiderio Soler, 16 years old, whom Chacón brings along like a son. There's another son here, Ezequiel Morales, 18 years old, his father dead in the wars. And those who arrive tell me about Rosa Moreno, the widowed campesina who sent her only son, Melesio, 16 years old, to Rabí: "Your father died in that: I can't go now: you go." They roast plantains and pound jerked beef with a stone for the newcomers. The rising waters of the Contramaestre are very murky, and Valentín brings me a jug, boiled and sweetened, with fig leaves in it.

On May 19, 1895, José Martí was killed during a skirmish with Spanish forces commanded by Colonel José Ximenes Sandoval. Though ordered by Máximo Gómez to stay back, Martí, with a raw recruit named Angel de la Guardia in tow, galloped into the Spanish line of fire. The battle took place at a ranch called Dos Ríos, within sight of the Contramaestre River.

His body was buried on the 20th, in a common grave in the nearby village of Remanganaguas. It was then exhumed by a Spanish medical examiner on the 21st, placed in a crude coffin, with a window over the face, and transported to the town of Palma Soriano, where it was publicly exhibited for several hours on the 24th. On the evening of the 26th, the body arrived in the city of Santiago de Cuba, where a number of people went to view it. It was laid to rest in the Santa Ifigenia cemetery there on the morning of the 27th. As the body was about to be placed in its sepulchre, Colonel Sandoval turned to the assembled multitude and asked, "Is there no friend or relative of the deceased here?" No one spoke.

AFTERWORD

José Martí lived in New York City for fifteen years. He didn't merely occupy space there; he came to grips with the city and the nation around it, plunged into the fray of its day-to-day doings, and wrote thousands of dense, impassioned pages about what he saw, heard, read, felt, and experienced. Today, one of New York's main thoroughfares, the so-called Avenue of the Americas—a name no New Yorker ever uses—cuts straight up through the heart of the city to end at the foot of a statue of Martí on horseback, at the moment of his death, clutching his chest and starting to fall. But among the thousands of people who stream along Central Park South past the statue every day (and who, if they are heading toward Columbus Circle, will soon pass a far more grandiose monument to the men who died onboard the *Maine*), how many have any idea who José Martí was? One of the things Martí found most dismaying about the United States was its iron-clad ignorance of Latin America. While that ignorance may have diminished since Martí's time, it still, for the most part, extends to Martí himself.

Who was José Martí? "Martí," wrote the great Cuban poet José Lezama Lima in 1953, the centennial of Martí's birth, "is, for all of us, the only one who succeeded in entering the house of alibi. The mystical state, the alibi, where imagination can engender event, and every fact is transfigured in the mirror of enigma."

Alibi, in Latin, means simply "elsewhere." Martí's was, in literal fact, a life lived primarily elsewhere, apart from the region he claimed as his own. More fundamentally, he seems, especially at the end of his life, to have gone beyond the ordinary realm of possibility into some remote terrain where life and literature are not separate from each other, where word and deed are one. The poet-politician is a particularly Latin American conjunction, and Martí was undoubtedly its most complete embodiment to date. And though Lezama's "mirror of enigma" was probably taken at the time he wrote it as a reference to the six decades since Martí's death, and the various strange outcomes history had given his work over the course of them, the true force of the words was prophetic, for the half century that has elapsed since they were written has deepened the enigma of Martí's destiny beyond all expectation or understanding.

Who was José Martí? This volume, too, strives to answer the question, or rather, to give English-speaking readers a real opportunity to answer it for themselves, for the first time since Juan de Onis published his masterfully translated anthology *The America of José Martí* in 1953. In choosing the passages from Martí's vast oeuvre that have been included here, I had three primary objectives: to provide an overview of Martí's life, and of the wide spectrum of his work, from poetry to journalism to political writing; to give as complete a picture as possible of his complex views on the United States and its relationship to Latin America; and to translate into English in its entirety, for the first time, his dreamlike final masterpiece, the *War Diaries*.

In making my selections, I was guided by Martí's own opinions, as outlined in his literary testament, and by the century of subsequent scholarship on Martí, which has singled out certain of his works for study. Given that this is a translation into English, destined primarily for an audience in the United States, I also tended to prefer those writings that resonate most deeply within the relationship between the United States and Latin America that has evolved since Martí's time, as well as those most relevant to the issues that currently occupy the foreground in the intellectual life of the United States.

Martí was a translator himself and commented very perceptively on the art of translation in his preface to his translation of Victor Hugo's *My Sons*. "Victor Hugo does not write in French," Martí wrote, "and he cannot be translated into Spanish. Victor Hugo writes in Victor Hugo, and what a difficult thing it is to translate him!" Like many of Martí's statements about other people, this one is doubly true of Martí himself. And (another enigma) it is truer of his prose than of his poetry. The profuse, intricate, luxuriant, and ornate sentences in which his journalistic essays (the *Diaries* are another matter) enveloped even the most dully prosaic subject matter are—and perhaps were explicitly intended to be, as his exile in the United States wore on and on—a kind of anti-English, an implicit rejection of the utilitarian notions of language that he would, nevertheless, sometimes claim to espouse. To pare this baroque style down into simple forms and staccato, declarative phrases would be to deny an essential feature of Martí's work. Yet a translation serves no purpose if it is not legible. I can only say that I have done my best to translate José Martí into José Martí, with as little sacrifice as possible of the sense of his words and the meaning of his style.

One word has always been especially problematic for Martí's English translators: *patria*, a word more important to him than any other. The more familiar English equivalents all miss the mark in one way or another: "homeland" is far too cozy; "native land" makes what, for Martí, was clearly a choice into a mere accident of birthplace; "motherland" is overly reminiscent of "Mother Russia," and negates the opposition between mother and patria that figures prominently, for example, in *Abdala*, while "fatherland" still echoes with Nazi jackboots. The English word "patria"—a relative newcomer to the language, first used by James Joyce in 1914—is less familiar, but that makes it all the more appropriate, for Martí's form of patriotism—absolute yet acutely critical, totally committed but never blind, selfless but never fanatical; a patriotism of bridges, not barriers—is not a common phenomenon. And "patria" has evolved a specialized meaning that made it particularly apt in this context: among Protestant theologians, "patria" denotes an idea of heaven as a place from which the soul is exiled while on earth and to which it longs to return.

A number of people have helped and encouraged me in my work on this project. I would particularly like to thank Eliot Weinberger; Richard Sieburth; Roberto González Echevarría; my kind and forbearing editor, Michael Millman; Alma Guillermoprieto; Roberto Tejada; Cecilia Vicuña; Michael Moore; Carlota Lozada; Carlos Ripoll; Manuel Tellechea; Lex Lalli; Wayne Furman of the New York Public Library; Reina María Rodríguez of the Instituto del Libro in Havana; and, most of all, Kim, Theo, and Jacob Landsman, my husband and sons.

—Esther Allen

NOTES

Unless otherwise specified, all texts were translated from the twenty-seven-volume edition of Martí's *Obras completas* published in Havana in 1975 by the Editorial de Ciencias Sociales.

LETTER TO HIS MOTHER FROM PRISON

1. *Rafael María de Mendive:* A poet and ardent advocate of Cuban independence and Martí's first and most significant mentor. He was the director of the Havana Municipal School for Boys, where Martí enrolled in 1866, and was so convinced of Martí's abilities that he personally funded the boy's secondary education. Earlier in 1869, Mendive had also been arrested. He spent five months in the same prison where Martí was held, and was then deported to Spain.

2. *This letter:* Martí and Valdés Domínguez each claimed to be the sole author of the incriminating letter, and both had signed it, but Martí gave the more vehement performance in court. Valdés Domínguez was sentenced to six months in prison; Martí to six years of hard labor.

POLITICAL PRISON IN CUBA

1. *Even men who dream:* An allusion to Spain's own attempts to form a republic and the contradictory stance of those Spaniards who favored a republic for themselves while denying Cuba its independence. Martí would explore this issue more fully in the pamphlet "The Spanish Republic and the Cuban Revolution" (1873).

2. *Taitica and Mamita:* Affectionate diminutives of "father" and "mother."

NOTEBOOKS 1–3

1. *North Americans:* It's worth noting that Martí had not yet visited the United States when he penned these views.

2. *Alphonse Karr* (1808–90): French satirist, critic, and novelist who coined the phrase *"Plus ça change, plus c'est la même chose"* ("The more things change, the more they stay the same"), and who famously responded to a proposal to abolish the death penalty with the words *"Je veux bien que messieurs les assassins commencent"* ("I would prefer that messieurs the murderers be the first to do so").

3. *Mikhail Bakunin* (1814–76): Russian anarchist revolutionary who believed that absolute freedom could be achieved through extreme individualism and the over-

throw of existing states and institutions. His clash with Karl Marx led to the disintegration of the International Workingmen's Association.

4. *Friedrich Wilhelm Josef von Schelling* (1775–1854): German philosopher who maintained that history is a series of stages progressing toward harmony. His work and that of Georg Wilhelm Friedrich Hegel (1770–1831), who was originally considered a follower of Schelling, had a great impact in Russia in the 1830s and was fundamental to the development of the Slavophile movement.

5. *Vissarion Grigoryevich Belinsky* (1811–48): Author of *Notes of the Fatherland* (1847); eminent Russian literary critic and essayist who influenced and helped to establish the reputation of such writers as Pushkin, Gogol, Lermontov, Dostoevsky, and Turgenev.

6. *Piotr Yakovlevich Chaadayev* (1794–1856): Russian philosopher. The mid-nineteenth-century Russian intelligentsia was dominated by the conflict between Slavophiles and Westernizers; Chaadayev was a leading Westernizer who converted to Roman Catholicism and caused a sensation by attacking Russian institutions such as serfdom.

7. *Ivan Kireyevski* (1806–56): Russian philosopher and critic, and a leading ideologist of the Slavophile movement, which held that Russian civilization was uniquely superior and should follow its own path of development based on values and institutions derived from the Russian Orthodox Church and the country's ancient past.

8. *Konstantin Aksakov* (1817–60): A founder and principal theorist of the Slavophile movement.

THE POOR NEIGHBORHOODS OF MEXICO CITY

1. *El Porvenir:* Mexico City daily newspaper.

2. *José Domingo Cortés* (1839–84): Chilean anthologist, biographer, and historian. The book Martí refers to is *América poética: poesías selectas americanas con noticias biográficas de los autores* (Poetical America: Selected American Poems with Biographical Notices on Their Authors) (Paris: Librería de A. Bouret, 1875).

SARAH BERNHARDT

1. *Victor Hugo's house:* On his first visit to Paris in January 1875, Martí called on Victor Hugo, who discussed the situation in Cuba with him and gave him a copy of his book *Mes fils* with a request that he translate it into Spanish. Martí did so with dizzying speed; the translation was published in Mexico by the *Revista Universal* just three months later, on March 17.

IMPRESSIONS OF AMERICA

1. *A very fresh Spaniard:* There is no record of why Martí chose, or was required, to write these "Impressions" in the guise of a "Spaniard"—the very national-

ity he was trying to be rid of. It seems likely that someone (either Charles Anderson Dana or Martí himself) had decided the articles would be better received if they were billed as having been written by a Spaniard—for nineteenth-century U.S. readers were always avid to see their country through European eyes. In any case, Martí gleefully used the imposture as an opportunity to take a few digs at Spain ("born as I am in a country where there is no field for individual activity") and to note the slavish devotion of the United States to all things European ("Frenchmen give the sacred word").

2. *Charles Anderson Dana* (1819–97): Influential journalist who, in addition to editing *The Hour*, was the longtime editor and owner of the daily *New York Sun*, one of the most admired newspapers of its time. In 1880 Martí contributed a handful of articles to the *Sun* as well, on literary topics such as "Flaubert's Last Work" (July 8) and "Pushkin" (August 28). On learning of Martí's death, Dana published a moving tribute to him in the *Sun* (May 23, 1895), writing, "He was a man of genius, of imagination, of hope and of courage. . . ."

3. *British Honduras:* When he was ten years old, Martí paid a brief visit there. He had been living with his father, who held a military post in the provincial town of Jaguey Grande. The elder Martí refused to turn a blind eye to certain clandestine disembarkations of slaves in which the local lieutenant governor had an interest; he was dismissed from his post and left quickly with his son on a boat that took them to British Honduras. (For what is probably another echo of this episode, see poem XXX of the *Simple Verses* on page 280.)

4. *Mark Twain:* In a later evocation of Mark Twain, published in *La Nación* (Buenos Aires) on January 11, 1885, Martí was to opine that Twain (who had published *Tom Sawyer* in 1876) had yet to fully develop as a novelist.

5. *Thomas Chatterton* (1752–70): English child prodigy who produced a considerable body of poems, many of which he falsely attributed to a fifteenth-century monk, before killing himself at age seventeen. To the English Romantics he was an archetype of the neglected genius.

PROLOGUE TO JUAN ANTONIO PÉREZ BONALDE'S
POEM OF NIAGARA

1. *Juan Antonio Pérez Bonalde* (1846–92): Though this Venezuelan poet also produced a well-known and beloved translation of Edgar Allan Poe's "The Raven," he is now chiefly remembered for the fact that Martí wrote this prologue to one of his poems.

2. *Ugolino della Gherardesca:* The penultimate stanza of Dante's *Inferno* depicts Ugolino in the ninth circle of hell, gnawing the nape of the man who betrayed and imprisoned him. Line 75 of that stanza suggests—though the point has been much debated—that Ugolino cannibalized his own children.

3. *Violent desires taken from Valbuena or leavings from Ojeda:* Bernardo de

Valbuena (1568–1627): Spanish priest and epic poet known primarily for his *Bernardo, o La victoria de Roncesvalles.* Alonso de Ojeda (1466?–1515?): Conquistador who accompanied Columbus on his second voyage in 1493.

FREE VERSES / *VERSOS LIBRES*

1. *Narciso Virgilio Díaz de la Peña* (1807–76): French romantic landscape painter, of Spanish origins.

NOTEBOOKS 4–15

1. *Jean-Louis-Ernest Meissonier* (1815–91): French genre and military painter.

2. *Adolphe Thiers* (1797–1877): French historian and statesman, president of France (1871–73), and author of histories of the French Revolution and the Napoleonic empire.

3. *Domingo Faustino Sarmiento* (1811–88): Argentine writer and statesman, president of Argentina from 1868 to 1874, whose *Vida de Abran Lincoln, décimo sesto presidente de Estados Unidos* was published in 1866 by D. F. Appleton, a company for which Martí himself had translated five volumes into Spanish, between 1883 and 1886. A great admirer of Martí's prose, which he compared to Victor Hugo's, Sarmiento was also the author of *Facundo, or Civilization and Barbarity,* a fundamental work of nineteenth-century Latin American literature.

4. *Pedro Paz Soldán* (1839–95): Peruvian romantic, author of plays, satirical poetry, and *Dictionary of Peruvianisms.*

PIN THE TAIL ON THE DONKEY

1. *Mariano Fortuny* (1838–74): Spanish painter and watercolorist who, in 1859, was sent to Morocco to paint scenes of the war between Spain and Morocco.

CONEY ISLAND

1. *Rockaway:* Here, as elsewhere in his descriptions of Coney Island, Martí's geography is a bit muddled. Rockaway Beach lies on another peninsula, across Rockaway Inlet to the southeast of Coney Island.

2. *Gable:* The town Martí refers to as "Gable"—the principal resort area of Coney Island—was in fact known as West Brighton.

3. *Antonio García Gutiérrez* (1813–84): Spanish romantic playwright, author of *El Trovador,* which Verdi reworked into the opera *Il Trovatore.*

THE TRIAL OF GUITEAU

1. *Oneida:* A religious community founded in 1848 near the present-day city of Oneida in central New York. Its members practiced a form of polygamy they called "complex marriage," raised their children in common, and made steel traps and sil-

verware. In 1881, the year of Guiteau's trial, the community was reorganized as a joint stock company engaged in the manufacture of cutlery and other metal articles, and abandoned all its religious and social experiments.

2. *John Humphrey Noyes* (1811–86): Founder of the Oneida community (see note 1), who preached the doctrine of "Perfectionism," which holds that man's innate sinlessness can be regained through communion with Christ. By 1879 internal dissension and outside hostility to the community had become so strong that Noyes retreated to Canada, where he stayed for the rest of his life.

3. *Moody and Shaddey:* Dwight Lyman Moody (1837–99), evangelist, religious educator, and founder of the Moody Bible Institute, conducted a series of highly successful revival campaigns in the United States and Great Britain in the 1870s with the help of an associate named Ira Sankey (whom Martí calls "Shaddey").

4. *Robert Green Ingersoll* (1833–99): A lawyer and one of the foremost orators of his day, he was known as "the great agnostic" for his antireligious beliefs. His lectures such as "The Gods" (1872) and "Some Mistakes of Moses" (1879) drew large audiences and provoked violent denunciations from the orthodox.

5. *John Alexander Logan* (1826–86): A Union general in the Civil War and a Republican senator from Illinois from 1871 to 1877 and from 1880 until his death. He was also the Republican candidate for vice president in 1884.

6. *James Gillespie Blaine* (1830–93): Republican politician. See "Blaine's Night" (page 231).

7. *Watched his party boil over and break apart:* During the presidential campaign of 1880, the "Old Guards," headed by Roscoe Conkling (1829–88), favored a third term for the incumbent, Ulysses S. Grant, while other Republicans supported the candidacy of James G. Blaine, Conkling's bitter personal enemy. A deadlocked Republican convention chose Garfield as a compromise candidate, with Chester Arthur, a Conkling lieutenant, as vice president to appease the Old Guards. Once in office, Garfield refused to grant Conkling any special patronage and further antagonized him by making Blaine secretary of state. The dispute climaxed when Conkling and another senator resigned from the Senate to protest Garfield's actions.

8. *M. de Z.:* The pseudonym under which Martí's early articles for *La Opinión Nacional* were published. After incurring the displeasure of the country's president, Antonio Guzmán Blanco (1829–99), Martí had been forced to leave Venezuela only a few months earlier, and he was still persona non grata there to a sufficient degree that his editors thought the use of a pseudonym advisable.

PRIZEFIGHT

1. *Fernand Cormon* (b. 1845): Sensationalistic Parisian painter known for his scenes of bloodshed. One of his most famous works was *Cain Flying Before Jehovah's Curse.*

2. *Netzahualcóyotl:* An emperor, poet, and priest (1402–72) of the Chichimecs, a group of peoples who inhabited the Valley of Mexico between the periods of Toltec and Aztec dominance.

3. In the original article, the description of the prizefight is followed by a lengthy tribute to the New York City industrialist and philanthropist Peter Cooper, whom Martí admired passionately.

EMERSON

1. *Edmund Clarence Stedman* (1833–1908): Successful Wall Street broker who was also one of the leading North American poets and critics of his day. Author of *Victorian Poets* (1876).

2. *Bronson Alcott* (1799–1888): Self-educated philosopher, transcendentalist, and advocate of educational reform, now best known as the father of Louisa May Alcott. Martí once wrote a profile of him called "Alcott the Platonian" and also profiled his daughter.

3. *Phrynes:* A Greek courtesan, the lover and model of the sculptor Praxiteles, Phryne was once accused of having profaned the Eleusinian mysteries and is said to have defended herself by opening her robe to display her charms to the judges.

4. *Tusculum:* An ancient city fifteen miles to the northwest of Rome, where Cicero composed his *Tusculan Disputations.*

5. *John Tyndall* (1820–93): British natural philosopher who studied the flow of glaciers and was a well-known popularizer of scientific theories.

6. *Pedro Calderón de la Barca* (1600–81): One of the great dramatists of the Golden Age of Spanish literature; author of *La Vida es sueña* (Life Is a Dream).

7. *Pindar* (522?–438? B.C.): Greek poet known primarily for his odes composed on commission to celebrate famous victors at athletic events such as the Olympic Games.

TRIBUTES TO KARL MARX, WHO HAS DIED

1. As originally published in *La Nación*, this piece began with a two-page description of the burial of the American poet John Payne and a paragraph deploring the pompous funeral given to a deceased pugilist, George Elliott.

2. *Liberty's power:* Martí's description of the memorial meeting in honor of Karl Marx has been published in English twice before, in *Inside the Monster: Writings on the United States and American Imperialism by José Martí,* edited by Philip S. Foner (New York and London: Monthly Review Press, 1975), and in *José Martí Reader: Writings on the Americas,* edited by Deborah Shnookal and Mirta Muñiz (Melbourne and New York: Ocean Press, 1999). Neither volume includes the first paragraph published here or notes the omission. Both also omit all that is subsequent to the account of the memorial meeting, though it is rather striking that Martí chose

to round out his account of Marx's memorial with a discussion of the education of women and a description of a lavish costume ball in a Vanderbilt mansion.

3. *Lecovitch:* Probably a mistaken reference to Sergius E. Schevitsch, a Russian of noble birth and former diplomat for Russia who became the leader of the Socialist Labor Party and editor of the *New Yorker Volkszeitung*, and was one of the first to speak at Marx's New York memorial meeting. (See Martí's subsequent allusion to him in "Class War in Chicago," note 5 on page 430.)

4. *John Swinton* (1830–1901): Managing editor of the *New York Times* during the Civil War and subsequently chief editorial writer for the *New York Sun*, in which he published an interview with Karl Marx on September 6, 1880. From 1883 to 1887, he published *John Swinton's Paper*, the foremost labor newspaper of the time.

5. *Johann Most* (1846–1906): German anarchist who spent years in and out of jail in Austria, Germany, and England; editor of the anarchist journal *Freiheit*. He, too, would figure in Martí's "Class War in Chicago."

6. *Théodore Millot:* Former secretary of Section 2 of the First International in the United States.

7. *Magure:* Probably Peter J. McGuire (1852–1914), born in New York of Irish parents. He took night classes at the Cooper Institute while an apprentice to a wood-joiner and eventually became a founding member of the Social Democratic Party of North America and one of the leaders of the American Federation of Labor.

8. *Henry George* (1839–97): U.S. reformer and founder of the "Single-Tax Movement," which held that since land ownership tends to enrich the owner at the expense of the community, it is the cause of poverty and therefore all taxes should be eliminated except the tax on land. (Though some—such as Massachusetts senator Henry Dawes [see page 157]—accused him of seeking to abolish private ownership of land, George never advocated any such remedy.) Martí alludes to George dozens of times throughout his work, always admiringly. George, he said in 1886, is "one of the sanest, most daring, and wholesome thinkers who cast their eyes on the muddled entrails of the universe today." "Only Darwin in the natural sciences has made a mark comparable to George's on social science," he wrote in 1887.

George's book *Progress and Poverty* (1879) sold millions of copies all over the world, and its influence extended across Latin America. An article titled "As Latin America Sees Us," in the December 1924 issue of H. L. Mencken's *The American Mercury*, cited a recent letter from Chilean critic Armando Donoso, who wrote, "Henry George has converted a fair percentage of our cranks to his single-tax theory."

9. *Edwin Dennison Morgan* (1811–83): U.S. merchant and philanthropist and one of the "war governors" of New York State, who held office from 1859 to 1863. A founding member of the Republican party, Morgan was the state's first Republican governor. As a member of the state senate from 1850 to 1853, he procured the passage of the bill that provided for the establishment of Central Park in New York City.

10. *Benjamin Franklin Butler* (1818–93): U.S. politician and Union general in the Civil War whose high-handed military governorship of New Orleans (May to December 1862) earned him the nickname "Beast" and who aroused similarly intense antagonisms throughout his life. After having served in Congress as a radical Republican from 1867 to 1875, Butler was elected governor of Massachusetts on a joint Democratic and Greenback ticket in 1882, but served only one term.

11. Disastrous floods had inundated Ohio in February of 1883, and in an article written that month, Martí had deplored the indifference of New Yorkers to the Ohioans' plight.

12. *Cambridge University:* Though women took university examinations at Cambridge in the 1880s, they were not awarded university degrees until after 1921, and their colleges were not admitted to full university status until 1948.

13. *College similar to Girton:* Barnard College was founded in 1889 as the women's undergraduate unit of Columbia and was incorporated into the university in 1900.

14. *Vanderbilt:* On March 26, 1883, the new mansion of William Kissam Vanderbilt—at 660 Fifth Avenue, on the corner of Fifth Avenue and Fifty-second Street, not far from Saint Patrick's Cathedral—was inaugurated with New York's first costume ball in a generation, attended by eight hundred guests. Designed by Richard Morris Hunt, the mansion was singled out in an 1885 survey of the leading architects of the United States as one of the three best buildings in the country, following H. H. Richardson's Trinity Church in Boston, and the United States Capitol. In the midtwentieth century it was torn down to make way for a block-wide office tower at 666 Fifth Avenue.

15. *Raimundo de Madrazo y Garreta* (1841–1920): Spanish painter, from a celebrated family of painters. In 1880 Martí had written an article about him that was published in *The Hour.*

The Brooklyn Bridge

1. At this point, five pages of very specific information on the measurements of the Brooklyn Bridge and its towers, its cables, the materials from which it was built, the history and methodology of its construction, and so on have been omitted.

Indigenous Art

1. *Bartholdi's statue:* The Statue of Liberty, or *Liberty Enlightening the World,* by Frédéric-Auguste Bartholdi, erected on Bedloes Island in New York Harbor and dedicated on October 28, 1886. Martí wrote an impassioned panegyric to the statue, published in the Buenos Aires newspaper *La Nación* on January 1, 1887.

2. *William Makepeace Thackeray* (1811–63): English novelist and satirist who first gained a reputation as a caricaturist and went on to write such novels as *The Memoirs of Barry Lyndon* (1844) and *Vanity Fair* (1848).

MEXICO, THE UNITED STATES, AND PROTECTIONISM

1. *As Nessus turned against his tunic:* In Greek mythology, Nessus was a centaur who rashly abducted Heracles' wife, Deianeira, and was then shot by Heracles with an arrow dipped in the Hydra's blood. As he was dying, Nessus gave his bloodstained shirt to Deianeira, telling her it was a charm to ensure her husband's love, but when she gave Heracles the shirt to wear, the Hydra's poison destroyed him.

GRADUATION DAY

1. *Jaime Balmes* (1810–48): Spanish cleric and philosopher whose manual of applied logic, *El criterio,* was widely used in schools throughout the Spanish-speaking world.

2. *Shooter of sepoys:* A reference to the Indian Mutiny of 1857 to 1858 in which British forces took savage reprisals against the native troops, or sepoys.

THE INDIANS IN THE UNITED STATES

1. *Henry George's:* See note 8 to "Tributes to Karl Marx" on page 425.

2. *Tremendous revelations about Lord Byron:* In 1869, Harriet Beecher Stowe (1811–96) published an article in the *Atlantic Monthly* alleging (correctly, many scholars now believe) that the poet Lord Byron had engaged in an incestuous affair with his half sister, Augusta. Stowe's popularity in England suffered from the resulting scandal, but she remained a leading figure in the United States, where *Uncle Tom's Cabin* sold more than three hundred thousand copies in 1852, the year it was published.

3. *Helen Hunt Jackson* (1830–85): Writer and champion of the rights of Indians in the United States whose famous romance *Ramona* (1884), an emphatic presentation of their plight, was regarded by Martí as so important that he translated it himself and published it at his own expense in 1888.

4. *Alice Fletcher* (1838–1923): Ethnologist, musicologist, feminist, and champion of what she viewed as Native American welfare. She was born in Havana, though Martí is unlikely to have known that.

5. *Erastus Brooks* (1815–86): Well-known journalist and former editor-in-chief of the *New York Express.*

THE WORLD'S BIGGEST EXPLOSION

1. *Brevet Major General John Newton* (1823–95): Fought in the Civil War with distinction but is primarily remembered for his removal of two of the largest obstructions—Hallets Point and Flood Rock—at the entrance to the East River from Long Island Sound. From 1888 until his death, he was president of the Panama Railway.

IMPRESSIONIST PAINTERS

1. *Knights of Labor:* Union founded by Philadelphia tailors in 1869, which grew to national prominence over the subsequent decade and eventually included

women and black workers. In 1886, the year this article was written, the Knights of Labor organized a strike against the Missouri Pacific Railway that ultimately failed; all in all there were 1,600 strikes in 1886, involving about 600,000 workers.

2. *Paul Durand-Ruel* (1831–1922): Art dealer and early champion of the Impressionists who began buying their works in the 1870s, when they were shunned by the art establishment. The 1886 exhibit of Impressionist art that Durand-Ruel organized at the National Academy of Design in New York City was so successful that he opened a branch of his gallery in New York the following year. Though advertised as a show of Impressionist paintings, it included works by the more traditional academic artists whom the Impressionists scorned as *pompiers,* or "firemen."

3. *Jean-Paul Laurens* (1838–1921): French painter, primarily known for his history paintings and academic murals.

4. *Alfred Philippe Roll* (1846–?): French painter, initially influenced by Géricault and Courbet. He became "official painter" to the French government and was given numerous commissions for commemorative pictures and the decoration of public buildings.

5. *François-Séverin Marceau* (1769–96): French general who vanquished the Austrians at Neuwied (1795) and was mortally wounded at Altenkirchen.

6. *Sir Lawrence Alma-Tadema* (1836–1912): British painter best known for his scholarly, meticulous paintings of scenes from Greek and Roman life.

THE CUTTING CASE

This article does not appear in the Editorial de Ciencias Sociales edition of Martí's *Obras completas* (Havana, 1975) but is taken from the valuable compilation of additional texts by Martí compiled by Ernesto Mejía Sánchez, *Nuevas cartas de Nueva York* (Mexico City: Siglo Veintiuno, 1980).

1. *Colonel Francis Cutting* (1828–92): One of the founders of the American Annexationist League, which was established in 1878 to promote the annexation of territories adjacent to the United States. Cutting was also president of the Company for the Occupation and Development of Northern Mexico and had deliberately had himself arrested in Mexico in order to provoke a war between the two countries.

The league's ambitions were not exclusively directed toward Latin America. In an article that appeared in *El Partido Liberal* on June 23, 1887, Martí described a New York meeting of the American Annexationist League attended by "delegates . . . from across southern and eastern Canada—delegates of no little note, since two of them are deputies in the Dominion's parliament" who declared that "in New Brunswick not a single citizen wants to be English . . . and all of Manitoba is annexation-minded."

2. *Thomas Francis Bayard* (1828–98): U.S. statesman of long and distinguished lineage, who succeeded his father in the U.S. Senate in 1869 and was secretary of state during the first Cleveland administration (1885–89).

3. *President of the Mexican Republic and Señor Romero Rubio:* Mexico's president at the time was Porfirio Díaz (1830–1915), whose dictatorship lasted with minor interruptions from 1876 to 1911, and whose ascension to power had been the reason for Martí's own departure from Mexico in 1877. Juan Romero Rubio was Díaz's secretary of state in the late 1880s.

4. *Robert Roberts Hitt* (1834–1906): Republican congressman from Indiana and longtime chairman of the Committee on Foreign Affairs. In 1871, before being elected to Congress, he was part of a commission that visited the Dominican Republic to investigate its resources, with a view to annexation. A treaty of annexation was negotiated and approved by the Dominican people, but the U.S. Senate failed to ratify it.

5. *Barbaric killings of Chinamen:* A reference to the massacre of Chinese workers in Rock Springs, Wyoming, when white members of the Knights of Labor brutally ransacked the Chinese section of the town, killing twenty-eight Chinese and wounding fifteen. Martí had described the events in detail in an article published in *La Nación* on October 23, 1885.

6. *1848:* The year when the United States invaded Mexico and annexed almost half of Mexico's national territory, now the states of California, Arizona, and New Mexico.

THE POET WALT WHITMAN

1. *Banned:* In March 1882, the Boston district attorney, acting on behalf of the Society for the Suppression of Vice, had written to the publisher of the sixth edition of *Leaves of Grass* accusing it of being "obscene literature." Whitman offered to make revisions, but ultimately the book was withdrawn from the Boston market and published later that year in Philadelphia.

2. *William Ewart Gladstone* (1809–98): British statesman who served as prime minister four times (1868–74, 1880–85, 1886, and 1892–94) and advocated home rule for Ireland.

3. *The work-people:* Martí, who generally translates quite accurately, places these lines in quotation marks, but there is nothing quite like them in Whitman's poetry, though three lines from different points of "Song of Myself" are similar: "The flap of the curtained litter—the sick man inside, borne to the hospital"; "What exclamations of women taken suddenly, who hurry home and give birth to babes"; and "the loud laugh of the work-people at their meals" (or, from "I Sing the Body Electric," "The group of laborers seated at noon-time with their open dinner-kettles").

4. *I will embrace him:* Here again, the lines originally appear in quotation marks as if they were Whitman's, but Martí has altered them. The lines of "Song of Myself" that more or less correspond to these are "Let the physician and the priest go home. / I seize the descending man and raise him with resistless will, / O despairer, here is my neck, / By God, you shall not go down! hang your whole weight upon me.

/ I dilate you with tremendous breath, I buoy you up, / Every room of the house do I fill with an arm'd force, / Lovers of me, bafflers of graves. / Sleep—I and they keep guard all night, / Not doubt, not decease shall dare to lay finger upon you, / I have embraced you, and henceforth possess you to myself, / And when you rise in the morning you will find what I tell you is / so."

In quoting from Whitman, Martí sometimes, consciously or unconsciously, creates poems of his own that allude to Whitman's work but are distinct from it.

5. *Lusts of Virgil for Cebes and of Horace for Gyges and Lysiscus:* Lysiscus, meaning "little wolf," engages in a predatory affair with the narrator of Horace's *Epodes,* who mention Gyges in passing as a pretty little boy with flowing hair. Cebes was a male slave belonging to Virgil's patron, Maecenas, who gave him to Virgil when Virgil took a liking to him—an incident recounted by Servius, one of Virgil's commentators. Martí may have selected these rather obscure examples of homosexuality in ancient Greece because each has a predatory or exploitative aspect, and that, rather than the simple fact of homosexuality, is perhaps what he finds "vile" about them.

CLASS WAR IN CHICAGO: A TERRIBLE DRAMA

1. *Howells . . . Adler . . . Train:* William Dean Howells (1837–1920), one of the leading North American novelists of the day; Felix Adler (1851–1933), author of many books on political and social ethics and founder of the ethical culture movement; George Francis Train (1829–1904), eccentric financier and supporter of the women's movement.

2. *Johann Most* (1846–1906): Notorious, frequently imprisoned German anarchist who emigrated to the United States in 1882, where he became symbolic in the popular mind of all the most fearsome aspects of anarchism. (See note 5 to "Tributes to Karl Marx" on page 425.)

3. *Eight legally permitted hours:* Though Ulysses S. Grant had signed a National Eight-Hour Law proclamation during his presidency, the eight-hour standard did not, in fact, become enforceable federal law in the United States until the Fair Labor Standards Act of 1938.

4. *Tinvilles, Henriots, and Chaumettes:* Like Robespierre, Marat, and Danton, mentioned in the previous sentence, and Saint-Just and Desmoulins, cited earlier, these men were participants in the French Revolution, all three known for their ultra-revolutionary stance. Antoine-Quentin Fouquier-Tinville (1746–95) was a pitiless public prosecutor for the revolutionary Tribunal; François Hanriot (1761–94), the commander of the sans-culottes forces during the Terror; and Pierre-Gaspard Chaumette (1763–94), the chief magistrate of the Commune.

5. *Schevitsch's . . . newspaper:* Sergius E. Schevitsch was the editor of the leading German-language organ of the Socialist Labor Party, the *New Yorker Volkszeitung.*

6. *Lyman Trumbull* (1813–96): U.S. senator from Illinois who said it was "about impossible that [the anarchists] should have a fair and impartial trial" in view of the nationwide furor.

7. *Fielden and Schwab had received their pardons:* Illinois governor Oglesby commuted their death sentences to life imprisonment. Along with Oscar Neebe, they were subsequently granted a full and outright pardon and released from jail in 1895 by newly elected governor John Peter Altgeld, who wrote a lengthy denunciation of the anarchists' trial.

8. *The Weaver:* The German-Jewish poet Heinrich Heine (1797–1856) wrote a dirge for the weavers of the Prussian province of Silesia in 1844, when they were violently protesting their intolerable working conditions. It was later translated into English by Friedrich Engels and was much admired in Communist circles. Here, it is translated from Martí's own Spanish translation, to reflect his understanding of it.

A WALKING MARATHON

1. *Peleus:* in Greek mythology, the father of Achilles.

2. *Steve Brodie* (1863–1901): Brooklyn bookmaker who became famous by supposedly jumping off the Brooklyn Bridge on July 23, 1886, and surviving, though rumors that he had used a dummy were persistent.

BLAINE'S NIGHT

1. *Events Martí alludes to:* See note 7 to "The Trial of Guiteau" on page 423.

2. *Joseph Benson Foraker* (1846–1917): American political leader who served in the Civil War as a young man and went on to become a judge. He was governor of Ohio at the time this article was written and was elected to the Senate in 1896. He strongly supported the McKinley administration in the debates surrounding the Spanish-American War and sponsored the 1900 Foraker Act, under which the United States instituted a civil government in Puerto Rico while retaining control of the island.

3. *Letters that proved he had criminally profited from his legislative position for personal gain:* Shortly before the Republican convention of 1876, a Democratic House committee alleged that Blaine had used his influence to secure land for a railroad in Arkansas and had then sold the railroad's bonds at a handsome commission. Proof of this lay in the famous "Mulligan letters" which Blaine privately got hold of before they could be placed on record. He never handed them over, but read portions of them before the House in his own defense. The scandal lost him that year's Republican nomination for the presidency.

4. *William Maxwell Evarts* (1818–1901): The lawyer who was government counsel in the abortive trial of Jefferson Davis for treason and who later defended President Andrew Johnson against impeachment. He represented New York in the Senate from 1885 to 1891.

A CHINESE FUNERAL

1. *Li-In-Du:* A mysterious figure. The *New York Herald* of October 30, 1888, devoted several paragraphs to the funeral of "General Lee Yu Doo," which it proudly described as "the finest Chinese funeral procession ever seen in this country outside of San Francisco." The *Herald* identified Lee Yu Doo as a "native of Annam, province of Tonquin, China" (a place Martí had written about in *The Golden Age*) and hailed him as a chieftain of the Black Flags, who, after having "inflicted repeated defeats upon the French troops during the recent Tonquin war," subsequently became a partner in several flourishing Chinese grocery stores in New York, the principal one at 28 Mott Street, and the grand master of the Lun Gee Tong Society, headquartered on Pell Street. (The "Tong" societies that sprang up in Chinatowns across the United States were then considered by outsiders to be a kind of Chinese Freemasonry.)

At the 1889 annual meeting of the American Folk-Lore Society, however, Stewart Culin delivered a report on Chinese secret societies in which he mentioned the October 1888 funeral of "a somewhat distinguished member" of the Lun-Gee-Tong lodge in New York named "Lee You Du." "He was reported in the newspapers at the time to have been a 'General of the Black Flags' in China," said Culin, "but in reality was only a poor clerk who had won the regard of the entire Chinese community by the probity of his character. He had held office as one of the councillors of the [Lun-Gee-Tong] and his funeral was made the occasion for a great demonstration on the part of the society."

Nevertheless, Martí's description of the funeral is far more detailed and extensive than Culin's or the *Herald*'s; he may well have had more and better information about the deceased than they did.

2. *Black Flags:* Bands of Chinese rebels who roamed the mountains of Tonkin, in what is now northern Vietnam, where they had been driven after the suppression of the Yunnan (1855–72) and Taiping (1850–64) rebellions against the Manchu dynasty. They took a leading role in beating back the French invasions of Tonkin in 1873 and 1883.

3. See note 5 to "The Cutting Case" on page 429.

4. *Tao:* Literally, "path." An ancient philosophical system stemming from the *Tao-te-ching,* a text written in the third century B.C., which instructs humans to abjure all striving. Martí's description of a peculiarly anthropomorphic Tao may be attributable to the nature of the information he was given by former Taiping rebels. Hung Hsiu-ch'üan, the visionary leader of the Taiping (Great Peace) Rebellion, in which Li-In-Du apparently took part, had studied Christianity for two months with an American Protestant missionary named Roberts and believed himself to be the younger brother of Jesus Christ. He subsequently evolved a syncretistic Taoism influenced by Christian theology, which even included a Taoist version of the Ten Commandments.

5. *Ts'ai-Shen:* Still one of the most widely worshiped gods in the Chinese pantheon, whose images are sold in the street during Chinese New Year.

6. *Kuan-Ti:* Another very popular Chinese deity, the God of Battle or of War, a historical Han general who died in A.D. 220 and was not deified until the sixteenth century.

7. *Victory at Nanking:* The conquest of Nanking in 1853 was the great victory of the Taiping Rebellion (see note 4 on page 432), one of the most massive upheavals of the nineteenth century, which brought death to upward of 30 million people.

8. *A law that would deport the celestial one:* The Chinese Exclusion Act of 1888 was one of a series of Chinese exclusion laws, beginning in 1882, which banned the immigration of Chinese laborers and jeopardized the status of the Chinese living in the United States.

9. *The eight pure insignia:* Here again, the anthropomorphic Tao that Martí describes is extremely anomalous. The insignia he saw probably referred to the life of one of the countless Taoist deities, though which one is not clear. Eight is one of the most auspicious numbers in Chinese religion, and Taoism has its Eight Immortals, but only three of them coincide with these eight insignia: the flute, the sword, and the flowers.

INAUGURATION DAY

1. *Lovely mistress:* One of the highlights of the first Cleveland administration was the president's 1886 marriage to Frances Folsom, his former ward.

2. *Samoa:* Since 1879 Germany, Great Britain, and the United States had all had ports in Samoa, though no single power had appropriated the island. However, in 1887 a civil war broke out over the succession to the native kingship; the Germans supported one pretender to the throne and the British and Americans supported another. In the course of the fighting, some fifty German sailors and marines were killed by supporters of the British and American would-be king. A tripartite treaty was signed in 1889, but the situation remained unstable.

3. *Panama canal company:* In 1878 a French company obtained a concession from the Colombian government for the construction of an interoceanic canal through Panama, and work on it began a few years later. On February 20, 1889, Congress had approved the incorporation of the Maritime Canal Company of Nicaragua, the "endorsement" Martí alludes to here. Work on a Nicaragua canal began in June of that year, but the company went bankrupt in 1893. The Nicaragua canal was widely considered the better route, but after the French company went into bankruptcy, the United States acquired its rights and property in Panama in 1903, and thereafter focused on completing the work the French had begun.

4. *Sheridan's widow:* General Philip Henry Sheridan (1831–88) was a Union general in the Civil War who was made commanding general of the U.S. Army in 1884.

5. *Surplus:* High import tariffs put in place during the Civil War had left the U.S. Treasury with a large surplus, and Cleveland had devoted the entirety of his 1887

message to Congress to the need for lower tariffs. The plan to purchase Cuba mentioned earlier in this article was seen, in part, as a way to use up the Treasury surplus (see prefatory note to "A Vindication of Cuba" on page 261).

6. *Our battles:* The Treasury surplus encouraged a great deal of "pork barrel" legislation that Cleveland generally vetoed.

7. *John James Ingalls* (1833–1900): U.S. senator from Kansas, who in the late 1870s was investigated on charges of having bribed and corrupted members of the Kansas legislature to secure his reelection.

8. *Melville Weston Fuller* (1833–1910): Prominent Chicago lawyer who was appointed chief justice by Cleveland and was also a member (1900–10) of the Hague Tribunal. Justice Fuller is not known to have published any poetry during his lifetime, or to have taken any special interest in poetry, and the question of why Martí describes him as "the poet Fuller" remains open.

9. *Hannibal Hamlin* (1809–91): U.S. vice president (1861–65), and minister to Spain from 1881 to 1882.

10. *James Gillespie Blaine* (1830–93): See "Blaine's Night," page 231.

11. *George Franklin Edmunds* (1828–1919): U.S. senator from Vermont.

12. *John Sherman* (1823–1900): U.S. senator from Ohio; sponsor of the Sherman Antitrust Act of 1890, the first congressional measure prohibiting trusts.

13. *George Frisbie Hoar* (1806–1904): U.S. senator from Massachusetts, a notable opponent of President William McKinley's imperial ambitions.

14. *Levi Morton* (1824–1920): Founder of the New York City banking firm of Levi P. Morton and Company, which became one of the most powerful banks in the United States. He served as minister to France (1881–85) before being elected vice president. He was later governor of New York.

LETTER TO EMILIO NÚÑEZ

1. *Calixto García* (1839–98): Cuban revolutionary who attained the rank of major general during the Ten Years War. When the enemy captured him in 1874, he tried to take his own life by sticking a gun into his throat, directly beneath his chin, and firing it. He bore the scar of the exit wound on his forehead for the rest of his life. After his humiliation in the Guerra Chiquita, he went on to fight once more in the war of independence and died in Washington, D.C., where he was negotiating with the U.S. government on behalf of the Cuban army.

2. *Emilio Núñez* (1855–1922): Cuban revolutionary who achieved the rank of comandante as a young soldier in the Ten Years War. In the aftermath of the Guerra Chiquita, he settled in Philadelphia, and wrote to Martí to thank him for having saved him from "certain death." In 1895, he was made chief of expeditions in the United States by the revolutionary army, and eventually held important positions in the Republic of Cuba, including the vice presidency.

3. *Bound for Cuba:* Martí's wife, Carmen Zayas-Bazán, did in fact leave him that October to return to Cuba, and took his son José Francisco with her. She returned in December 1882, along with the child, and stayed until March 1885, when she again left with the boy.

LETTER TO GENERAL MÁXIMO GÓMEZ

1. *Truly great:* On the back of this letter, Gómez noted an account of the incident that inspired it, and added: "This man insults me recklessly. Only one who knew the degree of sympathy I felt for him would have an idea of how acutely sensitive I am to his judgments."

A VINDICATION OF CUBA

1. *Joseph Benson Foraker* (1846–1917): See note 2 to "Blaine's Night" on page 431.

2. *Francis Cutting:* Leader of the American Annexationist League. (See Martí's 1886 article "The Cutting Case" [page 176], about Cutting's attempt to provoke the United States into war with Mexico.)

3. *José María Heredia* (1803–39): Influential Cuban poet who, like Martí, lived in exile in the United States and Mexico. He is best known for the poems *El Niágara*, an impassioned hymn to Niagara Falls, and *En el Teocalli de Cholula*, which evokes Mexico's pre-Columbian past. (See introductory note on page 43.)

4. *More than one American bled by our side:* Joseph Fry is one example of a North American who came to the aid of the Cubans during the Ten Years War. In 1873, as captain of the *Virgilius*, which was fraudulently flying the United States flag, he attempted to carry arms to the Cuban insurgents. He was captured by the Spaniards off the Cuban coast, and he and fifty-two of the ship's crew and passengers were put to death.

SIMPLE VERSES / *VERSOS SENCILLOS*

1. *López and Walker:* Narciso López (1798?–1851) and William Walker (1824–60) were both filibusters, backed by private armies of volunteers and mercenaries recruited in the United States, who invaded Cuba and Nicaragua, respectively. López was of Venezuelan origins but had lived for many years in Cuba and was a fervent partisan of Cuban annexation to the United States; he was captured by the Spanish authorities and put to death along with fifty of his volunteers on his last attempted invasion of Cuba. Walker, a native of Nashville, Tennessee, tried to conquer Baja California and Sonora in 1853–54; when that failed he set out for Nicaragua, where he succeeded in declaring himself president in July 1856. Less than a year later, he surrendered to the U.S. Navy, which brought him back to the United States for trial. Viewed as a national hero by many, he was promptly acquitted. In 1860 he made his

final attempt to conquer Central America; his life ended in front of a Honduran firing squad that September.

2. These and other lines from the first poem in *Versos sencillos* are well known to many English-speaking readers as the lyrics to the song "Guántanamera," with its famous chorus *"Guántanamera, guajira guántanamera."* (A *guajira* can be either a typical girl from the country or a certain kind of country song with a characteristic alternating rhythm; thus a *guajira Guántanamera* is a girl or song from the Cuban town of Guantánamo.)

The origins of the song are diverse. In the 1940s, a popular Cuban radio show was called *La Guántanamera;* its star was Joseíto Fernández, a well-known singer of *guajiras.* The different segments of the show were ushered in and out with a chorus of *"Guántanamera, guajira Guántanamera."* According to musicologist Tony Evora, the idea of using Martí's poem as lyrics for the "Guántanamera" song originated with the Spanish composer Julián Orbón (1925–91) who lived in Havana between 1940 and 1963, when he moved to New York and taught at the Manhattan School of Music. Orbón's student, Héctor Angulo, gave Orbón's version to Pete Seeger (and shared songwriting credit on Seeger's recording), and it was Seeger who first popularized the version of "Guántanamera," with lyrics taken from Martí's *Versos sencillos,* that is famous today. Later, a group named The Sandpipers scored a hit with the song on the U.S. pop charts.

The reference to the town of Guantánamo that the song attaches to Martí's verses is not irrelevant to its enshrinement as an unofficial Cuban anthem. Guantánamo is located on the southeastern coast of Cuba near the point where Martí and his five companions clandestinely disembarked in 1895. Since the adoption of the Cuban constitution of 1902, which included the U.S.-imposed Platt Amendment, giving the United States both the final say on many matters of Cuban governance and the right to build naval bases on Cuba, it has been the site of a U.S. naval base.

NOTEBOOKS 18–20

1. *Netzahualcóyotl* (1402–72): Poet and king of the Chichimec people who lived in the Valley of Mexico. (See note 2 to "Prizefight" on page 424.)

2. *Mitla . . . the Governor's Palace:* Mitla: a sacred city of the Zapotecs, near present-day Oaxaca in Mexico; its great temples are famous for their elaborate geometric decoration. The Governor's Palace, or "Casa del Gobernador": one of the central buildings of the late-classic Maya city of Uxmal, located on the Yucatán peninsula; it has some twenty thousand carved stone elements in its facade.

3. *Bryce and Noailles:* Viscount James Bryce (1838–1922) was the author of *The American Commonwealth* (1889), which Martí praised at some length in the course of a review of Max O'Rell's *Jonathan and His Continent,* published in *El Partido Liberal* in February 1889. Jules Charles Victurnien, duc de Noailles (1826–95), wrote *Cent*

ans de république aux Etats-Unis (A Hundred Years of Republican Government in the United States).

4. *Postrimerías:* Elusive Spanish word meaning, roughly, "last days," "final moments," "close," "end."

OUR AMERICA

1. *Juan de Castellanos* (1522–1607): Spanish poet and chronicler of the conquest of New Granada (now Colombia) in which he took part.

2. *Emmanuel Joseph Sieyès* (1748–1836): Author of the famous tract *The Third Estate* (1789) and leading figure in the French Revolution, who subsequently assisted Napoleon in his coup d'état.

3. *A priest:* Miguel Hidalgo y Costilla (1753–1811), an elderly priest, initiated Mexico's revolution of independence in the town of Dolores at the head of a band of Indians and with the help of the wife of the mayor of nearby Querétaro, Josefa Ortíz de Domínguez (1768–1829).

4. *Not the lesser one, turned back:* In South America, revolutions of independence emerged in 1810, in Venezuela, under Simón Bolívar (1783–1830), and in 1813, in Argentina, under José de San Martín (1778–1850). Bolívar's forces gradually made their way south, as San Martín's came north, and the two leaders eventually met in July 1822, in Guayaquíl. After that meeting, San Martín renounced his title as Protector of Peru and left South America to live in France.

5. *Bernardino Rivadivia* (1780–1845): Argentine politician who defended his country against English invaders and then fought for its independence. Elected as the first president of the United Provinces of Río de la Plata in 1826, he was forced to resign by the caudillo Quiroga and went into exile, living out his life in the Spanish city of Cádiz.

6. *Iturbide's Congress:* Agustín de Iturbide (1783–1824), Mexican general who initially fought against Mexico's independence movement. He later joined forces with insurgent general Guerrero to assure Mexico's independence. But instead of the liberal state envisioned by the insurgents, Iturbide ushered in a conservative one. When his soldiers proclaimed him emperor, the newly independent Mexican Congress, angry but cowed, ratified the proclamation (1822). A revolution soon broke out against him, and in 1823 he was forced to abdicate.

7. *Zorilla-esque:* A reference to José Zorilla (1817–93), a romantic Spanish poet. Martí did not share in the popular enthusiasm for Zorilla's work.

8. *Benito Juárez* (1806–72): Widely revered as one of Latin America's greatest nineteenth-century political figures, Juárez was a Zapotec Indian who was president of Mexico from 1857 to 1863, and again from 1867 until his death.

9. *Cemi:* A spirit worshiped by the Taino, an indigenous people of the Caribbean. The cemi (or zemi) is often represented in the form of a tricornered clay object.

The Lynching of the Italians

1. *Lalla Rookh* (1817): A series of four linked Oriental tales in verse by Thomas Moore (see note 28 of "War Diaries" on page 442), which tell of Lalla Rookh, daughter of the emperor of Delhi, who, on her way to meet her betrothed, is entertained by a young Persian poet who turns out to be her betrothed.

2. *Bourbons:* Most contemporary theories locate the origins of the Mafia in feudal times; the theory that it was formed to combat the Bourbons conflates it with the Carbonari, a secret society, possibly an offshoot of Freemasonry, which arose in southern Italy during the Napoleonic wars and fought a number of enemies, including the Bourbon king Ferdinand IV, in order to free the country from foreign rule and obtain constitutional rights.

The Monetary Conference of the American Republics

1. *Who does not speak Spanish:* Elsewhere in the article Martí mentions that the representative of Honduras at the Monetary Conference was a North American admiral's son who did not speak Spanish.

2. *A single tenacious and daring U.S. politician:* A reference to J. G. Blaine (see "Blaine's Night," on page 231) who, as secretary of state under Harrison, had organized both the Pan-American Conference and the Monetary Conference.

3. *Obscure, dangerous, and impossible alliances:* Blaine was in the process of negotiating a number of reciprocal tariff treaties with Latin American countries, though he was ultimately prevented from doing so by the McKinley Tariff Act.

A Town Sets a Black Man on Fire

This article does not appear in Martí's *Obras completas*, though he considered it one of his most important and listed it in the "literary testament" he wrote at the end of his life. It was first reprinted in the *Nuevas cartas de Nueva York*, edited by Ernesto Mejía Sánchez (Mexico City: Siglo Veintiuno, 1980).

The Abolition of Slavery in Puerto Rico

1. *That revolution:* The Ten Years War (1868–78), Cuba's first revolution of independence.

2. *"¡Viva la república!":* Spain's First Republic, which followed the abdication of King Amadeo in February 1873, lasted only until December 1874, when the Bourbon Alfonso XII was placed on the throne by a coalition of moderate parties. Martí was living in Madrid at the time of the First Republic. (See note 1 to "Political Prison in Cuba" on page 419.)

3. *Nicolás Salmerón y Alonso* (1838–1908): Spanish politician and philosopher who was the third president of Spain's First Republic in the year 1873, succeeding Estanislao Figueras and Francisco Pi y Margall.

4. *Julián Acosta* (1825–91): Eminent Puerto Rican politician, writer, scientist, and abolitionist.

5. *General Rafael Primo de Rivera y Sobremonte:* Spaniard of deeply rooted liberal convictions who was appointed governor of Puerto Rico by Spain's First Republic and served from March 1873 to February 1874.

6. *"La Borinqueña":* A popular Puerto Rican folk song. *Borinquén* was the Taino name for the island of Puerto Rico, and the tribe that first inhabited it was known as *Borinqueños.*

7. *Segundo Ruiz Belvis* (1829–67): Leading figure in the Puerto Rican abolitionist and independence movement who, with José Julián Acosta and Francisco Moriano Quiñones, was appointed to a commission sent in 1865 to take part in the Junta de Información in Madrid, to furnish information to the liberal Spanish government then in power about the Caribbean colonies' needs. A new government took over before the commissioners arrived in Spain; though it was indifferent to their cause, they presented it with a "Plan for the Abolition of Slavery in Puerto Rico."

The commissioners returned to Puerto Rico to find that the government there was preparing to throw them and other leading abolitionists out of the country. Ruiz Belvis and Ramón Emeterio Betances (see note 8 below) slipped out of the country on a ship that took them to New York. Ruiz Belvis subsequently embarked on a tour of South American countries to seek aid for the Puerto Rican cause. By the time he reached Chile, his health was seriously weakened; he died there in 1867.

8. *Ramón Emeterio Betances* (1830–98): A medical doctor who formed a secret abolitionist society in 1855 and later planned and led the Puerto Rican independence movement, which openly revolted against Spain on September 23, 1868, with the "Grito de Lares" (Cry of Lares), while Betances was still in exile (see note 7 above).

To Cuba!

1. *Humble worker's quota:* For several years, the tobacco workers had been contributing a percentage of their wages to the Cuban Revolutionary Party, to fund Cuba's revolution of independence.

2. *Seidenberg:* Seidenberg & Co. was the Key West cigar factory that was most aggressively pursuing the idea of a move to Tampa.

Letter to Manuel Mercado

1. *Arsenio Martínez Campos* (1831–1900): Governor of Cuba, who, as commander in chief of the Spanish forces in Cuba, had negotiated the Pact of Zanjón, which brought an end to the Ten Years War. On September 23, 1893, Spanish anarchists had attempted to assassinate Martínez Campos as he presided over a military parade in Barcelona. He remained in power in Cuba through 1895, but was replaced

in 1896 by Valeriano Weyler (1838–1930), who initiated the infamous policy of *reconcentración* against the rebels and the civilian population.

2. *Manuel Gutiérrez Nájera* (1859–95): Mexican poet known as "Duque Job." He founded the influential *Revista Azul* (Blue Review), and, like Martí himself, was an important precursor of *Modernismo*, the most influential Latin American literary movement of the early twentieth century.

WAR DIARIES

A great deal of work has recently been done on the *War Diaries*. This translation was assisted by the superb annotated and illustrated edition by Mayra Beatriz Martínez and Froilán Escobar (Havana: Casa Editora Abril, 1996), which clarifies many misreadings and ellipses in the original text and provides enormously useful contextual information. The edition published in Spain by Galaxia Gutenberg in 1997, with a prologue by Guillermo Cabrera Infante, a chronology by Enrico Mario Santí, and a glossary by Manuel Pereira, is also extremely helpful.

1. The girls to whom this dedication is addressed were Carmita and María Mantilla, the adolescent daughters of Martí's long-time companion Carmen Miyares (1841–1925), whose son, Manuel Mantilla, accompanied Martí on his journey to the Dominican Republic. The younger of the two girls, María, is said to have been Martí's own daughter, a fact that—according to María's son, the well-known film actor César Romero—Carmen Miyares confessed to a friend of hers at the time of Martí's death, and which that friend finally told María in 1935.

2. *The General, Collazo:* General Máximo Gómez (1836–1905), commander in chief of the Cuban revolutionary forces (see Martí's letter to him on page 257), and Enrique Collazo Tejada (1848–1925), who had attained the rank of comandante in the Ten Years War and had written an open letter very critical of Martí in 1892.

3. *Juan Isidro Jiménez:* A wealthy white Montecristi landowner and merchant, son of a president of the Dominican Republic, who went on to become president of the country himself from 1899 to 1902.

4. *Musié:* Foreigner; derived from the French *monsieur.*

5. *Castelarian . . . Zorilla-esque:* Emilio Castelar (1832–99), a Spanish politician known for the hollow pomp of his oratory; José Zorrilla (1817–93), a wildly popular Spanish romantic poet, author of *Don Juan Tenorio* (see note 7 to "Our America" on page 437).

6. *Guajiro(a):* A typical man or woman of rural Cuba.

7. *Idea I suggested in an article:* That article was "La Escuela de Artes y Oficios de Honduras," which Martí had published in *La América* in June 1884 and which was reprinted in the Dominican Republic that same year, under the title "Los maestros ambulantes," by the Dominican poet José Joaquin Pérez (1845–1900) in his *Revista*

Científica, Literaria y de Conocimientos Utiles (Review of Science, Literature and Useful Knowledge).

8. *Billini's presidency:* Franciso Gregory Billini (1844–98) was president of the Dominican Republic in the period 1884–85. He was a cousin of General Máximo Gómez, who was born in the Dominican Republic.

9. *February 14:* There are many problems with the dating and sequencing of Martí's diary; in several instances, he may have lost track of time or made entries retrospectively without being certain of the date. Here, for example, the entry appears between two others, both dated February 15, and speaks of a journey that, other sources indicate, took place on February 18.

While adhering to the dates noted by Martí, Mayra Beatriz Martínez and Froilán Escobar, in their masterful edition of the *Final Diary,* arranged the entries in a sequence that conforms to current documentation on the actual chronology of Martí's journey. Their ordering has been adopted here, as it gives the narrative a more logical flow, even if it means that the dates of the entries are out of sequence.

10. *Amargo:* A sweet made from bitter almonds.

11. *Divi-divi:* A small tree whose twisted pods are a good source of tannin, used to cure leather.

12. *Carlos Manuel de Céspedes* (1819–74): Cuban lawyer, politician, and revolutionary who gave the famous cry *"¡Viva Cuba libre!"* in Yara in 1868, unleashing the Ten Years War. He was president of the rebel republic from 1869 to 1873.

13. *Guanche:* Indigenous inhabitants of the Canary Islands at the time of their conquest by Spain.

14. *Haitian cannon:* In 1844 the Dominican Republic gained its independence from Haiti. Though the two nations that share it have differing colonial histories, the entire island of Hispaniola had been united under the Haitian flag for much of the first half of the nineteenth century.

15. *Ulpiano Dellundé* (dates unknown): Exiled Cuban doctor and patriot who owned a pharmacy at 33 rue Vaudeuil in Cap-Haïtien. Dellundé and his Puerto Rican wife, Dolores (Lola) Arán, were extremely generous to Martí during his visits to Haiti. They went back to live in Cuba after 1895.

16. *"Ah! gardez-ça":* "Oh, looky there: white man soldier too."

17. *Lilí:* Ulises Heureaux (1844–99), nicknamed "Lilís," dictator of the Dominican Republic from 1882 to 1884 and 1887 to 1899. General Aristide "Tilo" Patiño initially fought against him but Heureaux later made him governor of the province of Santo Domingo.

18. *"Mosié blanc pringarde":* "Monsieur white man, take care: they'll put monsieur in prison."

19. *"Bien sellé":* "Well saddled, well bridled: not a common man . . ."

20. *"Le chemin"*: "The road is transitable" ... "Oh monsieur, the aristocracy is always most welcome!"

21. *"On est"*: "One is a journalist"; "the aristocracy has no future in this country."

22. *"Comment, frère"*: "How's that, brother? There's no talk of money between brothers."

23. *"Ah, compère"*: "Ah, compadre, don't trouble yourself. That's not it, that's not it, friend. On the road, one fellow helps the other fellow. We're all Haitians here." ... the three children with whom "God has favored me." ... "Ah yes, when you speak of a friend's home, you're speaking of God's home."

24. *"Non: argent non"*: "No, no money: the book, yes." ... Of mud and straw ... is the "residence of Mamenette" on the road to Cap-Haïtien.

25. Lengthwise, along the margin of the original page on which the following paragraph appears, Martí noted: "(Here follows March 2's note on *Petit Trou*, interrupted after the part about Nephtalí, in Fort Liberté.)"

26. *Augustus (1826–1908) and Alice D. (1851–1910) Le Plongeon:* The first American archaeologist to explore Chichén Itzá, and his wife. Martí met the pair in Islas Mujeres, Yucatán, as he was on his way to Guatemala in 1877. Alice wrote a book about the couple's experiences in Yucatán, and Augustus was the author of several esoteric works linking the Maya to the lost city of Atlantis and the pyramids of ancient Egypt. Like several other archaeologists from the United States before and after him, Le Plongeon wanted to transport the pre-Columbian ruins he studied to the United States, stone by stone.

27. *Pantun:* Or pantoun, a Malay verse form consisting of four lines with an a-b a-b rhyme scheme. The first two lines allude figuratively to something that the last two lines state more directly. It was introduced into French by Victor Hugo in *Les Orientales* (1829).

28. *Thomas Moore (1779–1852):* Irish poet, author of *Lalla Rookh,* a narrative poem with an Oriental setting which Martí was translating in February 1888, though the translation was never published and has been lost. (See note 1 to "The Lynching of the Italians" on page 438.)

29. *La Regenta:* A two-volume novel published in 1884 by Leopoldo Alas, known as Clarín (1853–1901); it is considered the Spanish *Madame Bovary.*

30. *Jules Michelet (1798–1894):* French historian and man of letters, author of a history of the French Revolution.

31. *March 4:* That night Martí had left Cap-Haïtien by boat for Montecristi, where he would spend the rest of the month.

32. *Their enchantments:* The trip from Cap-Haïtien to Montecristi is not a long one, and the boat would have stayed fairly close to the shoreline. Voudou ceremonies are often held at midnight on the seashore, and because of the syncretic confluence of Voudou and Catholicism, Lent, the forty-day period leading up to Easter, is a partic-

ularly active time in the Voudou religion. Martí and his traveling companions may have been overhearing a Voudou ceremony on a nearby beach.

33. *Speaks of the caves:* Salas is describing the Caves of the Haitís, located between the mouths of the San Lorenzo and Naranjo Rivers, near the town of Sabana de la Mar, on the bay of Samana, which lies along the northeastern coast of the Dominican Republic. The cave containing the two faces is probably the one now known as the Cueva de la Cal.

34. *April 3:* On the night of April 2, Martí, Gómez, César Salas, and five others had boarded the schooner *Brothers*, out of Turks and Caicos, which they had purchased. Its captain had agreed to take them to the island of Great Inagua—a British colony, one of the Bahamas—and from there to Cuba. When they reached Great Inagua, the captain alerted the authorities to the expeditionaries' plans. The boat was searched, but all weapons and compromising objects had been carefully hidden, and nothing was found. However, they could not go on because two of the three crew members had deserted—only the cook, David Caley, remained—and the captain claimed he was unable to recruit any sailors to take their place. Finally, Martí persuaded the captain to return 400 of the 450 pesos that had been paid for the boat and the crew's wages, and went in search of another means of transport.

35. *Onboard the steamship:* On Great Inagua, Martí made the acquaintance of Heinrich Julius Theodor Löwe (1859–1935), captain of the steamship *Nordstrand*, with whom the expeditionaries reached an agreement. They returned to Cap-Haïtien on the *Nordstrand* and stayed there, hiding from Spanish spies, for three days. Martí hid at the home of Ulpiano Dellundé (see note 15 on page 441), where he had stayed on his last visit to Cap-Haïtien.

36. *Moctezuma . . . Cacama . . . Cuitlahuac:* Moctezuma II (1466–1520): emperor of the Aztec city of Tenochtitlán (now Mexico City) when the Spaniards, led by Hernán Cortés (1485–1547), arrived in Mexico. Cacama (or Cacamatzin): an Aztec prince put to death by Cortés. Cuitlahuac (or Cuitlahuatzin): brother of Moctezuma and successor to his throne, who dealt the Spaniards their worst defeat on the so-called *Noche triste*, or "Sad Night," in 1520.

37. *Tecuichpo . . . Cuauhtémoc:* Tecuichpo (or Techuichpotzin): Daughter of Moctezuma II who married her cousin Cuauhtémoc (1495?–1525), successor to Cuitlahuac and last of the Aztec emperors. He was tortured by fire in 1522 and hanged three years later.

The source of the information Martí gives here is unknown. Of the three Spaniards he mentions as having consorted with Tecuichpo, only Alonso de Grado is well known; he was given a title of nobility after the Spanish conquest of Mexico and married a daughter of Moctezuma.

38. *The baseness of our woman:* Martí seems to be alluding to his own marital

difficulties. In 1891, after almost a decade of separation, he had attempted a reconciliation with his wife, Carmen Zayas Bazán, who had been living with their son, José Francisco, in Cuba , where the child was being raised in the vehemently pro-Spanish atmosphere of his maternal grandparents' home. After a brief stay in New York, Carmen fled back to Cuba, taking José Francisco with her. Since she did not have Martí's consent to take the boy, she asked for, and received, help from the Spanish consul in New York in order to do so. "She has walked up the steps of the Spanish Consulate to ask for protection against me," Martí wrote. He never saw his wife or his son again.

39. *April 9:* At 2 A.M. on April 10, Martí, Gómez, César Salas, Francisco Borrero, Angel Guerra, and Marcos del Rosario reboarded the *Nordstrand.* The previous afternoon or evening, Martí had left his hiding place in Cap-Haïtien, waving good-bye to Dolores Arán ("Lola"), the wife of Ulpiano Dellundé in whose house Martí had been staying (see note 15 on page 441). A *jolongo* is a bag or pouch worn over the shoulder.

40. *April 10–11:* On April 11, the *Nordstrand* arrived in Great Inagua for a brief stopover. It then continued on toward Cuba, skirting the Punta de Maisí, Cuba's easternmost tip, and drawing as close as was prudent to the southeastern coast. At 8 P.M. Martí and his companions left the *Nordstrand* in a small rowboat, making for the coast, which they reached at 2 A.M.

41. *Blas, Gonzálo, and the "Niña":* The six men reached the home of Adela Leyva Rodríguez (the "Niña"), where they met with Blas Martínez, an emissary from the revolutionaries of Guantánamo. Guided by a member of Adela's family, Gonzálo Leyva Rodríguez, and a neighbor named Silvestre Martínez, they continued on their way.

42. *Ruenes:* Félix Ruenes Aguirre, chief of operations of the insurrectionary forces in the Baracoa region.

43. *Mambí:* A Cuban revolutionary was called a *mambí* (masculine) or a *mambisa* (feminine; plural: *mambises*). The same word was used for rebels on Santo Domingo. Various conjectures exist as to its origins, the most plausible of which is that it came from the Congo, where it means "bad man." It was used by Congolese slaves in Santo Domingo—their will bent to that of their masters—to describe runaway slaves, or cimarrons. The Spaniards then applied it pejoratively to those who fought Spanish rule. In time, the insurrectionaries proudly adopted the nickname that was intended to insult them.

44. *Caridad Estrada in Camagüey:* This story, also noted in Máximo Gómez's diary, appears to have taken place during the Ten Years War. After her home was attacked by a small band of soldiers fighting for Spain (the "guerrillas"), Caridad Estrada sent for insurrectionary General Manuel Boza and stirred his men with her revolutionary fervor.

45. *Flor . . . Maceo . . . José Maceo . . . Garrido:* Flor Crombet (1851–95), Anto-

nio Maceo (1845–96), and his brother José Maceo (?–1896) were three central figures in the Cuban Revolution and the leaders of a group of twenty expeditionaries who set out together from Costa Rica, stopped at Fortune Island, and clandestinely disembarked in Cuba from the schooner *Honour* on April 1, 1895. Crombet was killed on April 10 in a skirmish with Spanish forces led by Pedro Garrido Romero, whose men were known as the "Indians of Yateras."

46. *Poor Frank:* Francisco José Agramonte y Agramonte ("Frank") was another of those who arrived on the *Honour.* He was taken prisoner by Garrido's forces.

47. *Escuadras de Guantánamo:* A paramilitary body established prior to the Ten Years War by the landowners of Guantánamo to defend Spain and fight against the *mambises.*

48. *Voluntarios:* The Tercio de Voluntarios of Yateras, or "Volunteer Regiment of Yateras" (also known as the "Indians of Yateras," because some of its members were descendants of Cuba's indigenous people), was a regiment made of up Cuban "volunteers" who were actually mercenaries, fighting for pay against their fellow Cubans. They were also sometimes called "guerrillas."

49. *Pérez . . . Policarpo . . . Pérez:* Miguel Santos Pérez and Francisco Pérez were two soldiers who died during the Ten Years War, the latter at the hands of Policarpo Pineda, a notorious Spanish colonel.

50. *Letter to Carmita:* On April 28, Martí wrote a letter to his companion Carmen "Carmita" Miyares, describing his reunion with General José Maceo who had just fought a battle at the Arroyo Hondo bridge against the Spanish *guardia civil.* This entry must have been written at the same time.

51. *Manuel Fuentes:* Correspondent for the *New York World,* the famously sensationalistic New York daily edited by Joseph Pulitzer that gave birth to the term "yellow journalism" when it began coming out on yellow paper in 1893.

52. *Herald:* The *New York Herald,* one of the most influential U.S. newspapers of the day, had been a prime source for many of the articles about the United States Martí wrote during the 1880s and had published an interview with Martí in 1893. Martí gave Eugene Bryson, a *Herald* correspondent, an open letter and manifesto, signed by himself and Gómez, which the *Herald* published in its entirety on Sunday, May 19—the day Martí died. (See Martí's description of his conversation with Bryson in "Letter to Manuel Mercado" on page 347.)

53. *Because Flor:* During the planning stage of the expedition from Costa Rica, Antonio Maceo claimed he needed five thousand pesos to bring it off, rather than the two thousand Martí had sent. In February Martí had written to Maceo from Montecristi, telling him that since Flor Crombet assured him he could do it with two thousand pesos, he had decided to make Flor responsible for the expedition.

54. *Country, with its full dignity:* This dispute among Martí, Maceo, and Gómez over the form that the government of an independent Cuba would take was a rekin-

dling of an argument that had broken out eleven years earlier, in 1884. See Martí's "Letter to General Máximo Gómez" of October 20, 1884 (page 257).

55. The six pages of Martí's diary that correspond to May 6 were removed at some point after his death and have never been recovered.

56. *Arsenio Martínez Campos* (1831–1900): Commander in chief of the Spanish forces in Cuba during the Ten Years War and in 1895. (See note 1 of "Letter to Manuel Mercado" on page 439 and note 65 below.)

57. Martí left a blank space here, apparently in the intention of filling it in later when he had found out what the flagpole was made from.

58. Another blank space, possibly to have been filled in with the name of an animal.

59. *Donato Mármol* (d. 1870): Commander of the forces in Santiago de Cuba during the Ten Years War. In April 1869, he had just won a stirring series of victories and—at the behest of his cousin Eduardo Mármol and other opponents of Carlos Manuel de Céspedes, the president of the insurgent republic—decided to use his popularity to attempt to oust Céspedes and take over as supreme leader of the war, with dictatorial powers. At a meeting in Tacajó with Céspedes and other rebel leaders, including Máximo Gómez, Mármol was dissuaded from this ambition. He died the following year of natural causes.

60. *Moncada:* Guillermo (Guillermón) and Narciso Moncada were both veteran fighters on behalf of Cuban independence. Guillermo (1838–95), a major general, died of tuberculosis in the spring of 1895, after having led his region into war once again. Narciso, who inherited command of the Moncada regiment after his brother's death, was killed in action on July 13, 1895.

61. *El Morro:* The Castillo de San Pedro de la Roca of Santiago de Cuba, originally built to protect the city against corsaires and pirates and subsequently used as a military base and prison.

62. *Not obey him:* José Miró Argenter (1857–1925), then a colonel, and Angel Guerra (1848–96), a brigadier, were rivals for command of the rebel forces in Holguín.

63. *"Three wars":* That is, the Ten Years War (1868–78), the Little War, or *Guerra Chiquita* (1880), and the War of Independence (1895–98).

64. *"Horrible division":* Like Antonio and José Maceo and a number of other leading figures in the Cuban War of Independence, such as Juan Gualberto Gómez, Guillermón and Narciso Moncada were black.

65. *Protest of Baraguá:* On the morning of March 15, 1878, Antonio Maceo and a number of other rebels held a meeting at Baraguá with Arsenio Martínez Campos (see note 56 above), to discuss the Pact of Zanjón, an agreement on the cessation of hostilities that did not have Maceo's support. Maceo told Martínez Campos that he would not stop fighting until Cuba was independent, or, at the very least, slavery was

abolished. Martínez Campos left in disgust and the fighting continued, sporadically, for a while longer.

66. *Pati-peludos:* Literally, "hairy-feet." Derogatory term used by Spaniards for the Cuban rebels.

67. *Men of the Chamber:* Many military leaders of the Ten Years War blamed the rebel Chamber of Deputies for hobbling the military with its political trammels and, in particular, for acceding to the Pact of Zanjón (see note 65 above).

68. *Letter to Rabí:* General Jesús Sablón Morena, known as Rabí (1845–1915), commander of the forces in Jiguaní, was allegedly permitting cattle to be herded across his territory for sale to the Spaniards.

69. *James J. O'Kelly* (1845–1916): Author of *The Mambi-Land, or, Adventures of a Herald Correspondent in Cuba* (1874) who went to Cuba to talk to the insurgents in 1873, without permission from the Spanish authorities.

70. *Limbano . . . Reyes:* Insurgent General Limbano Sánchez was the leader of an expeditionary force that disembarked in Baracoa on March 15, 1885, to initiate a war of independence. Wounded, he was accompanied by one of his men, Ramón González, known as "Mongo," to the home of Gabriel Reyes, whom he asked for help. He is said to have been poisoned by Reyes, though another version of the story holds that Reyes killed him by stabbing him in the back with a machete. Mongo died in combat shortly thereafter, as did all other members of Sanchez's expeditionary force.

71. Gómez left the encampment on the 17th with thirty men to try to mount a surprise attack on a column of Spanish troops commanded by José Ximines de Sandoval, which was coming from the town of Bayamo. He returned on the 19th without having met them.

72. Here again, Martí left a blank space, clearly intending to fill in Avalos's first name later.

INDEX